Jazz Stories
From Katrina to Connecticut

A collection by Professor Arturo

Copyright © 2015 By Arthur Pfister aka Professor Arturo

All rights reserved. No part of this book may be reproduced or transmitted in any form or by any means – graphic, electronic or mechanical, including photocopying, recording or taping of information on storage and retrieval systems -- without written permission from the publisher.

ISBN: 978-0692473832
This book is also available in eBook under the same title,

Published 2015 by

MARGARET MEDIA, INC
PERFECT. PUBLISH. PROSPER

Margaret Media, Inc.
1425 Marrero Street
Marrero, Louisiana 70072
www.margaretmedia.com

JAZZ STORIES

From Katrina to Connecticut

by

Professor Arturo

Acknowledgments

A GOO-GOB OF BOO-COO BIG UPS 2 my editor, Paul Watson, a truth-telling giant of a gentleman with Jobian endurance and testicular fortitude; and

The people of Stamford, CT for their post-tempest kindness and support when they selflessly shared their hearts, homes, churches, wallets and bars; and

2 Tony Piazza, a Stamford, Connectican whose technical expertise rescued many of these stories from Katrina's wild, wet, windy, wretched wrath; my longtime colleague, dear friend, and lady of letters, Dr. Mona Lisa Saloy; and

XTRA-XTRA-XTRA SPECIAL thanxxxxxxxxxx 2 Mary Gehman, who healed, counseled, inspired, and fanned the flame of inspiration through her confidence and support of my work, her selfless dedication to the literary efforts of a diverse medley of authors, and her constant, conscious keeping of the faith.

Gracias, gracias, gracias 2 David Lotus for the back cover photo…

Author's Note

No . . . every microfiction in this collection is not necessarily "about" jazz or its players, although many are. The construct of most of these works is intended to reflect the essence of the music through the implementation of extensive improvisational "word riffs," multi-patterned phrasings, and extended linguistic solos.

This book is piction (poetic fiction). No resemblance is intended between any character herein and any person living, dead, or otherwise unembodied in the flesh. Any such resemblance is impurely coincidental. © 2015

To Aunt Sweet and Mama Rachel--

Pillars of Kindness

Amidst Seas of Insanity

". . . I am like a pelican of the wilderness.

I am like an owl of the desert.

I watch, and am as a sparrow

alone upon the housetop. . ."

-- Psalm 102

Contents

GENUFLECTION 8

Last Time I Saw Jeanine 9
A BIG, RED, CHICKEN-EATIN' MAN 24
The Great Chain of Being 48
Let Me Count The Ways 49
The Tree 54
Mama Rachel's Garden 81
The Last Second Line 85
Graveyard Love 97
The Funeral Poet 115
The Boy with the Cheap, Ugly, Green, Army Surplus Tennis Shoes 123
The Bugar Man 125
The Boy and the Famous French Quarter Lady Writer 128
The Boy with Two Heads 140
Yo! -- Dog! 144
The BIG TOO-DOO!!! 150
EPIPHANY 155
Sew, Sew, Sew 158
Don't Wish for What You Want 182
Epitaph 184

ADAPTATIONS 192

The Pound of Bionic Chronic (from *The Cask of Amontillado* by Edgar Allan Poe) 193
Handa Wanda (from *Cinderella* as told by Jacob and Wilhelm Grimm) 205
The Jewelry (from *The Jewelry* by Guy de Maupassant) 223
The Necklace (from *The Necklace* by Guy de Maupassant) 230
A Mardi Gras Mambo (from *A Christmas Carol* by Charles Dickens) 237

EJACULATIONS 259

Alice in the Afternoon, or *Up For The Downstroke* 260
On A Mission 273
A Living Doll 279
Jack Moore (Private Dick) *The Case of the Missing Draws* 283
Company Man 296

GLOSSARY 328

GENUFLECTION

Professor Arturo

Last Time I Saw Jeanine
(Confessions of a New Orleans Jazz Poet)

"We don't stop playing because we get old.
We get old 'cause we stop playing."
-- Satchel Paige

I hadn't seen her since Katrina, hadn't stared in stunned silence at her comeliness . . . hadn't tickled her tantalizing, teasing, inebriatingly tartish tongue; hadn't kissed her *Illicit Raspberry*-covered, intoxicatingly beautiful nether lips or savored the magic of her red-nailed fingers' touch . . . hadn't felt the vise-tight grip of her valley of pleasure, hadn't inhaled the unexpended aroma of her perfumed fragrance on the gossamer fabric of her negligee or her strapless, fake leopard print bustier . . . hadn't fingered her sheer, black *peignoir* (I *still* cain't pronounce it) . . . hadn't fancied her paper-thin yellow sweater or her dangerously-clinging, form-fitting tops accentuated with "come get me" heels . . . hadn't been blinded by the treacherous trance wrought by her beatific Vaseline tooth smile or her jaw-dropping, tutti-frutti gumdrop nipples on her bounteous breasts which stood up proudly and profoundly like WE, THE PEOPLE . . . She was a swell looker, a top-shelf girl, brain-bogglingly beautiful -- an obviously well-maintained cross between Marilyn Monroe, Pam Grier, Dorothy Dandridge, Dakota Staton, Sophia Loren, and Mae West. At any moment I expected Sweet Young Thang to say: "Is that a old-fashioned cell phone in your pocket, daddy -- or you just glad to see me?" *My* first words to *her* were: "Hey baby -- you into rheumatoid arthritis?" I was the Last of the Red Hot Poppas.

She was a stunnah. Meana than Katrina. Healthy, brown and manicured with a proud mane of pecawn-brown hair atop an old-fashioned Coke bottle shape. A postcard pretty devil in Dior. Hotter than a grand latte. She was big and (classically) fine as a B-29 (wunna them kinda wimmins they say Sam Cooke was runnin 'round with). I lost lifelong friends 'cause they got tired o' me talkin' 'bout that woman so much. They say I talked about that woman from sunup to sundown, from the new moon to the full moon, from Lake Pontchartrain to Lake Titicaca (I always like to say that word 'cause I can say *two* bad words at one time), at breakfast, lunch, dinner, brunch and snacks inbetween.

The valley amidst her mountains was a target-rich environment. Her cups runneth over. Her saucy, dark, oversized, smoldering eyes were inviteful, delightful pools of sizzling passion and desire. She didn't shop at secondhand stores . . . she shopped at *consignment boutiques*. She didn't use scissors . . . she used *shears*. She didn't drive a used car . . . she drove a *pre-owned vehicle*. She didn't use turlit paper . . . she used *bath tissue*. She didn't use a vibrator . . . she used *a personal massager*. And she *definitely* didn't fart. She . . . *pooted*. She had perfectly-arranged hair, ripe, ruby-red lips, gleaming white teeth, and *come hither*, erotic eyelashes. That young girl's grease was *way* too hot. I know you ain't supposed to judge a picture by the frame, but I loved that woman.

Male onlookers focused the totality of their attention on her while some wimmins gave her direful, green-eyed, envious looks 'cause the girl could *dress*. She could *rag*. They say they saw her in Katrina in front the Superdome, a brickhouse beauty shoehorned into a pair of fashionably-torn designer jeans and sportin' knee-high Yves St. Laurent-lookin' swamp boots, a high-end, sequin-festooned poet blouse, red, wraparound shades over a Cheshire grin, a Helen Kaminski "Cassandra Hat" tilted at a wicked angle -- and totin' a bubblegum-pink clutch. To my entranced, wide-open eyes (and nose) she was a queen in ruffled collars.

But that pretty woman could *lie*. Lawd, that woman could lie. I thought she was a great catch, but she was a net fulla minnows. She was a lady of perpetual liability with sinfully lush, lasciviously luscious, lying lips. The girl lied so much that if she were an abolitionist and advocate of women's rights they'd call her Sojourner *Lie*. That woman could *lie*. I was on the road broke one time and she said she sent me some money by Western Union ("It didn't go through"). She then said she sent it by regular mail ("It came back"). Then she said she sent it again ("I forgot to put the stamp on it"). Finally, she sent me some *cash* – and it was counterfeit! She was a *lyin'* woman -- a BIG, BROWN, *LYIN'* WOMAN**.** She lied about her weight, lied about her age, lied about her mens, lied about her chirrens, lied about her education, lied about her family, lied about her job and lied about her lies. If she was in the Bible her name would be Delilah. If she played baseball she'd hit nuthin' but line drives. Her surgery of choice was liposuction. Her favorite train was a Lionel train, her favorite singer was Lionel Ritchie, her favorite flowers were lilacs, her favorite *color* was lilac, her favorite big cat was Leo the Lion, her favorite dance was the Second Line, her favorite king was Richard the Lionhearted, her favorite Chinese leader was Chou En-lai, her favorite food was jambalaya, her favorite month was July, her favorite song was *Li'l Liiiiiza Ja-a-a-ane,* her favorite actress was Liza May Minnelli, her favorite legal offense was libel, her favorite exercise was line dancing, her favorite country was Liberia, her favorite place to meet mens was the library, her favorite oldie singer was Frankie Lyman, her favorite football team was the Detroit Lions, her favorite soap was lye soap, her favorite surreptitious activity was lyin' in wait, her favorite defendant in a double murder trial was . . . Orenthal James Simpson and her favorite U.S. President was . . . Richard Milhous Nixon. Her word was phonier and mo' fake than her cornrow extensions. Her sageless beauty and luxurious, curvaceous angles belied the breadstick brittle core of her heinously hardened heart, but I loved that woman. I loved that woman more than a heroin addict love a toppa-the-line, spankin' brand new, shiny syringe. Yeah. I loved that woman. I loved that woman way befo' Katrina was a distant swirl in the Atlantic. But I just didn't know what time it was down here on the ground. Watch what happens as time goes by. . . .

* * *

Saying our relationship was stormy is like saying Katrina was a light, summer breeze. According to her, I didn't "act up" – I per*formed* like:

1) that time I (allegedly) made her lose her job when she was workin' at the discount store
2) that time I (allegedly) made her so nervous she couldn't breathe
3) that time I (allegedly) brought her blood pressure up and her reputation down
4) that time I (allegedly) put her *and* her girlfriend out my momma' house

5) that time I (allegedly) embarrassed her in front of her entire extended family
6) that time I (allegedly) dogged her out at the restaurant
7) that time I (allegedly) almost made her have an accident while she was driving
8) that time I (allegedly) prevaricated about that li'l woman in the Ninth Ward and they bumped heads at my apartment when I was livin' in the French Quarter
9) that time I (allegedly) made her throw a hissy fit (that's when you sittin' in the middle of the floor, kickin' and screamin'), or
that time I (allegedly) made her throw a titty tantrum (that's a li'l stronger)
10) that time I (allegedly) made her throw an ethnic fit (that's when you gittin' ready to come out yo' ZULU bag)
11) that time I (allegedly) made her have a conniption fit (that's when you don't know *what* you carryin' on 'bout -- you just carryin' on)
12) that time I (allegedly) told her not to call me "as long as (her) behind point to the ground"
13) that time I (allegedly) told her, "You better close that window, girl! Them extensions gon' fly off yo' haid!"
14) that time I (allegedly) made her get off the elephant ride at the zoo that her life was becoming
15) that time she (allegedly) caught me sittin' in the audience with that li'l Ninth Ward woman when me and the fellas first started the Spoken Word/Jazzoetry Night gig at Sweet Lorraine's over on St. Claude right off Esplanade (certainly not Espla*nod*)
16) that time I (allegedly) promised to marry her (again) and ran off and was livin' with that li'l woman from the Ninth Ward, and of course
17) that time I (allegedly) made that baby with that *same* li'l woman from the Ninth Ward

-- which was nothing compared to her constant accusations, her persistent bitchiness and her lamentable, pitiable, perennially ghetto-dwellin' deportment as reflected by:

Professor Arturo

1) that time she told my podner (who had come over to pay me some money he owed me) that I was busy
2) that time she publicly shoo-shooed about how lowdown, dirty and ign'ant I was in fronta Henry, BIG HAROLD, Thomas, Biggy, Keith, Country, Wilfred and Willoughby
3) that time she called me and told me she was all hoochie-coochie with some doctor dude up in Virginia (He a doctor, but he still a man)
4) that time that gay sister was in her house and she was ironin' my clothes in her bra-*zeer* and slacks and I told her what the play was and she said I was crazy, then two months later the woman hit on her and she had to break down and call me and tell me I was right (Nobody rides for free)
5) that time she was leavin' my apartment and that married man next door (with his wife and chirrens inside) flirted with her and told her she got some pretty brown eyes and I told her I need to talk to homeboy 'bout that 'cause he got a wife and chirrens inside and knowed she was my company and was disrespectin' her and she said that it wasn't a flirt and I was just jealous (later on, she broke down 'bout that, too)
6) that time she wanted to go to the ZULU Club with Girlfriend insteada hangin' outside in the 1800 blocka Dumaine with me, Henry, BIG HAROLD, Thomas, Biggy, Keith, Country, Wilfred and Willoughby
7) that time she had me on my knees *beggin' PLEASE . . . PLEASE . . . PLEASE . . .* and the neighbors thought James Brown was in the house (I *hope* she didn't tell Henry, BIG HAROLD, Thomas, Biggy, Keith, Country, Wilfred and Willoughby)
8) that time she loaned Girlfriend her car when *she* had sumthin' to do for her*self* and Girlfriend was gone so long her life was on hold
9) that time she was gon' pick me up after work to cash my check and never showed up and the check cashin' place closed on me on a long 4th of July weekend and I missed Essence Fest with Henry, BIG HAROLD,

Thomas, Biggy, Keith, Country, Wilfred and Willoughby

10) that time she was supposed to meet me on payday and showed up two weeks later
11) that time she came to the club and stood in the back when I was onstage with the band doing that long love poem about that li'l woman from the Ninth Ward -- and left befo' I finished
12) that time she started all that foolishness with that dude who was shaped like a broad (his jock was *strapped*)
13) that time she got all gussied-up and told that li'l woman from the Ninth Ward that I bought everything on her back
14) that time I called the crib and a dude answered the phone and said, "**She's not available. Don't call here no mo'**," and I said, "That's alright, podner, 'cause *she* gon' call *me*" (and she *did* -- and *still* do)
15) that time she had me up all night and I missed the job interview
16) that time she cussed me out and told me I was too old for her (*Baby, what's 20 years?*)
17) that time she used me to write all them letters to FEMA for her then act' like she didn't wan' talk to me no mo'
18) that time we were in the store on Royal Street and she didn't like it when I announced to the who-o-o-o-ole world: **"GIMME A SIX-PACKA BUD AND A DOZEN EXTRA-LARGE PROPHALACTICS!!!"**
19) that time I told her about managing her time mo' betta and she told me she didn't need another daddy and I said I wasn't tryin' to be her *paw* -- I was tryin' to be her *friend*
20) that time I told her I loved her so much I'd pay her light bill *and* her gas bill and she looked at me like I was *some* kah-*goo*
21) that time I told her that you're not really familiar with somebody until you can pass BOO-COO gas around 'em -- and proved that flatulent speculation (repeatedly)

22) that time she told me about she thought she was pregnant and I asked her, "Is it mine?" and
23) that time she told me at the Dirty South Summer Block Party Jazzoetry Festival gig that she'd kill me if I didn't marry her by Christmas (What kinda proposal was *that?*)

I knew it was hopeless when she told me that I was the most exciting thing in her life.

* * *

I discovered what it means to miss New Aw-leens when the vagaries of memory brought to mind the unholy days of obligation rendered unto the city's folkloric exoticism by Katrina's howling, growling, fiercely whipping, BOO-COO BIG, HUMONGOUS, GOO-GOBBA winds and water that ravished and wracked the city that care forgot, transforming it from the Big Easy to the Big Greezy. The music Mecca, an inevitable city founded at the mouth of the Mississippi that boasted the jazzy regality of Champion Jack Dupree, The Royal Dukes of Rhythm, Queen Goody, King Floyd, King Bolden, King Oliver and Li'l Queenie, was a mere commoner to Mighty Empress Katrina. I remember trudging through unctuous knee-high waters in my Jazzfest shoes, with my *Bill Withers LIVE at Carnegie Hall*, the clothes on my back and 28 cents in my pocket, stumbling through the grim landscape's blighted sea of water-soaked Creole cottages . . . jagged mounds of bricks . . . mangled heaps of metal . . . tangled tableaus of dangling wires . . . packs of wild, hungry dogs . . . half-eaten bodies floating in oily waters of deserted, rubble-strewn streets . . . storm-torn buildings . . . overhead powerlines snappin', cracklin' and poppin' . . . emaciated, dehydrating babies . . . swaying palm trees (shaking like pom-poms) . . . gaily-colored Neoclassic homes now reduced to splinters . . . the deathlike pallor of neighborhoods of heartbreak awash in mud, grime and mold . . . days blending into days outside the Superdome (the designated shelter of last resort) . . . the extraordinary rendition of the elderly, the poor, the faint and the feeble . . . the simmering frustration of incessantly moaning mothers and wailing, parch-lipped babies under a blistering sun . . . United States citizens begging and pleading to humming helicopters for food and water (as though they were soliciting beads at a Carnival parade) . . . windswept debris blocking wrought-iron door entrances to formerly elegant, exquisite, dreamlike gardens and red-brick patios . . . and signs saying

    HELP

    HELP US

    WILL GO
    WITH
    CHESTER THE MOLESTER
    FOR FOOD

    FOOD
    WATER
    PLEASE

    HUNGRY   PLEASE   HELP

Husbands left wives and wives left husbands. Husbands *met* wives and wives met husbands. Husbands met husbands and wives met wives. They were all too-willing victims of hurricane romance. It was a swingin' time. They say that bass player I was with at Dragon's Den was in Houston after the storm and told his wife he was going out for a packa squares -- and they ain't never seen him since. They say he dumped her like a bad habit.

It reminded one of Atlanta in *Gone with the Wind,* for the toxic gumbo looked like a terrible, swift sword had come, gone and come again to cast our collective fates to the wind. The whole world was watching. I was so hungry I salivated at the sight of a matchbox from a seafood company. *We should all go to heaven*, I thought, *'cause it sho' look like we done lived through hell.* I'm writin' a lot of fiction about it now. Sometimes I rearrange the time sequences like light changes over in the southern skyscape in August. It's the same story no matter in which order the timeline is configured. You already know the end at the beginning (or maybe even the middle), but you check it out anyway. Like *I* did. It wasn't the beginning of the end or the end of the beginning. It was the beginning of the beginning and the end of the end (I *still* don't know what that meant).

Professor Arturo

* * *

    The last time I saw Jeanine was on a moon-kissed night just before me and the fellas went on for Jazzoetry Night at the spot. She stood like a glittering, golden brown, gilded ghetto flower just next to an overgrown, garbage-strewn thicket-of-a-lot choked with thigh-high grass, weeds, weed, moldy furniture and waterlogged ghettobilia in the baleful post-Katrina remnants and ruins just around the cornder off St. Claude Ave. from Sweet Lorraine's, relishing the attention her body brought from male onlookers (straight and crooked) and the covetous stares of lesser-endowed wimmins, the outline of her flesh clearly visible beneath the sheer fabric of her tight hottie wear (white see-through BALI bra, halter top and khaki "boy shorts"). Cross-hatchmarkings made by Day-Glo orange vest-wearing emergency teams were like eerie ghettoglyphs in testament to a torrent of suffering. The vision of her brought to mind that last time we spent time together before she was evacuated to Baton Roo-*ejj* and I found a haven in Houston. That (pre-Katrina) night me and the fellas had just finished down at Café Brasil -- that li'l Bohemian hangout on Chartres and Frenchmen that cater' to the coffeehouse crowd and a buncha Newer Left alcoholics. She was leanin' against a lamppost with a go-cup in her hand when she beckoned to me like a candidate for Street Corner Ho' Of The Year. That's why I loved her: She was so promiscuously wanton, shameless and heathen. She was a pretty slick number. If she starred in a spaghetti western it'd be called "The Good, The Bad and The Hottie." A car enthusiast would've described her as the perfect grill with a body by Fisher on a 5'6" chassis. A wino would've described her as "top shelf." A boxer would've described her as a first-round knockout. A baseball pitcher would've described her as a perfect game. A meteorologist would've described her as a perfect storm. A priest would've described her as the most heavenly of hosts. I could only describe her as sumthin' in which I should've never flicked my Bic.
    She said she wanted to get sumthin' off her chest. I wished it were that white, see-through bra demolishing that wafer-thin top. I salivated like one of Pavlov's minions at the thought. Unbeknownst to me, underneath that top was a heart like gold -- yellow and hard. "I see you still got that old-fashioned cell phone in your pocket," she vamped. We were a picayune item, indeed.

"Naw, I'm just glad to see you," I enjoined. I hadn't touched a woman in eight months, three weeks, five days, seven hours, six minutes and 32.5 seconds. It was divine intervention. I felt like Gomer Pyle -- SUR*PRISE*-SUR*PRISE!!!* GOLL-OLL-OLL-*EE!!!*

The next thing I knew, I was on a purple-cushioned, perfumed divan behind some red, black, and green beaded curtains with my lips on the business end of a pair of unsurgically-enhanced 38DDs, my firmness buried deep within the dark, mystic magic of her enchanted forest. They was a whole lotta shakin' goin' on. The fragrance of flickering, multicolored, scented votive candles seeped throughout the set as our words interblended with the ardor of our coupling's flawless precision.

"*I can't tell where the silky fabric ends and your skin begins*," I bullshot.

"Silly . . ."

"Hey -- it was a helluva line."

"We still gittin' married?"

"Married?!? Uh . . . uh . . . *uh* . . . I might be robbin' the cradle, but you ain't gon' be robbin' *me*."

"You-told-me-you'd-give-yourself-to-me-as-my-husband," she stacattoed. "You told me you'd marry me. Especially after all you've done to me."

"Marry?!? Done?!???! Give!!??!? 'Give' is a four-letter word. The only thing I'ma give you is a good spankin' . . . and a good tongue lashin'," I teased.

"Git off me," she said, making a strategic withdrawal. The sacred lips of the temple's inner sanctum were sealed. Then -- "I cain't *do* this no mo'. I cain't live like this."

"Like *what*?"

"You need a wife."

"A *what*?"

"A wife."

"I'm too old to marry you. I cain't be robbin' the cradle for no wife. I'm old 'nuff to be yo' paw. It'd never work. It'd never --"

"-- Age ain't nuthin' but a number."

"-- Tell that to my knees! I'm tired of people asking me if you my daughter. I'm tired of people looking at me like I'm some kinda dirty old man," I opined. Then, in pompous, Nixonian fashion -- "I am *not* a chronophile."

"A *what?*"

"A chronophile . . . wunna them old men who be runnin' round chasin' after wimmins half they age -- like they tryin' to find another daughter -- or the Fountain of Youth -- or sumthin'."

"Ain't nuthin' wrong with it. All my sisters married to men some twenty years older than them. A man my age cain't teach me nuthin'. You teach me a lot. You taught me everything I know."

"Yeah. *Bet,*" I said, reflecting on the carnal nature of my teachings.

Then she embraced me, kissed me and whispered in my ear, *"I told you what I was gon' do if you don't marry me."*

That was when I knew my life was worth about as much as a spoiled, leaky, plastic bottle of bargain-priced stool softener.

* * *

It was the day after Christmas, the first day of Kwanzaa, right around the time when Sweet Lorraine's got them metal-finished, bistro pub tables. Sweet Lorraine's had been part of New Orleans' musical soundscape ever since anybody still alive could remember. The Men of Labor, a renowned social aid and pleasure club, used the spot as its home base. Politicians, preachers, poets, mailmen (and mail wimmins), athletes, Pontchartrain Parkers, Easterners, tourists, ghetto-dwellers, painters, writers, waiters, hustlers, bustlers, hoes . . . *Everybody* went to Sweet Lorraine's. Everybody who was somebody (or thought they was) or who was tryin' to *be* somebody (that they mighta not done been) went to Sweet Lorraine's for its authentic music, food, and New Orleans ambiance as reflected by the framed photos, posters and paintings (by New Orleans artists) of many of the city's luminaries in the arts hanging in homage throughout its interior. A portrait of the present owner's mother, the venerable "Miss Lorraine," a long-deceased (but never forgotten) woman of illustrious achievement and community involvement, dominated the wall just above the bar to the left when you walked in. To the right was a glass display case featuring CDs, books, pictures and other music-related merchandise and memorabilia. On the wall in back of the display area was a gaily-colored poster of a long dead Old School New Orleans poet.

Me and the fellas, a first-call, second-linin', motley assemblage of music makers, were outside down the street towards Esplanade down near where them A-rabb cabdrivers be. The joint was jumpin' from hand-to-hand. The pungent aroma of marijuana smoke saturated the crisp night air as we smoked, joked and toked. "Doody" Duplessis, a Fifth District NOPD Morgan Freemanesque-looking homicide detective who moonlighted on Sundays as a preacher from the black lagoon, passed us by as he measuredly walked down the banket towards the club. He was working on a book of his poems he said he was callin' *Thou Shalt Not Kill* and was a longtime poetry lover ever since his pre-college days in Upward Bound when he was in the first summer session class Uptown at Loyola back in the summer of 1966. He hadn't missed the Jazzoetry set since we started it. "Where y'at?" he greeted me with practiced eyes as he strode by.

"Just out catchin' a li'l breeze 'fore we go on," I said, concealing the joint behind my back.

"The breeze kinda *strong* tonight," Duplessis jibbed.

"Yeah ya-right," I jabbed. I wasn't makin' no BIG TOO-DOO 'bout it. He shook his head, laughing slightly to himself, went down to the club, took his usual seat and ordered his uniform standard Rum & Coke setup.

"It's 'bout that time --" I announced to the fellas, "I'm puttin' this out," I told the cats, crushing the roach on the banket with wunna my 13-EEEs. "I ain't messin' with Doody Doop. You ain't gon' find *me* floatin' in the canal."

* * *

By the time we got inside the act just before us was rockin' and rollin'. Comedian Willy Lancelot was up that night (again) shooting himself in both brogans (again) with his usual and customary snippets of timeworn witticisms. He was doing a heckuva job. We heard the same jokes over and over so much we had 'em memorized and often accompanied him, mouthing his stale, stock humor as he moved the evening along at glacial speed. It was murderously embarrassing.

"Thank you for coming . . . just don't git it on the floor . . ." *Laughter.* "This show is dedicated to all our fighting men and women -- and I don't mean just married couples. . ." *A li'l bitta strained laughter.* "And I said to the li'l boy, 'You like trains?'... 'Yeah'...Well, come in the room and see yo' maw..." *Juvenilish laughter.* "A Louisiana state senator walks into a bar with a horse. The bartender says, 'We don't serve those in here'... The senator says, 'Why not?'... The bartender says, 'I was talking to the horse'..." *Besotted laughter.* "What do you call a woman who gives the President a handjob?... A Bushwhacker..." *Politically incorrect laughter.* "And man, were we po'... We was so po' we couldn't afford the last two letters. We weren't 'poor'... We was P-O...PO'!!!" *Impoverished laughter.* "And my father was mean. He was mean. He was so mean, he didn't leave a will... he left a *won't*... One day he said 'Let's go bungee-jumpin', son -- put this rope 'round your neck.'" *Pitifully paternalistic laughter.* "He was so mean, we didn't drink DOCTOR Pepper -- We drank INTERN Pepper..." *Medicinal laughter.* " Insteada Burger King, he took us to Burger *Peasant*... where he had it *his* way!" *Dictatorially dominating laughter.* "For holidays he didn't take us to grandma's house... he took us by the BIG, BAD WOLF... We asked for a vacation one summer... he gave us a pounda rice...'Make like you're in China.'" *Uncle Ben-ish laughter.* "What do you call a Swiss hooker?... a Heidi ho'..." "When it came to discipline, my father believed in the Powell Doctrine... overwhelmin' force." *Politically pugilistic laughter.* "Why couldn't Blackbeard the Pirate be a homosexual?... He didn't want nobody to take his booty." *Faintly gay laughter.* "If your mother-in-law and a IRS agent were comin' at you with guns in their hands and you had two bullets in *your* gun, who would you shoot first?...-- The IRS agent... Why?... Bizness before pleasure." *Mercy laughter.* "'Then there's these new cars... talk about sticker shock... I was electrocuted." *Li'l bitty, teenantsy, slightly shocking laughter.* "Eleven scantily-clad Amazon Warrior Women and one Buffalo Soldier?... SOMEbody's gonna git screwed." *Delicately profane laughter.* "I really like children's rhymes... 'Ding-Dong-Dell-Pussy's in the well'... Where's my swimmin' trunks?" *Wringing-wet laughter.* "Let's see if I can make you say a dirty word... One thing I really like is opposites... Republican-Democrat... North-South... just like the opposite of happy is 'glum'... the opposite of 'smart' is..." (Audience: "*Dumb!*") "... and the opposite of 'go' is..." *Non-socially* redeeming laughter. "Anybody got a daughter? I know a father who saw his daughter gittin' off the plane with a tall African in traditional garb and a bone in his nose and he says, 'I wanted you to marry a RICH doctor . . . a RICH doctor. . . .'" *Shrimpy laughter.* "What did the prophylactic sing to the weeny?. . . *'I've got you under my sk-i-i-i-i-iin'*. . . ." S*exually risqué laughter.* "What kinda hoes join the Marines? . . . GUNG hoes." *Miniscule laughter.* ". . . Again, thank you for coming . . . I just hope you brought your own towels. . . ." . . . *RELIEF*!!!

* * *

We started out that night with the band playin' the lead-in tune. The first call was "Impressions" -- that tune where everybody seemed intent on doing the longest solo in musical history ('specially when they old lady out there in the audience). Then I came on and did that long love poem with that "Voodoo Woman" bassline. Jeanine never *did* like that poem. After that, I did "MALCOLM" and the drunken, post-pubescent neo-nationalists sucked it up right in the middle of furiously fingering their Blackberries. Then I did a piece that was dedicated to motherhood and mothers *in* the hood (I didn't do nuthin' for yo' paw that night, 'cause he ain't never done nuthin' for *me*). I'm from the Sixth Ward (*Tremé* to the tourists). Then I did a new piece -- on Jeanine -- about how she was into that graveyard love and was talkin' bout killin' me that time. I did wunna my standards (the Louis Armstrong piece) then wrapped it up with that long jam about New Orleans that one reviewer called "a very evocative hybrid poetic story form, a passionate paean to the magic and mystery of the city that care forgot." He read the book, but he never *did* buy the album. That was the problem with a lotta New Orleans audiences. They always wanted to get your *sumthin'* for their *nothin'* and pat you on the back -- like that's gon' pay the bills (and they wonder why cats wan' live in New York). Then the band did their last two numbers and it was closin' time . . . time to breeze. I sold a coupla books, signed a coupla autographs, got my cut from the door (and my two free drinks), grabbed my poems and went out into the world's dark, perilous night. As I walked out the door a li'l young dude in a long, gray hoodie-type sweatshirt came from outa nowhere and asked me if I was who I was. I thought he wanted to buy a book or sumthin'. Before I could answer, he pulled a sawed-off, double-barreled shotgun from underneath his oversized shirt, stuck it in my face, said, *"This for Jeanine --"* and blew my head off. I then reentered the unfathomed abyss in the land of spirit and shadow from whence I had come.

* * *

About a week later, they found the youngster in a alley in the Sixth Ward (offa Robertson and St. Philip) with his throat cut and a broomstick jammed up his anal cavity. Soon after that, Jeanine got a visit from Detective Duplessis. He told Sister Girl he wanted to ask her a few questions. . . .

2008
Stamford, CT

Jazz Stories: *From Katrina to Connecticut*

A BIG, RED, CHICKEN-EATIN' MAN

Big Red was a chicken-eatin' man -- breasts, thighs, legs, wings, backs, necks, the gizzard, the liver, the heart, and . . . the-last-part-over-the-fence. He loved his chicken and he loved his bird -- barbecued, browned, ground, broiled, berled, fricasseed, *pannéed*, sautéed, smothered, stewed, grilled, fried, chilled, jerked, roasted, toasted, and raw. He loved him some bird . . . had to have his chicken (on earth, throughout time, and in the heavens above) . . . Alexis, Kentucky, Church's, Popeye's, Big Mama's, Chicken & Waffles, Wings N' Things, Chicken Delight, McHardy's, McKenzie's (Gentilly Store), Hayes Chicken Shack, and the H & K Oyster House. It cost quite a bit, but to him it was mere . . . chickenfeed . . . and he always managed to stick to a minimally chintzy budget . . . on a wing and a prayer. He even took up playin' the skins . . . because of the drumsticks. His favorite piano player was . . . Chick Corea. His favorite trumpeter ("trumpe*tier*" to the natives) was . . . Donald Byrd. His favorite saxophonist was . . . Charlie "Bird" Parker. His favorite First Lady was Lady Bird Johnson. His favorite part of the Bible was the part where "the cock crowed thrice." His favorite tribe (after the Wild Magnolias and the Yellow Pocahontas) was the *Chick*asaw. His favorite Civil War battle was the Battle of *Chick*amauga. His favorite peas were . . . chickpeas. His favorite con game was the Pigeon Drop. His favorite soup was Chicken Noodle soup. His favorite Chinese food was chicken fried rice & chicken chow mein. His favorite dance was the Funky Chicken, and his favorite nightclub in all of America and the free and unfree world was . . . Birdland.

The boy lived, died, and was born again for the bird. He loved chicken so much, you could go to his house any night of the week and find him with a breast in his mouth and a thigh in each hand (an odd configuration). Insteada Black Pride, he believed in Chisesi's Pride. He didn't drink highballs -- he drank cocktails. If someone were to ask him "What's the word?" he'd yell "*Thunderbird*!!!" His *nanann* once told him, "Boy -- you eats so much chicken, one day yo' behind gon' turn in*to* a chicken!" His *parann* once told him, "Boy -- you eats so much chicken, you gon' sprout wings!" His paw-*paw* once told him, "Boy -- you eats so much chicken, you gon' lay eggs!" And his maw-*maw* once told him, "Boy -- you eats so much chicken, one day a chicken gon' eat *you*!"

He was a big, red chicken-eatin' man . . . a big RED man. He liked red socks and red shirts, red shoes and red coats, red pants and red beans, red cars and red draws, red handkerchiefs and red hainkachiffs, red ink and red drink, the Cincinnati Redlegs, Red Lady 21 wine, and chocolate brown Sixth Ward wimmins (even though he was known to fool 'round a li'l bit in the Seventh Ward sometimes). He was a Hai Karate-usin', breast-stewin', leg-chewin', bird-buyin', wing-fryin', butter-ballin', turkey-callin', finger-lickin', bone-pickin', roach-fightin', bird-bitin', chicken-eatin' man.

He was a birdbrain, an egghaid. He didn't have a girlfriend. He had a "chick." His favorite mythical character was . . . Chicken Little. His favorite sport was cockfighting. His favorite brand of tuna was Breast O' Chicken. His favorite publisher was Bantam Books. His favorite cowboy was Rooster Cogburn. His favorite lawman wasn't Marshal Dillon, but Marshall Durbin. His favorite movie was "My Little Chickadee." His second favorite movie was "The Ghost and Mr. Chicken." His third favorite movie was "Birdman of Alcatraz." His favorite cartoon characters were Heckle & Jeckle, and his favorite cartoon was . . . anything with Foghorn Leghorn in it. He was a birdbrain who put boo-coo chickens in they grave. His favorite soldier was . . . Colonel Sanders. His favorite religious figure was not a nun, a priest or a monk, but a friar. His favorite game of derring-do was playing "Chicken," his favorite drink was coffee (with chicory), and his favorite Louisiana high school basketball star was Fred "Chicken Red" Hilton.

He didn't dance "cheek-to-cheek" but . . . "chick-to-chick." HE WAS A BIG, RED, CHICKEN-EATIN' MAN. He would love to take pictures and . . . watch the birdie. The bird-bird-bird, the-bird was his word. The boy ate chicken each and every day of his chicken-eatin' life. The boy ate more chicken than anybody in New Awlins -- and that's a *who-o-o-o-ole* lotta chicken! He was a chicken-lovin' man who believed in a chicken in every pot – and every man a king.

Even the boy's wimmins looked like chickens. He liked his wimmins with Catawba Pink chicken lips and li'l bitty teenantchee chicken legs -- nice and neat, short and sweet (and that chicken-looking' lacquered hairstyle they have with all that wax in they haids). His prized and preferred pastime was birdwatchin' the fine, young tenders on Canal Street, especially by the Saint Bernard bus stop by Krauss, the department store adjacent to the Iberville Project. The boy loved the bird -- any way, shape, form, fashion or passion. His favorite cheap champagne (sparkling wine) was Cold Duck. His favorite liquor was Old Crow, and his favorite chauvinistic stereotype was . . . Chick Eata Banana.

* * *

The streets of the city forgotten by care were woefully slow that September night. Hurricane Galinthia, a relatively light, category 1-level storm was lumbering across the Gulf, inching her wicked way landward, her winds whistling wildly through a cityscape of shotgun houses; trembling, quivering chineyball trees and ancient oaks. He turned the maroon, two-door Impala onto Claiborne Street (Claiborne Avenue to the tourists) from Orleans ("Basin" to the tourists), going towards Esplanade ("Esplanod" to the tourists) while swiggin' a half-full (half-empty?) bottle of Cold Duck. He mulled over which local watering hole he could duck into to ride out the winds and heavy rains of the storm (as was the custom in those pre-evacuation days). The party places in the region of his ancestral homeland near the Lafitte Project were so quiet that one could take a leak in the Orleans Avenue neutral ground and they'd hear it in the middle of Lake Pontchartrain ("Punchatrain" to the natives). Claiborne Street was dead. Wasn't nuthin' happenin' at Prout's. The Strip, a motley series of rum and coke clubs, was wanting and haunting that night. The Oyster House was closed, Scotty's was out-like-a-light, and his tightman had already hipped him that the band didn't even show up at Blunt's (down on Dumaine and Prieur). Club 77 was hoppin', and the Desert Sands had a li'l barroom band, but he had also gotten the word on Gloria's Living Room over in the Seventh Ward where, he was told, there were so many wall-to-wall wimmins that he'd be like . . . a wolf in a henhouse. . . .

The leaves of the Claiborne neutral ground's venerable, majestic oaks made merry music as they rustled, hustled, bustled and tussled under a wanton wind-maddened New Awlins nightscape, a warren of shops, bars, salons, restaurants, mid-19th century Creole cottages, and shotgun houses. Batches of hatches and windows were battened down with plywood and tape. Once brightly-colored, now faded strands of beads (left over from last Mardi Gras' Zulu parade) swung festively, mirthfully, from nutbrown, timeworn limbs. He munched on a piece of bird, took another swig, and noticed a cherry red chickaree squirrel scampering up the trunk of a tree on the far side of the neutral ground, but there would be no safe harbor in the treetops that night. Rising waters were lapping over grassy levees, covering Louisiana lowlands. It was worse than the night Otis Redding died. A marquee at the Clabon Theater ("THE SHOW" to the natives) asked "Guess Who's Coming to Dinner?" The answer was second-linin' in the wind.

New Awlins . . . the land of hot tin rooves and dance floor-packin' grooves. New Awlins. The Sixth Ward ("Tremé" to the tourists). It was an innocent age -- passionate and peaceful, yet violent; straight-out cut and dried; a city long unremembered by CARE. The howling, punishing wind was *rollin'-rollin'-rolliiiiinnnnn'*, whistlin' Dixie in the night air's song. Hurricane Galinthia would soon hit, spreadin' her big, black, cloudy behind all over everything and fottin' titanic tornados, but the creatures were stirring. The night people, the wanderers, the birds of prey, passage, and passion jitterbugged -- tippin' down, across, around and inandout the Crescent City's meandering streets. *The natives were restless.* Wasn't no *one* monkey gon' stop no show -- not in New Awlins!

He flicked on the dial. Ed "Screamin'" Teamer, Larry McKinley, Poppa Stoppa, Shelly Pope or *some*body would be jammin' *sumthin'* on *some* station on such a night as this, just as sure as Lafitte Project children ("Housing Development residents" to the politicians and newscasters) would soon be hiding from the hurricane's fury by cowering under red bean-stained Rosenberg's kitchen tables. It started raining-raining-raining -- lickin' like chicken. A plastic glow-in-the-dark statue of Jesus, arms outstretched, gazed at him from the dashboard. A set of oversized black and red-dotted, fuzzy, fake fur dice (and assorted Mardi Gras beads) dangled from the rear view mirror. He turned on the windshield wipers just as the Temptations, harmonizing like musical birds of paradise, sang:

Jazz Stories: *From Katrina to Connecticut*

>   *". . . Chicka-boom Chicka-boom*
>   *Chicka boom-boom-boo-oo-oo-oom . . ."*

Imitation silk-covered red and pink lace-bordered pillows quivered and quaked, trembling in the wake of two powerful back window speakers. He deftly reached in the glove compartment of the Chevy for a pack of Chiclets, stopped for a red light at Esplanade, and pondered the answer to the eternal question, "Why did the chicken cross the road?" The light changed. He went to the other side.

* * *

He continued down Claiborne, hit a left at Elysian Fields, and hit a right down to Spain Street. A sign on a corner shotgun house announced the presence of the newly-opened, soon-to-be-infamous "Gloria's Living Room." Rows of cars parked on Spain and couples hoppin' and-a hippin' and-a skippin' and-a trippin' and-a drippin' and-a tippin' through the rain told him that the set inside was kickin' like a chicken. The joint was jammin' and a-bammin' and a-jumpin' and a-humpin'. The poppas was a-poppin' and the honeys was a-boppin'. He parked the car, donned his canary yellow rain slicker, reached for his drumsticks, got soaked in the driving rain while dashing inside, entered the joint strutting like a Bantam rooster, and ran right smack into Bucky Melancon (that li'l heavyset red boy from the Seventh Ward --- look like Burl Ives), Poppa, Robichaux, Bubblegum, brogan-wearin' Burnell Barbarin, Magoo and Greenhouse. They was sho' nuff on the wild, totally outa wack, higher than giraffe bugars. They was sittin' there playin' it down, jokin' and jammin' in high cotton, cuttin' up like a brand new pair of tight, patent leather shoes. Drinks were going down faster than a European heavyweight champion boxing Muhammad Ali. He went over to their table where the "set-ups" they had ordered were being drained dry and took a seat with the fellas that afforded him a bird's eye view of the bar. He sat (tappin' his drumsticks in time with the tune that was blasting from the box) just under a poster announcing an upcoming comedy show with Redd Foxx, LaWanda Page, Skillet & Leroy, Blowfly, and Dootone XXX Party Records. There were so many blackfolk in the bar it looked like Canal Street. It was a sea of plaid shirts with butterfly collars, All Star tennis shoes (high top, low top and the new black All Stars), plain white T-shirts tucked into tailor-made pants, Ban Lon shirts, "Old Man Comforts" shoes, Edwin Clapps, two-tone wingtips, double-breasted blue blazers; slick, tight-fitting, iridescent suits; checkered, hip-huggin', bell bottom pants; skinny, rayon, clip-on ties; dimestore dark glasses, neckerchiefs, and more bouncin' brown and black breasts and butts than a Tarzan movie. They was *raggin'*. A Shorty Long list of all the local dwellers and denizens woulda showed who was there: Joe Young, Laughin' Man, Hammerhead, Black Bill, Lucifer, Crime Wave, Showboat, Textbook, Dopey, Shorty, Pinky, Sleezy, Pimpy, Stinky and Willoughby. Them superfine Six and Seventh Ward wimmins was there too: Paulette, Antoinette, Suzette, Halette, Georgette, Earline, Ernestine, Wilmarine, Jolene, Josephine, Arthurine, Bernadine, Dora, Flora, Cora and Isadora. They was dressed sharper than a brand new, unopened packa Gillette Double Edge Blue Blades. A gaggle of them nightclub photographers was goin' from table to table havin' people watch the birdie and snappin' they pitchers – like they was out there in Hollywood swingin'or sumthin'. Everything was Kool & the Gang. They wasn't standin' on the verge. They was gittin' it on.

"I see Greenhouse old lady let him out the cage for the weekend," Red cracked as the liquored-up commoners and nignitaries stunted and fronted.

"-- Yo' paw! Yo' pedal-pusher wearin' paw!" Greenhouse retorted. He was a very funny character. He *kept* people in stitches. "You heard o' the coffeehouse? The jailhouse? The po' house? The crazyhouse? The dopehouse? I'm the Greenhouse!!!" he boasted.

"-- More like the *Out*house!" Bucky kidded. " 'Crazyhouse' 'bout right. You need to be up on the third floor, Charity Hospital."

"That's why yo' maw borned you when she was locked up in Mandeville," Greenhouse gagged.

"Lighten up, 'House,'" said Barbarin, as he poured a Seven and Seven from one of the set-ups. Greenhouse helped himself to some Thunderbird and grapefruit juice. He had quite a snoutful.

"Wow! They got mo' young twat in here than Saint Mary's Academy," said Red.

"Say, bruh -- be cool with that. My sister go to Saint Mary's," protested Poppa. "Y'all always loudcappin' somebody."

"I ain't talkin' 'bout yo' tackhaid sister. I'm talkin' 'bout the school. You know 'bout them Saint Mary's girls. Them scabs done had mo' weenie in 'em than a Oscar Mayer delivery truck."

"That's why yo' maw be down in the French Market stealin' crabs every day," Poppa snapped.

"That's why *yo'* maw *catch* crabs every day."

"That's why yo' maw favorite record is *I Made a Mistake* and yo' paw favorite song was *It Ain't My Fault*."

"Magoo ain't seen his maw since the day he fell out her ass -- and he had to *smell* his way outa *there*!"

"Y'all keep messin' with me -- and my Injun gon' come out," said Magoo, adjusting his superthick spectacles.

"Damn, bruh! Looka Laughin' Man," someone said. "He still on that hair-roin. His clothes so raggedy he look like Robertson Crustoe."

"Yeah. He got a bad rep. He'll shove a shank in you in a minute."

"He so old he remember the old Claver Building when it used to be the French Hospital. He was wunna Ed's Cabs' first drivers. That boy old as the pyramids. He older than Jackson Square."

"I thought 'Bad boys die young'!?!"

"Naw, not in his case. He still out there livin' like a hermit. Then his old red ass got the nerve to be color-struck."

"His face so skinny-- look like he suckin' on a dill pickle," Melancon laughed amidst the ocean of Ivy League haircuts, flattops, and assorted goo-gobs of greasy kid stuff. Pimpish pumpadoos were fried, dyed and laid to the side.

"Man, y'all must be smokin' too many left-handed cigarettes," said Robichaux, coolly sipping a scotch and milk drink. A sober mind was about as scarce as hen's teeth and about as rare as a female *flambeau* carrier. The bar bees were Cissy Struttin', Jerkin', twerkin', Poonannyin' and justa shakin' they tail feathers. A sign on the spackled wall said:

Professor Arturo

EAT FISH
LIVE LONGER

EAT OYSTERS
LOVE LONGER

"Yeah. Yo' sister some fine," Red said. "That's how I like 'em -- young, tender, juicy, and golden brown. I bet her titties feel like two big catfish pressin' up on you. My Uncle Willie was right -- 'There's titties, there's *pretty* titties, there's *nice* titties, and there's *serious* titties.' Yo' li'l sister got some *serious* titties."

"That's why yo' maw go to the 'Hoe Mass' at Corpus Christi every Saturday evenin'."

"'Hoe Mass'?!? What's that?"

"That's the mass them bugar bat hoes go to 'fore they go work them tourists in the Quarters. They be prayin' not to git arrested, robbed, or killed."

"These matches complimentary?"

"No, they *free*."

"-- Gittin' back to Greenhouse' maw. . . her face so ugly she could scare a packa hungry lions off the meat truck." The revelers were sensuously, smoothly, seriously slow-draggin' as the untender night rocked and rolled on. The fellas were still comin' down hard on Greenhouse's momma. . . .

"Yo' maw like a meat market freezer . . . fresh meat go in her every day. They gon' lock her back up in Mandeville -- put her in the crazyhouse."

"How you git to Mandeville?"

"Act like him."

"Say, man --?!"

"What?"

"Chicken butt."

"You is a *fool*."

"They got too much ice in this drink."

"A whole lotta people git killed by foolin' 'round with ice."

"Hot ice?"

"No . . . *mawfiddice*."

"I'm tore up."

"I'm tore down."
"I'm drunk."
"I'm lit."
"I'm blackin' out."
"I'm toasted."
"I'm high as a kite."
"I'm low as yo' gran'nma."
"I'm fried."

"That wind sound like it's still blowin' some hard out there, yeah. Galinthia out there some bad."

"Man, this ain't nuthin'. I done been in a hurricane so bad it made a whole string o' boxcars look like a Slinky."

"I'm still at Clark runnin' track -- the 880 and the mile. What's *yo'* race?"

"Colored."

"Don't be callin' nobody no 'colored.' I'm *black*. I ain't no 'colored' and I for *damn* sure ain't no 'Negro.' I have knowledge of self, my brother. That's why I enlisted in SUNO."

"Enlisted?"

"Yeah . . . you don't 'matriculate' at SUNO . . . you serve time."

"SUNO?!? You ain't got no exclusive dibs on no knowledge. That's why I'm at Yale and you still down here in Pontchartrain Park."

"It don't matter where you go. It's what you do with what you git where you go."

"Man . . . shut yo' fonky face. You too light in the ass."

"You know yo' people -- put three of 'em in a room and you'll have four opinions."

"What *I'm* trying to do is to git me a new short . . . a T-Bird. I'm tired o' pushin' that Shivvalay. That's why I'm workin' overtime. I'm puttin' my ducks in a row . . . *now*. I'ma hold on to my money 'til the eagle grin. I'm gon' git that new short. I'ma be happy as a runaway slave. I'm savin' *my* dust. I'ma pluck every chicken feather I can. I'ma make my*self* happy," Red said to anybody whom he thought was listening.

"Yo' gravediggin', barhoppin', mudslingin', brick-layin' maw gon' be happy," instigated a voice at the table.

"Keep messin' with me . . . yo' ass gon' be grass . . . and I'ma be the lawnmower."

Professor Arturo

"You still at the slaughterhouse?" Bubblegum asked as he lit a KOOL Filter King with his stainless steel, flamethrower lighter.

"Man, I don't work at no 'slaughterhouse.' I work at the 'chicken processing plant.' I'm the head honcho. I just got a promotion. I'm the H.N.I.C. I'm The Man. I'ma *buy* that T-Bird -- cash on the barrelhead," said the newly-promoted poultry eviscerator.

"Aw, bruh -- the only thing you gon' ever own is yo' walk," someone ribbed.

"Tell that to yo' street-hustlin', cattle-rustlin', bush-whackin' maw!"

"Ain't no thing but a chicken wing," said Red as he coolly cocked his head back. "What time is it?" he asked Poppa.

"I don't know. I ain't got the time."

"Ain't got the time? *You* the one sportin' the Rolex."

"This watch don't work. I just wear it to pull some cock. I just wear it for the front."

"You some stupid. You just as stupid as yo' P-poppin' paw."

"I ain't stupid. I'm ig'ant. I'm a lover."

"Aw, man . . . you ain't had cock since cock had you," said Barbarin.

"Ain't had *what*?"

"*Cock*. Nookie. Cookie. Cat. Cooch. Pah-*yonn*. Trim. Snatch. Crack. Gap. *Panocha*. Poonanny. Poontang. Leg. Twat. I know it's been a long time . . . like forever for *yo'* sexually-challenged ass."

"Yo' maw! Yo' man-eatin' maw!"

"That's why yo' oldlady named 'Squirrel.' She gather nuts for a livin'."

"That's   raw."

"Man, what time is it? I gotta git to the gig. Who got the time? What time is it?"

"Cold Duck time!" somebody shouted.

"Half past the bear's azz . . . *Rookie* . . . The azz shall be *first* . . . and the first, *azz*."

"No, man. *Seriously*. What's all that fowl language about? What time is it? I gotta git to work. Who got the time? What time is it?"

"-- Ten to."

"-- Ten to what?"

"-- Tend to yo' own bizness."

"That's why yo' maw up there in Angola -- servin' triple life -- and *don't* wan' come home."

"That's why yo' maw got skid marks on her draws."

"Tell that to yo' cigar-smokin', truck-drivin', anklewhipper/brogan-wearin', mustache-growin' gran'ma." This latest unwise crack really laid an egg with Red. "Y'all some sometimey," he said. "Y'all need to quit givin' me all that static," he said as he peered through the smoke and bouncing booties, past the twisting, undulating orange and red blobs in the tables' lava lamps. "I gotta git on over by the London Canal. I gotta git to work and check on them chickens. Y'all drunk, fonky monkeys ain't gon' stop no show."

He thought he noticed an eerily familiar figure standing at the bar under a cloud of cigarette smoke. It was Maggie. Maggie Glapion, the li'l lady with the honey-colored eyes who was long-reputed to be the great-great-grandniece of Marie Laveau. She was a young woman with whom his intentions were not favorably regarded. They said Maggie G. had wooed and hoodooed many a male with that red gravy and her butterball turkey ass. Her ass was so fine and shapely you could eat a full course meal off it. You could put a mixin' bowl on it -- and it wouldn't fall off. Momma mia! She was a spicy meatball. The ooglebirds and wallflowers would watch in a daze for days and days as she danced the forbidden dance in delirious delight while the music's pumping bass swayed on. She was *fine*. The dark, raven-tressed beauty was Miss Hotpants, Miss Crescent City, Miss Tight Jeans, and Miss Ass of The Year. For Carnival last year she wore a purple Playboy Bunny suit -- with a li'l red tail and everything! She was *boss*. She was wunna them wimmins who spend hours stinkin' theyself up with all kinda exotic concoctions that she kept in delicately sculpted miniature bottles with fancy French names. Her cleavage entered the room before *she* did. That girl was so fine -- it looked like she was a Lifetime Charter Member of Thigh Beta Kappa. She was fine. They say she sent some pictures to JET for they center page, but they told her her titties and ass was too big. She was fine. Stunningly beautiful. They say she never let her men friends down: she always kept 'em up. You shoulda seen that pretty woman goin' under a limbo stick.

"Looka who I see at the bar," said Red.

"Who that? Who that?" asked Poppa.

"'Who'? 'Who'? You got feathers in yo' ass?"

"Huh?"

"'Who'? 'Who'? Is you a owl?"

"Say it -- don't spray it. Stop spittin' when you talk!"

"Yeah, bruh -- I showed the rollers a pho-to-static copy of my draft card. They *still* cuffed me and brought me to the Pink Palace. All I had on me was a matchbox fulla weed and a carpet knife. I told 'em I was on my way to work."

"-- At 3:30 in the mornin'?"

"You got a cigarette?'

"Uh-huh."

"You got a light?'

"Damn, bruh! You want me to smoke it for you?'

"Man -- you still strung out on that twat?" asked Poppa.

"She broke my heart in three," moaned Red.

"Well, me -- I ain't gon' be like you with all that. I ain't lookin' for no permanent, fulltime spoogie. Some horses just don't pull too good in a double harness."

"You don't know like I know what that woman done done for me," Red whimpered. "Don't be bussin' my rap. Quit cockblockin'."

"Aw, man -- when the broad say 'jump' you say 'how high'?" laughed Robichaux.

"I remember her . . . the li'l bowlegged one with the li'l gap in her teeth," said Poppa.

"That ain't the *only* place she got a li'l gap," smiled Red.

"All she did was put you in a trick bag. She got you on a jive-time tip. She put that red gravy and them black draws on you," Poppa persisted. "I heard she givin' up that pah-*yonn* outa three drawslegs."

"Why you bein' so skep' on her? Why you so skep' 'bout her?'

"'Cain't live with 'em . . . cain't live without 'em," quipped Bucky.

"Not in *this* camp," said Greenhouse.

Jazz Stories: *From Katrina to Connecticut*

"You robbin' the cradle again. I know you like I know the backa my rod. It ain't gon' work. You tried it before. Y'all from different sides o' the street. You cain't make a hoe a housewife," Poppa insisted.

"-- And you cain't make a mule into a thoroughbred," Greenhouse slobbered.

"Tough enough. But she so fine and shapely. She look like a big, fat government check – just waitin' to be cashed. . .. I'ma make a turn."

"-- A turn for the worst!" someone insisted.

"The only turn I'ma make is over to Prieur and Lapeyrouse -- over there at Joe & Jean's -- where they got that li'l fine red go-go dancer," yawned Barbarin. "I think I'ma slide over there."

"Bruh --" offered Poppa, "I cain't stop you, I cain't knock you, and I'm not gon' bump my haid. But you actin' like you on that happy dust. If you weak, you beat."

"If you slow, you blow," offered Barbarin.

"If they dumb, you come!" joked Greenhouse above the sound kicking from the jukebox.

"That's how I like 'em," mused Red. "Young, dumb and full of it!"

"Turkey!" spat Poppa. "She was just usin' you. You wasn't nuthin' but a popcorn . . . sucker john."

"That's bogue," said Robichaux.

"We just had a li'l fallin' out. A quail in the hand is worth two in the bush. I ain't chicken," protested Red, while giving his podners the bird.

"That girl used to have so much Indian Fire on her face, I wanted to play 'Connect the Dots,'" hollered Bubblegum.

"Body by Fisher -- Mind by Mattel," teased Magoo. "Yo' nose wide open."

"My nose closed. You cain't even see my nose. My nose closed."

"Naw, it's wide open. I see them big, green bugars in there."

"Aw, Magoo -- Yo' four-eyed blind ass cain't see the broad anyway," protested Red. "I just wanna go back and be her special man."

"**Let her have it**," baritoned Robichaux.

"Tighten up, Red," sopranoed Barbarin. "I thought you wasn't gon' work on Maggie's farm no mo'."

"Dealin' with wunna them scabs is like waitin' on a bus," chimed Bubblegum. "You always got another wunna them tackhaids comin'. You just punkin' out . . . tryin' to be on the rebound with that broad like that. You know she already took you for a ride. Sometimes you gotta put a statue of eliminations on 'em. Stop bein' so softhearted. When it come to wimmins -- I do 'em like vitamins -- one a day! It's a poor rat ain't got but one hole to run to."

"-- And it's a *real* po' chicken ain't got but one worm."

"Y'all be comin' down some hard on me tonight, yeah. I just want her to give the drummer some. I like 'em 8 to 80, blind crippled or crazy. I been layin' in the cut a long time for this. Look at her -- sittin' over there tryin' to ig' me with her fine ass in that black leather miniskirt and red flyaway scarf. I'ma take it like I find it or leave it like it is," said Red, rising from the table, drawn as if by a magnet to the U-shaped lavender bar where she stood stylishly nursing a drink. All the bold soul needed was a blue dashiki. Dyke & the Blazers were blasting in the background. Greenhouse got up and was doin' a Ninth Ward version of the Toulouse Booty (or was it the Seventh Ward Shuffle?) in a Soul Train line. They was cuttin' up and showin' out. On the wild. Shakin' 'em on down.

* * *

He strutted towards her like the Cock o' the Walk as she stood conversatin' and blah-zayin' with her gabby girlfriend Shitoya, her purple whipstitched imitation leather purse and shiny, gold lamé jacket slung over a bar chair. Her round, rubious lips were caked in slut pink lipstick and her ears boasted giant, gold plated hoochie hoops (way 'fore everybody else started wearin' 'em). Her raccoon eye makeup shone strangely in the bar's dim light, accenting her ultra-short miniskirt and snakeskin stiletto "I'm over here -- come git me" heels. She had on a ba-a-a-a-a-ad outfit.

"May I, baby? . . . What it is, Baby Doll? Let's talk a li'l turkey," he gobbled, eyeing the perky swell of her breasts as he stood there nervously looking around like a one-eyed canary in a tomcat show. He didn't wanna front himself off *too* much in fronta the fellas. He didn't wanna get caught out there with egg in his face.

"What it be like?" she bugalooed.

"What you drinkin'?" he shingalinged.

"Double rum & coke. Top-shelf."

"That's a lady's drink?" he asked, motioning to the barmaid and ordering for her.

"It is if a lady drink it," she capped, her pert, pecawn brown, rosebud nipples standing up like the Marine Corps Band, peeking thru her purple and pink paisley-printed blouse. Everything on the girl was brown and round, 'cept for her li'l bitty teenantchee chicken legs. They was nice and neat, short and sweet. She moved her butterball buttocks as smoothly as Gladys and the Pips. The girl wasn't nuthin' but lips and hips. Wunna them girls who went to Clark (y'all know what I'm talkin' 'bout).

"Girl -- you drink so much you gon' bust yo' bladder," said Shitoya, leanin' all up into the conversation. "Why you tryin' to drink like you some high-to-do fancy woman? A minute ago you was drinkin' Thunderbird and grape juice."

"Where y'at, Shitoya. How's tricks?" he signified as she stood by the bar with all that earl up in her haid. "That's yo' real hair?" he asked regarding the pedigree of her plumage.

"Old bullet-haid boy. Every time you open yo' mouth you don't know whether you gon' talk or shoot. Yeah it's my real hair -- 'cause I *bought* it."

"Well, *I* bought the lady a drink," said Red. "And she don't need no chaperone. Why don't you just zip yo' lip. This a 'A' and 'B' conversation. So why don't you 'C' yo' way out it!" Two stylish women lookin' like they was fresh off the block bogarted they way to the bar through a medley of smoky yellow eyes and sweating bodies. Sweet Thing #1 was in a tie-dyed, braless, crotchet halter and ombré pink peasant skirt with a yellow poncho. Sweet Thing #2 was so fine he didn't notice *what* she was wearing as his eyes had undressed her quicker than you could say "Richard Nixon."

"Don't come over here messin' with me," warned Shitoya. "I'ma call you a BIG, BAD, DIRTY WORD," she shoo-shooed, undereying him. This had been going on for a lo-o-o-o-ong time.

"Yeah. Just like you did when you told Baby Girl you saw me with some broad up in the Nightcap. You ain't had to go there."

"Uh. I'm scared 'o *you*. And it wasn't the Nightcap. It was you and that fancy woman up in Chez Helene -- over there on Robertson -- right down the street from Hank's. Put *that* in yo' pipe and smoke it." *I'd put so many holes in him, he be done whistled when he walk,* she thought. Maggie G. was just sittin' there with her mouth wide open like a Gulf oyster at low tide givin' him wunna them "Negro, *please* --" looks as she chomped and swagged on a platter of barfood.

"Why is that yo' bizness? You always gittin' in somebody *else* bizness. You need to loosen yo' wig cap," he said, turning and facing Miss Fine, his hardness straining against his tailor-made pants. *I shoulda worn my tight bellbottoms,* he thought. He was as hard as a Buffalo soldier in an Amazon movie. She had that kind of effect on men.

"-- Old pecawn-haid boy," Shitoya snapped. "Crack his big empty, humpty haid open – pecawn candy come out. That man so dumb he cain't find a drink on Bourbon Street. You need to go on 'haid and run off with the next man you see 'fore you go 'haid on with him." Just then, Greenhouse came over from the dance floor. "On second thought --"

"Look -- I don't know what yo' malfunction is, but I *do* know yo' ass so sluttish that if you walkin' down Canal Street and see some lollipops in the candy store window you gon' holler 'Practice'! . . . What's happenin', 'House?"

"Take a walk," he whispered. They went to the men's room to fire up a joint. "*Toodaloo*," Shitoya sang as the cats stepped away. The women then started conversatin' like two cackling hens, talking woman to woman.

"Girl --" said Shitoya. "That man sumthin' else. He some crazy, yeah. He need to be 'shamed o' his self. His chin need to be hittin' him in his chest. He got loose brains. You know how he perform when he git drunk. When my uncle drank, he used to drink a fifth o' hard liquor at a time. All you could do with him was put him in the house, lock the door, and hope for the best. Red just need to stop actin' like a Creature from the Black Lagoon. He need to be 'shamed o' his self. His wings musta done flopped." Then -- "He still married?"

"Girl, you know I don't fool with no married mens," Maggie said. "First -- it ain't right. Second -- I know how it feel to be the wife. I don't mess with no married man. Ain't no future in that. And I don't need no pitty party. I don't need no man workin' on my nerves like that. That man was gon' make me conk him in the haid. That's why I kicked him to the curve. And he ain't *never* had no money. He ain't nuthin' but a BIG WHEEL with a flat tire. Talkin' 'bout he savin' for some ride he been wantin'. Puttin' on airs . . . *I* was footin' the bills. *I* paid the cost to be the boss. *I* was the woman *and* the man o' the house. I can do good by myself. I don't wan' have no chirren underfoot with a man like that. Nuthin' in this world come for free. That man got champagne tastes with a beer pocketbook. He all sizzle and no steak. Talkin' 'bout he want us to live with his *nanann* in Boutté. That li'l town so slow they daily paper come once a month. I'm from New Awlins. I cain't live nowhere where they got roaches big 'nuff to name and pull on a leash! I cain't live just anywhere. Shoot." She shrugged. "I want a man with BIG BANK -- and one foot in the grave and both heels on a banana peel. I'ma git me a *rich* spoogie . . . not no bugar daddy . . . a *sugar* daddy -- a man who can give me a house with a swimming pool big as the Specific Ocean! Shoot. He always outa pocket. He be broke as the Ten Commandments. That man so tight he stand up and walk to the backa the church when they pass the collection plate."

"Yeah," said Shitoya.

"He done bust his draws with me. He flew the coop on me. Talkin' 'bout he was workin' offshore in the Gulf for two weeks out the month knowin' full well he was foolin' 'round with that li'l woman over there in Pontchartrain Park . . . had a whole outside family. And always got the nerve to be jumpin' salty with *me*. Like I'm some dumb cluck. He had the right key but the wrong keyhole 'cause that man could talk so smooth butter woulda done melted in his mouth . . . but I wasn't gon' train him for another woman. That's why I *been* done had a boot in my mouth for him. I just don't want no humbug. I ain't gon' say no act o' contrition for no man."

"Baby -- mark my words -- what's good for the goose . . ."

"Every time I think about that man I just bust out cryin'. He all issues and no answers."

"You need to bust his *haid*. That man boo-coo doofus. If you fool with that man again I'ma jump on yo' time," said Shitoya, nearly blowing a gasket. "I believe in Gawd, but don't lemme lay my religion down. I'll bust his behind for 15 minutes and pick it back up again."

"Ever since I done known him he ain't been doin' nuthin' but livin' on chicken and wine. Comin' to me hat-in-hand. But I'm time 'nuff for him. I git up mighty early in the mornin' – way 'fore the rooster put his underwear on. He be tryin' to put me under a microscope but be usin' a telescope with everybody else. He hurt me to my heart. I was some outdone. Shoot. That same bridge that took him over gon' take him back."

"He jump too salty with me and I'd slap him so hard -- I'd knock the yella off his teeths. I'd put some pain on him. He wouldn't be runnin' his haid and blowin' his top at me. I'd knock the red off his black ass. He need to stop bein' so flip by the lip. He ain't nuthin' nice. If you go back to that man, I'ma have a hissy. He gon' drop you like a hot potatuh . . . draggin' the streets when he need to be at work cuttin' up them chickens. Lawd, don't git me started . . . I'd give him a run for his money."

"Uh. That take the cake."

"With icing on it."

"How you like *them* apples?"

"They say 'The dog that bring tail take tail.'"

"What *that* mean?"

"I don't know. It's just sumthin' my gran'ma used to say."

* * *

"Bruh --" Greenhouse started, "I just think you and that broad being together is like tryin' to light a match in a hurricane. I unnerstand that one cat's sly is another cat's stone, but it just ain't gon' roll. You cain't be no husband and be a cockhound too. I saw how you was eagle-eyein' them two broads when they walked over to the bar." He choked as he pulled on the joint while letting out a prime example of the legendary, room-clearing, torturing toxicity of Greenhouse Effect flatulence. He was a true gentleman of distinkshun. He passed the joint to Red as they stood side-by-side at the double urinal, relieving themselves. "I'm just tryin' to keep abreast of the subject," Red said. "I know it went bad befo', but I'ma love her for the next 25

Jazz Stories: *From Katrina to Connecticut*

years to life. She the pearl in my life. I'ma love her as long as the trees be standin' on Claiborne Street."

"Yeah, but don't be tryin' to shuck and jive her. You know good and well you ain't no settler."

"-- But she gotta git ridda Girlfriend. That li'l heifer too nosey. She too saddity. She think with her ass. Always all up in somebody' bizness. All she be 'bout is perpetratin' and instigatin'. But with the broad -- all this ping-pong, merry-go-'round, yo-yo shit got to go. Enough is enough – and too much *stink*."

"Either way it go down, bruh --" Greenhouse said, leaning on the restroom's rusty, stained, $.25 prophylactic dispenser that had "Dump The Hump" scribbled on it in raging pink, getting the joint from Red "-- I'ma tell you sumthin', podner, and it ain't no lie – you gon' stay my main man 'til the day you die."

"'Yeah. 'Til the day I die, "said Red. "Let's book."

* * *

Greenhouse went back over to the fellas while Red tipped over to the bar, peacock proud, as chipper as a jaybird. It was 'bout time for the night's version of "He said-She said"...

They stood next to each other at the bar, staring at the imitation French provincial mirror that hung over rows of bottled pleasure and poison, seemingly dancing dangerously around each other like two fighting cocks.

"What's *yo'* angle, Mister Man?" Maggie asked, tauntingly, egging him on, knowing he was trying to hatch some chicanerous scheme.

"When you gon' come over to the crib for dinner some time? I could put some chicken on," was *his* opening line. *Old big-haid, liver-lip, coke-top-face, cabbidge-haid boy*, Shitoya mumbled as she made her exit.

"I don't *eat* dinner."

"Well then -- what about lunch?"

"Uh-uh."

"Breakfast?"

"No."

"Brunch?"

"Naw."

"Then how about a snack?"

"I cain't have no snack. I gotta watch my figure."

"I'll watch it for you," he flirted.

"You been playin' that alblum 'til it done long been scratched. Don't be talkin' un'neath yo' shirt to me."

"C'mon, baby. You sure you don't want a li'l company? Can we talk . . . for a minute?" Red asked Maggie, coppin' a smooch by sneaking a peck on her well-rouged left cheek (Y'all know how them mens be tryin' to git that free feel). *"Wow . . . the way you look tonight,"* he said. "Lemme keep you company. We cain't just stand here like a coupla ducks in a thunderstorm."

"I don't mind company. Company's alright with me every once in a while. It's yo' thing -- Do what you wanna," she said.

"It cain't be all bad. Is you is or is you ain't my baby? If I could see you one mo' time . . . I'm too far gone to turn around," he said.

"I'm downright disgusted," she said.

"What it is? What can the matter be? It cain't be too serious we cain't talk it over. Why you always mean to me? Why cain't we be friends? I wanta take you higher," he said.

"I'd rather go blind. I'd rather be crippled and crazy. You fightin' a losin' battle. You walk yo' way and I'll walk mine. Lemme walk mine," she said.

"I won't cry. I won't shed a tear. Everybody plays the fool. That's life. I'ma love the life I live and I'ma live the life I love," he said.

"Cool down poppa, don't you blow yo' top," she told him. "You act like you Gawd' gift to wimmins."

"You act like you the Devil' gift to mens."

"What about that li'l woman in Pontchartrain Park? I bet you love her too."

"That was my cousin."

"Cousin?!?!? I know what kinda cousin she was. Ain't that much 'cousin' in the world. I wasn't jerked up. I was *raised* up. You act like you was raised by a packa wild dogs. I'm climbin' on the safe side o' the mountain."

"-- But she *was* . . . I mean . . . *is!*"

"Cousin!?! If you think I believe that then you the biggest fool since Chicken Little. Who do you think I am? I don't want no pimp daddy. I want somebody who gon' love me for *me*. I'm sick and tired o' all y'all sorry-ass mens out here comin' all up in my face. Like you 'rate.'"

"Mea culpa. Mea culpa. Mea MAXIMA culpa."

"Don't be makin' no issues. You *way* off the beat. You got the wrong number. You ain't gon' drive me, no."

"I'm so in love with you. Time is tight. Talk to me. Try me. Don't leave me this way. I got the feelin'," he said. "I'm tellin' you now like I told you befo'. Don't leave me no mo'. You lose me again -- you gon' lose a good thing. You'll lose a precious love."

"Things does happen, but the thrill is gone . . . at last . . ." she said.

"I don't know what to do with myself," he said. "Don'tcha just know it?"

"Do what you gotta do. Do like you wanna. You can make it if you try," she said.

"There's always sumthin' there to remind me," he said.

"That's a real mutha for ya. It's too late, baby. Yo' good thing done come to a end. You cain't make me cry no mo' 'cause I'm fresh outa tears. You talkin' loud and ain't sayin' nuthin'," she said. "Ain't no way for me to love you."

"I'm sorry," he said.

"Sorry is a sorry word," she said.

"You lost that lovin' feelin'," he said.

"You don't know what love is," she said.

"I'm chained and bound. I'm chained to yo' love."

"There's a thin line between love and hate."

"If lovin' you is wrong," he said, "I don't wanta be right."

"Love don't pay the rent," she said.

"I'll be good to you --"

"You been a good old wagon, but you done broke down."

"It's like I don't even know you anymore," he said.

"If you don't know me by now, you'll never know me," she said.

"Baby, I'm for real," he said. "If you leave me, I'll go crazy. Let's straighten it out. It's sumthin' you got. There's sumthin' about you. For yo' precious love, I would do anything."

"Well then -- hit the road, Jack. I done got over you at last. We just cain't git it on, so take yo' dead ass home," she blahzayed, sashayin' away into the crowd, leaving him breathless, standing accused in the misty shadows of love 'round midnight, a one bass hit, takin' five, steppin' into tomorrow, tryin' a li'l tenderness with all his body and soul, tellin' it like it is, and always and forever beggin' *Please, Please, Please* for mercy, mercy, mercy.

* * *

The club crowd was thinning out. Galinthia's ferocious coils of winds had signs outside flapping and slates flying over towering chineyball trees. She was tearing the roof off the sucker. Most of the fellas had skyed and the bar bees were about as scant as hen's fins. "I'ma holler at cha," Greenhouse waved as he rose from the table, grabbed a go-cup from a nearby barmaid, and stumbled drunkenly towards the door like he was all hopped-up on sumthin'. Red still hadn't copped what he wanted to cop, but was a firm believer in the adage "When the going git tough -- git rough." Just as he was runnin' his last rap – the power went out. The sound from the jukebox was history. The barmaids quickly reverted to candlelight and the proprietor proclaimed, "It done got some bad out there! Drinks is on the house! Just drink what you *been* drinkin'!"

"So what you drinkin', baby?" he asked, easing up to Ms. Thang in a suddenly thirsty pack at the bar.

"I'm drinkin' what I been drinkin'."

"Come here and drink summa this," he said, reaching for her like he was Rock Hudson or somebody.

"Git off me! Don't touch me! Don't be gittin' no ideas with me!" she protested, as he tried to make his way with her. He persisted, provoking her to throw the remnants of her drink in his face. He was an unyielding believer in "an eye for an eye and a drink for a drink," so he splashed the remainder of *his* glass into her heavily made-up mug. She slapped him and he smacked her back, knocking her to the floor. An undersized swarm gathered, separating them. "If *I* cain't have you, cain't *no*body have you!" he barked (the dirty dawg).

She freed herself from the pack of people, fumbled around in her purse, came up with a small snakeskin satchel and a tiny container of salt and sprinkled the saline substance into a circle on the floor. She reached in the satchel, taking some guinea peppers out, and put them in her mouth while pivoting around three times and asking St. John and some long-gone saint or sinner for their intercession. She made the sign of the cross over and over while spitting the peppers into her hand and throwing them floorward into the circle of salt. In the flickering candlelight one could see a charm of roots, string and chickenbones around her neck. "Gimme-what-you-got-to-gitta-ridda-him," she chanted, her voice accompanied by a blaze of light. "Gimme-what-you-got-to-gitta-ridda-him. . . ."

When Red peeped this, it was time to take a powder. . . .

* * *

Outside, Galinthia's winds roared recklessly, brutally, screaming bloody murder, goo-gobs of debris flying treacherously through the sinfully sinister air. Sheets of rain raged relentlessly, stinging him, shoving, thrusting him about like a sunflower in a storm as he made his way towards the Impala. He still had to make it to the job (he had just been promoted to Assistant Overseer and *some*one had to brave the storm, feed the stock and write up a damage assessment), so he maneuvered up London Avenue through the rising streams of wind-whipped water (that was now moving like the Colorado rapids in springtime) towards the slaughterhouse near the usually foul, rotten egg-smelling canal adjacent to that last stop for generation upon generation of chickens.

He approached the side door of the corrugated tin-roofed facility, struggling against the wind's wretchedness as he reached underneath his raincoat for the key, then noticed that the door had been compromised by the storm's wilding winds. He heard the locomotive-like shaking, rattling and rolling of the all-to familiar sound of an approaching tornado, struggled unsuccessfully to open the door, but could not gather the potency or power to overcome the crashing, crushing, overwhelming force of the twister's absolute supremacy. A section of the plant's thin metal roof flew off, spinning, plummeting impiously and inevitably towards him, decapitating him, sending the tortured turkey's head off into the wild black yonder, blood gushing out all over the Seventh Ward. His goose was cooked. The answer was jitterbuggin' in the wind. The chickens had come home to roost.

* * *

They say that after the stormwinds died down them chickens was so hungry that they got out from there and was eatin' up anything and everything they could. They say them chickens was peckin' all over that boy's body like it was

Christmas dinner. Some folk even say they saw him out there rippin' and runnin' 'round like a chicken with his haid cut off.

August 2011
Stamford, CT

The Great Chain of Being

Once upon a time when the goose drank wine (and the monkey chewed tobacco on the streetcar line) in the midst of a vast ocean a school of fish was swimming in the briny deep and one of them spied a tiny shrimp floating in the water while feeding on a miniscule morsel of paltry, unpretentious plankton. The fish left the twisting, twirling, whirling mass, swooped down on the shrimp, and ate it.

"I am the mightiest fish of all," the fish boasted.

Then the fish sought out its sanctum of kinship and swam towards them. At that moment a larger fish descended upon the smaller fish and swallowed it whole.

"I am the greatest huntress in the ocean," the larger fish said.

The larger fish then saw an inviting morsel dangling nearby, grabbed it, and was snagged by a fisherman's hook. The fisherman reeled in the larger fish, detached it from the hook, and placed it in a pail of ice in the rear of his vessel.

"I am the best fisherman on all the seas and all the shores," said the fisherman.

Just then a pelican plummeted from the skies, scooped the fish in its bill, and soared across the waters to its nesting place somewhere in the horizon's wetlands.

"I am the most supreme, powerful creature on land, on the sea, or in the skies," the pelican boasted, while far above the ocean's mystifying waves, a slight wisp of warm, moist air that would eventually develop into a calamitous, catastrophic Category 5 hurricane rose in the heavens.

October 2012
Stamford, CT

Professor Arturo

Let Me Count The Ways . . .

"Who so loves believes the impossible."
-- Elizabeth Barrett Browning

    At first she was the sweetest rose in my life's garden, but she grew to be the most painful of thorns in my side. On our wedding day our marriage was a blissful and beauteous gateway to heaven. A week later it was a greased sliding board to the deepest, most abysmal expanse of hell. Whenever I hear our then-favorite song we danced to at the ceremony it now sounds like a funeral dirge and I have the urge to smash its source into oblivion whenever it raises its grisly, repugnantly unmelodious ugliness. Life is like a confused, beginning classroom teacher. First she gives the test -- then she teaches the course.
    She was my grade school sweetheart, but I now wished Cupid's arrow would've become encased in her impenetrably thick, nagging noggin rather than her heart. The same love that once made me laugh made me cry tears of longsuffering and despair.
    She had the sensitivity of a cremation urn and was surrounded by an aura of evil of Hitlerian proportions. She was one of those women who keeps you in the doghouse -- and runs you to the cathouse. Her face became a mini-map of Death Valley. Her once ripe, soft, melon breasts metamorphosed into withered, sun-dried rinds. Her relaxed hair seemed doomed to a state of perpetual slumber. Her self-hating pretensions reflected her desire to be a luxuriously-coifed champagne blonde. She was indeed a bugar bear. Sex with her became another adventure into plushophilia. She was the wind *above* my wings. She'd nag and nitpick about a toothpick in your behind while she had a giant sequoia up hers. Life with her became as tough as a two-dollar steak. It was more difficult than a tourist attempting to pronounce "Tchoupitoulas." I had more than enough of her relentless insistence that I do the Electric Slide at the corniest of carnival balls when I preferred doing the Wobble. . . . I dreaded her horse mane weaves and hair hats . . . the unorganized grime that was her closet . . . her morbid addiction to those "housewives" shows . . . her constant derision of and rabid

opposition to my friends and associates (especially Ricky, the cigar store owner in Puerto Rico I knew from grad school) . . . her accusations about non-existent affairs . . . her barbecue-grate earrings . . . her nagging, her snoring, her eyelash extensions . . . her pitiful attempts at being a social gadfly . . . her passings of gas that were like the winds of black death . . . her threat to inform the governmental authorities that I tore a label off a pillowcase and illegally copied a DVD . . . her constant correction of my grammar, spelling, and pronunciation . . . her elitist linguistic constructs coupled with words like "caveat" and "*ad hominem*". . her habit of smoking indoors which forced me to invest in a medley of humming humidifiers . . . her alleged pencil skirts that looked more like legal pads . . . her slimness-challenged shapelessness and the lasciviousness of her bargain-basement leggings . . . that bush league mistake of her charter membership in Colored Women for Obama and my having to shell out money for every Michelle knockoff in existence . . . her failed business enterprises such as the one where she tried to open a rockateria -- a washateria where patrons could wash clothes and dance . . . her attempts at gadgeteering and invention like the ink pen with a night light attached so writers could take nighttime notes without disturbing their bedmates . . . her insistence that I not eat white rice with my red beans . . . her constant post-Katrina home remodeling efforts . . . her tea sandwiches and garden parties . . . her vulgar careerist attempts to ride the mantle of my success . . . her dislike of my Amos and Andy movies and butterfly collar shirts . . . her driving me nuts with her habit of folding plastic shopping bags into tiny pyramidal shapes . . . her discarding of my GQ magazines before I had a chance to use the scented inserts . . . her pork roast stuffed with jalapeños that ran me straight to the turlit (making me feel like I had released a box of double edge razor blades) . . . her insistence that our household become "environmentally appropriate" and we had to flush just once a day to conserve water . . . *"no propellant spray"*. . . *"green products only"* . . . At least I was able to get a few hours respite and peace one night from Ms. Mother of All Environmental Issues when I deliberately used the most odiously pungent of bleaches to mop the kitchen floor and she vacated the chlorine-filled premises.

But the final straw that broke the crab's back was when she demanded that I permanently remove beer from my gastronomic preferences -- the beer -- that most sacrosanct of liquid pleasures, as historically and traditionally recognized by legions of men (and a buncha wimmins) worldwide as the holy of holies of mortal, worldly satisfactions. It wasn't time to get up. It was time to get *down*. She had to go. She just *had* to go.

I had long tired of taking her incessant verbal flack and dreamed of killing her slowly and softly, not with my song, but with my hands steadfastly clutched around her elephantine throat. Yes, there were a thousand ways I wanted to go Charles Bronson on her, but I had to settle for a Pee-Wee Hermanish approach to ridding the world of this most dastardly of demons.

Murdering her by the most agonizing means became more than a passing infatuation. Perhaps I could interest her in taking up an extremely high-risk activity. Our life and accidental death and dismemberment policy would well compensate me in the event that her eventual demise was expedited a mere trifle. Her well-deserved end had to be something more profound than tampering with her vehicle's brake system, attaching a bomb to her car, disabling the air bag then crashing her vehicle into a tree, or hanging her from the bell tower of St. Peter Claver Church.

I might be able to convince her to take a vacation in Spain and run with the bulls (*they'd* gore that heifer). I could have her "accidentally" slip and fall into a gumbo pot of bubbling, boiling water, or lop off her head with a remotely controlled, high-powered toy helicopter. The trouble was that she didn't know how to boil water and couldn't even handle a TV remote. How about inviting a serial killer over for a threesome? Naw, he'd probably dispose of me too. Maybe I could get her to take a 'round-the-world cruise on a Liberian tanker or remove the STOP signs at the corner of the city's busiest intersection, but unlike many death-dealing, hoodish thugs, I shunned involvement in the avoidable departure of innocents when the guilty was my target. I could bind her securely and force her to listen to Richard Pryor albums for days without end until she perished from fits of uncontrollable laughter; or have her stand in an open field in a lightning storm while holding a 20-foot-high metal rod. I could get a pack of rabid dogs to bite into her most vulnerable parts and consume her, but they would probably regurgitate at the mere thought of such nauseating morsels of such an object of volition. Helmetless motorcycling might do, but her concrete-hard skull would withstand even the most profound of headlong crashes into the most formidable of substances. It might be possible to contract with a prodigiously overendowed lover (so that she might die from dyspareunia due to impalement) or arrange for her to have anal intercourse with a stallion so she might die from peritonitis, but that wouldn't be tormenting or torturous enough. It might even be pleasurable for the horse hair-wearing, two-legged Clydesdale.

    I *could* manage to have her conveniently "trip" into a wood chipper or cut off her thumbs and stick them in her nostrils so that she could smother to death, but her blimpish, pimplish schnoz would need an entire fist for each opening. I could use some snow to block her car's exhaust pipes, but waiting for snow in New Orleans would be like lingering in line in Florida to cast a vote for Obama. A Zulu coconut to the skull at a Carnival parade might be appropriate, but they now hand out (rather than toss) the much-coveted former throws in this litigious age. Perchance I could employ an exploding bra, a poisoned douche, a radioactive sanitary napkin, TNT-spiked tennis balls; poisoned, heart-shaped Valentine's Day pancakes (but she didn't like pancakes or syrup); or exploding incense (but she wouldn't burn any due to her perennial seasonal allergies). I could have her conveniently fall while hanging wind chimes on the balcony, but we didn't have a balcony (or a stepladder). Conceivably, I might convince her to seek employment at the circus where a cowboy could shoot matches out of her mouth, have her apply for a position as food taster for a Middle Eastern potentate, or get a boa constrictor and train it to develop a fondness for her favorite perfume. Rat poison à la Faulkner's "A Rose for Emily" might accomplish the task, but an intellectually astute member of the local constabulary might have paid attention in a college level literature course (even if he or she went to SUNO). How about a public service -- like hurricane chasing (while skydiving)? I could shove her into a crawfish pond, but the bottom-feeding creatures might not have a taste for such abominable swill.

    Sport might be the most accelerated manner by which to expedite her termination . . . something like heli skiing, base jumping, free diving, swimming with sharks, bungee jumping, free fall parachuting, hang gliding, hot air ballooning (but she was afraid of heights), or a deep sea diving swimming accident (but the big, brown whale was an expert swimmer and captain of her college aquatics team).

After lengthy consideration of all of the above, I decided on a good, old-fashioned means of ridding myself of this snaking laceration in my heart -- a .38 caliber slug to her blubbery skull that would render me a life of orderly domesticity with no hassle in the castle of the two-paychecks-away-from-being-impoverished Eastern New Orleans oaklined subdivision. I didn't hear the sound of her customary snores when I entered the room that night, but she was there beneath an abundant bundle of covers. I crept through the darkness towards the bed and positioned the snub-nosed revolver just next to her thickset temple. That's when I noticed something odder than odd. She wasn't breathing. I leaned closer to her overflowing figure. Halleluiah!!! She was gone to the trashbin of the ages!

I immediately contacted the police authorities and the trumpet-playing coroner, went through the motions of being the bereaved husband, purchased the corniest (and cheapest) of flower coronets, planted her in the ground, and collected and cashed a rather prodigious insurance check. I was as happy as a gay sex addict serving triple life in Angola State Penitentiary without the possibility of parole. Within days I was on my way to Puerto Rico to hang with the loco senoritas and my podner, the cigar store owner. Just over a couple of hours into the flight the captain announced that there was a problem with one of the engines and a stewardess told us that we should fasten our seatbelts and say a prayer for our unfortunate souls.

. . .

June 2013
Stamford, CT

The Tree

(*a New Orleans tale of forbidden love*)

"For there is hope of a tree, if it be cut down,
that it will sprout again,
and that the tender branch thereof will not cease"
-- Job 14:7

"Storms make the oak grow deeper roots."
--George Herbert

Once upon a time when the goose drank wine and the monkey chewed tobacco on the streetcar line . . . before Tulane football's much-ballyhooed (and booed) Buddy System . . . before desegregation . . . before Nixon and Spiro's godawfully gross gyrations . . . before the 'Nam and the wars in the sands . . . before Ernest Kaydor Jr. was Ernie K-Doe . . . before the reconsideration of term limitation . . . before Bounce music and the neo-slave, blinding bling of raunchy, raucous, rapping mannequins of minstrelry . . . before the virtual unreality of the Internet . . . before jazzoetry . . . before Spoken Word at the Grammies . . . before times leana than Katrina. . . . Once upon that time, there was a boy and a girl who met in a Southern gentleman's home on Royal Street, their fate seven times cursed and seven times sealed. . . .

Armand Pierre LaFarge, present family patriarch, raised his Waterford wine glass in tribute to his long life and regeneration as he stood, occasionally pacing back and forth before the artifacts of his family's blood ties that adorned a marble mantel in a recessed corner of the crowded, whimsical elegance of the heirlooms, keepsakes and relics of an excessive era that were displayed and arrayed throughout the memento-filled family room of the galleried, Greek revival *grand dame* of a house with its sloping, red-tiled roof. As he did, he mulled over the distinction of his seed's impending extinction, surveying the sweep of history and the grand delusion that was his life, seeking the drunken bravery of liquid courage in what would be his life's endmost ancestral toast. The *Mouton Cadet* was a gift from his brother that he had been saving since his daughter was born. Over the

Professor Arturo

mantel hung a huge, glass-encased canvas with the family tree *of La Famille LaFarge*. He stood in his Rubenstein's lavender seersucker suit and two-tone shoes, reflecting on the splintered fabric of his inextricable linkage to his family, balancing himself on his thick, gentryman's walking stick (with its goosehead handle of polished brass). He held fast for a period of time under clouds of uncertainty, standing before the representation of his familial lineage and the issues of great contention muddling the frayed fabric of his life. A *fleur-de-lis* design enhanced a coat of arms with the LaFarge family motto inscribed in gold flake *(Famille, Honorer, Courage)* that was decorated with a hawk, a lion, a shield and coins.

Once upon a time, I had a fleeting thought of changing it to "Facta non verba." Tonight's maleficent events prove me right, he thought. A feeling of unmanifest destiny dominated the marble mantel and the gold-plated goblets on both sides. On its right was a plaque he had been given in recognition of his more than generous contribution of a new swimming facility to an exclusive Canal Street men's club (he gave it to 'em so he could join).

The walls were covered with exquisite gold and maroon *fleur-de-lis* pattern wallpaper. The polished granite floor bore grim, inglorious witness to his terminal libation as he once again reflected, ruminating over the deeds (and misdeeds) of his predecessors -- and himself, whom he considered a devout Southern gentleman who kept a customarily conventional distance between himself and a proper lady while dancing. He was viewed by his contemporaries as a man of honor and respect, as a gentleman of stirring oratory (for public consumption), but now found himself speechless. In fact, if he were of his great grandfather's generation he might even mull over whether he should beat his slaves.

He breathed the aroma and the dust of decades residing in the richly-appointed room and deliberated with himself on the intended consequences of the ghosts in these gay, yet spectral surroundings. The fates were conspiring. *It is a wise man who knows where honor ends and stupidity begins*, he thought of the unnatural selection and insatiable cruelty just demonstrated and so eternally prevalent in this rent and ripped fabric of the Confederacy's cradle.

Jazz Stories: *From Katrina to Connecticut*

He reflected on the hatred and bloodlust, the conflict in his heart, the social insecurity of Southern discomfort, his life of ostentation and great luxury. He stared at a Confederate battle flag next to a huge oil painting of a sword-clutching ancestor (General P.G.T. LaFarge) in a grey uniform, laden with medals and epauletted-down. They say the old Bourbon and Balls general led his men in romantically daring, dashing charges over heaps of battlesmashed bodies into direct enemy fire with nothing but "nuts and a sword." A Union army cannonball hit him dead-on in battle and that was about all they found of him and his unmagnificent obsession with fool's bravery. *Such a man would surely have reveled in the bloodlust so apparent in the garden's unpleasant implications.* . . . A Regency gilded and painted *recamier* was to the picture's left. A patinated, bronze figural clock was nestled between ornamental Charles Robert mirrors.

Armand Pierre LaFarge was the youngest of twelve children in that then-latest rendering of the LaFarge clan, a wealthy, prominent, dogwood and magnolia, old money, highborn New Orleans family whose lineage extended back to before the Louisiana Purchase. Theirs was a life of thick rugs and dripping chandeliers, windswept palms, gardens of ivy, the Civil War (they conveniently forgot that they had rebelled – and lost), the stubborn pride of their faith, cherub fountains with goldfish and turtles; idyllic, passionate views of the midnight fog on the Mississippi (and the secrets lying amidst its unforgiving beauty), statues of heroes of an ungodly cause, grand passages of pelicans of the wilderness, grassy oak-lined avenues, slave quarters (antiseptically and clinically-dubbed *"servants'* quarters"), glowing gas lights, lacy grillwork, silver candelabras, velvet-roped restaurants, black-jacketed waiters, paid household servants and (unpaid) slaves, silver-trimmed, leather saddles; carriages with pairs of blooded horses, antique guns, rare coins, fireplaces, billiard rooms (when they knew they liked pool halls), well-appointed evening excursions on flagstone sidewalks, doll collections, handshake agreements, the relaxing charm of outdoor cafes, spiral staircases, evening clothes and winding carriage roads, "unmanageable" Negroes who were born in bondage but craved freedom, silver watches, ornate white columns, whimsical, spacious homes with tall front porches and leafy enclaves; the authentic feel of tradition in the architectural triumphs of courtly,

Uptown manicured neighborhoods, antebellum mansions in the unfaded grandeur of their former elegance of Doric columns, fine wines, exquisite cuisine, and long, luxuriant curtains collecting dust as they kissed the lustrous, hardwood floors in room settings that exalted the spirit and inspired the imagination of mistresses, missys and masters; gas-lit, cobblestone alleys. *Memories that haunt like hungry flies around a pile of dog feces* . . . Sleepy Southern towns and cities steeped in tradition amidst the tortuous ghosts of the past such as the pall of guilt, everlasting hellfire and damnation, emptiness and impotence that still (and forever) would torment Armand Pierre LaFarge about the death of his long-dead wife (and mother of his only child), a flame-haired beauty whose company and comfort he lost in the flower of her youth, for she was too delicate-boned to have babies and died in childbirth. His greatest loves were his daughter and going antiquing in the colored sections where he would come across a plethora of riches that the uninformed coloreds would surrender for the most miniscule, teenantsy fees. . . .

These were Armand Pierre LaFarge's lucid recollections of his family's blood-tainted past, its private and public sins and the impending, emerging impotence of a dream destined to be deferred. *All this over a jig,* he thought. . . .

The LaFarge ancestor cult was typical of a society built on kinship relations among the most rarified social circles in New Orleans; and it was often said that LaFarge children were born in a field of shamrocks with eloquently-crafted, metallic spoons in their mouths; but words about the weeds and thorns of familial dysfunction amidst the ranks of those silver spooners were often left unspoken. He shed a tear for those yet to be born as he contemplated the pedigree of this, his present life, before the murmurs and whispers grew to a deafening roar. . . . There was Great-Great-Great-Great-Great-Great Uncle Luis, one of the most venerated patriarchs in the family tableau, and the Biblically-proportioned tales of daring dues (and don'ts) of the blood of men who braced the wilderness at his side and fought the beasts and MERCILESS INDIAN SAVAGES of the forest (and tales of the women whose assignment it was to clean up the blood). It is said that he sailed with René Robert Cavelier, Sieur de la Salle, when he was looking for a water route to China, and he was so far in the family's past that he was one of the first white men the

MERCILESS INDIAN SAVAGES encountered. There was always great consternation and discommode at family gatherings about the historical accuracy of whether he was actually with la Salle or whether he and Bienville cleared away the thickets of riverfront canebrakes to lay out the city's French Quarter where streets were named Royal, Bourbon, Chartres, Conti, and St. Louis to adulate the French court. But there was no doubt about whether he chained escaped slaves to swamp trees and left them for the gators. *Was the family saint actually a heathen? What manner of atonement can correct such deviltry?* he asked himself.

There was Uncle Leonne, whose barnstorming adventures as a dead-reckoning, seat-of-the-pants pilot in the War to (purportedly) End All Wars was humongously legendary in the family chronicles and tall tales. He named his daughter "Lorraine" after his service in France. His stories about the banks of nooses he saw in villages that were razed by the Germans long titillated the imagination of the family's eldest of elders. Armand recalled Uncle Leonne's war story about how he was shot down and a colored soldier came to his aid when his Curtiss JN-4 "Jenny" crashed into a pocket of tangled woods and he hadn't had solid or liquid nourishment for a week. "Thunder!" Uncle Leonne yelled, giving the password as he heard a disturbance in the bush. "Lightnin'!" he heard a voice yell back as a colored soldier suddenly and inexplicably appeared like a phantom angel from the shadows of the forest and killed two German soldiers who had come upon him and were setting up a Maxim gun, then offered him waters of salvation and sustenance from his kitbag's canteen -- when at home they couldn't even drink from the same fountain. He said he was "never so happy to see a goddam nigra in all (his) life." *What would he think of the barbarism in the garden's stormy sea of implications?*

Then there was Uncle Laurence (lovingly re-dubbed "Uncle Poo-*Pooh*"), maker of toilets, spittoons, and an assortment of bedroom vessels and chamber pots (usually de-euphemized as "pisspots" or "slopjars"). He was everybody's # 2 Uncle. He enjoyed farting around with the fescennine work in spite of the crappy disposition of some of his customers. He often joked that while he was in the military he was cited for "conspicuous gallantry in holding the fart -- under extreme duress." *Knowing him,* Armand Pierre LaFarge told himself, *he would indeed take extreme displeasure in a most distasteful fashion at such a fecal matter as the prospect of a new, disparate branch on the family tree as has just been revealed to me. . ..*

Then there was healthy, wealthy Aunt Lola, a spinster and adventuress and "lady of extinguished modesty" who was known to keep large sums of money (and monied men) about the premises. They say she was a *modiste*, but she must have sewn a whole lotta dresses to maintain the lifestyle to which she accustomed herself. They whispered that they had to stop her from engaging in a scandalous, embarrassing lust affair with one of her slaves that threatened to stain the family honor and blemish the lily-whiteness of their blanched, ancestral line of descent. She left New Orleans for New York (with her manservant) and nobody had seen hide nor hair of her ever since. . . . *Her love, like my beloved, darling daughter's, knew no boundaries. . . .*

Grampa "Big Poppa" Lucien Lafarge reportedly served as an aide to William Charles Cole Claiborne, who was appointed by Thomas Jefferson to serve as governor of the Louisiana Territory and was the first governor of Louisiana as a state. Grampa Lucien was one of the founders of The Grand Knights of the White Carnation, described in its charter as "a group of brave patriots who shall perpetually involve the bold firmness of their manhood in defending the moral righteousness of the Confederacy's just cause, its sacred honor, its fertile soil and the virtue, purity and grace of its women." *And I thought he was a shining hero. . .*

He recalled that the family honor, devotion to duty, cloaks of respectability and flags in the dust of a long-lost cause survived the Great Pandemic of 1918 when the scourge of influenza broke out, affecting some 14,000 people and killing more than 800 in the city. Armand Pierre LaFarge speculated on the pathological ignorance of family members who fought in 1874 in a race riot known as The Battle of Liberty Place which bechanced to come about on Sept. 14, 1874, when the White League, a group of outraged, prominently-blooded New Orleanians seeking to restore pre-war, white "home rule," fought 3,600 policemen and black militia troops, deposed a standing governor, installed their own governor by force of arms, and ran the state government for three days. Thirty-nine were killed and 79 wounded.

Then there was Aunt Lucinde, one of the family's most heroic figures and heroine of the Great New Orleans Fire of 1788, who died a tragically terrible death of severe, lethal burns she received while rescuing her first-grade students from certain, horrible demise on that Good Friday afternoon as they were making their final preparations for a passion play to be held that evening.

Paw-Paw Leo was a hero, too. He saved a colored woman and her two children from drowning in the hurricane of 1915 by helping them aboard his skiff. When other white men saw them in the boat with him, they thought there was a situation unbefitting a Southern gentleman, shot holes in the vessel, and the woman and her children drowned. He inevitably drowned himself in drink and committed suicide in the former, faded glory of what was supposed to be the incorruptible surroundings of the family home's lush, shadowy, courtyard garden – a garden garnished with resplendent, Italian marble statues, a huge, live oak, mysterious Spanish moss, aromatic mint foliage and clasping, clinging, climbing vines of ivy. They say his last words were: "I'm too blessed for this mess." Armand Pierre LaFarge recollected Paw-Paw Leo confiding in him as a child, telling him what he could relate to no adult in the family, for to do so would have been to be inextricably labeled with that indelible epithet -- *"nigger-lover"*. . . about how one of the little colored children told him as they sat shivering in the boat -- "Thank you, mistuh. Thank you for saving our life. Gawd bless you. I love you, mistuh." *How would Paw-Paw Leo feel about the dreadful, unblessed mess that just occurred outside?*

Finally, there was Great Uncle Leopold, a petulant, petty rapscallion and a rogue-of-a-man, an evil shell of a human being who was less than temperate in his eating and drinking habits, and whose brash discord and brittle exterior were living proof that you can't make a silk purse out of a sow's ear. He was tall, dark and stupid with a disagreeable disposition, a man not easily governed. He had a face that looked like 10 million miles of back country road. He was living proof that the LaFarge family didn't have mere skeletons in the collective consciousness of its closet -- it had a whole graveyard. He was so dumb that if you asked him to make an "X" to indicate his signature -- he'd make an "O". He was a grizzled, burly, bear of a man with soupbone hands, icy, bay blue eyes, a strong back, a pencil moustache, and more than a touch of larceny in his soul.

Professor Arturo

His was an unremarkable, hardscrabble life of dark barrooms, shadowy alcoves, fast women, horseflesh, low-stakes gambling, canebuck liquor, bathtub liquor, and bourbon for breakfast -- forever stranded in poverty and ignorance. He had the intellectual achievement of a lawn jockey. He fancied himself a rather gay fellow and considered himself quite the adventurer during his lifelong cascade of ill-fortune, but his legacy to the lineage always manifested itself as one episodic misadventure after another of ne'er-do-well, dirtbag living and ongoing satisfaction of a man's lower pleasures. His past wasn't checkered . . . it was chessed. He had an ironclad grip, but his reach (usually) far exceeded his grasp. He was a flimmer, a con man whose main game and claim to fame was his mastery of mumblety-peg.

He was the son of cousin Louis (the gunsmith) and a spitfire music hall entertainer who often sang (and played) in riverfront piano houses. He never overcame the circumstances of his birth or the bittersweet flypaper of the wretched residue of his life. A jackoff of all trades, he was a saddle bum, a cotton-chopper, a polecat slavecatcher, a bullwhacker, a hod carrier, a medicine show foil, and the first family member to be expelled from Fork Union Military Academy in Fork Union, Virginia, for "inappropriate behavior fueled by an alcoholic binge." "Fork you!" they say he told Colonel Desdunes, the academic dean, on the day of his departure. Because he was a LaFarge, he wasn't *officially* po' white trash: he was gar-*bajj*.

But the LaFarge family's most maleficent, immortal and original of sins, its deepest and most bitter of wounds was Great Uncle Leopold's murder of the innocent, unarmed lover of a free woman of color with whom he fell in love upon first sight at a Creole cottage near Rampart Street where young women of color were presented to mannered (and usually married) gentlemen of distinction in that arguably most curious of Southern social institutions, *plaçage,* an extra-legal system where Southern gentlemen of privileged birth and honor entered into chattel marriage with women of color after being "introduced" at extravagantly well-appointed quadroon balls. Even today, many white New Orleans families of civic prominence and social prestige are shocked and frightened by the presence of mixed-race forebears in what they thought was their milk-white, pureblooded lineage ("Sumthin' in the milk ain't clean!").

* * *

Desireé was a free woman of color, a copper-toned woman with coconut-brown, ripe, soft, dazzling breasts who was reputedly of royal lineage, born and raised on an indigo plantation on the Bayou Road. She was a fashionably-dressed woman, one of the wealthiest free women of color in New Orleans, a headstrong woman who usually wore her abundant head of raven tresses *au naturel* in the style of the African. The mocha-hued beauty was an ocean of loveliness and men swooned in her wake. Her house was a late Victorian three-bay shotgun with a high, wooden fence. She sold hats, bonnets and read cards to proper ladies dressed in high fashion. She was a woman of funkadelically delicious, bewitching physical beauty (watermelon lips, champagne bottle hips). They say she was the most beautiful free woman of color in New Orleans. Some say she was the prettiest colored woman in all the Southern states -- some, the most beautiful woman of *any* color *any*where. At times she wore her hair in a *tignon* -- a headdress with seven points tied "just so" -- in the manner of the women of color of those days. Men of all complexions and stations in life were concerned not with her hair, but with what sweetly succulent secrets lie beneath the mysterious and dark domain of her petticoats. Many were her suitors who promised to keep her in coffee and cakes if only she would satiate their present, immediate or past-due carnal desires.

On many a blistering-hot Sunday afternoon, Great Uncle Leopold watched from a distance as she danced the *Calinda* in Congo Square, whirling gracefully to ancient drumbeats and whistling wind instruments, enchanting, intoxicating him with her movements as she and other colorfully-clad, dark and sultry women undulated to the rhythms of faraway lands and memories. Swooning in pleasure at the vile debauchery and wicked delights of her dance and the pecawn-brown vividness of her tall, tanned, untamed form, Great Uncle Leopold, a man with a lustful disposition and ridin' high and handsome in the catbird seat, was drawn to her beauty like a drunken moth to a flame. He realized that actually falling in love with her was BOO-COO taboo, but (to him) she was prettier than an unopened gallon o' bourbon. It was a shameful state of affairs indeed. Some say he was hypnotized by her midnight-black hair. Others contend that she put that red gravy on him, burned a candle on him, or sprinkled something in his shoes. Eventually, he made her an offer of concubinage, an immodest proposal of regular deposits into her accounts of all the folding money his poke satchel could bear losing. They agreed on times, places and frequencies of their trysts. It was an indefectibly delightful arrangement.

But there was a problem. One of her alleged suitors, a free man of color said to be from the land of her parents' birth, was her one, truest love. Great Uncle Leopold recognized the power of their passion when she spoke of him, and so he often confronted her with jealous words wrought by his bacchanalian forays into drunkenness and displeasure. One clean, crisp, starlit night he and the free man of color encountered each other as the black man left her house. An argument ensued and the man reputed to be from her ancestral homeland was shot dead by Great Uncle Leopold.

There was, of course, a show trial, a not-guilty verdict, and a gnomish fine arranged and paid by the powerful LaFarge family, and to their well-compensated corps of judges, accountants and lawyers. After that, Great Uncle Leopold took a small apartment below the Esplanade, became a talented French Quarter *saucier*, was dismissed from his duties due to chronic inebriation, and lived in an open-faced, one-room tarpaper shack in the woods with only a cot in a corner of the dwelling. Eventually he married an equally pleasure-addicted, cash-poor woman with fish-belly white skin, uneven, smoke-stained teeth, and an uncertain reputation coupled with a questionable virtue who was as broke as the Ten Commandments.

They say after usual and customary explosions of his compulsive, fiery temper he killed two men under the dueling oaks in *affaires d'honneur* -- one with a pistol (after a political argument in a ballroom) and one with a *colichemarde* (for putting his chair too close to a "lady" he was escorting) -- and it is rumored that he and his companion shack dweller once killed a black baby and drank its blood for its potency. They eventually burned to death in a downtown hotel in a brutal fire of unknown origin....

* * *

But there was another tree. It was a massive, breathtakingly beautiful, magnificently gnarled live oak tree, well over five centuries old, that stood in the courtyard near a carbon-encrusted red brick barbecue pit, a whitewashed garden table and chairs, and two grass-green, iron lace benches. Its oakwood-hard, strong, beautiful grain wood and wild, aggressive root system had survived mushrooms, termites, the Great Fire, a child's swing, the pee of generations of New Orleans revelers, a goo-gobba hurricanes and the coloreds getting the right to vote.

Elegant and sturdy at a height of more than 100 feet, it stood in omniscient observation of all that occurred above, below and around it. The tree had no leaf unrustled, no secret untold. Its gnarled branches draped with hanging Spanish moss, extending outward from its center adjacent to a garden of ivy and mint; pink, purple and blue hydrangeas; four o'clocks, *gardenia jasminodes*, elephant ears and orange and yellow marigolds in front of the sun window of a well-appointed drawing room. They say that runaway slaves could tell which way North was by lookin' at the moss on such a tree.

Soon it would be time for another transition. It would be time for its nine-lobe leaves to turn golden brown and no longer would the small, yellowish, green flowers be prevalent among them. Caterpillars feasting on the leaves would often fall on startled children playing in its shady succor. Its acorns fed generations of squirrels. Its birth and blossoming was an undulating rhythm that would surely and inevitably survive the fleshly existence of anyone living. Birds, mosquito hogs, butterflies, cool riverfront breezes and the secrets of all around her found sustainment in new, uncharted havens of its large, brown, sturdy arms.

* * *

LaFarge House, an antiques, furniture, collectibles and gift shop that had been under the family's auspices since before the Civil War (located near the French Market's stalls on an engaging corner of Royal Street at Bienville) was a stylish, wood-frame, three-story Greek Revival mansion with free-standing spiral staircases and pull cord bell systems in both the shop and the family quarters. For generations, the manageable slaves had slumbered on wooden pallets on mud floors of their quarters near the rear of the house, far away from the business's maddening

Professor Arturo

crowds of customers. These days the servants and other hired help changed back there. Huge cypress beams held up the flooring of the house. Cast iron front galleries above the shop windows overlooked the narrow, vaginal tract that was Royal Street. In the same block there was a liquor store, two sleazy bars, a barbershop, a girl's high school, a music and dance conservatory, a tenement, a home for juvenile delinquents, a Freemasons' lodge, and slivers of specialty shops also featuring antiques, furniture, collectibles and gifts. Street vendors (usually the vejitibble man) on horse-drawn wagons could be heard going to and fro from the French Market to the colored sections touting their wares. ("*I got bana-na-na-nas. . .water-mell-ell-ell-on. . .sweet pa-too-tee-ee-ee. . .*")

A sign on a little square of cardboard posted in the window of a curio shop on the river side of the street said:

>   NO DOGS
>   NO JEWS
>   NO NIGGERS

Among the inventory at LaFarge House, which operated primarily as a consignment agent for a galore of New Orleans auction galleries, were maps, 19th-century English needlepoint carpets, all manner of lacy wares including both gentlemen's and ladies' lace-edged silk handkerchiefs (created by dark, dexterous, unseen hands of dedicated, devoted craftsmakers); antique tapestry pillows, shoebox Easter baskets, rare coins and jewelry, bed sets, glassware, candles, curtains, sofas, dinnerware, Tiffany lamps, real estate inventories, 19th-century armoires, and a plethora of notions, gift items and home accents for the fortunate members of the close-grained, properly-blooded citizenry who appreciated (and could afford) living quite visibly, and opulently, well. Indeed, the generationally-observed and honored motto of the LaFarge House was:

>   "Where OUR people meet THEIR people"

* * *

A block away (on Bourbon Street) the French Quarter was a glitzy Gomorrah of glamor and grit: shadowy bars; a queer, exotic gumbo of architecturally diverse structures; the cultural amenities of uninhibited imbibement and vile exploration of the lower extremities of (and exercises in) the carnal pleasures of rented sex and gluttonous gastronomy by just, noble, and honorable men. Broadway was America's favorite street, but Bourbon was its favorite gutter. It was the Golden Age of Burlesque, a politer precursor to the art of low-down, Dirty South, shake dance strippin'. It was something like what Stagolee and Shine was befo' Rap. *Nymphs de pave* prowled the thin bankets promoting their own antique profession that catered to the natural calamities of human nature. "B-drinkers" and exotically interpretive dancers abounded in this gilded age of Burlesque: Bambi Brooks, Candy Barr ("The Perfect Texan"), Lilly Christine ("The Cat Girl"), Rita Alexander ("The Champagne Girl"), Linda Brigette ("The Cupid Doll"), Blaze Starr (according to the guv'nuh -- a *real* redhead), Evangeline ("The Oyster Girl" w/ seaweed green hair), Kalantan ("The Heavenly Body"), Sandy Loren ("The Girl With the Twin 45s"), Patti White ("The Teacher Turned Stripper" -- who performed in a mortarboard and academic gown) and Evelyn West ("Biggest and Best, The Girl with the $50,000 Treasure Chest" -- insured by Lloyd's of London).

It was a time so publicly, raunchily raw that Catholic school girls riding the bus to and from the French Quarter-located academy for colored girls were directed by the Sisters of the Blessed Sacrament to cover and close their eyes when passing through the Quarter to ward off the potential infection to and corruption of their vulnerable, defenseless, angelic souls. Amidst it all, Sam Butera was playing his sonorously sweet saxophone to holidaymakers from far and wide in the dance dungeons in which progenitors of his profession plied their melodious trade ever since anyone alive could remember. Wives of the colored musicians had to sit (separately and unequally) behind their husbands' Bourbon Street bands on stage amidst the alcohol-soaked debauchery.

That was the world in which the boy and girl met and fell in love. . . .

* * *

Their innocent, youthful eyes engaged and their hearts interblended when they first encountered each other in the house's great hall. His mother, Mrs. Lula Mae Lavalais, a domestic servant for the LaFarge household, went about her daily duties that included dusting the girl's deceased mother's doll collection, making floral arrangements, cooking, advising, sewing, mopping, waxing and tending to the moments of mayhem, madness and merriment inherent in maintaining the smooth running of such a large household enterprise. One of his marbles rolled under an armoire as he frolicked in his gilded playground of antique furniture, flowing curtains and the residue of a grander age. As he crawled under the masterfully-crafted, anciently ornate cabinet he heard a prepossessing, youthful female voice just over his shoulder saying, "I think I can get that chiney for you."

She bent to her knees in her periwinkle blue dress, crawled under the dowdy, dated wood of the armoire, and rescued the handmade eyeglass marble from a potential dust-covered eternity in that graveyard of a land where such children's trinkets often ultimately disappear. They exchanged pleasantries in the manner and innocence of children their age; shared some stick candy; discovered secret, hidden, hallowed places in the rooms of the house amidst huge, gold-framed canvases of Civil War generals and (publicly) fair maidens; and became lifetime best friends enjoying their fortuitous, benevolent bonding and the curiosity of their youth. She was a red-tressed, Frenchified, Southern white girl; a *jolie jeune fille,* a flower of the South, white as a white-feathered hen's egg, in her earliest days of a lifetime of admirers, suitors, wooers, starers and watchers.

Eventually, the boy became infatuated not only by the physical beauty of her first full flower of adulthood, but by the virtue, humor and truth that she so often made evident during their tenderest of years of discovery, epiphany and joy, oblivious to the implication and history of some of the house's artifacts -- such as the huge chains attached to the walls of the basement that had once been used by her forebears to chasten the behavior of unmanageable slaves.

Their friendship was the most politic of strange bedfellows. She taught him the antiquated etiquette of a bygone era. He learnt her about skatin' trucks, mosquito hogs and tumblesettin'. She instructed him on the intricacies of crystal, china, and flatware patterns. He schooled her on the ways of his own faraway world of gospel, greens and authentic, downhome grits and gumbo.

In time, however, the old ways and traditions of bygone (and eternally omnipresent) generations had to take over. The two young hearts had blossomed into that latter time in their youth when their friendship would certainly be deemed inappropriate by the socially-sanctioned authority of a system of mastery and servility; a system that demanded that such matters as young love in bloom not disturb the fabric of legacy and tradition mandated by the living and dead progenitors of appropriate breeding within, of, and for the Southern gentry, lest the boy dare take the boldest of steps and enjoy the flowery Southern maiden's forbidden fruit.

As was the custom, their years of comradeship were abruptly and officially ended just prior to their pubescence and her first full flower of adulthood as she grew into the most fetching young socialite in Louisiana. They say she was so pretty all she had to do was bat her eyelashes and she'd start a stampede of male suitors. Eventually and inevitably, she was sent upstate for tutelage and instruction at an institution wherein young ladies of appropriate lineage and uninterrupted bloodlines learned proper hygiene, how to personalize their wardrobes, nutritional conventions, proper sitting and standing techniques, literary criticism, personal grooming, conversation (how to "jib and jab"), introductions, telephone and table manners, the importance of body language, speechmaking, interviewing skills and other timewashed conventions of the Southern gentry. He was assigned to work in the home and its well-maintained gardens of ivy amid rich, onyx soil, and fragrant flowers beneath the mighty oak, perpetually pondering the bittersweet wine of their parting.

* * *

It was her first Christmas home from school and the fine gentlemen of the Grand Knights of the White Carnation (of which her father was treasurer), a blooded band of hog-wild compatriots comprised of a dwindling fraternity of men with unimpeachable public reputations, exploited the occasion to throw her a spouseless, non-concubinish dinner party with a fancy-food, sit-down repast in the house's great room, replete with fountains of "giggly water"; platters of fresh leaf spinach salad, glazed pork loin medallion, fruit *tartelette* and finger sandwiches; bowls of chips and pretzels; red beans, rice, and Regal beer on ice; "boo-coo" bottles of Southern Comfort and Jim Beam Bourbon and a lotta swing and jitterbug music. It was a grand affair, indeed. There were enough drunken white men in there to make a Viking movie.

Some of Louisiana's most colorful populist politicians greeted each other with a secret handshake that was a sign of the brotherhood who clung to their guns and religion. There was Senator Broyard, the folksy-drawled blowhard, absinthe distiller, hotelier and founding father of a white-shoe law firm; Roughneck, a discontented, unsettled rogue and childhood friend of Armand LaFarge who worked at Lincoln Beach, the colored amusement park located on Lake Pontchartrain's shore a stone's throw from Hart's, the seafood restaurant on stilts where colored merrymakers would devour healthy portions of "berled" crabs, shrimp and a medley of Po-Boys after a day on the rides and poolside pleasures; Judge Claiborne, an eminent, ruthless legal scholar widely known as the kind of jurist who kept law and order with a rope; Dandy Andy LeBlanc, a bawdy house owner, Uptown butter and egg man, saloon proprietor, and procurer of colored women, whose devotion to haberdashery was legend at downtown men's stores such as Rubenstein's and Meyer the Hatter (the emporium on St. Charles and Canal that touted itself as "the largest hat store in the South"); and of course, a corps of black-jacketed Negro waiters moonlighting from their trade at the Roosevelt Hotel . . .

. . . and the boy -- now a well-toned, muscular young man, whose present appointment it was to cheerfully serve every slightest whim of the multitude of self-appointed, crapulent patricians while maintaining a cool-headed composure as he and the other *garçons* served drinks and replenished trays of finger food in spite of the slivers of niggeristic jocularity ensuing from the night's sea of men's laughing faces, faces of men who hadn't had such a good time in a montha Sundays:

"What's a shine's idea of foreplay?. . . 'Open up dem legs -- or I'll cut you, bitch'. . . What did the parish sheriff call the nigger who was shot 20 times?. . .Worst case of suicide he ever saw . . . I've kilt 12 men in my lifetime. . . . . I thought it was 18?!? . . . I don't count the niggers. . . . The nigger wouldn't, but the pecker would. . . . I never met a nigra that was half as reliable as a horse. . . . You oughta see how dumb the ones over at the riverfront is. . . . They was all lined up for about two blocks. . . .

Jazz Stories: *From Katrina to Connecticut*

I went out and told 'em I needed a hundred RIGGERS!!!! . . . RIGGERS!!! . . . We don't make it a habit o' hirin' 'em 'cause next thing you know they'll be sittin' in the White House. . . ."

It was then that he saw her.

He could only watch furtively, discreetly, as she glided across the hand-polished floor, noticing that the pouting sex kitten had grown into a growling lioness. She schmoozed, politicking for a while with her father's comrades, and summoned him with a raised hand indicating that she wanted a drink of bubbly. He made his way to her through the crowded, drunken mass of men, noticing the natural intimacy of her lips, gazing soulfully into what he saw as the pristine beauty of her ocean-blue eyes, recalling that first time they met as children when he had lost his marble. She slipped him a note on a crumpled napkin, strategically indicating that he should read it. It said:

Meet me out back in the slave quarters in ten minutes

It was on. Ten minutes, three-point-five seconds later, they barred the door of one of the ancient, limewashed wall shacks and found themselves passionately embracing, examining the difference in their hair and the texture of their tongues, canoodling on a wooden pallet that once served the nocturnal needs of the family's former chattel. They were speechless, going at it hammer and tongs. He was tryin' to scratch that cat 'til it purred. He licked the pink areola of her olive pit-hard, goody-goody gumdrop nipples through the thin fabric of her straining, overstuffed bra, exploring the secrets deep in the walls of her cleavage.

"Girl -- if yo' paw saw me doing this --" he said, as he yanked her bra straps loose with an iron grip on her young, fresh firmness, then gently nudged the elastic waistband of her panties between his teeth and slid them down her smooth, oddly "ghetto-fine" thighs. She cocked her limber limbs wide open, providing him effortless entry into the mysterious, enticing, fiery, candy apple red wisp of fur barely covering the quivering lips of her channel of charm and delight.

"*I learned a lot while I was away*," she whispered. "*I'm free, white and old enough to know. . . . Ain't no li'l colored gal EVUH gon' give you what I'm 'bout to*," she panted, grabbing the bull by the horn, ignoring the certain, inevitable peril of which they dare not speak that her actions in sharing her forbidden fruit could render unto them both. But this was true love, and true love recognizes neither peril nor terror when it comes to its sweet, seraphic consummation. "God laugh when thief steal from thief," he joked as he entered her, the unmanacled, irony hardness of his thick, rigid member invading the pleasure path of her soft flesh, flooding the harbor of their lust, her monogrammed, silver-plated ankle bracelet jingle-jangle-jinglin', their passionate embrace melting into the blackness of the night as they cast their inhibitions and age-old taboos aside. They got *down*.

The li'l white girl was hotter than the lowest abyss of Hades. He felt like a searing, sizzling-hot link of Vaucresson's Creole Hot Sausage immersed in a newly-opened can of fresh, warm, PET Evaporated milk. She was white, tight and outa sight. He was strong, black, in love and soaked with her juices. She whimpered helplessly, haplessly, as he held her in his sinewed arms. She was moonbeam light, plump, huggable and hungry for affection. They purred, cooed, and made tender, sweet love for what seemed like an eternity, her moans echoing through the walls of the humble dwellings of the ghosts of the now-nameless, ill-fated unfortunates who slept and dreamed of the dawn of a happier day in this same ignoble place.

* * *

That following summer when she was home from school, she (with her father's consent) asked him to accompany her on a shopping expedition, for she expected to be laden with booty from a foray into several disparate stores of then-thriving downtown Canal Street, arguably the city's premier shopping hub. They went to Maison Blanche, a department store within walking distance from the house, with him trailing in her wake (as was the custom in those days). While there, she bought herself some stockings, garter belts and panties, and made several discreet acquisitions of clothing for him, indicating to the clerks that the garments were actually for her brother who was about the same size as her man-in-waiting.

They stopped at an ice cream parlor and she went in and bought several scoops of vanilla ice cream for him and chocolate for her. They then stood at some distance from each other, enjoying her mirthful attempt at gallows humor. She said it reminded her of an earlier time during their childhood when she snuck him some cake and ice cream for a birthday party thrown in her honor that the omnipotent Southern credo of segregation didn't allow him to attend.

The next day after the shopping spree *he* decided to show *her* a bit of the world in which *he* dwelt. They went to Lincoln Beach. She wore her flame-red hair tied in a *tignon* in the manner of women of color (so that, with her tan, she wouldn't be recognized by anyone who might report their illicit outing to her family) and planned to wear a swimming cap while in the amusement park's large pool lest someone discover her surreptitious jaunt with her dark and secret love. "If somebody see you, they just gon' think you wunna them Creole girls from the Seventh Ward," he assured her.

"What do you think about monogamy?" she asked him as they sat behind the yellow sign-- FOR COLORED PATRONS ONLY -- on the lake-bound Elysian Fields bus as it crept through the city's darker section.

"I'm really into oak. It's a way mo' prettier wood. It lasts longer than most," he replied. Then -- "You gon' like our beach. It's right on Lake Punchatrain. It got a view that's better than the one at the Specific Ocean."

"I know. I studied its environs in a class with a friend at school. She's studying to be a cartographer."

"What she wan' spend all them years in college for just to take pitchas o' cars?" he queried, puzzled.

"Silly! *Cartography* . . . map-making." He hadn't had much learning in the academic graces. They disembarked and he met her outside the designated dressing areas by the pool after dodging the stinging jets of water emanating from all angles in the entrance area between the locker rooms and the pool through which one had to maneuver to get to the liquid gratification. One of his uncles had told him that the white men who set the pressure at the entrance/exit calibrated the spray so that the Negroes using the pool would be painfully stung as they entered and left the area. Such were the ways of gentlemen of breeding and honor during that most dreadful of times.

"Wow!" she exclaimed when she saw the mass of brown, black, and bronzed bathing-suited bodies in and around the pool.

"There's enough colored people out here to make a Tarzan movie."

"That's what I like 'bout you. You *some* funny, yeah --" he said, taking her by the hand and leaping into the water.

They stayed a while in the water, playfully enjoying its coolness and comfort amidst the sizzling heat of an oppressively hot New Orleans summer day, whispering the language of love to each other, in that truly unique tongue that only true lovers understand. Later, she tied her hair and they explored the varied booths offering stuffed animals, candy, or trinkets as prizes; rode the Tilt-A-Whirl, fiddled around in futility with a glass-enclosed toy derrick, shared a towering cotton candy cone, and spent a minor fortune at the shooting gallery where he showed off his skill as a carnival marksman by landing several shots on the brown bears that rotated inside the display on a go-round at the back of the exhibit. After rippin' and runnin' and exhausting themselves on the rides at the amusement park all day they went to the Clabon Theater on Claiborne and Ursulines Avenue in the Sixth Ward and saw *Imitation of Life*. They were thinking about going to the Carver over on Johnson and Orleans, but the Clabon was a much closer walk to the French Quarter for her and was unlike the movie houses on Canal Street, where he would have to sit in an upstairs balcony while she watched the same screen from down below (such was the state of American apartheid at that most tenuous time). He followed her up St. Philip Street as far as Rampart to assure her safety, and reversed his steps at the designated line of demarcation. On that dark, rainy evening as oily water ran in bright rivulets down the rain-soaked bankets, he returned to his pitch-dark world and she to the faded glory of hers, unaware that unseen eyes had observed their surreptitious assignation in the waters, lights and fantasy of the separate and unequally-maintained amusement park and beach designated for the city's colored, tax-paying subjects.

* * *

The following day, her head carefully wrapped so as not to reveal her non-native identity, they met outside an oyster bar on the corner of Claiborne Avenue and Dumaine Street, just across the avenue's broad expanse and its canopy of live oaks in the neutral ground that provided shade and aesthetic grace to the historic district. The area boasted an abundance of businesses including doctors' and dentists' offices, bars, scrolling wrought iron and wooden porches, and an array of gambling houses, pleasure palaces, schools, churches and colorful residents.

Suddenly, a Second Line, a parasoled sea of dancing, jumping, gyrating color, noise and mayhem burst forth from the French Quarter side of Dumaine Street, snaking its raucous way past them up Dumaine and erupting toward City Park. The multitude of perspiring merrymakers dipped, stepped, strutted and danced in unrestrained jubilation, mad with joy under a clear, blue sky. Silver and brass trombones shimmered brilliantly under the oppressively hot mid-afternoon sun. The bold, sassy backbeats of the music and the undulating, sweating, dancing, dark bodies stirred an ancient jungle lust in her and she soon joined the unconstrained, impromptu parade doing some of the things that a properly-bred white woman of the time wouldn't or shouldn't do (at least publicly). The girl danced, jiggled and wiggled so much that her headscarf came off and was picked up by one of her fellow second-liners while she waved her crimson locks wildly, wickedly, wantonly raising her hands in the air and yelling like she just didn't care.

They rented a room in a hot sheet motel that night on Claiborne near St. Bernard Avenue and made love until the dawning of the next day. "Some kinda way, we gon' leave from down here, git married, work our land, raise fat chirrens and --" he started.

"-- live happily ever after," she cooed, hugging him closely.

"Me and my nigger-lover," he said.

"Me and *my* nigger *lover*," she enjoined.

Little did they know, the outcome of their affair's consuming passion was a forgone conclusion.

* * *

"I don't mean to be stirrin' up no trouble, Brother Armand," Roughneck told the girl's father at the counter in LaFarge House the next day, "but as a lifelong, dues-payin' member of the Grand Knights of the White Carnation -- there's sumthin' I think I should relate to you."

He said it cautiously, for such matters were not easily related to the father of one of the South's delicately fragile flowers. With grim determination he told the girl's father what he saw at Lincoln Beach where he had been working that day: The illegitimate couple was frolicking in the water and proudly and quite openly promenading through the lights, fantasy and fanfare of the designated colored amusement park. He conveyed his displeasure, telling him how his cousin Boudreaux swore on his dead grandmother he'd seen her dancin' and cuttin' up with the dreaded darkies in the middle of Claiborne Avenue like some drunken jungle slut in a Johnny Weissmuller movie. He said how ashamed he was to see a white woman out there with 'em -- "Actin' their color." He told him how such a proposition was intolerable for the daughter of an officer of the Grand Knights to be involved in and that he should do something about it before it put a stain on the honor of the men of the organization who not only were dues-paying members, but who also avidly patronized his business enterprises as clients of commitment and loyalty. He also related what he had heard emanating from the slave quarters when he left the party briefly that night to get a little fresh air away from the cigar smoke-filled great hall of the house.

"Sooner or later the worm'll turn," he said. "I *do,* however, understand that it's hard to call yo' own monkey ugly. Besides, some of the brothers are sayin', if you don't do what has to be done about it -- you gon' be a gone goose. I'm jess tryin' to steer you right. They's more than one way to tree a coon."

With a swarm of profanity featuring an expletive indicative of poultry excrement and human buttocks, his impertinence was duly noted and he was chased out of the LaFarge House by Armand Pierre LaFarge, who later went about his functions that day questioning the propriety of immediately dismissing the colored boy from his duties as soon as humanly possible on the word of such a lowlife specimen of low-blooded white trash as was Roughneck. After closing that night he dismissed the boy without explanation, and in fact, thought about firing Miss Lula Mae, too. Still, something inside him refused to believe such a thing about his delightful, blameless, undefiled daughter. *A tonic might help,* he convinced himself, as he later retired to a sleepless, sweating, agonizingly long night in which his spirit was torn between loyalty to the cause and the love of his dear, sinless, uncorrupted daughter: a night in which the deepest sleep could not quell the rumblings of discord in his heart.

He approached her the next day and told her why he had ended the employment of the boy in the family garden in which he had so faithfully toiled ever since he was an uninitiated, unversed and unpracticed colored child. "You must listen to your father in things of this sort," he counseled her.

"I have to listen to my heart," the dutiful and obedient child said.

That same day he had a visit from Judge Claiborne, who said that he wanted to see him on a gentleman's matter of fierce urgency. The Judge then stated his judicious opinion that he felt that firing the boy wasn't enough demonstrable action to make clear to the rest of the Carnation men that LaFarge was committed enough to continue as an officer of the clandestine collection of Southern patriots.

"He took *more* than an improper gander at her. It was the vilest of indignities. He violated her purity -- *all* our women's sacredness and purity -- with such unnatural affections. I wish no harm to befall you, but how do you think the other members gon' feel if you should remain in a position of authority havin' any sorta say-so in our proceedin's -- especially with *our* money?"

"My honor is at stake?" asked Armand Pierre LaFarge.

"Right now, your 'honor' ain't worth a pincha snuff. He's threatenin' the fabric of public safety. He shoulda *been* put off the face o' this earth -- the first time you got wind of the . . . *affair*. It's my ethical obligation to tell you . . . I know it's a tough pill to swallow, but we got him dead to rights. He took freedoms with her. He was consortin' with your daughter . . . a white girl . . . raisin' a rumpus with the niggers out there in the middle of the street like some brazen wench . . . and *him* with his pants down and his willy hard. . . . They was seen by more than one upstandin', unimpeachable gentleman in more than one compromisin' situation. He was makin' time with your daughter . . . a nigger boy . . . the son of a goddam maid! We need to git a California collar 'round his neck. . . . I'll never believe any different until my soul vanishes from this earth -- then I'll hate niggers in heaven, too . . . if any of 'em ever *git* there. If it was *my* daughter, I woulda been on him like buzzards on a dead mule. . . . I'd give him fifty mo' holes to breathe outa. . . . They'd hafta wrench the noose outa my cold, dead hands. . . .   Godspeed."

The next few weeks' receipts at the LaFarge House were dreadfully pitiable. It was a time of profound economic anxiety. His cash flow was considerably affected. The same men in the grey seersucker suits (whose progeny would later rail at the boycotts during the civil rights era) were boycotting his store. Evidently, the righteousness of a given struggle was defined by whose ox was being gored for the village feast.

Eventually, Armand Pierre LaFarge decided after much consideration of all that his forebears had gone through and all the fortune his family had amassed, that one vanished spook more or less was nothing but another speck of dust in the ashbin of history, and that he couldn't threaten the livelihood and honorable name of the family over a single nigger life. He had a surrogate contact the boy, telling him to come to the house on an appointed night to discuss possibly getting his job back after reconsideration of this most embarrassing, though not-yet fatal situation.

The magic show was over. The rabbit was out of the hat.

* * *

It was an old-fashioned, low-tech lynching attended by a clandestine collection of ghostly figures, some of the citizenry's most prominent men, who waylaid and set upon their unsuspecting target like lion hounds, rendering him helpless as he entered the house at LaFarge's invitation that night. Three plug-uglies set to beating him bloody with long-unused chains from the slave quarters, a fountain of blood issuing forth onto the once-green ivy gardens adjacent to the tree, now bathed in the moon's shadow as it kissed the starlit sky.

"He ain't gon' never see sunrise again!" shouted one of the voices in the darkness. "Quit stallin' and git busy," bellowed another bloodthirsty ghoul. They tossed a noosed rope over the mighty oak's branches. "He gon' join his cotton-choppin' paw! He ain't gon' never agin see nighttime neither -- *never*!" swore another player in this uncarefully orchestrated dance of death. "He gon' hang there 'til he swell up like a dead hog in the sun!" "Cry *blood,* nigger! Cry *blood*!" another voice spat.

As he dangled from the rope, his body was doused with gasoline and motor oil with fingersnap-fast, ruthless efficiency. An ogre stepped forward, cut off his penis and stuck it in what was left of his bloodied mouth, a customary act in such matters that was usually a post-mortem addendum. There was still a flicker of life in him as he writhed on the rope.

The girl appeared as if a lightning flash out of nowhere, a tsunami of tears flowing down her porcelain cheeks, her teardrops moistening the ground beneath them, flinging herself at his feet, grasping his body as it swung like a pendulum on the rope in a futile attempt to support his near-lifeless mortal remains lest the rope snap his neck and effect a death even more certain than that planned and executed by the valiant Knights of the White Carnation, protectors of all that was good, wholesome and essential to the ongoing struggle of Southern manhood in defense of the virtue and purity of their womenfolk.

The imperiled heroine knelt under the tree, drowning in her own tears, holding his body, begging him, pleading with his spirit not to abandon his flesh, her red-rimmed eyes sprouting even more rivers of tears, her body quaking, her mind paralyzed with grief. He was as dead as Good Friday, but still she tightened her grip, clinging to him, imploring him to never leave her, pleading with him not to abandon this life, pledging that she would be with him forever, astonishing the crowd of fiendish onlookers with her apparent fineness and finality of feeling for a mere nigger boy. *How could a white girl do that?* they asked themselves.

She held him all night throughout their curses in the dark until the moon had returned to her corner in the heavens and the sun was expected to rise. "Cut him down and throw him in the river!!!" a voice ordered from somewhere in the murderous crowd. But none took heed. They were instead entranced by her uncanny, unearthly physical strength in holding his body up for hours and hours all through the night, her heavenward pleas and the torrent of lover's teardrops falling like rain from her face as the Southern sky gave passage to the brightness of the rising sun's witness to the grim business that had happened in such a fruitful place as this beauteous garden, while (unbeknownst to her) he had long slept the sound sleep of the dead.

One by one, the murderers dawdled away from the scene of the crime, leaving only the girl and her father to contemplate the melancholy madness of this most sobering of scenes. Finally, she turned to her father on sore, tear-drenched knees and between near-drowning in a flood of her own tears, confessed to the unsuspecting, expectant grandfather: "*I have his baby inside me.*"

Armand Pierre LaFarge then realized that in killing the boy, he merely hastened his own doom, for when he saw that the lascivious lot's hatred and curses in the dark during this night's depravity could not douse the inexplicable, living flame of love (for love recognizes neither the nobility or ignobility of a lover's birth, their station in life, their age, family fortune or fealty, or the time-tested tradition of ancestral politics and polemics), he realized that one might as well have tried to cease the swirling currents of the mighty Mississippi from flowing to the Gulf.

Looking like a one-faced totem-pole, he slowly and deliberately entered the house, stood before the family tree on the mantel in stunned silence, contemplated a while, dusted off and finished a bottle of wine given to him countless moons ago by his brother, took off his family crest ring (adorned with the LaFarge coat of arms) and cast it aside, took out his pocket gun, wrapped the awkwardly-bent, arthritic finger of his right hand around its hairpin trigger, pressed it to his temple and joined the eternal dance of his ancestors as the bullet passed through him and shattered the transparent glass frame of the family tree.

The girl left the family dwelling house (never to return), changed her surname by adding a "u" after the "g" (thus *LaFargue*), gave birth to the child and named him "Uriah" ("Light of the Lord"). Eventually she met and married Gonzalez Francois Dumas, a cornetist of Mexican, French, Houma Indian, and African descent from a family of musicians; moved into the Seventh Ward just off London Avenue; became one of the area's most acclaimed and skilled *modistes,* and read her son to sleep each night from books she acquired from her patrons (for the city's libraries would not then admit those citizens who identified themselves as -- or were identifiable as -- "people of color").

The tender branch's strange fruit grew strong, became a mighty oak, attended Morris Brown College in Atlanta, lived in the light of the Lord and prospered. He became an architect, a builder and a financier, designing and constructing buildings on Canal Street and throughout the Tremé District that were the most preeminent in the building trade of the entire Southeast. They say he built the family grave (*La Famille Dumas-LaFargue*) in St. Louis Cemetery #2 "with his own hands," constructed an immense family home on Music Street, married a virtuous woman, fathered several children from that one wife, and lived a prayerful, contemplative life of great austerity, achievement, social commitment, kindness and harmony (during which he founded several institutions to serve the sick and the poor), established a home for colored waifs and performed numerous, selfless acts of charity such as bringing samples of the local cuisine (carefully wrapped in pristine white *serviettes*) to the sick, the infirm and to the prisoners confined in the parish prison. They say he died a heroic but hideous death of a malady contracted while he was ministering to the homeless. The people of New Orleans had such fondness and respect for his public-spirited deeds that they erected a statue in his image (of stone imported from France) on a street in the Tremé District of the city, a street now called LaFargue Place.

And his light shone forever with the brilliance, brightness and blessings of a thousand suns. . . .

August 2008
Stamford, CT

Professor Arturo

Mama Rachel's Garden

My grandmother's garden in the yard in back of the late-Victorian, bayed cottage with the masonry-fronted, recessed side gallery (on Iberville just off Galvez) was a delightfully passionate, pulsating cornucopia of living things: butterflies, birds, bees, juney bugs (my cousin from California called 'em "love bugs"), snails, slugs, and swarms, seas, clouds, oceans and swirls of arrow clubtail mosquito hogs (my cousin in the Seventh Ward called 'em "dragonflies") that miraculously and mysteriously appeared on clotheslines, the ancient oak or the chineyball tree. Mama Rachel's yard was a gathering place for caterpillars, snakes, spiders, scorpions, daddy longlegs (our folks in California called it a "prayin' mantis"); those large, papery, multi-colored flowers (I think they was hibiscus); vivid and vibrantly painted ladybugs, rose bushes, Easter lilies, hydrangeas (with their big pink, purple and blue flowers), camellias, colacasia (we called 'em "elephant ears"), azaleas, egg shells, coffee grinds, faded, lost marbles ("chinees" to the natives), and long-discarded, discolored carnival beads.

It was a patchwork of foodstuffs. There were snapbeans and squash, tomatoes, collard greens and okree, plums, pecawns, peppers, onions, garlic and cucumbers. With all that food -- there was a lotta ants, too. They had sugar ants (the li'l teenantsy, brown ones), black ants (they called them another word, but that wasn't a word li'l boys was supposed to use), and red ants (them ones with them big hooks in they mouth that bit you).

Flowering yellow cat's claw vines jutted from a corrugated tin-roofed cinderblock wall at the rear of the yard amidst a patchwork of emerald and olive. There was summa them plants with the pointy leaves that my uncle used to dry out and put in his cigarette papers to smoke. He told me not to go nowhere near 'em 'cause they was poison ivy, but I often wondered *How could he smoke 'em if they was poison?* My gran'ma told me my uncle woulda had *ten babies* if I ever messed with them plants.

There was a bay leaf tree adjacent to a pecawn tree by a four-foot tall chain link fence that separated my gran'ma's yard from the less than art deco façade of the backa Miss Pie's house. We called her "Miss Pie," but they say they called her "Sweety Pie" back when she was a flapper. A rusted barrel in which my daddy and uncles burned gobbidge sat in the middle of the yard. An occasional runaway chicken from Miss Beulah's backyard chicken farm would sometimes abscond into my grandmother's yard under the aged, wooden, rusty-nailed, chickenwired fence and fulfill its unintended culinary destiny. (My gran'ma, who came to New Orleans from Napoleonville, used to say she was a "real woman" and ate her chickens "standin' up" or "on they feet.")

She never used a measuring cup and didn't really like too much that was store-bought -- except for Holsum bread which she would have me go 'round the cornder on Galvez to get where they sold them BOO-COO BIG "mammy cookies" and day-old donuts. She'd stand on the front gallery and watch me comin' and goin'. Sometimes she'd wave to Miss Mattie who lived in the big house across from Miss Doris (the school bus driver) on the Uptown side of the street (where they say Cassius Clay stayed before the hotels was integrated). I could feel the timeworn gleam of her loving eyes as their saintly power protected me from the pedestrian danger and sinful secrets of souls now living and dearly departed whom she prayed for at every Novena since she and my aunts moved to the city from Napoleonville so long ago that nobody could remember. (I still don't know who I loved the most -- her or Aunt Sweet.)

They were the ones (they say) who started the family tradition of watching the parades around the cornder on Galvez and Canal every year on the Sunday before Carnival Day. She watched Walter Cronkite EVERY EVENIN' -- *EVERY* EVENIN' (I didn't understand why until Vietnam came 'round). I once inquired as to why she ate a halfa advocado (with vinegar and earl) every day. She told me, "You're not supposed to eat anything that Gawd didn't put here for you."

I thought for a while and asked, "What about Budweiser beer? You drink wunna them every day." She came back with, "You don't count that."

She never flew and would get airsick steppin' 'cross a linoleum floor. There wasn't a cut or bruise caused by nature or humankind that she thought Mercurochrome couldn't cure. They say she always liked the Dodgers and Jackie Robinson 'cause his wife's name was Rachel too. They even say when she was young

-- she rode a horse on the levee bareback. I thought that meant the horse didn't have no saddle!

I guess we all got a history.

* * *

For a wide-eyed, short pants, shirtless, barefoot child, her red brick-framed garden was a laboratory of ages-old, wizened womanwisdom. It was mysterious, magical and majestic. It was a wonderful world.

* * *

As she tenderly tended to her garden, I learned of the internal, external and eternal secrets of life's Great Chain of Being from her age-old adages and advice: "The mosquito hogs eat the mosquitoes . . . the birds eat the mosquito hogs . . . the cats chase the birds . . . the dogs chase the cats . . . and everything eat the chickens. . . ."

"Uncle Thaddeus eat a whole lotta chicken," I said. "Where he at? Where he been?"

"He gone to Angola."

"Angola?! He gone to Africa?"

"No. He gone to Angola."

"Angola in Africa, ain't it?'

"Boy, hush. Quit that lollygaggin'."

"Lollygaggin'? What's that?"

"Bullshootin' . . . shootin' the bull . . . 'talk behind the barn'. . ."

"Huh?"

"Boy, move over. Lemme pour this dish soap down there to kill them critters."

"At least they gon' die clean."

"That's what yo' grampa used to say. He always wanted to die clean, dirt-free as his jitney cab. He always said he wanted to be buried with his brass duckhead walkin' cane."

"Grampa got buried? You went to his funeral? He died? I thought he went to live with Jesus."

"He did. He went to live with Jesus."

"A lotta people go to live with Jesus. He must have a big house."

"He sho' do. He sit high and He look low."

"All them dead people done moved in with Him? That's like the time Aunt Anna Mae and all her chirren got put out and had to come stay by *our* house."

"That's what happen when you don't pay yo' bills. You git put out. And everybody know it 'cause all yo' furniture be out in the street."

"Why they got put out? How come they so po'?'

"'Cause they don't never wan' do no work. If you can walk -- you can work. They don't wanna work. The li'l money they *do* git -- they drink it all up."

"Oh -- I'm sorry," I said.

"Don't be sorry. Be careful -- and you *won't* be sorry," she cautioned. "It's better to be nice than sorry."

"I'ma be nice," I said. She looked at me, smiled, and tenderly told me that she knew I would as she reassured me with her firm but gentle hand.

* * *

"Why people die?" I asked her in the garden one day.

"Well, when God close a window, He open up a door. If you live long 'nuff you gon' see a who-o-o-ole *lotta* people go. If you don't -- they'll see *you* go. They always tellin' me 'bout 'Have a good day.' Every day above ground is a good day."

Decades later, she died in her sleep.

* * *

After Katrina, when we went to inspect the rancid shell of the house and its shattered garden, we discovered that the storm's wayward winds and waters had uncovered some of the yard's long-held, primordial, silent secrets -- long-lost marbles, tossed-away toys, abandoned game pieces, and exotic, unfamiliar flora. Underneath the uprooted chineyball tree we found a withered and rotted, brass duckhead walking cane.

August 2011
Stamford, CT

Professor Arturo

The Last Second Line

After the storm his daughter, who lived in a well-heeled, upscale, gated community across the river that was relatively untouched by the rude rawness of nature's supremacy, drove him and his vibrantly-colored, intricately-beaded sun hat, Pork Pie snare drum, and wooden tip drumsticks over to the Sixth Ward's scarred landscape where he surveyed the Southern discomfort of the storm's incalculable damage and chaotic aftermath to blocks and blocks of haunting houses and unfettered, unfulfilled lives of the Big Uneasy. They arranged to meet later at an appointed time on Claiborne and Dumaine by the I-10 where the old H & K Oyster House used to be.

The neighborhood, an apparitional labyrinth of splintered wood and twisted aluminum, looked like one huge, desecrated cemetery vault. It was as quiet as a churchhouse mouse peeing on cotton. Clusters of FEMA trailers stood on the steamy, inhospitable, silent and sad wasteland dotted with overgrown lots where he once heard children's laughter. There was no neighborly chitter and chatter, no Double-Dutching with whipsnapping extension cords, no middle of the street baseball with broom or mop handles and rolled-up newspaper tied with string. Hollowed-out shells of houses were caked in toxic mud. Streams of Mardi Gras beads hung from ruptured limbs of splintered, shattered trees that were snapped like twigs. Gunmetal gray skies loomed over the mirthless, deserted, urban killing fields as unspoken streams of profanity emerged from the cold glare of his age-worn eyes.

If trouble was money, he thought, reliving past glories of the princesses and pagans, already living in the bleakest of circumstances, to whom fate had dealt an unkind hand. The landless peasants, now homeless, were scattered to the winds.

His 80th birthday was far back in the rearview mirror. He wasn't a man of current fashion, wasn't into Prada loafers and Rolexes, but preferred Timex watches, White Owl cigars, and Gold Toe socks. He was tall and silver-haired, a rank sentimentalist who still used Hai Karate, English Leather Lime, and Brut (every year he bought his cologne after Christmas when it was on sale, in the gift packs). He still wore leisure suits, butterfly-collared shirts, camel hair coats, double-breasted blue blazers, pocket squares, ascots, cummerbunds, and platform heels. He was sartorially resplendent. Sharp. He *ragged*. He never wore white shoes after Labor Day, and (unlike many New Orleanians) always sent his children to school before then. His tailor-made, lace-edged hainkachiffs had been in every Second Line from when Louis Armstrong was the Zulu king to when white folks started turnin' out. They waved in the winter winds or summer steam at the president and the pope, dried scores of pairs of crying eyes at funerals and wiped up gallons and goo-gobs of spilled wine (and other spirits) at weddings.

He was a clever and careful man with an unflagging enthusiasm and insatiable passion for Old Man Comforts Stacy Adams shoes, two-tone black-and-white wingtips, sharkskin brogans, fishtail Chryslers, titty-pink Cadillacs, Ford Galaxie 500s, 1975 black-on-black-in-black Cutlasses (with the 8-track tape), Bicycle playing cards, PET Milk on peaches, houses with rope bells on the gates, pickles and potato chips, washtubs and wringers, Betat bikes (from over on Broad Street), rum & Coke-filled nights, and the Latin Mass. He still called credit cards "charge plates," ate his oysters off the halfshell, sprinkled salt in his beer, and had seen hair trends go from processes to ivy leagues to Afros to jheri curls to Git-it Girls to shaved heads to Natty Dreads. He liked his hot sausage sandwiches "dressed" (no cheese, please), didn't use those newfangled "phone cameras" and instead preferred Kodak Instamatics.

He was from a generation not prone to profanity and didn't "slap five"; he gave handshakes. He was a charter member of ROMEO (Retired Old Men Eating Out) and remembered when a pack of M&M's was a nickel, bus fare (with a transfer) was six cents, and the police first introduced "radio cars." He was a "man's man" who read *Argosy* and was a devoted fan of Bob Cousy, Jerry West, Oscar Robertson, Wilt, Elston Howard, Sandy Koufax, Audie Murphy, Z.Z. Hill, and Henry Hank. He called watches "timepieces," binoculars "field glasses," strippers "shake dancers," shaved with a cup and brush, and used "headache powder" insteada aspirin. He still said "London Avenue" insteada "A. P. Toureaud Avenue." He was one of the few cats who liked *The Temptations in a Mellow Mood* (when it first came out) and firmly believed in the spirits of the lore of yore: Old

Spice, Old Hickory, Ancient Age, Old Taylor, and Old Grand Dad. *The older the drum, the stronger the song,* he often said.

He was a sober and discreet man, and many things by choice, but he was a drummer: a trapsmith by trade (back there with Frank Parker, Earl Palmer and Idris Muhammad). He was a seriously talented professional musician with the slickest of licks, a master of his instrument good enough for triple scale and cartage, who came of age long before the era of "Thou shalt not hit helmet-to-helmet, ride without the seatbelt buckled, tie up your dog in the yard, use the paddle in school, or ride in the fronta the bus." He was out there when colored people had to go through the back to get into the movie theater on Canal Street and when the night parades ended at Municipal Auditorium (way before Pontchartrain Park was "open").

His father, a man who pulled out his own teeth with a set of rusty pliers, spoke with measured wisdom and often beat him like a rented mule, and had a "white man's job" in the French Quarter -- tallying watermelon and vejitibble shipments. Like his father before him and his father before him and *his* father before *him*, he was from the *oldest* school, always had a job and a side hustle, was his "own man" who footed his own bills, and left his father's house when he was 19 years young -- and never looked back.

His first real job was throwing watermelons in the French Market, then he painted coconuts for Carnival Day. Eventually he became wunna the first colored supervisors at Boh Brothers, the New Orleans-based construction company founded at the turn of the 20th century. He was lucky, too. His feet started going bad right around the time Hush Puppies first came out. His dogs was *barkin'*.

He thought profound thoughts, but liked simple beer. He was a Jax, Dixie, Regal and Falstaff man. He liked his steaks rare enough to hear the cow "moo" and knew how to find the "soul" radio stations in far-flung, unfamiliar cities (just listen for the Sunday mornin' church show or the Cadillac and skin bleachin' commercials). He never used a food processor and chopped his vejitibbles by hand. He knew a whole *lotta* ladies called "Ma Dear," but ain't never hearda no "Madea" 'til the movie came out.

He considered himself fortunate for a man of his age, for he had only rheumatoid arthritis and one loose tooth while his contemporaries suffered from several medically-complicating conditions such as shortness of breath, dizziness, chest pains, palpitations, difficulty concentrating; out-of-control, overpampered grandchildren; and death. His heart was as sound as a prewar dollar.

During the war (back when he had his habits on) he was stationed in Paris where he fell in love (well, with the idea of love) while sampling and savoring the unearthly delights of the most syrupy-sweet, finest French pastries a Sixth Ward boy could ever imagine. That part of his life's novel was a special chapter. He remembered the heat and passion of those long ago horizontal refreshments plying the expertise of their profession amidst the heave and ho of bellying up to the bar for top-shelf booze as he immersed himself in the counterfeit romantic attentions of the licking, flicking, teasing, tantalizing, scantily-clad Parisian women who often wore nothing more than a beaming, inviting, milewide smile. In his off- and on-duty hours he habitually took acute pleasure in the gentle banter of the gash-for-cash girls who knew a trick or three.

The youthful western warrior was impassioned by the raw yet refined sensuality of the deep, dark pools of their eyes; their velvety, moist, pouting lips, painted faces, scented knees, pancake makeup and coquettishly flirtatious poses, and their thrill and delight at meeting a black American named "Francois."

He and his sergeant lived in a hotel with a to-die-for view of the Seine and rocked, rolled and romanced their way through lingering hostilities in the carnal company of a baker's dozen premium package of a worldly assemblage of wanton, war-weary, welcoming women's well-seasoned buns -- and just two weenies. Back then he was harder to hold than a hand fulla bumblebees and as happy as a fat pig in the sunshine. He had so much fun in Paris, he wished they'd fight again.

They couldn't keep him down on the farm no mo'.

He met a pillow-lipped, curvy-hipped, buttercup-nippled, young Parisian "glory girl" over there who turned him on to Edith Piaf and what she called "the alphabet system," a kissing technique (used in the most intimate places) that employed every letter of the alphabet from A to Z. She was a woman of interdependent means who had a name like a cheap perfume and he nicknamed her "Candybar" because she always wanted him to melt in her mouth -- not in his hand. He couldn't believe she ate the who-o-o-o-ole thing. They performed in more positions than an orgy at a contortionists convention. She was a real pretty woman and he always claimed she looked like Gina Lollabrigida. Her body was a perfect storm of lips, dips and hips. She was a real pretty woman. The romance died on the vine when he discovered that she snored too much -- and he kicked her to the curve. He used to love her, but it was all over now.

After the war, he packed his seabag, returned stateside and was going at full gallop but slowed his roll when he started bringing courtin' candy to Lorraine, a li'l lady from the Seventh Ward who was broad in the mind and working on a bachelor's degree in Home Economics at South Carolina State College. She sure rated with him. To him, her eyes shined like new money (fresh from the printer). She cured him of his commitment phobia and wanted to make him a better man with a better plan. *If you don't slow yo'self down in life, life'll slow YOU down,* she used to say.

He took pride in the fact that he was the first to press the love button that was her puckering rosebud and always joked that she had a Zsa-Zsa Syndrome: You had to marry it to *smell* it! She kept him on a short leash, but she loved him so much, she cherished washing his dirty draws . . . by hand. She was more than a two-night stand at a time when public demonstrations of affections were taboo.

He married "up" and their progeny made him a nah-*noo* 18 times over and he was eternally devoted to each and every one of his grandchildren. She was a genius with a smoothing iron and dirty-drawsed that man for over sixty years. She even loved the salt and pepper hair around his bald spot. He treasured her graying, peroxide mane and he never let the good girl find out about what the bad girls did. She turned out to be well-fixed, making sure all their children had college degrees and jobs before she died. There wasn't no sunshine when she was gone.

They lost a son in Vietnam whose arrogance of youthful, patriotic invincibility made him volunteer for that futile foreign adventure after he left Tuskegee Institute and accepted a commission in the Army as a second lieutenant. The son's longtime dream of fidelity and devotion to duty was abruptly deferred when a bullet punctuated the occipital plane in the back of his skull. The Army said that his son was "a true hero in the defense of freedom" and presented the patriot's parents with a ceremoniously-folded U.S. flag.

* * *

He was in a haze of disbelief now, as he stood on Orleans and Roman across from the boarded-up units of what was left of the Lafitte Project, a now-barren monument to the generational damage done to the lives of those AMERICAN CITIZENS when the levees failed. It was a legacy of saccharine-tongued politicos (the kind who played power politics long before Rome floated) and a public education system that once cursed those AMERICAN CITIZENS' precursors by legal prescription that prohibited them from going past the fifth grade. Giant coils of razor wire sat silently atop a chain link fence awaiting the first scene of the final act -- making the city safe for gentrification. It was an immortal sin for which there was no absolution or plenary indulgence.

He was weary and worn, as wound-up inside as a 25-hour clock and as jumpy as a bag of fleas. He felt like Hip Van Winkle as he toted his drum while stumbling through the vagaries of memory past the roll-down protective storefront gates and bare concrete slabs where slaphappy, nappy homes once stood, bearing silent witness to the storm-tossed swell that had made the once gaily-colored, now flood-ravaged houses unsafe for human habitation.

He felt like he had a head fulla stale liquor, longed for a pep pill and thought he could use a li'l pimple cream. The filth, fear, and fetid stench of death arising from the eerily silent ruins and the mournful choir of quietude offended the hubris of his prickly pride. He thought that what was left of his mind was playing tricks on him.

He strode past the weathered remnants of a once-white, vine-covered Greek revival cottage on Prieur Street where as a child he witnessed an elderly lady pitifully perish after her nightgown caught on fire as she leaned over the stove. She had run out of the house and was screamin' and quiverin' and shakin' like a leaf all over the banket as people crowded around, her coffeecolored skin melting like candlewax. Being an altar boy-in-training, he ran down to St. Peter Claver's rectory and got a priest who gave her the last rites (way back when the church was brick-red -- and not its present-day tan outer).

That was the same church where -- a Mardi Gras season or so later -- he was in the church's cloak room changing into his cassock and surplice and discovered a priest and a nun in a rather compromising (missionary?) position. They banished the priest to a Lower Ninth Ward place of worship and she was exiled to Nun Siberia.

Then there was the unoccupied, gray, plastered-brick Creole cottage (bookended by overrun vacant lots) where the cardplayer was killed over some humbug involving a woman. He had more holes in him than a fat honey hive. His slaying attracted a crowd that made the crime scene look like the Zulu parade on Orleans and Claiborne on Carnival Day. Five-Oh came, nobody talked, and they concluded that it was a suicide. *He musta been playing solitaire and cleaning his gun,* the police said, and chalked that one up to the audacity of dope. People said he sold somebody a whammy and they found out the dope was fake and they had to do what they had to do.

Then there was the other hot spot next door with all them stacked-up, faded newspapers (them dopefiends ain't never had no heat, so they had to sleep un'neath 'em) and them layers of glassine envelopes out front. It was a "bad-luck house" (that was reputed to be a powder shop) from which prolonged outbursts of gunfire often erupted at any and all hours.

Next to that was that the now-ghostly, eerie, galleried shotgun house down by that bar called the House of Joy, down from Joseph S. Clark Senior High School (the home of the MIGHTY, MIGHTY BULLDOGS!!!). In that house a 15-year-old curly-haid boy fought the police (when that kind of thing wasn't fashionable, usual or customary). The prowl cars ran up on Miss Marie's rosebushes and they ain't never bloomed since. Two years and six months later, he come out the jailhouse switchin'.

The white, classically-styled, side-hall, shoe box shotgun house where the elderly twin sisters lived was also despoiled. No one saw Miss Mary and Miss Martha after the storm and nobody never heard from them again. The cheap cinderblock hot sheet motels on Ursulines had sustained minimal damage and were going about their business as unusual.

The pink and red, double Creole cottage of that evil, hoo-dooish woman nobody liked was barely impinged on by the hurricane's gruesome bizness. She used to have her hands in that hall on St. Bernard where they supposed to done had the "brown paper bag" test for the darkskinned negroes (if your skin was darker than a brown paper bag, you couldn't go in). Her roughneck, longshoreman, clodhopper shoe-wearin', riverfront plate-eatin' husband came home early from workin' on the water out in the Gulf, caught her nekkid in the booty and the beast couple's own bed with his older brother, strangled her poodle, shot up her fur coats, and pistol-whipped his brother within a incha his life.

Days later, after they kissed (or whatever they did) and made up she cooked him his favorite meal (trout with butter sauce), loved him up 'til he fell asleep, got the gun, and shot him in the haid. She was so cold-blooded -- she didn't even call the police. She called her furrier (and began a lust affair with *him*). She didn't tell nair soul that her spouse was dead, hid the body in the garage out back, and was back with his brother befo' the husband' body was cold in the ground. She died a coupla years ago in jail. But they did give her husband a BIG TOO-DOO at his send-off and everybody say his ghost be walkin' 'round in there every year after nightfall on the anniversary of the killin'. Urban legend also had it that she killed her *first* husband by bammin' him over the haid with a big-old loafa frozen French bread, thawed it out, ate it, and got away scot-free. That was the same place where them cats was hangin' out in the backyard and gave that young boy that bleach to clear out his system for the drug test before he went to court -- and he died that evenin' from drinkin' almost a halfa gallon o' Purex. Nobody else ever lived in or went anywheres near that house again.

The clarinet player's purple, orange-framed, two-level, four-bay house was just gone with the winds. They said after the storm he got real-real low-sick and died of bone cancer (everybody knew what kinda "bone"). After he died, the bodybuilder with all them Alaskan sled dogs moved in there and started shrivelin' up too. People said it was just a ba-a-a-ad house.

He paused at the spot where his li'l cut buddies long ago had dared him to drink a whole quart of Muscatel -- straight down, an irritating episode in his life's adventures. He imagined that he still saw the stains on the bricks on the side of the

Professor Arturo

schoolteacher's now-faded, yellow, late Victorian frame cottage, the result of his abrupt and predictable upchuck of the cheap, rotgut pluck.

That was right down the street from where Vampire Man drank the blood of a fella with whom he had a dispute in Miss Peggy's bar, a storied and revered community institution (down from where LaBranche's Drugstore used to be) that was once across from the barbershop on the cornder of Dumaine and Derbigny where they sold chirren $.59 quarts of beer "out the wall" for their parents and (presumably) other grown folks. Vampire Man was under the illusion that drinking the blood of his victim would keep the police away. Everybody figured it did, 'cause he way up there away from NOPD *now* -- way up in Angola. Some people from Uptown moved in Vampire Man' house after that and their son was killed on Jefferson Highway 'fore day in the mornin' when he was in his truck on his way to the water to catch some big ones. That po' boy was jess dyin' to go fishin'.

Then there was the concrete slab where the fun house was -- the six-bay, common wall, double shotgun where that woman used to live who liked that happy dust and always had delicately-painted, hot-red nails (and a naughty, pouty-lipped smirk). She looked like a million, but she only cost' a dime. She was bright enough to "pass" and worked nights as a shake dancer at a high-end French Quarter jiggle joint where she shed her clothes along with her inhibitions. She demonstrated her more than marketable skills on a stripper's pole, sported jinglin' belly jewelry, shaved her engaging forest's prime evil, and would nude sunbathe on Sundays in her back yard.

She would greet the ice man, the milk man, the rent man (or somebody' uncle, daddy, brother, grampa, boyfriend or husband) in a leather or lace leotard with fishnet stockings and harlot-red heels, her hair pulled back in a nappy ponytail. Sometimes she'd be wearin' nuthin' but lipstick and nail polish.

The house brought to mind a memory of his uncle who went over there when he got paid one Friday and she was posing provocatively on the side gallery in a red leather bustier, a chilled bottle of Bali Hai in hand, and a naughty grin. His uncle was listed as missing in action for over two weeks.

He trudged on towards the former family abode next door to the music teacher in the middle of Dumaine between Roman and Derbigny on the Ninth Ward side of the street, recollecting that when they first moved in they had to take a million nails out the walls. They imagined that it musta been some kinda place for some kinda racket or some hoodoo people. A magnet of misery drew him closer to the double camelback shotgun house with the French doors that he had opened up into a single. A thin veil of windblown, foreboding clouds moved swiftly across the sky. He was as scared as halleluiah to enter the mangled wreckage and shambles of ghastly, ghostly relics of the grand adventure of his life, gravely alarmed at the sobering reality of the unrecoverable fragments of his family's muck-covered possessions. The terrible, sickening site was about as useless as an empty can of shaving cream. It was change he couldn't believe in.

He placed his drum and sticks on the green and white front steps, swallowed the pride of his passion and crept cautiously through the now-doorless entrance. Inside the semi-darkness was a wealth of forensic evidence: his waterlogged, padded leather armchair; the roll-up desk and drop leaf table from his office space, a crumbled couch, file cabinets filled with sopping papers, water-torn, warped record albums; the remains of the glass-walled, penthouse bar he had installed himself; the sodden, soggy remnants of his treasured *Love and Passion,* Edith Piaf's boxed set given to him by his eldest grandchild the first day it hit the store; broken glass-framed wall pictures of Huey Long, JFK, MLK, RFK and a torn and tattered, trampled photo of his dreaded sister-in-law's liver-spotted face.

He almost blew a gasket when his eyes adjusted fully to the shadowy gloom and he bore witness to the distressed state of the space in which he had expected to continue living out his retirement in modest comfort. He knelt dumbly, dispirited and defeated, amidst the dust and debris, sifting through the rubble of the bruised and battered shards and remains of his life. He felt like Mr. Pitiful as the fragility of memory brought back evenings of rhythmic rug-cuttin' by the Magnavox console stereo and that time when no other than Gov. Earl Long gave him a turkey, a ham, and a sacka potatoes right there outside the house. (There was a lotta colored babies born named "Earl" that year.) Amidst the green mounds of mold he came upon the long, embroidered robe his wife had given him the Christmas before she passed and the leopard print dashiki his daughter had made for him for a 50th wedding anniversary gift.

I guess it's good to be on this side o' the dirt, he thought, contemplating the maddened mystery of his history. He heard a slight rustling noise coming from the kitchen, pulled his protection (it's better to be caught out there with it when you don't need it than to be caught out there without it when you do) and thought *Whoever back there betta come out grabbin' air! I'll pop a cap in you!*

A humongous river rat scurried, cowering in a tangle of wires in a cornder as he stood ramrod rigid speculating on why these bitter bells had tolled for him. He couldn't believe he had actually thought about remodeling after the storm.

He pocketed his pistol, stood soldier straight, walked with a restrained elegance into the outside world's sunwarmed pools of water and sunken-cheeked addicts, then slowly, expertly reached for his snare drum and sticks. He checked his timepiece. It was almost the appointed hour for him to meet his daughter in fronta where the old H& K Oyster House used to be anyway.

He started playing his favorite Second Line tune with uninhibited, polyrhythmic passion, stepping, strutting, prancing, romancing, dancing through the monochromatic palate of the neighborhood. He used his overdeveloped "Popeye arms" and arthritis-gnarled hands to play with the dogged tenacity of his twilight years, snaking his way down Dumaine Street towards Claiborne, evoking the spirits of those long-departed, dead, rotten and so often forgotten (his feet couldn't fail him now). Each and every body was there. The whole neighborhood turnt out as the magic of his well-polished chops stirred up the joy and delight of incalculable numbers of natives, now buckin' and shuckin' in tune to his pounding beat in a sea of familiar souls and psyches, recalling his days (and nights) as a Second Line Grand Marshal in eye-popping, colorful suspenders, bowler hats, and rainbow-colored parasols. They was cuttin' the bodies loose. They was huffin' and-a puffin', humpin' and-a jumpin', screamin' and-a creamin'. . . burnin' down the house. They was workin' that sucker to death. He pursued his life's passion in communion with the strength and wisdom of his aging, playing for their untender mercies and morsels of mortal pleasure. He was makin' merry music (for all his friends) as he trotted riverward down Dumaine under the I-10 on Claiborne Street (where the trees used to be), now numbed by evening traffic. He stood there, playing tenaciously in the terrible tunnels of time, tapping his tightest tune on the drum's, tired, tattered, wellworn, ancient skin for whirls without end. He was back in stride again.

He then heard a familiar voice that seemed to come from amidst the merrymakers' magically marauding midst. "Daddy -- Daddy --" the voice said. "What *are* you doing?"

It had been a one-man charade of a parade.

That night, someone in the well-heeled, upscale, gated community across the river heard a loud *Pop*! in his daughter's garage.

August 2011
Stamford, CT

Professor Arturo

Graveyard Love

In the graveyard on Claiborne Street she and her wistfully cool thoughts were netherworlds away from the madness and badness of the low-rise housing development known as the Iberville Project -- its bell pepper green-painted, crumbling screen doors; its red-brick, bullet-pocked facades, its worn pathways and spent shell casings; its discarded, clear, glassine envelopes; its used prophylactics and syringes, broken 40-ounce beer bottles, roaches, curses, advanced cases of housatosis, sweltering, brick-oven heat; earsplitting beat boxes, rusty storm drains, goo-gobs of giant hoop earrings; ratty, cheap linoleum floors; grey, ashen faces; nicotine-stained teeth, generationally-sanctioned poverty and the temporally contemptible ign'ance of some of its permanently underclassed dwellers in that quarter of the shiny jewel at the bend of the river. It was Baghdad on the Bayou.

Angela Armour was a fish and French fries girl with a cherubic countenance, a plump and perky, doe-eyed womanchild, a sensitive vessel of song, her skin, the color of iced coffee, her Afro-puff hair blowing in the breeze of a smoky, hazy sky's spitting drizzle on her wildflower-freckled face. She was pretty from teeth to toe. Her legs was so fine, they used to say she looked like she was from Thigh-land. She walked in beauty and harmony like the dawn, as pretty as a new shotgun. A beauteous ghetto blossom in blue jeans, the long-legged sapsucker's eyes flickered and fluttered as she sang and dreamed of calm winds and warm, windswept, looking glass waters lapping against the ebb and flow of the tides on sandy, quartz beaches; crystal clear skies over rugged coastlines, sun-baked cliffs and sweeping landscapes; duckweed-filled ponds, cobalt blue water sailing and racing, lush tropical island forests; green, undulating hills; silk chiffon evening dresses, windmills spinning in the distance, evening vespers at a timeworn and venerable basilica, heavily-wooded walking trails, oversized windowboxes stuffed with flowers, exotic lingerie, beachside pavilions under canopies of trees, swamp sparrows and riverbank cattails; breathtakingly postcard-pretty, passionate views of the Mississippi; red leather restaurant booths, a simple, K & B-purple shotgun house with orange trim; wind-driven, snowy landscapes; the riveting orchestration of swelling strings and brassy climaxes; moonlit, starry skies; artfully-prepared meals, the gentle currents and pastoral tranquility of turquoise waters of faraway lands of song and romance, seaborne breezes, thick-layered curtains of mist in the shadows of fog-shrouded mountainous splendor, bugling wild elk, marigold garlands enhancing the enchantment of her waist, sculpted gardens, diamonds, winesweet kisses, silk stockings and pearls, forested slopes, lustrous strands of fabric and romantic strolls down Royal Street -- all things she thought bright, impassioning and resplendent -- as thin, grey wisps of clouds rolled overhead bearing witness to her sonorous song. She had always wanted to be a singer and relished the solitude of the ancient graveyard just across the street from the Iberville Project apartment she and familial generations before her called home.

    The decayed bodies in the concrete tombs, above-ground vaults and marble crypts constituted an ever-silent retinue of listeners, long departed but savoring the euphonic sustenance she provided their souls as she expressed the divine spark of her sultrier side. She sang to the tomb dwellers and their bronze gates, brass urns and vases as often as she could, memorizing the notations of their final dissolution from the world of the living's toil and tales of love, wars, and rumors of war as reflected in the graveside relics of grief set in stone:

A ROSE IN A WORLD
OF THORNS
Nov. 13, 1925 – Oct. 28, 1982

AUGUSTINE
DEATH CANNOT SEPARATE
THOSE WHO ARE BINDED
IN THE BOND OF LOVE

LABEAU
CONTENTMENT AND GODLINESS IS GREAT
GAIN. WE BROUGHT NOTHING INTO
THISWORLD AND IT IS CERTAIN WE CAN
CARRYNOTHING OUT. DON"T SAY FAREWELL
FORSOON, HEREIN WE ALL MUST DWELL.

FRANCOIS
Now the labourer's task is over;
Now the battle day is past;
Now upon the farther shore
Stands the voyager at last.

PVT. MILTON T. LOMBARD, U.S.M.C.
KILED IN ACTION ON OKINAWA
MAY 21, 1945

UNTIL THE DAY BREAK AND
THE SHADOWS FLEE AWAY

LIFE SIMPLY CHANGES FORM

TO KNOW HIM IS TO LOVE HIM

OUR BELOVED SON
LT. ANDREW J. BOUDREAUX, JR. U.S.A.A.F.
KILLED S.W. PACIFIC
AUGUST 22, 1944. AGE 23 YEARS

SGT. JAMES A. NOELLE
U.S. INFANTRY
Co. F 36th ARMORED DIV.
Born NOV. 13, 1913
KILLED IN ACTION
SOMEWHERE IN FRANCE
ON AUG. 11, 1944

MICHAEL J. BROUSSARD

Jazz Stories: *From Katrina to Connecticut*

LOUISIANA
SP CO A 28 INF DIV
VIETNAM
OCT 24, 1947   OCT 17, 1967

BORN A PIMP
DIED A PLAYA
Sept. 20, 1979   Aug. 18, 1995

One simply said:

MOTHER

* * *

When the day's euphonious rendition was over, she noiselessly returned to the lodgings of the living, that curious and quirky world of the walking dead souls in the project across the street. The twilight was gone, the songbird was no longer singing and Bill Clinton was making an indelible stain on the country's oral history.

* * *

Angela first met Dick on the night of St. John's Eve when she (quite literally) ran into him coming out the door of the drugstore. The store was right 'round the cornder from the Iberville Project on Canal and Robertson where she was pickin' up that weird contraption they had, the one them neighborhood girls was using to put in they arms for they birth control.

At first, she refused his advances (*You talkin' un'neath my clothes? You hittin' on me?*), but his smooth tongue and niggardly-handsome, hood-tough looks (including an expensive grill of gold teeth, representative samples of verbal illiteracy, dangling gold chains and ceaseless, unremitting vulgarisms) were all the rage at that age and time. Shortly after, she was *whipped.*

She didn't usually welcome all comers, but she welcomed Dick. It was lust at first sight when she saw him in his see-through, imitation silk, "wife-beater" T-shirt, as she smiled more than a mid-level, black female government administrator taking a picture standing next to Barack Obama. About a week later, as she shucked her duds after turning the picture of Jesus around on the dresser (so He wouldn't see the lowdown lewdness that would transpire during their first late-night hookup) and tossed them on a dingy bureau in her project apartment.

She was luvstruck blind over Dick and reveled in the delectation and pleasure in the libidinous predicament of their relationship. It was a prickly deal.

She basked in the physical pleasures Dick provided her carnal cravings, for she was entrapped in a net of his comings and goings-on that (to her) were as irresistible as her unearthly vocal forays into the graveyard adjacent to the project. Lawd, that girl was crazy 'bout Dick! She was *whipped.* To her, the moon rose and the sun set over Dick. Her favorite beer was Dixie beer; her favorite supermarket was Winn Dixie. At the Roosevelt Hotel (where she changed linen and cleaned rooms) she developed an addiction for Eggs Bene*dict*, and a fondness for a recording duo called Dick and Dee-Dee. She was straight-up, strung out *whipped* over Dick.

Her favorite comedians were Dick Gregory and Dick Smothers, her favorite neckwear was a dickey, and her favorite snack was Dickey's Potato Chips. She even savored a movie called *Whatever Happened to Dick & Jane?* And her favorite part of the Catholic liturgy was the bene*dic*tion. Lawd, that girl was crazy 'bout Dick! To her, the moon rose and the sun set over him. It wasn't long before she had a tattoo painfully, inexpertly pricked across her chest in HUMONGOUSLY BOLD, bugar green and K & B-purple letters that simply said:

DICK.

It was a match made in Purgatory

* * *

Unbeknownst to her, there was an aspect to Dick's life of which she was totally unaware, for (like many of his male contemporaries) he was living a double life of contradiction and untrue declaration. During the earlier daze of their romantic attentions he had told her that his father had died, leaving him a rather handsome sum (even though he didn't use *them* words) which purportedly afforded him the funds to be perennially "laced-up" in the proletariat-supported industry's latest sneakers, to purchase his hoopty, gold teeth and jewelry, and to keep himself and his friends in 40-ounce beers, weed and overpriced gitups of high-end fashion apparel designed by people named *Ralph, Giorgio, Liz, Calvin, Tommy, Perry, Donatella, Coco,* and *Yves* for folks named *Towanda, Tamika, Paprika, Ghettosha, Latrina, Easy Money, Shorty, Shotgun, Smash & Grab* (the brother from the Seventh Ward -- look like Richard Boone), *Kingpin, Weenie, Red Willy* (he the one look like Raymond Burr), *Street Life,* and *Ringworm.* In spite of his immaculately-dressed, sartorially resplendent outer, his life was about as phony as the congratulatory smile on the mascara'ed face of a beauty pageant runner-up.

    She didn't know it, but her beloved Dick was a walking crime wave whose main zest for life and for living was the courage of his ignorance. They were a classic Beauty and the Beast couple, for he was accused, tried and (sometimes) convicted of some of the most heinous offenses known to man, woman, child, ghost, beast or goblin.

    He was a man of deep convictions (mostly for armed robbery and assault) whose criminal activities and enterprises included (but were not limited to) forgery, passing bad checks, cruelty to an animal, cruelty to a juvenile, cruelty to the infirm, simple escape, complex escape, and jess plain bein' simple. Then there was abuse of a corpse, possession of human body parts, bein' chintzy with his Mardi Gras beads, tellin' his momma he wished she'd drop dead (two days later she whipped him down the street, went home, laid in the bed and died), removing the "Do Not Remove Under Penalty of Law" label on a pillow, carjacking, disturbing the peace, penetration of a body with a foreign object while using a drug, resisting a police officer, disarming a police officer, simple battery, complex battery, BOO-COO battery, niggravated battery, aggravated assault w/intent to be stupid, aggravated aggravation, and just plain bein' aggravatin'.

    People said the police had him up for serial public masturbation, malicious castration, criminal neglect of family, desecration of venerated objects, erectile blissfunction, foolin' 'round behind his oldlady' back and bullshooting in the "umpth" degree. He had a goo-gobba chirrens -- 12 different chirrens by 12 different li'l wimmins (ain't *none* of 'em had his last name).

His world was one of wine, wimmins and thongs. If there were an award for such a thing, he'd be unanimously elected Sperm Donor of the Year. His favorite plant was a pussy willow, his favorite clothing was booties and his favorite "old school" year was '69. He looked at wimmins as soulless creatures with the intellectual and creative sensibility of plastic blowup dolls. His permanent motto-of-choice was "No Hoe Left Behind."

Her only crime (like many of her female contemporaries) was to love a complicatedly cruel, no-good man.

* * *

There was another li'l shorty in his life. Buttermilk. She was a "born hoe" -- a sushi-eatin', up and comin' rising star on the rock scene, a pumpkin pie-complexioned hot momma from the project, a walking sperm bank whose father died from "acute drug intoxication." That girl was some hot in the tail. Her momma was wunna them wimmins who invented them lap dances and used abortion as a form of birth control. If sex were a library, Buttermilk'd be an open book. She was a fonky li'l thang, a sleazily-painted slut, a skankawank.

One time she was actin' up in a corner store on Claiborne and Dumaine and a policeman came to check it out, saw her, and refused to arrest her and put her in his cruiser because he thought she woulda stank it up too much (and he was driving a K-9 unit!). She was so skanky she couldn't get laid at the Million Man March. But that was what Dick liked (y'all knows how some mens like dat).

They say she was wunna them wimmins born with a "Roman toe" -- wunna them middle toes that's longer than the others. You could always see hers through them Ben Hur sandals she liked to wear with them camouflage, "Hammertime" parachute pants. They say that Roman toe is what makes them kinda girls so horny. She was hot as fresh milk. Chastity to her was about as rare as a white RTA bus driver. Her life's foremost philosophy was to beg, borrow and rip off every dime she could get and every inch she could take. She was a born hussy whose only claim to fame was that "No white man ever touched me." She didn't have issues. She had the whole subscription.

Yeah. Buttermilk was living proof that hoes was indeed born -- and not made. If she'd been religious, she'd have started an organization called "Hoes for Christ." If she were in college she would enjoy giving oral presentations (probably at Ball State University). If she were one of the Sisters of the Sacred Sacrament, her favorite form of prayer would be ejaculations as she sang Hosannas in the highest. Her favorite extinct hominid would be *homo erectus,* her favorite expression upon seeing a man would be "Where's the beef?", and her favorite candy store would be Chock Full o'Nuts. Yeah. On her tombstone there'd be a sign:

HERE LIES A BORN HOE

Angela was a housekeeper at the Roosevelt Hotel, which was located within walking distance of the project so that she didn't have to salt away change for the bus. It had changed its name to the Fairmont, but change came slowly to oldtime New Orleanians, and their sons and daughters and daughters and sons still called it "the Roosevelt."

Her duties were to maintain the hotel in an orderly, clean manner; be a physically-fit employee (so that she could "turn" mattresses, make beds, and organize soiled linen); clean halls, rooms and bathrooms; dust, vacuum, arrange and prepare sample sales rooms, banquet halls and rooms; and all duties as designated by the Deciders. She worked hard for the money.

One day at lunch, Winsome, one of her white-uniformed coworkers, sat at a table in the lunch area engrossed in a book and taking notes while she chucked away on a hot sausage po-boy (dressed -- plus pickles) as Angela sat across from her. "What you readin' like that?" Angela queried.

"Homework."

"Homework?!? I thought you was finished school. I thought you finished at Clark. You goin' to night school?"

"Yeah, I finished. I'm goin' to Delgado. I'm goin' there at night."

"Oh -- that college over there by City Park . . ."

"Yeah ya-right," Winsome said, napkining away a spot of mayonnaise from her uniform. "I was over at UNO for writin', but they didn't have nobody in the whole department understood what I was tryin' to do. Plus Delgado cheaper anyway -- and it's closer to the 'hood," she added.

"What you takin' up?"

"I was takin' up writin', but now I'm down with General Studies. I'ma get my grades up and try to get a scholarship to Loyola for music."

"You play music? You sing?" inquired Angela.

"Yeah. I'm at a coupla clubs on the weekends. I work with a band right off the Quarters, too . . . right over there on Chartres and Frenchmen . . . mostly on the weekends but sometimes during the week when I ain't gotta study."

"What kinda music you sing?"

"Jazz."

"Jazz? You mean like Kenny G?"

"No . . . *jazz* . . . like Dakota Staton . . . Ella Fitzgerald . . . Sarah Vaughan . . . on the *real* side."

"Wow!" Angela said, wide-eyed. "I hearda Ella, but I ain't never hearda the resta them singers, but I sing, too. I sing all the time. I sing to every body." Then -- "You know what kinda music I like?"

"What you into? What's yo' roll?"

"I like what I call 'graveyard music'."

Winsome momentarily ceased partaking. *Each to her own . . .* she thought.

"But I wouldn't mind goin' to school to learn all them people."

"Look -- we got a few mo' minutes then we gotta hit-it and quit-it. Lemme run it to you, baby. . . ."

Winsome schooled her, explaining her reasoning for attending Delgado, a two-year institution, rather than first going to Loyola, a four-year college. She expounded on the application process, the demands of budgeting one's time and the rewards of a higher education to a woman's social development, self-esteem and financial independence. That done, she loaned Angela a disc of *Under Her Spell: Phyliss Hyman's Greatest Hits* to check out.

That night Angela donned her yellow, above-the-knee, crinkled silk chiffon dress with the empire waist and collar, took her Sony Discman portable CD player to the graveyard, listened to the songstress' sweet strains deep into the thrill of the night, mused on a vision of grasping her diploma and laudatory bouquet upon graduation from college, and conjectured thoughts that her life would no longer be a dream deferred.

Jazz Stories: *From Katrina to Connecticut*

     Soon it was her first night of classes at the sizeable acreage of the community college campus adjacent to City Park's green bayous, mosses, and ancient oaks. It had been founded as a normal trade school for young white boys by Isaac Delgado, a 19th century Jamaican immigrant and benefactor. Her unimaginable dreams had become a reality.

  That night she dressed for her first class in majestic fashion -- turquoise peasant skirt, matching bejeweled tank top, freshly-braided hair and those Bernardo Leopard Patent shoes she knew she couldn't afford but just *had* to have for such an extra-special occasion. Her first class that night was a course in Composition 101 in which she was asked to write a diagnostic essay that was to be entitled "Why I Am Seeking a Higher Education." She wrote:

> *Why I Am Sekking a Higheur Education*
> *i am trying to better my chances at life. and wunt to got to college to do that. When i first hear about college from my friend i knew what i had to do to be sucess i my life. i don't have a baby andi wunt to be a singer like my favorite singer Fillis Hymen! Whenever i hear her songs It make me wunt to be bettr at my life and what all ican be to do all the things i dream of which is to go to a bigger school for music and to lift myself from the project where all them things be happen that just ain't not write like they be shooti and fighting and they always fusing about nothing except killing up each others i just cannot take it no more and want to be the best i can be by making more of myself and increasing my self of steem. There has been many words that have been heard about it in the media and the murder rates is to much. when wills the violent end? another thing i would like to say is i want a colleg degree because they don't let you do nothing in today's society without one. My boyfriend Dick always try to do somethnig but he keep all to his self when i aks him what it is he be about when i be at work.and now i'm in school. i want to marry him one day and have a baby but i can't make it on what i bring in from the hotel even though i will try my very best to get all i can be for me him and the baby*
> *That's if he let me have one.*

> *In cunculsion i would like evrybody to know that i am on my way and nothing going to stopp me from being the world best singer – except for*
> *Fillis Hymen.*

Just after she and her fellow classmates finished the essay she received a text message which she stealthily read so as not to disturb the instructor in her illuminating and edifying now-nightly sermonette. It said:

I LOVE YOU BITCH

* * *

Around midterm that oppressively long first semester she arrived home from work and saw an open letter left atop the VCR in the living room. It was from the State of Louisiana, Department of Social Services, Office of Family Support. It said:

> *". . . had sexual relations with the mother on or about 10/94 which resulted*
> *in the conception and birth of the child. . . ."*

She couldn't read any further. She didn't need Maury Povich to tell her what Dick didn't tell her. He already was a baby' daddy. Then she found a glittering "door-knocker" earring in the bathroom's medicine cabinet. The next time he came over, he'd have some 'splainin' to do.

* * *

"What you mean, bitch -- askin' me if I had some hoe in here while you was at work?!?" he blustered, a bagged 40-ounce of Old English 800 beer held securely in his grasp.

"-- Or at school."

"School?!?!! Don't be frontin' and stuntin' on me 'bout no school!!! Ain't nuthin' but a buncha educated fools back there," he spat drunkenly. "Ain't nunna them white folks gon' do *nuthin'* for yo' ass! Ain't *no* white folks gon' do nuthin' for *no*body! I don't wan' hear nuthin' 'bout no white folks! I don't eat no white rice! I don't think the President should live in the White *House* and I don't use no white cleanser -- but I *do* wear white draws and use white turlit paper . . . I don't even drink no white milk . . . I just drink . . . *Buttermilk*," he mused.

"What about the baby?"
"What baby?"
"The baby that -- the baby I read about in the letter."
"You saw my mail? You read my mail?"
"It was sittin' out. I couldn't help but see it."
"But you read it --????!!?!!??"
"It was by accident."
"Accident?!? I'ma 'accident' yo' ass!!!"

He then proceeded to give her the latest version of a Rodney King asswhippin'.

* * *

The physical abuse continued until about time for that semester's final exams. Between the beatings, the demands of her job and the pressures of that first semester, she was a quintessential nervous wreck.

She decided to go see Miss Ruby.

* * *

Miss Ruby Lee Thornton, aka "Madame Ruby, the Jewel of Gentilly," was widely known as a fortune teller, healer and peddler of all manner of dolls, cures, contraptions, notions, potions, prayers and lotions. She was a gypsy woman, a practitioner of the darkest of arts, the spitting image of the lady who usta be on the pancake box. They say she was the one Major Lance made that record "Gypsy Woman" about. When she wasn't foretelling one's future she made a living cleaning rich folks' houses in Metairie and the French Quarter -- which afforded her access to the most ancient of family secrets and most embarrassing household turmoil. Many a prosperous citizen, thus, became her best clients.

It was pourin' down rainin' while the sun was shinin' that day Angela went to see her. The devil was beatin' his wife and marryin' his daughter. Angela wore a pair of French Market-purchased knockoff sunshades, a gauzy white embroidered blouse, and a tye dye khaki skirt. She knocked at the door of the late Victorian, double bay shotgun house and a pair of familiar eyes peeked carefully out from the half-drawn blinds of *Madame Ruby's Luxurious Antique Shop and Spiritual Temple*.

Miss Ruby opened the door and gave her a BOO-COO BIG hug and a wider grin, her floor-length floral dress dragging over the less-then Dali-ish design of the room's well-worn linoleum floor. Her head was wrapped in the manner that the women of color were once commanded to do by legal prescription of the Northern occupying forces.

She beckoned for Angela to sit on the plush, worn, red-patterned, velvet-covered pleather sofa by the window near the river side of the house. The music of Miriam Makeba percolated strangely from the next room as a thick shroud of red bean and ricey smells rambled through the candlelit, heavily-incensed room. A cheap, velvet, wood-framed picture of Kennedy, King and Kennedy hung over a mantel covered with all shapes and sizes and colors of candles.

After a while, Angela and the healer spoke. "Miss Ruby," she began, "I didn't tell nobody I came to see you. And I know, knowing you, you already know what I come here for . . ."

"-- Man trouble," Miss Ruby affirmed.

"How did you --" Angela started, beset by an unease that bewitched, bothered and bewildered her.

"-- I been doin' this for a long time. I wasn't jerked up -- I was raised up. I did it for yo' momma. I did it for *her* momma. I mighta even done it for her momma's momma. I don't rightly know sometimes, but I do know I been doin' this ever since I was a li'l bitty baby. They say I was born with a veil over my face. It's just the way things always been. Now what can Miss Ruby do for you today, baby?"

"I'm in love with a man who don't love me."

"That's the worst kinda love."

"He don't love me. . . . He never did."

"But I see he done whipped up on you," Miss Ruby said, taking a studied look at her eyes through her *Serenghetto* sunglasses.

"How do you --"

"-- Why else you gon' wear sunglasses in all that rain outside? The sun ain't shinin' *that* much. Take them glasses off, girl." She complied.

"I love him but he done tore his draws with me. He even beat me up one time when I was 'sleep . . . but I'm *still* gon' love him 'til the day I die."

"Well, Miss Ruby, time-and-a-half for him. I could pray over some candles, give you sumthin' for his shoes -- or for his food or --"

"I still love him, Miss Ruby. I don't wan' do nuthin' to him. I just don't wan' live without him. I love him to death. I like-ted him every since I first saw him. When I first met him I was tickled-tickled-tickled. He so fi-i-i-i-i-ine."

"Ain't no biggy, Boo, but ass and face wear out. One link cain't rattle by itself. You needs the whole chain!" Then -- "Girl -- reach that White Owl cigar box over there by the chiffarobe -- the one with that aluminum ferl all over it -- then come over here and sit over at the table. I'ma read you yo' bones."

They sat by the light of a red candle in the center of a round table in a corner of the room. Miss Ruby, eyes aglow, opened the cigar box, mumbled some incantations and spilled a bunch of dried chickenbones onto the tree-green tablecloth, staring at each position in which they landed.

"What the bones say, Miss Ruby?" Angela asked, unsure if she really wanted to know the answer.

"Bones say the boy just *dumb* . . . he just *innately* dumb. His paw was dumb. His maw was dumb and everybody in that whole entire family is dumb. He just born to *be* dumb. Bones say you cain't make a mule a thoroughbred -- 'specially a mule like him."

"Throw 'em again! Throw 'em again!"

Miss Ruby collected the bones, put them back in the box and shook them animatedly, appearing trancelike, disengaged from her body, and tossed them tableward.

"What they say, Miss Ruby? What the bones say?"

"Bones say you done really chucked a monkey wrench in the gumbo. Bones say that boy ain't 'bout nuthin' but some 'graveyard love'."

"'Graveyard love'? What's that? What you mean by that?"

"'Graveyard love' . . . that kinda love that grab holda yo' heart and take it and bring it off somewhere and next thing you know you done landed yo'self in the graveyard. Stop tryin' to be wunna them 'I-think-I-can' wimmins."

"Huh?"

"Like the li'l train --'*I-think-I-can*' . . . --'*I-think-I-can*'. . . --'*I-think-I-can*'. . . You cain't change the spots on no leopard --

just like you cain't change a colored man' skin . . . unless you Michael Jackson," she added. They laughed.

"It just caught me up short, Miss Ruby. I found a letter sayin' he had done made a baby with another girl and I found a earring in the house -- then he whipped up on me."

"What goes on in the dark . . ."

"That's what *you* say? What the bones say?"

"Baby -- bones tellin' me he ain't the one. Bones don't lie. Bones ain't *never* lied. They's other mens out there. I know a nice young man -- went to LSU Dental School and can tell you everything you wan' know about yo' teefs. He so smart he could talk the fat outa butter. But I guess a woman want what a woman want. You cain't tell 'em nuthin' when they love that kinda man. I guess sometimes you gotta kiss a lotta frogs to find that prince. They ain't no behind-whippin' like the one the Lord'll give you."

"But I love him . . . and he say he love *me*. What can I do?"

"Change your hair . . . make yo' face up different . . . change yo' life. You cain't be in mournin' for somebody still alive. That's all that kinda man wan' do is lie, steal, drink, run the streets, jackroll, rob, fool with that dope and jump in and out the bed with a buncha wimmins just as no-good as them. Don't trust what he say. Mouth say anything. I loved a man like that once. He called me 'bitch' so many times I started thinkin' my *name* was 'Bitch.' Old bell pepper-head man . . . but my momma put me to the wise . . . told me he wasn't nuthin' but a baker cryin' for bread in the baker shop . . . but I went deaf in the ears and still stayed with him . . . even if he was a li'l long in the tooth. . . . He was in the rackets. Tryin' to talk sense into that man was like tryin' to nail Jello to a balloon. They found him all shot-up dead in the street one mornin' . . . all kinda holes up in him. Ain't left me two pennies to press together. Ain't left me a dime. All I got was tragedy money. Gawd don't sleep, baby and as the Lawd is my secret Judge -- all I'm sayin' is -- don't clean nobody' back yard if yo's ain't clean."

"Miss Ruby -- it make me sick to my heart what you sayin'. I just think you got a suspicious mind."

"Bones ain't 'spicious. Bones don't lie."

"It's just that with school and everything -- I just cain't take the pressure right now."

"Ain't but two things in my life that *can* take a tunna pressure and still do what they hafta do -- a bus seat I got my big backside on and a big-old, fat woman like me' high heels." They both laughed as the weight of the matter was at least momentarily managed. Miss Ruby packed away the bones and Angela gave her a box of commodity cheese she had brought for her services.

"Thank you, baby. You sho' knows what I like. This the best cheese they ever done made for macaroni and cheese. The guv'mint sho' knowed what they was doin' when they put *that* one out there. Guv'mint cheddar make it betta. . . . And you do good in school, baby. I don't celebrate no C's."

* * *

She had just finished her first midterm exam (rather quickly) that semester, left class after only about 30 minutes and headed home that night on the City Park bus as the autumn leaves had fallen and winter was finally rearing its ugly head. She walked the short distance from the bus stop by the project just before the Canal Street stop on Basin and Canal and maneuvered through the plethora of wolf-whistles and caustic comments cast her way regarding her bodily image and scholarly pursuits. *Yo! Schoolgirl! . . . Come learn me sumthin', baby . . . I gotta book for you, girl . . .*

She opened the door to the apartment and heard some compromising banter emanating through the bedroom's closed door. On the living room sofa she noticed a pair of women's tortoise shell glasses, a female-style, pink bubble jacket; a pair of stringy, needing-to-be-washed panties; a strappy, low-cut tank top; a sky blue "shorty robe," a pair of black fishnet hose, a red bijou bustier, and a large pair of imitation gold "hoochie hoop" earrings. It was on. She listened for a while. *C'mon, baby . . . we got about a whole hour mo' . . . The bitch takin' a test tonight . . . She gon' be there for a while . . . Git down on it, baby. . . . Throw that ass!!! Throw that ass, hoe! . . . Heave, hoe!!! . . . All I ever wanted her to do was slob on my knob, anyway. . . .*

The next thing she knew her earrings were off, she had a big kitchen knife in her hand, the door was knocked off its hinges, and she saw that Buttermilk was on toppa him -- nekkid as a boulder. "You been freakin' my oldman!" she niggerwomaned, the knife raised murderously over the illicit-loving couple.

"You the one! You the one been freakin' my oldman! I'ma kill *botha* y'all up in here!"

"Baby . . . baby . . . *please* . . . slow it down . . . slow it down," Dick cried as Buttermilk cowered naked in a corner. Angela approached him, knife in claw. "Baby -- it ain't what it look like!" he pleaded.

"It ain't?!??!!! Ain't but one thing it look like --" she snarled.

"Slow yo' roll! Slow yo' roll!" he pleaded. She stared at him as if moonstruck, with a look that could kill an already dead man. Buttermilk saw an opportunity for her exit and left the stage lest the impromptu performance end in her demise. She was gone and vanished before he could say "Bitch -- !"

Angela walked toward him slowly, deliberately, with the knife poised dangerously in an "I'ma-'bout-to-slice-and-dice-yo'-ass-up" position. He implored her not to kill him, shedding the tears of a lifetime as she approached. The boy was beggin' mo' than Keith Sweat. He sounded like James Brown, too . . . *Please . . . Please . . . Please . . .* His eyes was red-red-red with tears. "Un-ass it, baby . . . put it down . . . I love you, baby . . . Please, baby . . . Please don't do it, baby. . . Please! Please, baby . . . *Please*!!!"

Then something in his demeanor and his voice struck her deep somewhere inside. She lowered the knife, dropped it on the bed, said, "Baby, I'm sorry. It wasn't you," and opened her arms to him.

Then the leopard sprang into action -- "You snubnosed bitch! What is yo' malfunction?!?!??? You 'bout to git you another Rodney King asswhippin', bitch!!! I'ma whip yo' ass like Jesus in *The Passion*!!!"

"Baby --" she cried at the prospect of the inevitable, "-- we already livin' po' . . . why we gotta live like this?"

"Too late, bitch -- that's yo' ass, now!" He started off with a full-fisted punch in the face, knocking several of her teeth to the floor as blood sprinkled on the sweatsoaked mattress. Then he kicked her in her midsection. "Pulla knife on *me*? I'ma show you howta pulla knife on *me*!!!" Then he grabbed her by her beaded, braided hair, disjoining a clump of locks and smashing her head against the wall. He then grabbed the knife and started stabbing her viciously and with all deliberate speed. "Yeah, bitch! *This* how you use a shank, bitch!" he said as he counted out each stroke:

One . . . Two . . . Three . . . Ten . . . Twenny . . . Thirty . . . Forty . . . Fitty . . . Eighty-six . . . Eighty-seven . . . !!!!!

"Uh-huh!!! Yeah! You dead now, huh bitch!!! You dead, huh!!!" the banshees in his brain clamored. "Yeah, bitch! You ain't gon' never pull no knife on nobody no mo'!!! But you ain't got me yet!!! You ain't got me yet!!! And you *ain't* gon' git me!!! I ain't gon' end up spittin' on nobody' joint up in the joint! I ain't goin' to no Angola behind yo' monkey ass!!! I'ma see you in jussa 'bout a minute! Just wait right there in hell . . . *bitch*!" he said to her, now passed out and cold to the touch.

He went in the living room, still naked except for her blood, reached into his imitation leather shoulderbag for his instrument of salvation, went back to the room, stood over her now lifeless body, pressed it to his temple and ridded the world of another mound of monstrous flesh just usin' up oxygen.

* * *

The police and the trumpet-playing coroner's folks soon arrived, decorated the courtyard with yellow crime scene tape on the old oak trees, put him on a gurney as the people cheered, and tried to estimate the number of stab wounds on what was left of her earthly remains as she continued her eternal, beatific and beauteous ride on death's dark chariot.

They say that when you tiptoe past that graveyard over on Claiborne Street -- you can still hear that young girl singin'. . . .

August 2008
Stamford, CT

Professor Arturo

The Funeral Poet

At first, the poets in New Orleans weren't really into doing it that much. Sometimes they would put you on the program to spit a poem if you were a friend or family member, but nobody was really into having career aspirations as a funeral poet. It just wasn't the most economically-sustaining or traditional thing to do in a city that cherished anything old (if it weren't living, breathing flesh and blood). Preservation was a highly-charged political issue and convention and custom were the most sacrosanct of cows. For me, reading poems at funerals wasn't about burying the dead. It was about comforting the living. The first time they asked me to do it, it was a job. The second time it was an adventure.

The first funerary poem I presented was for a fancy woman in dookie braids who worked a shake dancer gig on Bourbon Street. She was wunna them streetwalkers who concealed razor blades under their tongues to defend themselves against disgruntled, unsatisfied johns and janes. She departed this life when she accidentally ingested a Gillette Blue Blade. They gave her a big sendoff at her wake where she was laid out in an orange-fringed, solid cherry coffin in her favorite orange and emerald tea dress. She was the prettiest dead body anyone ever saw and she looked like she was sleeping (the only difference was she wasn't snoring).

All *kinda* mens showed up. There were more men there than the Million Man March. They even had her son there -- a prisoner in chains flanked by two somber Angola State Prison guards. Some dope-dealin', gold-teeth sportin', designer fashion industry-supportin' young hooligan was there during her memorial service at Louisiana Undertaking and after I read the poem for her he hollered -- "WHY DON'T Y'ALL HURRY ON UP AND SEND HER NO-GOOD ASS TO HELL!?!?!!!" Her despondent family members and menfriends didn't take too kindly to his outburst and a big humbug broke out in the backa the funeral home. The po' li'l lady wasn't even in the earth yet. About an hour after she was laid (to rest, this time) they started arguing over the insurance money and who was gon' git the furniture and her costume jewelry. It was a grave situation.

One thing I found out from reading poetry at funerals was that people die in a whole lotta different ways. They choke to death on ballpoint pens, expire from roach bites, get sent to their Maker by exploding champagne corks, arrive at Cloud Nine from being banged upside they haid by wayward baseballs, get strangled by bras, give up the ghost during lovemaking sessions and get to those pearly (or hot iron) gates by imbibing too much beer. My newfound side hustle hipped me to the fact that every year more people are killed by donkey kicks than airplane crashes and that there's more departures from the realm of the living due to medical practitioners' negligence than firearms. People die from being shot in hunting accidents, falling off stepladders, being stung by bees, getting bitten by fleas, plunging into vats of gumbo, contracting the avian flu from parakeets, being decapitated by those huge, metal window fans that are so prevalent in older Crescent City homes, and from just doin' something really stupid.

I worked funerals from Metairie to Marrero -- Uptown, Downtown, Backa Town, Fronta Town, Cross Town, In Town, Gert Town and Outa Town -- Christian, Jewish, Muslim, Agnostic, and Satanist. I was an Equal Opportunity Poet. I've partaken in poetics at *Janazah*, read rhyme at *Shemira,* and chanted verse to *Yama* at Hindu cremation ceremonies. I consoled and comforted families and friends of the dearly (and sometimes *un*dearly) departed with my reassuring literary (often fictional) renditions while emphasizing the brighter aspects of their former lives -- even for the murderers, molesters, dope fiends and hoes.

Sometimes I had to tell a who-o-o-o-ole lotta lies. At one funeral service for a shot-up, gang-banging, tatted-up youngster (who was dead proof of the adage "Bad boys die young"), I gave my shallowest condolences and knocked 'em dead by spittin' the lyrics to his favorite "Bounce" rap song. Some attendees squirmed in their seats at the profanity-laced elocution while others recited right along with me. They per*formed.* Somebody said that they was glad he was in the bosom of the Lord. Somebody else remarked that he just might be in the Lord's *ass* -- 'cause that's about all he chased during his brief tenure on the planet.

Professor Arturo

I've read poetry at rich folks' funerals ("spiritually-based transfer ceremonies") and poor folks' funerals ("homegoings"). I've seen the most expensive 20-gauge, solid bronze coffins (almost big enough for my ladyfriend in Baton Rouge) and permanently-discounted cardboard boxes. I've read at funerals with throngs of photographers and some with only one more person than the deceased.

I've been to memorial services where brass bands blowed in Second Lines that were so on-the-wild that when the pallbearers rocked the casket so the deceased could dance one last time -- they spilled the cadaver on the ground.

I've been to some services so tediously boring that the tenor of the occasion could lull the dead to a deeper slumber, and I've read words of passion and praise for stillborn babies and great-great-great grandparents. I performed at one funeral for a cat from the Sixth Ward named "Chicken Red" who was cremated with the urn prominently displayed at his homegoing ceremony and that Bagneris boy from the Lafitte Project joked that he was "Chicken-In-A-Box." Quite a number of his family and friends were a bit fried about that.

One time there was a mix-up at a closed-casket service with the wrong body in the coffin. At the end of the ceremonies the husband finally stirred up enough courage for a final view of his badly-disfigured wife who was killed in a horrific car accident not long after their 50th anniversary. When the funeral director opened the casket, staring at the husband was a Girbaud shirt-wearing, gold-grilled gangsta rapper with "LOVE" and "HATE" tattooed on his fingers and "THUG 4EVER" in boldfaced, money green lettering across his forehead. The husband had a heart attack and died on the spot.

I've presented poems on the dead at a slew of humble, unassuming inner city churches and at some of the most elegant structures in the western world. I was commissioned to read a poem at St. Louis Cathedral for a rich Garden District lady who was interred in a custom-made, pink-trimmed obsidian coffin (for protection and good luck) in the shape of a late model Ferrari. One lady who was a shroudmaker had herself laid out in a coffin in the shape of a Singer sewing machine.

A notorious French Quarter madam had a custom made casket in the form of a prophylactic package. Guitar Willie was buried in a Gibson Guitar funerary box -- complete with real strings. There were coffins reflecting every possible aspect of the living: patriotic flags, cigarettes, pets, sports equipment, boats, firearms, foods, occupations and an assortment of iniquitous indulgences.

    I usually read my work near the end of the Order of Service after the Blessing of the Body and Placing of the Pall, the Opening Prayer and Blessing, the First Scripture Reading, the Responsorial Psalm, the Second Scripture Reading, the Homily, the Prayers of the Faithful, the Presentation of Gifts, the Lord's Prayer, the Communion, the Obituary and Words of Expression and (if it were a Catholic service) a seemingly eternal recitation of the Holy Rosary. I don't really have anything against Catholics. I was raised Catholic. I just think it rather odd to go to a house of worship where they have something called "Ejaculations."

    I read at funerals on days so clear that one could see forever and ever (amen) and on occasions when low, gray, threatening clouds loomed overhead, moving inland from the Gulf in commanding, circular motions. One thing I noticed was how the living fell out of tune with reverence for the late friend or family member despite the weather or one's station in life. Brawls broke out between surviving lovers and spouses. Churches, mosques, and temples became battlefields. Long lost relatives showed up to demand their dibs on the property or personal possessions of the recently departed. Wives, husbands, phantom friends and "outside children" (that no one ever heard of) would magically appear at some of the sites -- sashayin', shoo-shoo-in' and hissy-fittin' with the best of 'em, the faux authenticity of their tears inundating many a structure's floorboards.

    I discovered that the ones who did the least for someone while they were alive were often the ones doing the most conniptionin' at the funeral. I found that some lowlifes would check the obituaries in the paper and attend observances of people they didn't even know -- just to get a (free) New Orleans-style meal at the Repast. Then there were the charlatans, brigands, thieves and self-appointed saints (aka "men of the cloth") who discounted the fees for their churches' funerary services for bereaved mothers, spouses and acquaintances (who couldn't afford the secular fees of their houses of worship) and engaged in ungodly exchanges of sexual favors in lieu of assuaging those vulnerable, mourning women's capital deficiency as an aggravating factor in their bereavement. It was tit-for-tat. It was cold-blooded. Curtis Mayfield was right-on it: If there's a hell below, they're all gonna go.

After bearing witness to the unsaintly shenanigans of it all, I decided on a course of action that might expose their unholy scams and shams so that those legitimately distraught, moaning mourners and ingrate pretenders could at least become privy to those who saw their murmured weeping as prospective prey for the intended consequences of their fraudulent deceptions.

I decided to have my *own* funeral.

* * *

I conspired with a mortician for whom I had done several funerary poems, related my desire and justification for the proposed hoax, and we rigged the velvety maroon interior of a coffin so that I could breathe, see and hear when it was unhermetically shut at my own closed-casket memorial service. I was a bit skeptical at the prospect of inadvertent suffocation and expressed some lingering doubts I might have had. He reassured me of my safety by deadpanning: "It's your funeral. I'll be the last one to let you down." He was quite the comedian.

We arranged for a pallbearing crew from his staff whose members would not be privy to the surreptitious scheme, placed an obituary in the daily paper and effected a militarily-precise undertaking to get me to the church on time.

The scene outside St. Peter Claver Catholic Church (on St. Philip between Roman and Prieur) was a mournful assemblage of family members, friends, former classmates, poetry lovers, neighbors, clergy with whom I had worked, co-workers, debtors, runnin' podners and ex-girlfriends. The casket should have been waiting for them at the foot of the altar when they arrived, but (in truly classic form) I was late for my own funeral as the usual grace of the motorcycle officers' rolling roadblocks was interrupted by an I-10 traffic jam.

Upon my arrival I could hear them (at least the ones not hangin' on the cornder in the bar) as they stood by the church's black, wrought iron-laced fence reminiscing about some of the more public of my life's misadventures. Such as that time my podner Big Wayne and I were riding on Canal Street after an afternoon and evening of libation on Bourbon Street and in the casino -- and I upchucked out the passenger side window for blocks and blocks -- from Maison Blanche to Krauss (in fronta the who-o-o-ole known world) then literally crawled, sneaking up the series of steps to the house -- thinking I was foolin' everybody (but myself). Or the instance when those two women I was precariously juggling showed up at my French Quarter apartment at the same time and flipped their wigs at my long-running romantic ruse.

The attendees jibbed and jabbed jocularly about that time I went with my cousin to her friend's jam-packed hairdressing shop across the river, used the restroom, dropped a ghastly load that overflowed the commode, asked to use a mop (which the proprietor didn't have), went across the street to the dollar store and purchased one, and cleaned the putrid liquids and solids on the establishment's flower-themed linoleum floor as the stunned customers endured the hideous stench.

My runnin' podners just *had* to bring up that time they dared me to swig a whole bottle of Muscatel in one guzzle and I took the challenge and seconds later permanently stained the red brick banket on the side of the schoolteacher's house on Roman and Dumaine. They even remarked on when I was out there in the street runnin' in and out them hot spots (actin' a major league fool) and mentioned how they knew such nocturnal activities would lead to my untimely demise. Little did they know -- I was time enough for 'em.

The somberly-berobed parish priest and two black-cassocked altar boys, one holding a five-foot cross, escorted the casket cart to the front of the floral arrangement-encased altar as the onlookers filed in to pay their respects to my earthly remains. After completion of the usual and customary Order of Service for a Mass of Christian Burial, an infinite recitation of the Holy Rosary, and the infernally choking incense smoke I had to endure, it was time for the testimonials and tributes.

I almost bellylaughed in my gruesome hideaway and gave away the scam as a series of eyewitnesses to my life's often gory story approached a mic near the coffin and spoke eloquently about what a kindred spirit I was, the wisdom and wit of my being, the friendship and fealty I fostered among friends, the valor and gallantry that were unique to the tableau of my life, and the

Professor Arturo

high merit and integrity at the core of my immortal soul. It was enough to make the dead run out the graveyard.

Then the services were finally over. It was time to come to full disclosure.

I vigorously pushed at the hood of the casket, forcing a collective gasp from the crowd as the pall fell floorward. I arose from my intended eternal home, took a bow, and approached the mic.

"Good afternoon, y'all. Where y'at!" I said to the stirred, shaken, stunned and surprised listeners. "Many of you are here to sincerely bid my earthly remains goodbye. But today there will be no farewell. There will be no goodbyes . . . no 'Hasta la vista, babies,'" I Schwarzeniggered. Then --

"Some of you are indeed here out of sincerity, some out of curiosity, and some so you can git that down-home meal at the Repast in the hall around the cornder. The point is that many of you are here out of some sort of perceived obligation, some feeling that attending these such ceremonies can absolve you of the sins you commit without hesitation or shame in your day-to-day activities amongst yourselves and towards others.

"Like you, Bill -- When you plan to pay me that $260 you been owin' me -- for fifteen years? Or you, Gas Haid -- you done made six babies with that woman out there in Pontchartrain Park and ain't bought nair Pamper . . . and Brenda -- you been out there ho'in for over 40 years -- and still ain't got nuthin' to show for it -- 'cept for a big green and purple tattoo with yo' double life sentence-servin' pimp daddy' name in BIG BOLDFACE letters 'cross yo' chest . . . wearin' all them turtlenecks in the summertime!

"And Taquisha -- you supposed to be somebody' momma and *you* still rippin' and runnin' the streets, too . . . carryin' on with that woman' husband like that. . . . And you, Jackie -- with yo' BIG, RED, BEEFEATIN' ASS -- with them ghetto-dwellin', dog hair, dollar store braids . . . and them cheap, imitation cotton-polyester blend, red outfits . . . all that lyin' to that man 'bout you gon' marry him -- when you know that man ain't never wanted nobody but you . . . talkin' 'bout you gon' keep yo' weight down . . . eatin' up everything on the menu . . . just like yo' BIG, FAT SISTERS and yo' BIG, FAT COWORKERS. . . . Y'all *needs* to be gittin' them big alligator-eatin' jaws wired shut. . . .

"And Miss Pearl Tongue -- tryin' to put that baby on that man when you knowed all the while it wasn't his. . . That's why yo' life is what it is today . . . the same thing it was yesterday . . . and *gon'* be tomorrow. . . .

"And Reverend Everhard -- the righteous reverend -- ain't you the one called that lady and asked her to go out after you saw her phone number on that check she put in the collection plate -- *at the altar*? Didn't you stop goin' see that man who was dyin' of cancer when the doctor stopped givin' him them morphine pills you like so much? . . . sittin' up in here prayin' and kneelin' when you *really* out there layin' in the cut -- stealin'. . . with your philanderin' facade of marital respectability . . . foolin' 'round yo' wife' back with her youngest sister' daughter. . . .

"And Mr. Cousteau -- Mr. Schoolteacher -- I'm quite sure the gatekeepers of hell are reserving a grand suite in its lowest space for yo' two-faced, lyin' soul . . . frontin' and stuntin' like you a pillar of the community . . . still at that junior high school over 40 years so you can hit that dope with them li'l underaged girls . . . I saw you coppin' over there on Dumaine Street . . . My li'l niece told me 'bout you. . . .

"And Melvina -- I don't know what *you* laughin' at -- you out there bad, too . . . with all that shake dancin' out there in the East on the weekend . . . sleepin' all day Sunday -- and too triflin' to git yo' chirrens up for school Monday mornin'. . .. cryin' at that man' funeral last month -- after *you* the one 'caused all that confusion and got him all shot-up. . . . You got so many chirrens out there by so many different mens -- they don't say 'Happy Father's Day' -- they say 'Happy Baby Daddy Day'. . . .

"But that's aw-ite," I said. "I ain't judgin' nobody -- 'cause I don't wanta *be* judged. All I'm sayin' is y'all better tighten up y'all act 'cause one day *y'all* gon' be layin' up here . . . and I ain't gon' be the One y'all gon' hafta face," I cautioned. "So you' best git yo' life together -- or life gon' git *you*."

That said, I walked up the aisle towards the church entrance, took a refined, elegantly executed bow, buttocks high and heavenward, and they never saw me again in this life.

August 2011
Stamford, CT

Professor Arturo

The Boy with the Cheap, Ugly, Green Army Surplus Tennis Shoes

My father was a room service waiter at the Roosevelt Hotel (we called it the "Rooza-belt") and my mother worked "out the house" takin' in sewing. We didn't have everything that we wanted, but we more or less had most things that we needed. If we didn't, we just "made doo." We stretched the beans and baptized the gumbo when an unexpected playmate or family member would linger around for dinnertime, bathed some of the children two-at-a-time (to conserve water), and re-used the Dixie cups until they crumpled and the bottoms dropped out. We used every bit of clothing we had possession of in the most economical manner we could and thanked God (and big tippers at the hotel) for what we had. We were grateful for the least bit of hand-me-down clothing items my mother would get from the children of the ladies she sewed for, and (after whatever necessary alterations) treated them in as prized a manner as we would custom-made clothing from the finest tailor shop.

I recall that season when my father was getting stiffed on tips and the cupboard was bare. I had worn out the tongues and heels of my PF Flyer sneakers (we called 'em "tennis") down to where they were missing in action. After the cardboard I placed in them to salvage whatever life was left in their pitiful rubber and canvas carcass wore out -- they were officially KIA. It wasn't like we could go to the shoe repair shop on Prieur and Orleans (across from the Lafitte Project) or by Wilfred's daddy's shop (out in Fronta Town) and put a half sole and heel on 'em. To describe them as shabby would be akin to saying Katrina was a mildly placid waft of wind.

After work one day my father and I walked over to the Army Surplus store on Rampart Street where we had gotten the canteen, commando knife, utility belt, hatchet, and cans of Sterno when I went to Boy Scout camp one summer at Indian Village. Among the leftover stockpiles of goods from the war was a display counter stacked with heaps of cheap, ugly, green Army Surplus tennis shoes.

I winced at the thought of showing up for school (and basketball practice) in something so coarse and bugar-green that it looked like it should be covering an army truck, but my father --

and THE BELT -- were the indisputable legal authorities in my young life, and I had to defer my dream of donning a pair of Converse All Stars, U.S. Keds or even another pair of el-cheapo PF Flyers. I regretted my unavoidable fate as the designated laughingstock of St. Peter Claver Academy's entire schoolyard at the following day's recess.

The next day in school I gathered up my budding, boyish nerve and faced the music, prepared for an unrelenting medley of criticism for my perceived sartorial *faux pas*, but none was forthcoming. I was expecting a peanut butter sandwich, but I got a chocolate cake. The other children marveled at my inadvertent groundbreaking, trend-setting fashion statement, asked me where I had purchased my pedestrian adornment, and vowed that they would pester and beleaguer their parents until they coughed up and procured a pair. Suffice it to say that I strutted around school showin' off and showboatin' for the rest of the afternoon.

On my way home I saw a li'l boy from the Lafitte Project's Johnson Street court. He smiled as he walked with a proud, confident stride, pulling a little red wagon on which he had collected knicks and knacks from French Quarter trash bins and rubbish piles. On his crusty, sockless feet was the pair of tattered, worn and raggedy PF Flyers I had disposed of after we purchased the cheap, ugly, green Army Surplus tennis shoes.

August 2011
Stamford, CT

The Bugar Man

It was around the time when a halfa dollar was more than a rapper with a buncha holes in him and it could buy a coupla comic books, a rubber baseball and a 16-ounce Big Giant Cola. It was a time when a coupla bucks could get you a slingshot, a bag of marbles, ice cream cones from the Dairy Queen, a pack of Bazooka Joe bubblegum (with the baseball cards), a bag of Dickey's Potato Chips, and a bag of Chee-wees. Although we were as broke as a Commandment tablet, we had each other.

Me, Peanut, Head and Willie were walking on Roman off St. Philip Street after an afternoon of prepubescent basketball when we came upon the holy grail of childhood hunger and thirst assuasion just on the other side of an ancient, hurricane-battered wooden fence -- a loquat tree with low hanging branches and delightfully orange, tasty, succulently sweet, soft, oval fruit with red-blushed skin that could be peeled to reveal a heavenly exotic flavor of citrusy peach and mango. "Wow!" proclaimed Peanut, "a misbelieve tree!"

"It ain't 'misbelieve'," insisted Head. "It's 'misbo*leaves*'. . .because of the leaves," he added.

"Y'all some stupid," cracked Willie. "It ain't 'bout no leaves. It's 'misbe*lief*' 'cause if you eat too many you ain't gon' believe nuthin' nobody tell you. Not even no priest."

"All y'all stupid," I prescribed. "That's a Japanese plum. A loquat. I read about it in wunna them magazines my momma bring home from the lady she work for in the French Quarter."

"Loquat?" questioned Peanut. "My auntee call it a 'kumquat'. . .and she go to SUNO," he added proudly.

"Well she *definitely* don't know then!" capped Head.

"I tell you what. . ." I said. "Either way we gon' go in there and *git* some."

"Yeah ya-right," agreed Peanut.

"Sho ya-right," concurred Head.

"I know *that's* right," affirmed Willie, then added, "But who gon' go over that fence? You know who live there, don't you?"

"Who?"

"*The Bugar Man*," he deadpanned, pointing to an array of raggedy, hand-painted wooden signs nailed to the side of the shabby, wind-battered fence. The signs said:

GO AWAY...THIS MEIN YOU

NO TRUSPASSEN

STAY OUT!!!

PRYVITTE PROPIRTY

"Bruh, I'm in the sixth grade. I don't believe in no Bugar Man," maintained Peanut.

"I saw him once when he came out to pick up his newspaper early one mornin'. He got big, green bugars -- all over his face -- and his skin look like a old, fonky, worn-out alligator shoe," said Willie.

"I ain't scared o' no Bugar Man," professed Peanut. "I got my slingshot." He displayed his unusual and customary weapon of choice. "I ain't scared."

"Well, bruh -- since you *ain't* -- *you* climb the fence," I suggested.

With his man-boyhood being potentially threatened, he agreed and we boosted him up and over the fence on the quest to extract the tempting, mouthwatering holy of holies. We peeped through a knothole to witness the courageous undertaking of the valiant knight in the diabolically deadly dangerous realm of the reptilian monstrosity.

He reached the grounds of the outer stronghold with a mispronounced *thud* and dusted himself off. We jockeyed for position to witness the imminent destruction of our youthful comrade by boulders of bugars that would saturate his dwarfish frame in a torrent of gluey, grey slime and green nose poo.

As he went about his business of negotiating the vividly textured composition of the tree's short trunk and woolly leaves while stuffing as much of the fruit into his pockets (and mouth) as was inhumanly possible, a tall, wizened figure appeared at a side window of the camelback shotgun house.

"Git outa my yard 'fore I shoot you! Git away from here!" the figure bellowed. "I don't want nobody 'round here messin' in my tree! Git away! Leave me 'lone!" he shouted, "I'ma git my shotgun!!!"

With that, the adventurous knight nosedived from the tree, hurdled the fence, and landed on us. We stared wide-eyed as The Bugar Man came out the back door in a sea green camouflage shirt, shotgun in hand, and scared us within a millimeter of our lives' last breath when we saw the streams of scars on his face, his crumpled cheeks, reddened eyes and missing clumps of hair.

We never went anywhere even remotely near that block again.

* * *

Months later I was in my black cassock, going about my duties as an altar boy and serving a funeral. The creepy organ music, the recitation of the Sorrowful Mysteries of the Holy Rosary, the candles' dancing light at the altar, and the rising incense bore weighty witness to another woeful, melancholy, flag-draped ceremony marking the life's end of another St. Peter Claver parishioner. As the funeral director and his assistants rolled the coffin towards the altar and the handful of mourners mourned, I was wishing it were a wedding so the groom or best man could give me a tip (sometimes we even got five or ten dollars).

They positioned the coffin at the foot of the altar and opened it as I held a towering cross to the heavens and peeked at the uniformed body in the casket while Father McNamara sprinkled holy water on the departed. It was The Bugar Man.

Later during the service, Father Mac spoke eloquently of how he was a fearless, brave hero who led his men in battle, how he risked his safety by dragging seven of his wounded men across a minefield through reams of barbed wire under formidable, intense enemy fire, about the horrible wounds he suffered and how and why he became an aged shut-in. . . .

While holding the cross over the flag-draped remains in misbelief at our childhood fears, folly and fantasies, I came of age that day. . . .

October 2012
Stamford, CT

Jazz Stories: *From Katrina to Connecticut*

The Boy and the Famous French Quarter Lady Writer
(to FPK)

"In one drop of water are found all the secrets of all the oceans; in one aspect of You are found all the aspects of existence."
(Khalil Gibran)

It was around the time in my tenderest of years that the neighborhood grocer's cocker spaniel bit me and I had to git 16 rabies shots in my stomach at Charity Hospital. I learned how to detach my mind from my body in order to endure the perceived physical pain I feared would make itself manifest in such a precariously delicate dimension of my boyish, unseasoned physical self. The well-manicured doctor told me I couldn't flinch during the procedure or the needle might break, so I remained silent and still, squeezed my eyes shut, assembled every iota of courage I could muster, and took it like a man.

That skill would sometimes serve me well later in life when my father would administer immediate and unrelenting corporal punishment by laying a leather strap (THE BELT) to my behind and beating me like a borrowed mule. My survival strategy would often fail because of his desire to not only inflict pain, but to also bear witness to that literally burning discomfort that would be evidenced by a progressive sequence of my high-pitched screams as confirmation of the agony and torment amassed from his punishing tanning of my hide.

The lollipop reward the doctor gave me after each visit helped a bit. I missed three weeks of school at St. Peter Claver Academy and had to accompany my momma to work at her job as a domestic for a preeminent, critically-acclaimed, reputable, well-traveled female author who lived in what (to me) was an immeasurably gigantic, well-preserved, antebellum home in the French Quarter. I wanted to stay by my grandmother's house during the series of stressful ordeals, but the two adults who were the immediate commanding powers in my life determined that I was more than a handful for her and the world community's peace would be much more assured if I were to join forces with my white-uniformed momma as she went about her cleaning, polishing, washing, and dusting duties in the quill pusher's time-honored domicile.

The next morning I donned my buckle-up Buster Brown shoes, a pair of knee-length baggy shorts, a plaid-patterned shirt, and my black felt Hopalong Cassidy cowboy hat. I and my Mattel Fanner 50 Shootin' Shell cap gun were ready for a day of exploration, discovery, and fantasy subsequent to my medical appointment.

The home, a spectacular slice of Southern culture and a monument to the region's time-honored architecture located across from a former nunnery, had a medley of adaptations effected during its duration as a testament to structural sanctitude. It had served as the home of a Southern Civil War general, the birthplace of a world chess champion, a wine warehouse, a hostelry, a civic meeting place, a rest and recuperation center for soldiers of the Confederate conspiracy, the summer retreat of a world-ranked chess master, and as the restored dwelling of the romance novelist whose books were on the shelves of many highbrow, cultured and urbane readers worldwide (at least that's what her book jackets' back covers said).

Momma changed into her work clothes in the lower region of the house in a servant's room adjoining the concrete-floored basement, under a rear wrought-iron upstairs gallery that extended the building's entire distance end to end. My auntee told me that five men met their maker on the covered passage in a shootout involving the notorious Black Hand when that underworld society was attempting to extort a former owner in the prior century. I noticed huge chains she had told me about fastened to the walls of the one-time wine cellar, where "unmanageable" captive Africans were tethered and secured because they might get away and do bad things to the people who made them work so hard.

After Momma finished donning her well-starched accoutrements and apron she allowed me to pursue play with my little green army men in the landscape I had so often heard about at mealtime conversations and garrulous gossip sessions. Admonishing me not to touch, scratch, or otherwise disturb anything, she permitted me to explore the panorama of the residence's sweeping region and its legend and lore.

The graceful architecture of Doric wood columns lorded over the edifice's street entrance. A flagstoned courtyard with a triple wrought-iron pagoda near a double stone staircase leading to the rear gallery was framed by immaculately-clipped boxwood hedges. Ivy planting beds and magnificent magnolias flanked each corner of the quiet, idyllic garden-pathed surroundings. Bubble-eyed colorful goldfish resided with painted turtles in a cherub-themed cast-iron fountain in the middle of the enclosure near iron-railed granite steps. To me the courtyard was an occupied French village that my army men had to take before my momma got off work. The slave quarters, now empty of the flesh of its human bondage, sat ghostly and grim, the accumulated dust therein attesting to the souls of those who once endured lives of malady and want within its now-reverential confines.

Living quarters for the one percent reflected a life of freedom, fancy and fortune in an era of conspicuous prosperity in Southern custom, creed and tradition. Gaslight fixtures hung merrily under wired-glass skylights in a grand ballroom with gaily-colored Spanish tile-covered walls. An iron lace winding staircase near a handsome parlor set dominated a room where, my momma told me, the old Creole general spent his honeymoon soon after the war's ceremonious conclusion. Legend has it that he was buried in his stocking feet after he died the next week and he now rides a ferocious steed through the halls demanding that someone bring him his boots. I heard my momma and the cook talking about how a slave woman, who cost $350 and was given to him as a present by the bride's family, also haunts the halls while hiding the general's boots from his ghost.

Another story I listened to (without permission) was about what they called a "sittin' room" that eventually became the site for the suicide of the present caretaker's wife, who came upon her husband in a compromising position with the colored cook, then tightened a plastic bag over her head and breathed her last.

While later conducting research for a paper on Louisiana history in high school I learned that a nearby parlor-reception room was rumored to have its own apparition of a couple that returned every year to the scene where their Civil War-interrupted private wedding was to take place. The would-be groom was killed in action in 1862 when men under the command of Union Flag Officer David G. Farragut battled past Mississippi River forts and took control of New Orleans, the Confederate legion of indecency's most transcendent port and trade center. Further academic probing on the chess champion's life indicated that he often used the well-lighted room for marathon practice sessions, its aura reminiscent of rediscovered romance fueled by memories of past pleasures.

"Howdy, partner," I heard an unfamiliar voice beckon to me as I went about as playful as a guppy, leaving no stone unturned in my fanciful journey of this newer and bravest of worlds. I was playing near a Georgian inlaid mahogany tall case clock that sat on a French provincial carved elm double door armoire accented by a pair of centennial .900 silver urns in a sitting room designated for editorial conferences. (I didn't know the room's pedigree at the time; it just looked woody and shiny to my unsophisticated eyes.)

I turned and saw a bespectacled figure clad in a canary yellow, rounded neckline waist length blouse; a classically-wide, full-looking, natural-waistlined, cream yellow skirt; maroon kitten peep-toed heels; and a navy blue fascinater hat accented with a handmolded rose. It was an outfit that later legions of retro-fashionistas would literally and quite willingly give up the ghost for.

"You must be --" she started.

"-- And you must be Miss -- " I began.

"Yes. I guess I am who I am," she said, offering me an ambiguous handshake.

"You the lady writer!" I exclaimed.

"Yes." She shrugged. "I imagine that's an apt description of me."

"My momma work for you. She clean up everything," I said.

"Yes . . . Leola is quite a help around here. What school do you attend?"

"I go to St. Peter Claver . . . wa-a-a-ay away from here . . . in the Sixth Ward," I told her. I relaxed and removed my cowboy hat and let it dangle on its cord. "I can touch my ears with my toes," I blurted. "Watch," I said demonstrating my elastically supple skills. "I can make my ear click too," I said, taking my right ear between my fingers and making a series of synchronized snaps.

She hesitated, reminisced, then said, "How interesting. There was a time when I could do that too."

"Now *you* try it," I challenged.

"I don't think that -- "

"Who dat? Yo' boyfriend?" I asked, pointing to a picture of a well-dressed gentleman of another age and era that was hanging on a mantle over a set of French three-branched bronze candelabra.

"No. That's someone I'm writing a book about. He was a chess player. He was born in this house."

"I was bornded in Charity Hospital," I offered.

"Well, he was born here. This was his favorite room. He'd play practice games of chess here."

"Me and my Uncle Willie play checkers, but he always cheat. Did yo' chess player cheat?"

"No. I doubt it. He was awfully good at the game. I'm emphasizing how good he was in the book."

"*Wo-ow-ow-ow-ow* . . ." I stared, wide-eyed. "A real lady writer . . .*Wo-ow-ow-ow-ow.* . ."

"Yes," she reflected, peering at me through her professorial glasses, "A real lady writer". And then under her breath, "When I can think of something to write."

* * *

The next day I was playing with my army men, a slight river wind blowing billowing floor length curtains, when I heard highheeled steps coming towards the doorway.

"Hi again," the lady writer greeted me. I ceased my play and approached her. "I see you're playing with your toy soldiers," she said.

"Yeah. I like my army men. I don't see my friends at school no mo', so they my *new* friends. . . . What you doin'?"

"Oh . . . I'm just undergoing a little writer's block and just taking a break."

"Writin' blocks? What's that?'

"It's kind of . . . kind of . . . kind of like when you run out of stories to make up for your toy soldiers."

"I *never* run outa army men stories. I let *them* make 'em up."

"Hmmm," she murmured. "Perhaps I'll try that too."

"Where you goin'?"

"I was just about to check on my doll collection."

"You got dolls? You play with dolls?"

"No. I just collect them."

"Why you got 'em if you ain't gon' play with 'em? You just got 'em and don't play with 'em? You just look at 'em?"

"You know . . . that's a very good question, young man. Would you like to see my dolls?"

"I don't play with dolls. I'm a boy!" I charged.

"You need not play with them. I just wanted to show them to you. They're collector's items."

"You must have a lotta money . . . mo' money than my uncle. He got a *lotta* money," I whispered. "He got a girlfriend always givin' him money. She come from the country, but now she a BIG CITY woman. She dance on Bourbon Street. She ain't supposed to."

"Why not?"

"You *kno-o-o-ow* . . ." I started.

"No, I don't. Explain."

"She colorstruck. She colored, but she makin' like she white," I said, reflecting a generational comprehension of official edict. "She see us on the bus and don't even say nuthin'."

"Oh," she said as she ushered me through the great hall to the room containing her doll collection.

* * *

We entered the room where her treasured assortment of antique and then-modernesque dolls lived their motionless, silent lives. The space was accented by period furnishings, a doll's bedroom suite in French pine, and shelf upon shelf of collectibles of every size, shape, nationality and age. There were Asian dolls, Hawaiian dolls, Gothics, mammy dolls (one of which resembled my Aunt Willameena), Madame Alexanders, Marie Antoinettes, Little Miss Angel, Miss Nancy Anne, Storybook and Dress Me dolls, ballet dolls, hard plastic walking dolls, and a Bourbon St. B-girl doll.

"Wow! You got a whole room just for yo' dolls!" I said, astonished.

"I have two rooms full at my home in China," she said.

"You got *another* house . . . in China? That's where chineyballs come from! You so lucky. You got a big house with turtles and everything! I still don't like yo' dolls, but I *do* like yo' turtles."

"You've seen the turtles in the fountain?"

"I play with 'em all the time.... My daddy and my uncle showed me how to kill a turtle.... First, you take a hanger ... put some meat on it ... put it in front him ... and when his haid pop out he gon' grab it and he ain't gon' let go.... That's when you take a big knife ... or a hatchet ... and you chop his haid off ... he be squigglin' in blood all over the flo' ..."

"Oh my. Goodness gracious!"

"It ain't so bad. The lady turtles have eggs in'em. They *some* good."

"I imagine they are.... What do you want to be when you grow up?'"

"I wanna be a magician -- like Poppa Red."

"*Musician* ... Poppa Red? You know about Poppa Red?"

"He my uncle.... He do jazz music 'round the cordner. He play the washboard, the clarinet, the drums ... and he sing too. My momma and daddy cain't go see him, but when my auntee go she gotta sit on the stage in backa the band. She don't like that. He sick now and ain't got no money for the hospital. They say he gon' die.... What's that?' I asked pointing to a long, scarred wooden, boxlike object in the corner of the room.

"That's a period piece," she explained.

"A period piece? They got question mark pieces?"

"You know," she said dryly. "One day you're going to be a great comedian."

"What is it? What's up in there?" I asked, indicating the elongated container.

"I'll show you, but you have to promise not to touch."

"OK. I promise. My momma told me never to touch anything in the whole house. But she say I can play with the turtles if I be real careful with 'em."

She stepped to the case, sat it on a table near the window, opened it, and my uninitiated eyes were dazzled at the sight of a recently authenticated and appraised, bejeweled Confederate staff and field sword that she lifted from the blue velvet interior of the carton. It shone dazzlingly in the afternoon sun that streamed through the curtains. "It belonged to the general who lived here ... a long time ago," she said.

"Wow! That's wicked! I wish Thaddeus could see this!"

"Thaddeus? Who's Thaddeus?"

"That's my friend. He live next do' to us. He always beatin' me at sword-fightin'. We don't use *real* ones like this. We use gobbidge can tops and old mopsticks. Sometimes when we don't have the nickel to git a baseball -- we roll up some newspaper, tie a string around it -- and it's *on!*"

"That's quite creative," she said, tucking the sword back in its casing and placing it carefully into the protection of its almost century-old home. "I wish my creative juices could be so easily stimulated."

"What you mean?"

She sighed. "Oh, never mind." She glanced at a polished aluminum electric wall clock. "It's just about lunchtime. Why don't you run and ask your mother if you can go around the corner with me to pick something up. Be sure to ask her what she'd like to have. The cook's out today."

"You have a cook? You got somebody to cook for you? Why cain't yo' momma cook?"

"Because -- " she began to respond, then politely "-- just go and get Leola's . . . your mother's permission for you to come with me. Be sure to ask her what she'd like."

"OK," I said and scampered off to get my momma's consent for me to accompany the lady writer to a nearby store for some of the delectable neighborhood cuisine that the city forgotten by care (but remembered by cooking) had to offer in practically every block of every proximity.

* * *

After I found my momma and received her permission, her directive to be certain to hold hands when crossing the street, and her order, the lady writer and I headed for a corner market across from the outer garden's red brick, soaring walls. We paused to read a sign indicating the day's menu outside of the store's windowfront amidst a dangling display of varied brands and breeds of sausages, spices, vegetables and cheeses. It said:

– FOOD –

STEAK AND POTATOES	$1.40
HALF CHICKEN	1.25
PORTION CHICKEN	.75
OYSTER LOAF	1.25

OYSTER SANDWICH	.50
BARBECUE	.75
HAM	.40
HOT SAUSAGE	.30
WEINER	.30
MUFFALETTA	.40
STUFFED CRAB	.35
PORK CHOP	.40
HAM, EGG, GRITS, BISCUITS	.60
MEAT BALLS AND SPAGHETTI	.50
EGG, SAUSAGE, GRITS	.60
STEW AND RICE	.50
COFFEE AND MILK	.10
SOUP	.25
GUMBO	.35
CHICKEN DINNER	.75
SOFT DRINK	.05

A sign attached to a hitching post at a washateria next door to the store said:

WE WASH FOR WHITE ONLY

We were about to enter the store when I told her, "I cain't go in there. I cain't go in that sto'."

"Why not?" she asked, puzzled.

I pointed towards another sign. It said:

NO COLORED

"That is ridiculous. . . . Come on," she said, taking me by the hand.

We went to the counter to place our order with a man in a crop top purple sweater, a coat that looked like it belonged on a camel, and slicked-back, greasy Elvis Presley hair. "And just whattaya think y'all want?" he asked with the sunny disposition of a crypt keeper.

"We'd like to place our order. Give me a --" she began.

"*He* cain't come in here. We don't have that here."

"What do you mean?"

"We don't serve ni-- *colored*," he said glancing down at me as I surveyed the mountainous medley of colorful penny candy in the display case next to the counter.

"He's a *child*," she protested.

"He's *colored*. We don't serve colored here. Let him go where he came from. In here we don't have no dogs, no Jews and no niggers . . . not even no pickaninny nigger chirren."

"But I'm -- "

"I know who y'all is. You's wunna them Northern scallywags done come down here and don't rightly unnerstand how things *is* and *gon'* be. So you best git outa my place o' business or I'll call them paddy boys with the wagon on you!"

* * *

We returned to the halcyon haven of her home, prepared a lunch of finger sandwiches and sat in her office contemplating and discussing the afternoon's caustic confrontation. "What do you know about politics?" she asked me. "Do you know what that word means?"

"I won the spelling bee at my school," I boasted. "I know a *lotta* words. I can spell 'anti-disestablishmentarianism.' My sister cain't even *say* it! I done even memorized the Decoration of Independence."

"Awesome . . . I'll bet you have," she said thoughtfully.

"Ooh --" I beamed. "These sammiches *some* good. This the kinda food make you wanta slap yo' momma."

"Why would you want to hit your mother?" she asked.

"No . . . not like *that*. You wanta give her a slap on the back 'cuz it's so good."

"Oh -- " She laughed. "But do you know about politics? Do you know why people do bad things to one another?"

"Politics? I know I like Ike."

"You 'like Ike'? Why?"

"Cuz my daddy' friend gave me a pretty button with that on it. I can read."

"But what do you think about what happened today? Doesn't that feel hurtful? Don't you feel sad?"

"No," I said shaking my head.

"But you *do* know that people are mean sometimes for no reason . . . or at least for a reason they might think is OK . . . like what the . . . *gentleman* . . . told us today."

"I'm still li'l." I spoke with wisdom far beyond my years. "I just make bad things go 'way. I make the bad things go 'way from my haid . . . like the time I went to git some water at the playground Uptown by my cousin' house. They had a sign over each wunna the faucets. One said 'COLORED'. . . the other one had 'WHITE' . . . I thought the 'colored' water was gon' taste like KOOL-AID . . . but it didn't . . . it was just like water from the 'WHITE' fountain. . . . If I coulda changed it, I woulda. . . . I don't work at the water place. . . . Why you sit there all day and be writin'?"

"That's a good question. I often wonder about that myself."

"You got a big house to play in, turtles, good sammiches . . . all you need is a bike."

"I probably do." She laughed. "Perhaps exercise *will* generate some ideas."

"What you writin' on now?"

"I'm just doing a little work on a project."

"Project? Which one? The Lafitte? The St. Bernard?" I asked, alluding to two of the city's public housing developments.

"No." She laughed again.

"They's a who-o-ole lotta things to work on besides a project," I said.

"Yes," she said thoughtfully. "There are. There are many, many more things of much greater import."

That afternoon I overheard her as she ordered her secretary to cancel an appointment with an up-and-coming city councilman involving a new nine-story addition to a downtown hotel for which he was lobbying, a project that would guarantee her a 300% profit on her initial investment. He was assured the prospect of becoming mayor if the deal went through.

"The old windbag, white-shoed, Pat Boone Special-wearing klutz can attend to his themed fundraising events without me," she told her secretary. She also made inquiries on founding a medical facility for financially-strapped musicians. Later, I found out, she donated quite an expanse of time reading to the children of St. Peter Claver, and began work on a soon-to-be-heralded novel about race relations in the Deep South.

That same afternoon (and many naps, night visions and years later) I dreamed of the house's spirits known and unknown . . . of the ghosts of the couple whose marriage was deferred by the onslaught of imminent hostilities, the chess player whose birth took place in the same superannuated bed in which I napped . . . the luckless slave woman donated as a dowry . . . the general and his raucous rides through the hall in search of his boots . . . the caretaker's wife who took her life . . . the tortured souls of the African captives as they dwelled in an unfeeling abyss . . . the Black Hand's bullet-riddled bodies . . . and the two flesh and blood beings, dissimilar in the artificialities of time, race, age, sex, experience and station in life, whose animating forces once and forever interblended in an antiquated age on a tiny droplet in infinity's ocean.

August 2012
Stamford, CT

The Boy With Two Heads

At first, the doctors at Charity Hospital thought we were twins, but I was born with an extra head protruding from the back of my neck. I had a front head and a back head, an odd configuration that inspired my parents to inevitably and creatively designate my brother and me as "Front Head" and "Back Head." My (our?) parents, family members and friends would eventually call me (us?) "Head." No known surgical procedure could address the situation, for we were inextricably linked, immortally and permanently connected to each other by conjoined brain tissue that fused us at the most critical portions of that most essential organ.

Separating us would certainly assure our demise, for it wasn't a matter of us sharing body parts that could be safely disassociated; we were one thinking, singular ensemble with such a vital interconnection as to make us intertwined until death did us part. It was a strange marriage indeed.

At first it was a pleasant curiosity. There were at least two sides to every argument and two sides to every coin, but I (we?) had the unfortunate dilemma of being born with two heads and two distinct personalities and perspectives on life and living. He was radical. I was conservative. He preferred jazz. I liked R&B. He was homosexual. I was straight. When we went swimming at Lincoln Beach he preferred the backstroke, but I was a breast stroker who dove in headfirst. Although life dealt us a difficult blow I felt fortunate because I was more or less Head #1 (since I was the front head) and he was Head #2, the back head.

The 1800 block of St. Ann Street wasn't the most desirable of places to come of age while having two heads. Whoever coined the phrase "Two heads are better than one" should be shot in the head or at least have his or her own head examined, for our life was living proof that two heads are *badder* than one....

We lived near the Lafitte Project and would often get into turf-related teasings and altercations with many of the young toughies from its environs. On more than one occasion we were jumped by a group of degenerate, fratricidal guttersnipes from a nearby court who were showing us less than brotherly love. We tried to fend them off, but there were so many of the unmindful ghetto-dwellin' creatures that it was both politic and prudent to sometimes effect an expedited withdrawal. One day as they chased us down a sundrenched side street Back Head was yowling, "Hurry up!! Hurry up!! Put the burners on! They all up in my face! I don't wan' git my head bashed in!!!"

"Don't worry! We rollin'!!! We rollin' on out!!!" I assured him. "I ain't gittin' my butt kicked!"

We headed for the haven of home and hearth with all deliberate speed. Sometimes we sprinted away from the two-legged varmints. Sometimes we battled. Sometimes we won. Sometimes we lost. Suffice it to say that we didn't generally turn the other cheek, for we really didn't know which one to turn.

But there were advantages to having two heads. As altar boys at St. Peter Claver Church we could simultaneously face the tabernacle and the congregation, affording us the opportunity to both perform and participate in Catholicism's ritualistic renderings. During official church services we could light prayer candles while leading the assembled flock in the Mysteries of the Holy Rosary as they lifted every voice and sang.

In grammar school we discovered that we could read two books at one time and never had a problem with our academics. In high school we were involved in organized sports as a four-letter man (men?). We excelled at football, basketball, track, and baseball and even sang in the school choir (although we had to stand at a rather odd angle to get the full effect of our voices). I remember running towards the end zone in umpteen gridiron contests with my brother urging me, "Faster! Faster! They're gaining on us!"

Back Head was also useful on the track team, for the runners behind us would be so unsettled by our appearance that they wouldn't concentrate on the task at foot. There was hardly anyone on opposing basketball teams who could steal the ball from us, for our forward and rear vision proved more than effective in thwarting such a play. When I was up to bat in baseball Back Head would detect the catcher's signals and relay them to me through a telepathic connection we had cultivated since birth. I was a pitcher and it was unfeasibly unimaginable to steal third base on me because my brother's dorsal vision added to my anterior sight of the batter at the plate.

When someone on the corner said, "Heads up!" (because the police were approaching) we'd be the first to discern from which direction they were (ahem) headed, and head out because we just didn't want to be accused of street corner slingin' or get into anything over our heads.

But there were disadvantages to having two heads. In one early season football contest I made a headfirst dive towards the goal line, got hit really hard, suffered a concussion, and we both had to co-suffer the consequences by not participating in any contact sport for the remainder of the fall term.

Sometimes opposing teams would challenge our school's athletic contingents for having "too many men" on the field/court. Or when one of us received after school detention we would both have to sit silently staring into space in silent detainment.

When we first started school we had to pay for two lunches, but a social worker stopped doing her nails all day and intervened, and we eventually settled that unsettling issue. Sometimes I had a hunger for a hot sausage po-boy, but my brother had a taste for an oyster loaf, so we had to settle for "half-and-half" sandwiches.

My brother would complain fret, fuss, wail and whimper whenever we had to have a sit-down session with a commode, for having the hindmost set of nostrils he would be subject to some of the more offensively noxious odors known to humankind. If I dared to construct an unreasonably transparent prevarication to my parents, my father would tell me I was a two-faced liar and THE BELT's next shattering session would be twice as vigorously applied.

We would be charged double admission for a movie or dance. In the theater we had to sit sideways so each of us could gaze at the silver screen's leading ladies and men. At the prom I had a girl for a date while my homophilic brother had a guy. It made for quite a configuration on the dance floor. "Tell yo' boy to ease up back there and stop bumpin' and rollin' on my booty!" I protested during one slow drag encounter.

But the most challenging thing about having two heads was trying to get some sleep at night. Back Head suffered from sleep apnea and snored like a drunken sailor. When I was dog-tired and headed to Dreamland his sawing-wood wheezing would keep me up for daze. My folks got him diagnosed and we discovered that he had something called "complex sleep apnea," an unmelodious mixture of obstructive and central sleep apnea. At bedtime he was angry and irritable. He was tossin' and turnin' all night, having nighttime awakenings and waking up breathless. His memory and concentration became extinct vestiges of an earlier time. He was restless, moody and would arise just after dawn with morning headaches. We kept a sleep diary, took video and audio recordings, and avoided alcohol, sedatives and caffeine while attempting to maintain reasonable and regular sleeping hours. We propped our heads up and had our seamstress mother sew tennis balls to the back of our pajamas, but nothing brought any progress to our efforts at even the most minimal level of dormancy. Night after aggravating night he'd curse himself and me while urging me to commit suicide, that most ultimate of disembodiments. Being Catholic, we knew there was an extra-special place in hell for one who took one's own life, but at least we wouldn't be alone after committing the ultimate of Mortal Sins. Eventually and inevitably we both couldn't stand the torture of our fated fusion and decided to enter into a pact that would finally sever our inexplicably enduring quandary.

On the appointed night of our scheduled departure we sat at bedside, my (our?) father's equalizer in hand, pondering the destiny of our circumstance and summoning the courage to finally sever ourselves from the world and each other. Then we tossed a coin to determine which head would be blown off first.

June 2013
Stamford, CT

Yo! -- Dog!

I was the cutest, cuddliest, little ten-pound ball of fluff you could ever imagine, descended from a pedigree that is said to have originated in 17th century Tibet. My Shih Tzu forbears survived the Communist Revolution in China (during which we almost became extinct), were popular in the courts and sleeping quarters of empresses and kings, and my lineage eventually found its way to America via soldiers returning stateside after WWII. None other than the American Kennel Club officially recognized our breed in 1969.

My short muzzle; long, silken, golden, flowing, lustery coat; powerfully built hindquarters; compact, rock-solid body; curved tail over my pert backside; and the adorable little blaze of white on my forehead made me the most cherished housepet in the history of my human providers and protectors.

They appropriately and accurately bestowed the name "Snooty" on me the moment they saw my large, deep, dark eyes encouraging them to become my humans, as they stood in front of the glass display in which me and my brothers and sisters were put on view in the suburban mall's upscale pet emporium (dogs like us weren't sold in "stores"). My bulging dark eyes and gleeful playfulness made me the perfect pet for any pack of humans who could find my tastes and requisite refinements affordable. They even adored my farts, or as they called them -- "poots." It was a doggone good life.

I was the epitome of the four-legged, pampered, constantly-petted family favorite and enjoyed a life of honey and almond shampoo sessions (when I really preferred the melon and cucumber cleansing), $60 five-pound bags of organic free-range chicken or beef treats, interactive puzzle toys, Waterford Crystal water bowls, daily brushing and maintenance of my luxurious golden caramel coat, noiseless nail grooming tools, hooded robes, a monogrammed set of "companion stairs" (so I could access my humans' bed at will), bedtime bones, squeaking toys and frozen pup treats. My humans made my life one of comfort and contentment as I laid back on my comfy-cozy pet couch, ultra-plush bed or paisley-printed Medici chair -- living the life of Riley amidst grooming trips to the doggie boutique, outings to the veterinarian, and the sky-high maintenance of a cherished companion and costly creature of comfort.

Then the hurricane came. . . .

* * *

My humans and I abandoned our non-air-conditioned, heat-heavy home when the skies' mighty winds howled heavily at the windows and dumped copious amounts of rain so that churning floodwaters rose. Earlier, the dominant female of my human pack had her military unit activated and she was deployed to a marshaling site in the northern part of the state.

After the storm subsided and the waters ceased rising, the rest of my people pride donned their hip-wader boots and waterproof gear, then navigated the flooded, steaming city's back alleys and soggy thoroughfares -- trekking towards a more promised land, leaving with what they estimated were adequate provisions for their relocation to wherever they were destined to arrive. It was so hot that when I scurried off into an alleyway and urinated, it evaporated when it came out. Standing there in my matted, unkempt coat, I articulated a slight protest yelp in disapproval of the indignity of it all then scampered back to where I'd left my humans. To my surprise and distress they were gone, disappeared, nowhere to be found.

I surveyed the deserted desolation so prevalent in the wasteland. They were about as lost as the Vietnam War. I found a hideout near a ransacked corner store, desperately dug a cubbyhole in a pile of moldy, unassembled cardboard boxes, and faced the fact that I was alone and insecure in a most treacherous, unforgiving world -- cold, hungry and dog-tired. I was so famished I could eat a buttered cat's claw.

I heard roving packs of now-homeless canines wandering the streets in search of the slightest semblance of victuals. So I secreted myself further in my hideaway and prayed for deliverance from this doggone mess in which I presently found my four-legged self. I had no desire to be late-night dinner in such a dog-eat-dog world.

* * *

I awoke the next morning to the sound of scavengers sifting through what was left of the former meat market/po'-boy sandwich shop. I cowered in the corner closest to a mildewed wall as they searched frantically for any remnant of food, alcohol, booty or beer. My scruffy caramel coat was itching annoyingly due to the crawling, hopping critters that had taken overnight residence all over my unpampered, unwashed body.

I heard a jagged voice shout, "Wow! Look what the wind blew in --!!!" and was scooped up by a grimy chocolate hand connected to a tattered, toothless face with "NOONY" tattooed vertically on the left cheek and three teardrops under the right eye. The face beamed at the prospect of acquiring a monetary reward for the return of a creature of my obvious breeding.

"He a Shit-Sue," a gnarled voice bawled doggedly from another warm body. "They poo on people furniture -- and they sue you!" said Mr. Dog Hollerer.

"Yo' -- Dog!" Noony grunted while placing me in an empty Budweiser 12-pack carton as though I were some common cayoodle. I wanted to snap out and bite him, but I was afraid I might catch some incurable, communicable disease.

"Noony got him sumthin' nice *now!*" he triumphantly woofed. The dysfunctionally illiterate being couldn't comprehend the name on my personalized, hand-embroidered collar and my inadvertently-adopted human dubbed me simply "Dog." *I have a name,* I barked. *How about if I named you "Hey Stupid"?!?!*

* * *

The dwelling where he and his cohorts resided (and got loaded) was a medley of methodless madness. It was a doggish, tormented, torturous site where he was the top dog and the supreme (human) being in an unholy region. Everybody had been to jail. Noony had been to jail so much they named a wing after him.

Everybody was into the act. They rolled these brown, green and gold flower buds in Optimo cigar paper (and smoked them), ate something called "picklemeat," and used words like "Rockweiler" (for Rottweiler), "Amtrak" (anthrax), "Walmark" (Walmart), "alblum" (album), "conversate" (converse), "Star Track" (*Star Trek*), "cornder" (corner), and "fornificate" (fornicate). They didn't have usual and customary human names (like my real family); they called themselves things like "Doony," "Poony," "Boony," "Bootsy," "Li'l Black," "Pasooky," "Nooky,"

Professor Arturo

"Pooky," "Doody," "Wooty," "Bugar," "Bitch," "Hoe," "Migga" (I think that's what it was), "Too-*Too*," "Mah-*doo*," "Nay-*Nay*," "Nee-*Nee*," and "Noo-*Noo*." About a dozen human males in their extended pack had the same name -- "Baby Daddy."

Empty-bellied, shirtless, crying toddlers in soiled diapers were bawling, screeching, creeping and crawling over every inch of what meager possessions passed for furniture (rusted plastic and aluminum lawn chairs, milk cartons, third-hand mattresses, plastic-covered wooden crates, and mountains of foul-smelling, dirty clothes).

In what they called a home there were no paintings, no books or magazines, no computers, no genteel, silkysmooth jazz; no Xavier, Delgado or Dillard pennants (not even SUNO); no innocent, playful banter; no carpet or linoleum or tiles to adequately cover the openings in the floor through which one could see the trash on the ground under the meager structure. They didn't even have a picture of Martin Luther King or the Kennedys.

Like other homes after the storm, there was no electricity, but they acted as though they were accustomed to life by candlelight and Noony swore that he wouldn't be evacuated from the house that his overextended family had rented for 67 years. Somebody said something about "kibbles and bits" and I thought they were talking about dogfood -- but they were referring to a miniscule amount of something called "crack" that someone down the street named "That Dirty, No-Good Muthafucka" sold them.

One afternoon somebody outside hollered for "Snooty" and I thought that my liberation was at hand, but they were referring to *"Li'l* Snooty" (as opposed to *Big* Snooty -- who lived somewhere in the rear section of the house that was so sinister and forbidding that I dared not enter). I thought I had long ago perished and gone to the lower depths of Hades.

One day some genius had the bright idea of shaving off my body hair and putting a tattoo on my underfed frame. Noony approved the procedure and allowed Li'l Black, who had attended two weeks of college (barber college) on Canal Street, to give me a Tide laundry detergent bath and straight razor shave. To say I was frightened at the prospect of someone shaving me who had a history of mental illness (and had disrupted judicial proceedings by coating his face with his own feces in open court) is about as much an understatement as declaring "George Bush doesn't care about black people."

After he gave me a bare back, another genius held me tightly while Bitch (whose name they used a great deal towards practically everybody of the species' female gender) gave me a jailhouse tattoo on my bald back with the name Noony had assigned me: "Dog." I winced, squirming and whimpering as she engraved a vein-purple D-A-G on my exposed flesh. As they put it, they were doggin' me out. They dogged me out some bad. They was *wro-o-o-o-ong* for that.

In lieu of giving me my preferred brand of distilled water in designer doggie dishes, they filled empty Blue Runner Red Bean cans with Olde English 800. For solid provisions they mixed chicken bones and eggshells with moldy, stale bread – and sometimes sprinkled gunpowder on top.

They threatened to put me in deadly dogfights with opponents named "Bruiser," "Hammerhead," "Mr. Big Stuff," "Lucifer," "Teeth," and "Iron Chest Charlie" -- if nobody (with a reward) showed up to claim me. They dogged me around. They blew clouds of laughter-inducing smoke from blazing blunts in my face while "signifyin' 'bout how they wish they had a cookbook with instructions on making "Shih Tzu gumbo," and terrified me with the possibility of being dropped off at the pound where my inevitable, dogged demise would be virtually and unavoidably guaranteed.

* * *

"Every dog has its day -- and some dogs have two" is an adage as ancient as the blood flowing in my canine veins. My day came one sweltering afternoon. Day-Glo-vested rescue personnel were (finally) going house-to-house strongly urging residents to abandon their abodes to whatever locales were out of harm's way. They knocked resolutely on the door and explained their orders that they were to evacuate everyone from any structures that might be determined to be "unfit for human habitation," a depiction that accurately described the state of the house's composition even *before* the storm. *It was a doggone shame*, I thought.

It was then that I heard the familiar, welcome voice of my pack's uniformed, dominant female. She stood there, mouth agape, stunned by my presence and appearance, then opened her arms to me . . .

. . . and we lived nappily ever after.

August 2011
Stamford, CT

The BIG TOO-DOO!!!

I really don't wanna raise no big stank about it, but my momma' funeral was a whole lotta BOO-COO BIG TOO-DOO!!! This was way after when they stopped havin' wakes and my favorite girl was layin' there in the fronta the church in that elegantly-crafted, white lace shroud and fire engine red lipstick -- lookin' some fly. Them Boissiere boys at the funeral home sho' did her right.

When I saw her I told her, "Go 'haid, girl!" Some people thought it was irreverent, but it was just me bein' her li'l boy again.

The first thing happened was Miss Emmaline comin' up to the church door and tellin' me (and the sax player and my podner, the opera singer who grew up next door to us and live 'round the cornder from the church, and my nephews and they wives and they chirrens and my brother and my brother-from-another-mother) that she had done forgot her teeth (again). Down the street from the church, the li'l corner store where we used to cop beer and pluck and git drunk before (and sometimes during) the service was gone. Katrina took a lotta the fun outa goin' to a funeral.

Li'l chirrens was out there playin' in the schoolyard behind the church where they still had them same stringless iron backboards with the netless rims on the li'l basketball court that was there way befo' Motown. I even saw Mr. Frank, the former janitor (now "maintenance engineer") who was workin' there when I was in kinnygarden. He still recognized me and knew my name. He said he knew thousands and thousands of chirrens (now grown) by name.

That's what kinda people they was. All our folks had been buried through St. Peter Claver Church where I was an altar boy and made my First Communion and Confirmation, but Momma' funeral was some different. I remember momma' and daddy' 50th anniversary they had in the church, but I didn't really think a singular, fleeting thought that Momma could ever die -- even though I knew how sick she was.

She suffered a lot. My brother knew she was losin' it when she started callin' "cowboy food" (scrambled eggs with turkey weenies, mushrooms, green onions, garlic and two cheeses) "astronaut food." My sister knew she had lost it when she got a li'l rusty in the joints and stopped sewin'. I knew she was on the way out when she was talkin' 'bout how her and daddy' friend, Mr. Sonny Boy, was a "good provider."

All the irregulars was there, even though some family didn't come because of the potential for a big humbug over sumthin' that happened in the annals of familial antiquity that everybody but them forgot about. All the great-grandchirren was there and my Momma' friends too. Miss Pearl was there. Miss Rose was there. Miss Camille was there, and Miss Dickhaven, the lady who was her supervisor at the store on Canal Street (where she sold foundations) was there. She never gave Momma no big raise, but they was still on speakin' terms. I guess that job was better than working as a domestic and shoving suppositories up off in that French Quarter lady's well-traveled ass.

My friends was there too, and I sat on the right side of the church with the fellas while the family was on the left side. Ain't nobody said nuthin' 'bout that . . .'til later -- behind my back -- like they usually do. I didn't really want no pitty party, but I was glad that all my closest podners and comrades was there. It ain't but once that yo' momma die.

I didn't tell that crazy, red woman 'bout the funeral 'cause I knew if *she* showed up she was gon' be some humbuggish -- because I was down South in Florida for a gig that time and didn't go to Baton Rouge to see her. I knew if she woulda come there she was gon' act bad-bad-bad. I just decided to leave her 'lone, 'cause like Uncle Peter said: "The mo' you stretch it, the mo' you can stretch it out" (whatever that meant).

That female from 'round the cornder from my uncle in Gentilly, whose daughter got clinked-up for sumthin' I don't even wan' mention here, was there. She the one put her*self* in jail -- way out there in Angie -- and her people frownin' up at you 'cause you don't wan' be all up in that tryin' to git her out -- like *you* the one obligated to wipe her behind. She expressed her deepest condolences to me for the loss of my "luv-ded one" then asked to borrow 22 cents so she could jump on the bus to git to wherever she was goin'.

My podner from down the street was there. He was the one who was the neighborhood's fashion innovator. He started wearin' "Gilligan" hats way 'fore anybody else in the Sixth Ward even thought about it.

I was happy as a wino at a wine-tasting conference when I saw my brother. He was the one who was working with Uncle Warren, Uncle Herbert and Uncle Peter at that new hotel when all the models was in town and they didn't wan' send the older room service waiters on the floor where they was dressin' and sent him because he was just 18 and didn't know what to do with it anyway. Suffice it to say that if that weekend was a sex education class, he woulda made the Dean's List.

Shantiqua, that youngster my momma made the weddin' dress for, was there too. She the one left her husband and went back East and married -- get this! -- his *sister*. Her sister was the one who would git my momma to make all kinda weddin' gowns for her friends on-the-cheap and always complimented my momma on her red beans and rice and potato salad so Momma could make it for all her git-togethers. That woman wasn't 'bout nuthin' but game, and they couldn't even see it. My momma really liked her because she was the best friend of my cousin who husband got killed in Vietnam and my momma would always feed Shantiqua' chirren way befo' her own grandchirren. She was my momma' li'l friend, but she was messy-messy-messy.

I saw my podner from Upward Bound at Loyola and we did our secret "Mule Shake" -- a clandestine handshake whose meaning we swore never to divulge some four decades earlier. Big Harold came in his work clothes -- a sign that somebody really wan' come to a funeral when they do that. That politician who grew up down the street was there. He ain't never forgot where he came from.

Miss Henrietta almost fell out her wheelchair when they was rollin' her in the church because somebody had left a baby stroller in the aisle and a truck passed in fronta the church on St. Philip Street, shakin' the church, and the stroller rolled right into her heavily-stockinged legs. She didn't feel nuthin' from it. My uncle said she ain't felt nuthin' down there since the Korean War.

Black Willie was in the backa the church drunk -- recitin' summa that jailhouse poetry he know so much about. I held wunna my nephews' li'l baby named "Alexandria" after where my brother's wife's folks was from. She was all wrapped-up in a blanket I had sent her and looked just like her daddy. I guess every uncle say that. Some babies you just look at -- and they just babies. But that li'l baby was sumthin' else. Anybody who had real eyes could see it. My Momma' friend saw me holdin' her and told me that when I was li'l I was *more-than-a-handful*. I wondered what I did to them po' people like that.

Among my dozens of cousins I saw my cousin Keshonda there. That girl had done got so big I didn't even recognize her at first and I cracked that I thought she was a extra hearse. They say she use a whole roll o' turlit paper every time she go to the baffroom . . .'til she started usin' them Bounty paper towels . . . She buy 'em by the trainload . . . and I do mean *load* . . . That girl done got so big that every time she git on the bus, she gotta git on sideways -- and the driver make her ride in the middle so she can balance the load. One time she tripped on Canal Street and landed in Baton Rouge. When she got up to deliver a tribute to my momma after all that kneelin' and genuflectin' and standin' up and sittin' down (why cain't Catholics make up they mind?), she read the version in the program that I corrected, insteada the one they (family members who think they Random House) had written with people bein' married to theyself, 4-5 different typestyles in one list of the pallbearers' names, and some of the worst writing since Tyra Banks' widely-touted "fierce, new novel."

Some functional illiterate got up and announced that the Ave Maria would be sung, except she pronounced it the *Avuh Maria*. I guess it was all about good intentions.

My podner who sing opera flubbed the words to *Amazing Grace*, but got back in stride again by the time the Communion Hymn and the *Lord's Prayer* came 'round. I did a li'l piece on my main girl with a sax player who told me later that his momma was born on the same day and in the same year as my momma. *Small world.* . . . After the Recessional Hymn it was all about gittin' out there to Mount Olive Cemetery in backa Dillard.

At graveside after the prayers and after everybody left I stood staring at my mother's coffin in the January afternoon sun. That's when it hit me. I wouldn't be able to tell wimmins I was jugglin' that I was with my momma all day on Valentine's Day. I wouldn't see her through the screen door in the backyard feeding a huge flock of all kinda birds by the clotheslines like it was the

Song of Bernadette or sumthin'. She wouldn't be there to console, counsel and encourage.

I would never again hear her singin' that Etta James piece -- *At Last* -- as she went about creating enchanting culinary concoctions in the kitchen in our half of the humble shotgun house on Dumaine Street. Never again would she be at my table at literary functions chanting "That's my son -- that's my son" as I returned from reading the poetry she inspired within my soul when (prior to my formal education) she taught me how to read.

Standing at her grave alone -- with just the music of the wind, the sun, and the essence of her memory -- I again became one with her in the unending dominion from which she transformed my ever voyaging spirit into bone, blood and flesh.

It was a BIG TOO-DOO.

August 2011
Stamford, CT

Professor Arturo

EPIPHANY

"Some days you the pigeon; some days you the statue."
-- Aunt Sweet (circa 1960)

I remember that chilly, breezy day in that exquisitely fantastic, magical, mystical, elemental world of clanging, low-rumbling streetcars, po-boy sandwiches and parades. It was the thirteenth day of Christmas. It was king cakes, shattered, gaily-colored glass ornaments, and now-dulled tinsel fragments and bone-dry Christmas trees piled up for collection along the city forgotten by care's bankets. It was back to life, back to reality. Post-yuletide bills were floating (unfreely) in the U.S. mail. The wooden and metal frameworks of scaffolds for reviewing stands were already going up for the season's Carnival parades. Department store Santas had reverted to their usual and customary pedigree's propensities for odiferous breath and reddened noses resulting from a jumbled, gumboed mixture of Thunderbird, Wild Irish Rose, Ripple, Night Train, Muscatel, MD 20-20, Boone's Farm, Catawba Pink, and Bali Hai.

Me and my momma had done finally Christmassed ourselves out, and I was going home and couldn't wait to wear out them new skates I got for Christmas so my daddy and me could go on the backyard steps and build a skatin' truck (my cousin in the Seventh Ward called 'em skate*mobiles)*.

I had on my navy blue, woolly, brass-buttoned winter coat with the fake fur collar, velvety cap with matching earmuffs, and buckle-up Buster Brown shoes. We had gone shopping after we left Charity Hospital where I had gotten the last of my 16 rabies shots in the stomach I had to get after I petted that dog on the corner where the schoolteacher lady used to live.

My momma and me had just left Maison Blanche Annex and were waiting for the City Park or the St. Bernard bus under the arched windows on the river side of Krauss, the Italianate style building housing the department store where your momma might let you put the credit card in the pneumatic tubes that would magically shoot upstairs to the billing office. It was a nickel for a fare and two cents for a transfer, but a child my age could get on free. We were in THE BIG TIME.

Mr. Bingle, the elfin, cone-hatted puppet snowman who ritually appeared in a Christmasy scene each yuletide in the large display window of Maison Blanche (the main store on Canal St.), was gone back to whatever polar refuge or storage room from whence he came. We shopped at the annex behind the main store, anyway. This was the After-New-Year's-Annual-White-Sale, but I ain't never-ever seen no sheets.

I stood, staring, silent and still (an odd combination for a child my age), and perused a statue -- a figure of a tall, caped man with a sword -- in the neutral ground on Basin between Iberville and Canal Street just across the street from the side of the store where the lady had told my momma she could buy a hat she had wanted, but couldn't try it on. Unbeknownst to my blameless, youthful eyes, it was the Simon Bolivar monument, a gift to New Orleans from the people of Venezuela. I smiled, grinning oddly at the statue as it stood proudly against the city's slate grey skyscape. *Was he Catholic?* the self inside myself asked my selves.

"Who dat?" I asked my momma as she warmly cradled my hand, her brown pillbox hat and demure, closed, sensible shoes being my then-permanent point of reference and anchor of protection.

"That's Simon Bollyver," she said. I sensed the same tone in her voice she had that time when she told me about my grandfather, the bricklayer who had built the family grave "with his own hands" in St. Louis Cemetery No. 2. She smiled, beaming at the twelve-foot-high, cast granite sculpture in the small plaza ornamented by a pool, fountain and tiled waterway. "He was a great man. He freed his people down in South America."

You mean New Awlins ain't South America!?!? I thought.

Just then a City Park bus came, stopped, and went *SH-SH-SH-SH-SH-SH-sh-sh-sh* . . . like wunna them funny sounds Uncle Peter' stomach used to make when he ate or otherwise imbibed a bit too much. My momma fumbled in her purse for the fare as I crept around to the front of the bus and looked fixedly at the statue as our fellow travelers crowded around the vehicle's open doors. I soon discovered that I had lost sight of my momma and her hand's warm, tender grasp in the rush of tree trunks of giant legs and the towering forest of fabric, flesh, and faces.

Professor Arturo

I turned and saw a man in a well-tailored suit, chocolate brown fedora, and bottle green coat with lots and lots of buttons. He was an adult and (being a dutiful child) I mannerly approached him, tapped him gently on his arm, and spoke to him politely as I was taught to do by everyone in my world who loved me.

"'Scuse me, mister --" I started. "I cain't find my momma."

He glared at me with stone cold, soulless eyes (I remember still) and swatted my hand away. "Git your goddam hands off me! Git away from me --

-- *nigger. . .*"

he said.

November 2003
New Orleans

Sew, Sew, Sew
(to Momma and the Mardi Gras Indians)

Roy Rogers was the King of the Cowboys, Lash LaRue was the King of the Bullwhip, and Jax, Dixie, Regal and Falstaff were the molasses of the masses. The Cisco Kid was a friend of mine. Four O' Clocks, chineyball trees and giant swarms of mosquito hogs (my cousin from over 'round London Avenue by St. Aug called 'em mosquito *hawks* -- anything but "dragonflies") were in abundance then.

A two-parent household was the norm, "Please" and "Thank you" hadn't gone outa style, Catholic school kids ended the Pledge of Allegiance with "One God, one country, one flag," and tourists were callin' New Awlins "New Aw-*leens.*" My gran'ma ate her chickens "fresh off the hoof" from Miss Beaulah's yard next door ('cross the basin on Iberville Street) and Fury was "the story of a horse . . . and the boy who loved him."

Mr. Cassidy was hoppin' along, Bugs was doin' the Bunny Strut, and Aaron Neville was sho' 'nuff tellin' it like it was. Miss Ginny was stompin' and 'rompin' 'round the room, Morgus and Chopsley were performin' fantastically frightful experiments involvin' all parts of the inhuman anatomy, Gene Chandler was the Duke of Earl, the Three Stooges were committin' malice in the palace, and Dorothy was off somewhere chasin' a Black & White rainbow.

Parents terrified and titillated their children with local lore and tall tales of The Bugar Man and The Gown Men (them mens in them white gowns up 'round Charity Hospital who were rumored to whisk children away to some distant, bedeviled haunt where they would execute all manner and mayhem of unspeakably atrocious acts on their bodies, youth and innocence). It was a wonderful world.

It was a time when thongs were sandals and upwardly mobile men (and some wimmins) of color were longshoremen, electricians, bricklayers, carpenters, plumbers, teachers, preachers, nurses and mailmen (wasn't no such thing as mail*wimmins* back then). Lionel trains, Fanner 50s, Robbie the Robot and Chatty Cathy were the Christmas gifts of choice, baseball was played with wooden bats (and real balls), and Roy Campanella was an eternal 39. I was the # 1 fan of Sandy Koufax

Professor Arturo

(and what he didn't do on Yom Kippur). Nelliebelle, Bullet and Trigger were all in the family (c'mon, baby, the good times was rollin').

It was also the time of "race movies" like *Imitation of Life, I Passed for White, Pinky,* and *I Crossed the Color Line* (at the Carver, the Circle, the Clabon and the Gallo). The Incredible Shrinking Man was the only "shorty" we knew. It was a time when the guv'nuh rode a white horse up the capitol building steps 'cause they didn't wan' buy him a Cadillac (*You are my son, Shine*). Pontchartrain Beach and Pontchartrain Park weren't "open" yet. Jessie Hill's *Ooh Poo Pah Doo* was out there creatin' disturbance in yo' mind and high schools were named Carver, Lincoln and Washington.

It was a time of shotgun weddings and shotgun houses. It was when the vejitibble man unroutinely snaked through the twistin', shoutin', animated streets of the city long unremembered by care, euphoniously hawking his everfresh wares. Al Johnson's *Carnival Time* was all over the airwaves and *real* New Awlins cooks were makin' goo-gobs of gumbo until they were too pooped to pop. Champion Jack Dupree was a boxer, a spy boy for the Yellow Pocahontas and barrelhouse piano professor (*Momma, move yo' false teeth; Poppa wanna scratch yo' gums*). New Orleanians were drinking in (and regurgitating) the sweet wine of their long-revered tradition of gaiety and merrymaking. Mardi Gras Day, the most fabulous and fattest of Tuesdays, was approaching. For 24 hours all would be disremembered and forgiven in the city that care forgot. It was Carnival time, just befo' Mardi Gras Day, and all my momma did was *sew, sew, sew*.

My momma sewed. She was a master (mistress?) seamstress. A dressmaker. She learned how to sew from her mother who learned from *her* mother who learned from *her* mother (and I really cain't remember back no further than that). She "took in" sewing befo' colored wimmins of her particular pedigree could even *think* about workin' at Haspel's.

She was a lady of lineage, delicate in her language and skillful in her craft who knew mo' stitches than a combat medic. She sewed for some rich white lady writer who had a big house in the French Quarter and who used to always ask momma what some term meant when she said something (and then wrote it down); the racketeer man' wife (she had the first Mercedes-Benz

I ever saw); Mrs. Moorehead, the wife of an old beer, bourbon and balls general (Momma and 'em used to always laugh when I called her husband a "Frigidaire General"); and a buncha other fish-white wimmins with names like Amber, Elspeth, Pilar, Penelope, Zoe, Heather, Phoebe and Chloe who used to take the dresses and stuff she made and have her sew in the label of some faraway, fanciful, fashion designer so they could front 'em off, sashayin' and promenadin' at the segregated balls and charitable affairs they would grace with their charming Southern presence.

Although formally unlettered and informally schooled, she mastered the complexity of the most demanding and exacting Simplicity patterns, humming softly while surrounded by a sundry assortment of cloth-covered tables, cedar robes and chiffarobes. Her world was one of thimbles, pins, needles, tape measures, rulers, ribbons, scissors, spools of thread, yards of material from bolts of fabric of all patterns "on account" from Mr. Levine (the rag man), zippers, buttons and notions of all manner and stripes that she got from Krauss, McCrory's, Woolworth's and Maison Blanche Annex.

Her Singer sewing machine sang sweetly as she sewed curtains, Carnival costumes, formal Mardi Gras ball dresses, prom dresses, plastic book covers, beautillion dresses for a mélange of debuts, elaborately bejeweled crowns, doilies, drapes, slipcovers, foundations (whatever that was), sportin' gals' and fancy wimmins' outfits, flannel baseball uniforms, patches on Boy Scout uniforms (the Beaver Patrol), denim satchels for chinees ("marbles" to the uninformed), moo-moos, First Communion gowns, liturgical and ecclesiastical vestments, baby doll pajamas, sequined turbans for Oliver and Charles Brown of the Royal Dukes of Rhythm (which always assured momma and daddy the most prominent, boo-coo good seats at Carnival balls and an assorted array of their gigs), wedding dresses, bridesmaids' git-ups, christening gowns, death shrouds, cassocks, surplices, (and eventually and inevitably) bold, blue, paisley print dashikis and a pietistic patchwork of all things delightful and delicate. My sisters just enjoyed stringing the spent spools of thread and making shoestring necklaces.

Local legend and common gossip held that a notorious lady in red, a fancy woman who used to ply all kinds of trades on Orleans Avenue, had her wake right there next to where momma sewed by the Magnavox console stereo in the front room of the late Victorian two-bay, camelback, shotgun clapboard house, its tripartite window cornices crowned with pierced-work cresting and gaily-fluted window frames as ornamental devices. Right there on Dumaine Street it was -- two blocks from where Fats Pichon, the piano professor, used to live. They say this lady was laid out right there in the livin' room -- all in red -- restin' on a bed of pink satin and all decked out in her favorite red Carnival gown. They say she was the prettiest colored woman you ever saw.

 Light and shadow were amplified by the house's jigsaw surface variations above its green, slime-covered, slick brick alleyway. Momma always liked to work by the front room's project-green hurricane window because the light there was so good.

 Inside the house's front room, poo-brown French slidin' doors (my uncle in the Seventh Ward called 'em "pocket doors") opened to the next room where a pitcher of Jesus stared solitarily above a lamp by the bed. First Communion and Confirmation photos, graduation portraits, baby pitchers, photos of WW II veterans, assorted ribbons, fadin' plaques, and images of long-dead ancestors hung on the mantelpiece above the unused fireplace's iron grate.

 My momma's longtime client and friend, Miss Rosa Belle Boudreaux, sat on the plastic-covered, imitation French provincial sofa under the window's beatific light and genteel gusts of riverfront breezes that stirred the billowing, gold and green Fleur-de-Lis curtains my momma had made. It was *some* airish in there! The ornate floral print of the well-worn linoleum floor covering's pattern was a vast canyon where unbroken-backed cowboys and the creepiest of critters roamed as I crept and crawled, absorbing all that was around me. Miss Rosa Belle Boudreaux, and my Aunt Sweet (Aunt Sweetie's eldest daughter), and my momma discussed the wisdoms and wonders of their universe. How my gran'ma once rode a horse bareback on the bayou (I always thought "bareback" was about the horse not havin' a saddle), about that time my uncle was gittin' off the troop ship and got all tangled up in the scramble net on the side and spent half the war in the hawspital. (They said, knowin' *him*, he probably did that on purpose.) They also told about how Mr. Tee-

Jazz Stories: *From Katrina to Connecticut*

Tee was a good provider because everytime he'd come home from runnin' on the water he'd pack the icebox and pay up all the rent.

And they told about how just 'cause people is old that don't make 'em no classic; about how "All yo' skinfolk ain't yo' kinfolk" (and other age-old adages); about that time my *parann* and *nanann* was tryin' to git work in the aircraft factory in California during the war and my *nanann* turnt around in the diner and saw she was sittin' next to Nat King Cole (and fainted); about the time they was out in California and they didn't want to hire my *parann* because my *nanann* was bright-skinned and my *parann* was dark-skinned (and they thought he was married to a white lady). The colored lady at the table pulled my *nanann*'s coat and told her to git in the other line and they hired her on the spot.

There were other short and tall tales of Sixth Ward (Tremé) New Awlins' sewin' and conversatin' in that precious, precocious age. They talked about knowns and unknowns and the things that they knew that they knew (which were the known unknowns) -- which is to say that there were things that they knew they didn't know. But there were also unknown unknowns that they didn't know they didn't know.

I thought about these things as the City Park bus shook, rattled and roiled the unadorned splendor of the tiny half-a-shotgun house, as the bus's timeworn, rusting, aged hunk perilously made its way up the one-way vaginal thoroughfare that was Dumaine Street to the end of the line at the park, where, I knew, it would idle near the former plantation's swampgreen, oak-laden expanses.

Miss Rosa Belle Boudreaux was a flame-haired, pink pedal pusher-wearin' beauty with canyon-deep décolletage, well-coiffed hair, flashy gold jewelry, sensible shoes, seafoam green eyes and a sky-blue, knitted pillbox hat, who liked to make grand entrances like Loretta Young. She was *some* shapely! She was living proof of my (usually drunk) Uncle Sleepy's sayin' that "Wimmins rule and mens drool." The room's light kissed her gently on her gingerbread skin. She was always all dolled-up and had a megawatt smile that would overload any straight-up man's circuits. The mens said she was so fine -- she put the last three letters in class. She was always all gussied up and had a face (and chasmic, cosmic cleavage) that could make a grown man weep and a newborn baby cry for mo'. She would always say some politician named "McKeithen" could kiss her kitten, but I don't remember her ever havin' no cat.

My Aunt Sweet was a gentle, loving, scapular-wearing, plainspeaking, matronly soul who would give you the smile off her lips or the socks off her feet. She predated Miss Rosa Belle Boudreaux by a generation and enjoyed the veneration of our entire extended clan. She was mother confessor, confidante, familiar friend and intimate to any who were blessed enough to encounter her sacrosanctity, for she wasn't just wunna them wimmins who party they whole life away runnin' the streets and then find Jesus when all they looks is gone.

She was a homespun philosophress who seemed to have a saying for everything, from "The Lawd don't like ugly" to "*Everybody* happy on weddin' day" to "Don't rock the boat -- 'specially when you sittin' in it" to "If they wasn't no losin' they couldn't be no winnin'" to "A hard haid make a soft behind." Then there was "It ain't what people call you; it's what you answer to"; "The dog that *bring* tail -- *take* tale"; "Better a educated *fool* than a *un*educated *tool*." Or "Don't shoot all the dogs 'cause one of 'em got fleas"; "You find yo' bottom when you stop diggin'"; "Never compare *yo'* insides to somebody else's *out*sides"; and "If you wanta see a rainbow you gotta put up with a li'l rain."

She also made the best pecawn candy (certainly not *pray*-leens) in New Awlins and had a big-old pecawn tree right there in her back yard on the corner (she always said "cornder") of Johnson and Lahopp (across from where them nuns used to live). We would make a pit stop there with our bikes on the way to baseball practice in Gentilly, pick pecawns from the tree in her yard, and have fresh pecawn candy and the world's greatest red beans & rice waiting for us after we returned and checked books out at Nora Navra Library over on Prieur and St. Bernard.

My world on the floor next to the rich cherry woodwork of the sewing machine's bottom drawer was dominated by a Kit Carson covered wagon set, squads of green army men, a Luzianne coffee can fulla chinees, and a cookie can fulla gaily-colored buttons of all sizes, shapes, designs and surfaces.

That day, as I played in my brown playsuit with the blue bear momma had stitched on, it was the green chinees vs. the blue chinees. First, second and third base were round white buttons and home plate was a BIG, BLACK button. I think the green chinees won that day while my momma was sewin' some Chinese "coolie" costumes for her, daddy, my uncle and my aunt for an upcoming Carnival ball. (Can you imagine Uncle Bubby in a yellow and black coolie costume -- complete with conical sedge hat and long, black platt in the back?)

That Mardi Gras my sister wanted to be a "snow girl" (a figure skater) and my momma was workin' feverishly tryin' to complete her costume, too. That afternoon I interrupted my mother's anointed tasks and reproached her, bawling, "You don't love me no mo'. You just sit there all day and sew. That's all you do is *sew, sew, sew*. . . . But yo' baby still love you 'cause you just so pretty. . . . You a glamour girl, a bathin' beauty, a movie star and a nun. . . . You prettier than Matty Monroe and Jayne Mamsfield. Mammy Van Doren ain't got *nuthin'* on *you*, girl," I bullshot.

"Lawd, 'outa the mouths o' babes . . ." remarked Miss Rosa Belle Boudreaux.

"Well, I'll be John Brown!" Aunt Sweet declared. "That take the cake! Lawdy-Lawd! I ain't never heard nuthin' like that in all my years o' livin' on this-here green earth! He sumthin' else! Did you hear what that boy said?" howled Aunt Sweet. "Jayne Mansfield? Mamie Van Doren? What he know 'bout that? That boy some ticklish!"

"Truth be told -- he just like his paw," my momma said. "That boy just like *Big* Ernest. He like his wimmins top-heavy in the bust. He know mo' than you *think* he know. He was *borned* with it." She laughed. "You oughta see how he spread them JET magazines all over the kitchen floor and look at them middle pages all day long. That boy cain't *wait* to see a Tarzan pitcher -- with all them li'l girls jumpin' up and down with nuthin' on top. He just like his paw. Just like him."

"The chineyball don't fall too far from the tree," my aunt offered.

"You the prettiest lady from here to Er-leens Avenue," I continued as my momma reached down from her work, extending me a hug and a smile as she laughed. She held me tightly for a moment, then placed me back on the floor to my world of cowboys, army men, chinees, and the cookie can burgeoning with buttons and baby boy fantasies. (It didn't take much to satisfy me back then.)

"That's all he want, is for you to hold him for a minute and then he go right back to what he was doin'," my momma said. "That boy some sperled." My aunt and Miss Rosa Belle Boudreaux howled with laughter, marveling at this curious thing.

"I wish Tee-*Tee* was like that," said Miss Rosa Belle Boudreaux. "I wish *he* was that easy to handle. That man ain't nuthin' nice," she sizzled. "I don't know what that man' malfunction is! Lemme tell you what he done done *now* -- 'cause he done cut his water short with *me!*" she shoo-shooed. "I wanted to bust him up side his haid with a Daniel Green slipper the other day. That old helmet-haid man *some* kah-*goo!* Here he got *me* and don't even know what he *got* -- and *he* livin' the life o' Riley! That man got a halfa dozen, brand new, Banlon shirts -- every color o' the rainbow!"

"-- He sittin' up in the baker' shop cryin' for bread!" my aunt suggested.

"Everything he need is right here -- and he don't even see it," crabbed Miss Rosa Belle Boudreaux. "He couldn't even blow his nose if he had dynamite for brains. He so fulla cah-*cah* -- his eyes is brown! He still makin' a BIG TOO-DOO 'bout nuthin'," she sneered. "That man used to be the hand I fan, but now he out there galavantin' with You-Know-Who -- "

"We all sin and fall short. . . . Who gon' love her when her looks is gone? No matter how pretty she is there's some man somewhere who cain't stand the sight of her. When you love a man and he act a fool -- let him," Aunt Sweet offered, lickin' her chops at the trauma of the drama. The intoxicating sound of a practicing trumpet player pierced the air, serenading us, its bewitching aura radiating exotic enchantment and unhurried intimacy.

"Sweet --" Miss Rosa Belle Boudreaux began "-- you can be so heavenly-minded you can do no earthly good. . . . I done caught him out there right in the middle of Dooky Chase Bar with Buttercup -- that li'l low class, no class hussy with the bubblebutt be over there in the Green Room all the time -- and over on Rampart Street – on the 'Ramp'!?! That li'l hoochie-coochie momma' behind hot as a truckload o' fresh cayenne peppers in the berlin' hot sun in the middle o' August! That li'l woman sumthin' else! She just young enough to be his daughter and smart enough to be his dog! *I* knows *that*! -- and I don't know Miss Thing from Adam's housecat! He can hit the road, Jack! That man must be out his mind if he think *I'ma* keep on singin' that same old-same old, sorry, sad song. Then he gon' lie and tell *me* what *I* done seen! Gon' tell me what *my* eyes done uncovered! I know Tee-*Tee* was havin' ideas with that woman. I knowed it soon as I was crossin' the Er-leens Street neutral ground goin' over to Dooky's from the Lafitte! I don't need no leftovers! I don't need no constellation prize! Don't be givin' me no pitty party! Tee-*Tee* grease ain't hot 'nough! He keep doggin' *me* around -- he gon' be a gone pecawn 'cause he best be done learnt -- 'Ain't nuthin' kill you faster than a old man or a young woman.' He ain't gon' just kick Miss Rosa Belle Boudreaux to the curve."

"Well, you know you can catch mo' flies with honey than you can with spit," my aunt proposed.

"Honey -- he done bought that li'l strumpet from up off the Ramp a brand new washer-dryer *and* a color television set!"

"No he *didn't??!!!???*" my momma said, the hum of the sewing machine pausing a bit. "He bought her a television set? A color television set? A *real* one?"

"He been givin' her money she cain't even spend. He done made Miss-Lookin'-Like-A-Elephant-Comin'-Out-The-Boxcar-Backwards well si-tu-a-*ted*," Miss Rosa Belle Boudreaux stacattoed.

"Uh-huh," my aunt said. "What don't come out in the milk gon' come out in the rinse. Sumthin' in the milk ain't clean," she suggested. "You know -- you cain't throw just anything in the pot and call it gumbo. . . ."

"Yeah-ya-right! -- Talkin' 'bout how he saw me kissin' Willy 'cross the fence and heard me tellin' Willy he didn't have no sense! He *think* he done put me in a trick bag, but I'm ti-i-i-i-i-i-me 'nuff for him," Miss Rosa Belle Boudreaux seared. "Always talkin' 'bout a splinter in *yo'* behind when they got a telephone pole up *theys.*"

"*Oh-oh-oh-oh-oh. . .*" my mother dragged.

Professor Arturo

"Yeah," continued Miss Rosa Belle Boudreaux. "He all 'bout snatchin' and grabbin'. Tryin' to put some sense in that man' haid is like tryin' to drink water with a fork! But he ain't gon' be rainin' on *my* parade no mo'. I don't wan' make no big blah-*yay* 'bout it, but I'm serious as a hungry crab walkin' over a bare behind!

"Tee-*Tee* act like he done just got off the plantation! Actin' a fool -- and here it is almost Carnival Day! He sho' done outdid his self! He act' mo' of a fool than Anus and Andy! Out there with that gold teef, tackhaid, bugarbat, ill-formed, streetwalkin' hussy . . . with her floozy, tart-brown hair! It ain't my fault! All that meat and no potatuhs!

"Then he was at that other woman' funeral last week -- that li'l red woman from 'cross the river -- and did he per*form!* All over the casket like a fool -- and me sittin' right there in the church with everybody under-eyein' me up and down -- like *I'm* the other woman! I didn't know that li'l heffer from Adam's *daddy'* housecat, but I *do* know he done footed both they bills. I know he was in cahoots with her. He always gotta have a woman between him and his mattress! He ain't got no skeletons in his closet! He got the whole graveyard! That man got mo' mess with him than Mesopotamia -- and I got the right to sing the blues 'bout it 'cause he sho' nuff think he in high cotton!

"Talkin' 'bout he look like Major Lance! I'll Monkey Time his behind! Back there in the project livin' like some kinda hermit -- older than Noah -- and *he* was 400 when the flood came! Like -- like I done told him -- 'If you cain't take it -- don't bring it!' He can put me *out*, but I ain't gon' *let* him put me *down*!

"Talkin' 'bout me and him gon' go to California and git some work in the shipyards. I ain't goin' to no California -- to Los Angeleez -- and no kinda points inbetween -- not with *him*! He ain't gon' be havin' *me* sleepin' in no Murphy bed the resta *my* days!

"I don't like no California anyways. Them people out there drinks you under the table -- and don't feed you nuthin'. He ain't gon be takin' *me* way out there and flyin' the coop on me! Talkin' 'bout I don't know my role as a woman. I knows my role as a woman. As long as he can walk in from work -- or wherever he done been -- and have some food cooked and some clean clothes and some good lovin' . . . that's my role. . . . That's my role as a woman," she wailed.

"Baby," my Aunt Sweet admonished, "'Don't set the blanket on fire for a flea.' You fattenin' the frog for the snake. One monkey don't stop no show. You much too young a woman to be with that foolishness."

"Foolishness?!? Foolishness!?!? Y'all ain't *seen* foolishness 'til you done seened Tee-*Tee* git pissy drunk! Law-aw-aw-awd, that man did some clownin' the other night. He was *some* clownish! That man clown-ded mo' than Bozo!"

"*Whu-u-u-u-u-ut*!?!??!," chimed my momma and Aunt Sweet.

"We out there the other night ridin' up Canal Street -- rollin' right up from the river -- I'm drivin' and he juiced-up-tore-down drunk," she started. "We right there in fronta Maison Blanche and Lover Boy decide to start upchuckin'. Got vomit all over his pumpadoo hair. Tee-*Tee* had done drunk a gallon o' Gallo, a whole halfa G o' Thunderbird and two whole quarts o' Bali-Hai (regular *and* pineapple). Here I am tryin' to git us home -- and he actin' a fool! Out there like some character! All out the car window throwin' up from the fronta Maison Blanche all the way down Canal Street to Krauss. He *did* some cuttin' up! He was *some* stupid! Then he gon' be callin' his self gittin' salty with *me*.

"Tee-*Tee* was tore up from the floor up and needed a checkup from the neck up! He was in rare form! That man almost brought my Injun' out! They needs to put him in a home for the feeble-minded! He so fulla his self! Gon' call me 'country'! Got the nerve to call *me* 'country'! He need to watch how he waggle his tongue! He ain't gave Theodora all that mess when *they* was married!

"My daddy ain't raised no fool! I'm Mr. Buddy B. Boudreaux' daughter! I'm Miss Rosa Belle Boudreaux, and chile -- I'ma tell it like it is, 'cause I'm here to tell it *to* you! Then he just blew a fuse! Callin' me everything but a childa God! Always talkin' 'bout I'm always diggin' in his haid -- like I'm gon' mess up my nails in all that pumpadoo hair! Like he the Count of Monte Crisco -- all that earl up there!" she said, a smile erupting across her face. "Tee-*Tee* ain't got a pot to pee in -- or a window to throw it out," she blabbed.

"Whoop-dee-*doo!*" Aunt Sweet sang. "When you throw a rock at a pack o' dogs, the one it hit is the one that holler."

"I'ma put the hurt on him. He ain't gon' be treatin' me like some popcorn, sucker John. I thought it was about beans, but it musta been potatuhs," Miss Rosa Belle Boudreaux simmered.

"Ain't that a shame!?!" my momma said.

"I'm gon' git up, make my groceries, git on that Roper stove and do my li'l cookin'," Aunt Sweet said, rising from the couch as red bean smells wafted gently, smoothly, through the window. "I think the City Park bus done just 'bout made it back 'round from Er-leens Street. Lemme go haid on and git on the backa that bus. Baby --" she cautioned Miss Rosa Belle Boudreaux as she was leaving "-- you better leave that poke chop sandwich alone." She then bade us farewell and went out into the world as she knew it, far from immaculately manicured Uptown lawns.

"But I love him. I love that man. He's the man I truly, truly love," said Miss Rosa Belle Boudreaux to my momma. Her face seemed drawn, sullen and sad. A teardrop teased her left eye. "I love that man mo' than anything. I don't know why I love him like I do, but I sho' does love that man. If he would just be true to me . . . I know he didn't come into my life by accident. God don't make no mistakes. The last thing I wan' do is be a old, broke, lonely, colored woman when I kick the bucket."

I looked up at her from my universe, contemplating what I perceived, crept over to her, climbed on her perfumed lap, huddled close to her sweet-smelling, talcum powdered, warm, pecawn brown bosom, and slept to the sound of Miss Rosa Belle Boudreaux's heartbeat and the soothing music of my mother's Singer sewing machine at the end of a long afternoon of existential discontent.

* * *

There was another member of my family who sewed . . . my cousin, Brickhead Red, an appellation bestowed upon him by our family and his (usually criminal) associates due to his shaggy, crimson head of hair that matched the color of the bricks of the Lafitte Project. They always said his head was about as hard as a project brick, too. We usually called him "Red" or "Brickhead" or even "Brickhead Red" as opposed to Prickhead Red, Dagoe

Red, Cherry Red, Icepick Red, Brickhouse Red, Trickhouse Red, Bugar Red, Boogie Red, Panama Red, Tampa Red, Uptown Red, Ninth Ward Red (the original), or Red Red. Yeah. He was my head-smashin', teeth-crackin', buck-jumpin', hardhead, humbuggish, in-and-outa-jail, always-fightin'-the-police-in-the-street cousin. . . . "Brickhead Red . . . Kill 'Em Dead!!!!!"

They say he was so mean he'd pop a cap in Jesus while He was on His way to Calvary -- and stick a shiv in Mary for cryin'. That boy loved the jailhouse -- he'd rather fight than switch. The only thing unarrested about him was his social development and his chronic halitosis. When he came by yo' house you had to always check the medicine cabinet to see if he had snatched up summa yo' momma' and daddy' pills.

He'd fight anything walkin' and cut anything breathin'. He was a character, a young toughie from by the basin who was livin' his adulthood in his childhood and his brief life was testimony to the adage "Bad niggers die young." They say he started that club they called the Halfa G's -- where you had to drink three halfa gallons o' pluck in one day to join (one for breakfast, one for lunch and one for dinner) -- and not throw up. He drank three *full* gallons befo' 12 o' clock noon!

His past wasn't checkered. It was chessed. He was the *white* sheep of the family. He got in so much trouble that his favorite record was *Old Man Trouble,* his second favorite record was *Nobody Knows the Trouble I Seen,* his third favorite record was *I'm In A World of Trouble,* and his favorite movie was *Trouble In Paradise.* If he had ever held a job he woulda been a troubleshooter. If he woulda had an eventual choice, his favorite song woulda been Marvin Gaye's *Trouble Man,* but suffice it to say that his favorite song actually was *Jailhouse Rock.* When he went to jail they'd say he was "away at school" (Scotlandville Junior College or Angola State University). He was "away at school" so much that he had to be the most educated human being in New Awlins history. He was living proof of the aphorism "If you don't want a nigger to steal something -- put it in a book," but knew mo' versions of *Shine, Stagolee* and *Shoo-Fly -- Don't Bother Me* than the Signifyin' Monkey. He knew every word and nuance on the *Gene Chandler: Live at the Regal* album and was the only person (besides the Duke of Earl) who could hold that note on Part 2 of "Rainbow '65."

His favorite sports were bullshootin', robbin', stealin', fightin' and goin' to jail where his motto was "Blood on my shank or shit on yo' dick" (and other sayings unrepeatable in polite company).

If he had finished high school he would've been voted "Most Likely To Go to The Penitentiary." He thought Hai Karate English Leather-Lime was expensive cologne, and once told me, "Life is like ridin' in the Zulu parade every Carnival season and bein' on the same side of the float and seein' the people gittin' older and older a li'l teenantsy bit every year until you don't see 'em no mo'."

I *still* don't understand what he meant, but that's what he said to me in the springtime of my youth, for in spite of all he did and all that was said by and about him, he was my spiritual teacher and guide, propagator of the faith and keeper of the flame. He learnt me how to pull my pants over my knees when I sat down so they wouldn't "bend in"; how to walk in green slime-slickened, New Awlins brick alleys (*Don't walk natchally . . .* ***pat yo' feet and walk***); how to pour beer (*Tip the glass to the side, bruh -- so it won't foam over*); how to put a box together; how to keep my hands outa my pockets when I grow up and walk the streets (*Always keep yo'hands out yo' pockets 'cause you never know who or what might be comin' at you*); and all kinds of hip things to say like:

> *Niggers and flies I do despise*
> *One bring disease; the other bring lies.*

and: *On my honor I will do my best*
to take what they give me – and steal the rest. . .

and: *It's Howdy Doody Time*
It make yo' booty shine. . .

and: *Ashes to Ashes*
Dust to Dust
Yo' momma got a ass
like a Greyhound Bus. . .

and: *Fat and Skinny was layin' in the bed*
Fat rolled over and gave Skinny some head

and: *I went downtown (Too-way pocky-way)*
to see Miss Brown (Too-way pocky-way)
I gave her a nickel (Too-way pocky-way)
She sucked on my pickle (Too-way pocky-way)
I went uptown....

and: *My nigger, my nerve, my jelly preserve*
You my ace boon coon, my pride and joy
You a ugly muddafugga
*But you **still** my boy...*

and: *I was walkin' thru the jungle*
with my dick in my hand
a bad muthafucka from the Congo land
I looked in the tree -- and what did I see?
-- a black muthafucka tryin' to piss on me...
I picked up a rock and hit him in the cock --
You shoulda seen that muddafugga run 24 CITY
BLOCKS!!!

and: *The monkey chewed tobacco*
The elephant ate grass
If you don't be-leeve me
you can kiss my big black --
*-- **ask** me no question*
I'll tell you no lie
If you don't be-leeve me I'll
I'll fuck you 'til you die...

and even: *I took my girlfriend to the show*
and sat her on my knee-ee-ee-ee
That girl FOT so hard she split her draws
-- and shit all over me....

  He learnt me how to Second Line and buck jump, how to give somebody a knife (*Handle first, bruh*), how to give somebody a light (*Give THEM the match and let THEM light it. Always keep yo' hands free*), how never to put after shave on my privates (*Ouch!*), how to pick up boxes by bendin' my knees so I wouldn't rupture myself (*Lift with yo' legs, 'cause yo' legs is the*

Professor Arturo

strongest part of yo' body), how to work with a Tandy leathercraft kit (like he did in jail), how to sing a halfa dozen versions of *Li'l Liza Jane* (he picked up on that in jail, too), how to sword-fight with a garbage can top and a broomstick, how to make a baseball outa string and paper, how to clean the "dead man" from a crab (*Don't eat that yella part*), how to throw a knife, how to buy cheap wine, how (and why) a man should always put his big bills on the inside (*Let 'em see yo' ONES -- not yo' TENS*), and how to build a skatin' truck (my cousin 'cross St. Bernard called 'em "skatemobiles").

He even cold-slapped me in my politically unastute brain with an explanation as to why I couldn't be in the Soapbox Derby (*That's for them **white** boys -- not **you**!*) and told me that "Just 'cuz you go to the Celebrity Lounge -- that don't make you no celebrity." Yeah. He schooled me in a whole lotta ways.

He was raised up in the Sixth Ward and lived right there 'cross from the Lafitte Project on the corner in a small house with an oyster shell alleyway. (It's a grocery store now -- Hung Wang had it, then that A-rabb, Brother Muhammed, got it.) It was on Er-leens right down the street from the award-winning Willie Mae's Scotch House and up the street from the world famous Dooky Chase Restaurant and Bar.

His world was one of cowbells, whistles, tambourines, Second Lines, fire water, handclaps, jumps, shouts, hollers, fried chicken, gasoline, wine, rum & coke, Kool Filter Kings, all kinda bars (cordner and jailhouse), the Nightcap Lounge, the Dew Drop, the Cozy Corner, Prout's, the Green "O" Liquor Store, swaggin' on berled strimps and crabs, joints, go-cups, scars, scams, schemes, secret stitches, sewin', cursin', stealin', robbin', shuckin' and jivin', doin' the Alligator, tellin' Injun' stories, smoke, drums, calumets (peace pipes), shanks, stocking caps, doo rags, day-old doughnuts (from McKenzie's on St. Bernard and Galvez -- right 'cross the street from Corpus Christi Church), Ray Charles, jailhouse slippers, gold teeth, Hush Puppies, fistfights, dope, hypodermic syringes and a plethora of injection site reactions (tracks). He was indeed a character, one of those social incorrigibles that St. Aug didn't want goin' there -- or anywhere *near* there.

In spite of that, in spite of his sins, assorted mayhem and too-numerous-to-mention criminal offenses, there was a light that shone in him. Three or four Mardi Gras seasons after the shoo-shooin' sewin' session I talked about a li'l earlier . . . about three or four Carnival seasons after that I was allowed to enter Brickhead Red's inner circle of joyous, festive sew-ers and reapers as they set about finishing their Injun costumes for Carnival Day which was less than a week away.

It was that time of year when all they did was sew, sew, sew in their annual effort to "mask Injun." Most of 'em carried the flambeau flame and picked up that li'l change in the night parades befo' Mardi Gras Day, but their main delectation and delight was to dance and prance in the flashing, regal, brilliant plumage of their radiantly-colored Injun costumes on the day of days that was the culmination of the Mardi Gras season, that wild, unbridled day of fun, frolic, and festivity.

Red always said he liked to sew by oil lamplight or candlelight (he probably had to inasmuch as the bill wasn't paid). That night, as I sat in my Hopalong Cassidy sweatshirt, black ten-gallon hat and two-gun holster while perusing my cousin's needle & thread handiwork, his band of cutthroat (and sometimes comical) characters and creatures from the Sixth Ward Lagoon were solemnly sewing their colorful Injun costumes ("suits") along with him.

It was around the time right befo' Mardi Gras Day when Red had busted my cousin in the pool hall over on Claiborne Street (it's a church now) when he was supposed to be at the football game and Red didn't even tell his momma and daddy on him. On the pool table Red himself was a master of the three-cushion shot and an eight-ballin' ace his self, but his main racket in life was sewing the splendorous, colorful costumes with great virtuosity and veneration on those holy days of obligation right befo' Mardi Gras Day.

Every year, 'specially 'round Carnival time, all Red would do was *sew, sew, sew.* It was a solemn and (sometimes) hallowed event. Every year he and his tribal comrades in flash and feathers would sew a new suit as a means of outshining other Injun tribes and as a way of honoring seemingly ancient traditions. Every year at Carnival time he made a new suit, as did his father befo' him, his father befo' *him* and his father befo' *him* as far back as anyone living could remember. If he was a character, then his fellow tribesmen comprised a cast of characters who probably embodied the most notorious sewing conclave in the history of the craft. His sewing circle consisted of Sixth Ward Lagooners such as Snake, Darkhorse, Turtle, Bulletproof (who had mo' holes in him than a strainer fulla water), and Blood & Wine. Everybody had a nickname. Everybody wanted to git into the act. A *States-Item*-covered white enamel slopjar sat in the cordner near the rickety door as the wind howled wildly, wickedly, outside. It was so cold that Mardi Gras season that you could take a leak and lean on it.

The light of a green kerosene lamp and several strategically-placed candles danced hellishly off the room's bare walls, illuminating the work of the men as they stitched their secret stitches, each and every one unique to its task. My cousin sat workin' on his headdress at a table with a white sheet thrown over it, a shoebox top fulla herb, some wine bottles, and Blackie, his old cayoodle, sleepin' at his green Army Surplus Store tennis shoe-clad feet (my cousin from over by the London Canal called 'em "sneakers"). He was raggin' in a purple Banlon shirt, brown iridescent tailor-made pants, a near-toothless grin (with one shiny gold tooth complete with diamond star) and his (usually) obligatory stocking cap and pumpadoo hair slickened down by Murray's Hair Pomade. They always said his long platts made him look like a *real* Injun. Six tattooed teardrops hung menacingly on his cheek just under his left eye. A big brown New Orleans roach took its good sweet time scurrying back and forth 'cross the table in the room's lusterless light.

He was busily, sensitively, gracefully sewing, his "LOVE - HATE" tattooed knuckles caked with tiny beads of sweat, a cigarette wedged behind his ear as he delicately concocted the elaborately-colored suit that he would proudly don on Mardi Gras Day -- that day of mirth and merriment on which they would all be transformed into dazzling, shaking, swirling, whirling, stuff-strutting, befeathered, bejeweled, orange-purple-green-gold-yellow-blue-red, sartorially resplendent peacocks of all that is, was and would be their pain, passion and pleasure.

Snake was standin' behind a chair in immaculately-pressed jeans givin' Darkhorse a linin' (that boy always liked to keep his hair nice) with his dirty, dexterous hands while Turtle, Bulletproof, and Blood & Wine busied themselves with the demands of their craft and tellin' Injun stories.

Jazz Stories: *From Katrina to Connecticut*

They say Darkhorse's claim to fame was that he held the world record for the longest version of *Shoo-Fly -- Don't Bother Me*. Blood & Wine was makin' a Bone Man outfit with a goo-gob o' dried turkey bones and a big hambone. Every year Blood & Wine was a Bone Man. He used to always go 'round scarin' every li'l child in the Sixth Ward singin' "Ashes to ashes, dust to dust -- You best straighten yo' life or you gon' see *us*. . . ." (That was when them kinda cats used to tell the children in the neighborhood to stay in school and don't end up like them.)

Bulletproof and Turtle were workin' on something the likes of which I'd never seen befo'. All I remember was that there was a lotta sequins, rhinestones and stitches so teenantsy you'd think that a newborn baby roach made 'em.

Snake, who was the Wild Man one Mardi Gras and worked for years as an oyster shucker at H & K Oyster House (over on Claiborne and Dumaine), was widely known as the most adept bladesman in the Sixth Ward with a straight razor or a beechwood oyster-shuckin' knife. They say he learnt how to do hair from the legendary Joe Mitch the Barber over in the Seventh Ward and how to shuck oysters from his daddy.

"Bruh -- my haid *still* hurtin' me! I got hit by a truck the other day on Er-leens Street!" Snake said, standin' in a white sweatshirt and anklewhipper, high water pants, his thin fingers skillfully handling the straight razor at the base of Darkhorse's neck, a wicked smile pasted to his lips displaying a grill of cigarette-stained gold teeth. "The nurse tell me: 'It *oughta* hurt! You done got shot in the haid!' But I told her I *ain't* got shot in the haid! I got cut and hit by a truck on Er-leens!. . . I been broke up and messed up 'most all over my body! I done just had chemicals in both my eyes from tombstone cleaner. They operated on me and was talkin' 'bout they wanted to spearmint on me and gimme some kinda corny transplant. . . .

"I'm leavin' from over there by my momma and 'em house . . . I gits to Er-leens and Prieur, gits cut, gits hit by a truck on Er-leens and Johnson -- that plate in my haid saved me -- and gits picked up by the po-leece on Er-leens and Galvez! I had a syringe in my sock, cocaine in my system and a unopened halfa G o' wine! All I heard was ZOOM!!! And had blood all over my shirt! Next thing I know I wake up in Parish Prison! I gits there and *they* tell me I didn't git cut -- I done got *shot*! You cain't win for losin'!"

"Here he go. Now he gon' start talkin' 'bout his paw! That boy was the worst cellmate I ever had," mumbled Blood & Wine as he stitched away.

"My paw had a 'scorched ass' policy," began Snake as he deftly used the scissors in the candles' odd glow between swigs out of a paper cup fulla wine. "He didn't take NO prisoners. My paw' favorite tune was *I Gits A Kick Outa You*, his favorite drink was punch and his favorite 'musement park was *Punch*atrain Beach – even tho' we couldn't go there. His favorite game was 'Truth or Consequences.' If you didn't tell the truth -- you paid the consequences." *Laughter.*

"My paw used to talk to me in Morse code," he said, shadow-punching the air, "DOT-DOT-DOT-DASH. . . DOT-DOT-DOT-DASH. . .. My paw even had pet names for his punches -- the Backhand Slap, the Delaware Punch, the Hatchetchop Killer, the Nut Buster, the Ass Buster, the Punches Pilot, and the Stay-Still-While-I-Kill-You-Son." *Swig. Laughter.*

"One time I asked him about my rights as a chile. 'Rights?' he said. 'I'll give you some rights -- and some lefts, too!' Yeah, he was mean. He whipped my ass every day -- *every day*! When I was bornded and my momma was layin' up in the hawspital holdin' me in her arms he came in, looked at me and hollered, 'Wow! Thanks, Bessie Mae! -- A new punchin' bag!'." *Swig. More laughter.*

"I ain't had no 'daddy'! I had a '*paw*'! The difference between a 'daddy' and a 'paw' is that a daddy build *mens* and a paw kill *boys*! My paw whipped my ass one day -- said BAM! 'That's for what you did last week!' Then BAM! 'That's for what you did yesterday!' BAM! 'That's for what you did today!' and BAM! BAM! 'What's them for, daddy?' I asked him. 'That's for what you *gon'* do tomorrow!'" *Swig. Boo-coo laughter.*

Suffice it to say that all Snake's father ever gave him was a daily asswhippin', an empty safe deposit box (when he died) and a proclivity for alcoholism.

There was a knock at the door. "Who dat?" queried my cousin. "Who dat?" he shouted again. "Who dat bammin' on the do' like dat?" Gittin' no response, he arose from his tenuous task, went to the door, opened it a teenantsy bit and peeked through. It was Yum-Yum, wunna them nighttime broads, wunna them nocturnal, painted birds of easy virtue from offa Claiborne Street.

"Hey, baby! Where y'at?!?" said Darkhorse, lookin' up from his chair. Silence. "You can say 'hello.' I ain't gon' eat you," he ignified.

"Well maybe I shouldn't say 'hello'," the soiled dove of the night cooed.

"Look, bruh, we up in here sewin' -- and *that* got to go back where it came from," Red said, indicating the woman in the crack of the door. "Plus -- all that cold air gittin' in here.... She cain't be comin' in here, anyway. We sewin'! She cain't be up in here! I don't want nobody -- 'specially her -- to see *our* colors and *my* stitches!"

"*Yeah* ya-right!" said Bulletproof.

"*Sho'* ya-right!" affirmed Blood & Wine.

"I know *that's* right!" assented both Turtle and Darkhorse.

"Bu-u-u-u-u-ull*shit*!" objected Snake defiantly, the straight razor poised menacingly in his rail-thin hand. "All the broad wan' do is come in and cop!"

"The bitch cain't come in! We sewin'!" shouted Red. "She can be Eleanor Roo-ze-velt! She can own the whole Roo-ze-velt Hotel -- but the bitch ain't comin' up in *here*!" yelled Red, still blockin' the partially open door.

Blackie stirred uneasily, got up and quietly sauntered to the backa the house as though she knew what was comin'. "The bitch cain't come in," Red repeated. "She ain't comin' in here and bogardin' *nuthin'*. That's just my personal idiotsyncrasy. No bitches in here while we sewin'!" he barked as he loomed forward, leanin' on the door.

"I ain't no bitch! I'm a hoe!" the hoe protested in her state-of-the-profession, tartish git-up.

"I can smell *that*," murmured Darkhorse, lookin' up momentarily. Laughter.

"I'm tellin' all y'all studs -- I ain't *sellin'* no dope tonight," Red explained. "I'm *sewin'*. *We* sewin'. Y'all know what we gotta do. The Chief ain't gon' like it if we ain't ready Tuesday moanin'. The bitch --" he started.

"Why she gotta be a 'bitch'?" Snake challenged. "I know that broad. That's Yum-Yum. She from Backatown. I know her people," he said. "I feel to believe you bein' too hard on the hoe -- callin' her a bitch and all, bruh."

"She a 'bitch' 'cause them hoes is always bitchin' -- bitchin', bitchin, bitchin'! Bitchin' 'bout *this*, bitchin' 'bout *that* – bitchin' 'bout my stitchin', bitchin' 'bout my kitchen -- bitchin', bitchin', bitchin'! Then the first thing they wan' do when they gits 'em a *real* man -- they wants to make *him* a bitch! Ain't *that* a bitch?!?. . .

"The bitch ain't comin' in here -- not for all the vagina in China. Let the bitch stay out there on the hoe stroll -- the *bitch*!" For a moment there was silence. One could almost hear the ships rollin' on the river, for when Brickhead Red talked, *everybody* listened. Then --

"*I know who actin' like the bitch*," mumbled Snake. Stillness. Silence. No one in history or farflung memory had ever signified, ignified, nignified, intimated or outright stated that Brickhead Red was a "bitch" -- and lived. The six teardrops under his eye attested to that.

"Say *what*?" asked Red, slammin' the door and walkin' over towards Snake as he backed away from trimmin' Darkhorse's hair. Red tensed, swept me out of his path with a gentle hand and approached Snake.

"Bruh -- I'ma 'bout to put so mucha you on the flo' -- they gon' think it's the blood bank up in here," he said as he reached in his sock for his favorite (ergonomically-designed) shank. "I'ma cut the black off yo' ass!" he threatened. Me, Darkhorse, Turtle, Bulletproof and Blood & Wine froze forthwith. We knew what was comin' next. "*Mawfiddice*" -- he began, "You let a li'l gum-smackin' skankawank piece o' trim git us off what we supposed to be doin' -- all 'cuz you smellin'up on a li'l twat -- wan' git up in a li'l piece o' crack -- a li'l poonanny -- when you knows what we gotta be 'bout doin'. . . *Mawfiddice!*" he repeated. In the world's whole wide creation he wasn't gon' bow down, not Red.

"Who? Snake asked provocatively. "Mawfiddice? Who? Who?"

"'Who'?" mimicked Red. "'Who'? You got feathers in yo' ass?"

"Huh?"

"-- Feathers in yo' ass! Is you a owl? -- 'Who? Who'?" Red signified. Muted laughter. Nobody wanted to git into the act. No one wanted their static to cling.

"Say, bruh -- " protested Snake.

"Look here, stud -- I'm 'bout to put my foot in yo' stinky, black, alcoholic ass -- I'm 'bout to put a big piece o' 13 Triple E foot dead up yo' prison wallet," Red threatened, displaying his weapon of choice. I felt like I was in a Shane movie as I peeked over the shoebox top fulla herb by the album cover, the half-empty wine bottles and the paper cups atop the white-sheeted table.

"Don't be draggin' on me! I ain't no alcoholic," Snake protested. "I'ma dope fiend!" he nignified. "I'm sorry, bruh -- I don't have the itch to fear man, woman, child, ghost, beast -- or bitch . . . so if you feel like a frog -- *jump!* You ain't puttin' *me* on no tip!" he undereyed as he brandished the straight razor in his long, killer fingers. "I'ma shave up that red haid o' yo's!"

"I ain't no erster you gon' be shuckin'," menaced Red, steppin' closer.

"Look, bruh -- " Darkhorse cautiously chimed in at that crucial moment. "I know this yo' house, Red -- and I ain't disrespectin' that," he said, slowly movin' aside. "But we gon' have a *real* problem if y'all start humbuggin' in here and mess up all we done done so far. Why don't y'all go on 'haid and settle this outa range where the blood don't spill all over the material. We done put a lotta time in this," he offered.

"If you cain't git along -- git it on," instigated Bulletproof.

My cousin thought a second, looked over at me, and ordered me to git a large bandana from the chiffarobe in the next room, which I dutifully did. "Y'all gon' settle this right -- Injun style," said Bulletproof.

Red and Snake agreed. I followed them as they went to the neutral ground (that island of grass, banana trees, palm trees and other native flora in the middle of the two-way thoroughfare) on Er-leens across from the Lafitte where Bulletproof tied their left hands together. It was on. They sweated, bled, cursed, cut and slashed each other (with extreme dispatch) like it was goin' outa style. There was a whole lotta hoopin' and hollerin' during the butchery and bloodletting of the profane, protracted, running orgy of stickin', slicin' and stabbin'. You wouldn't think that much blood could come from a human being' body! They fought all the way down Er-leens, leavin' a lake o' blood all up from Dooky's down to Prieur Street where they say the paradegoers had tore up the float for souvenirs back in 1949 when Louis Armstrong was the King of the Zulus. They was knife-fightin' out there 'til 'fore day in the moanin' -- right there in the middle of the neutral ground with people all crowded around like it was Mardi Gras Day on Claiborne and Er-leens. My uncle said they *both* was stupid and shoulda sold tickets insteada fightin' for nuthin'. Eventually, the po-leece (who cared little about the spectacle of two natives cuttin' up each other in the middle' o' the street) finally arrived in a coupla prowl cars, dashboard lights flashin', si-reens blastin' through the droves of people, and whisked 'em away off to Charity where they patched 'em up, then brought 'em *both* to jail. I don't know if they took 'em to the Pink Palace in the First District or to Tulane and Broad, but I *do* know they went to jail. I didn't see my cousin again 'til I came home one summer from college.

I'm not gon' be the judge of his deeds and dastardly decisions. That's not my role as a man. All I know is just befo' every Mardi Gras I think about those remarkable spirits and souls I grew up around who protected, nurtured, cradled, comforted and counseled me in my life's infancy and youth.

Every year I remember them and pay them homage -- their often undearly departed souls; their joy, pain, sunshine and rain; their long-suffering fears and tears; their moments of loving, madness and mirth; their humanity and insanity; their jocularity and imagination; the humility of their prayers and the futility of their struggles; their yesterday hugs and kisses; their deferred dreams; their blessings and bereavement in sadness and sorrow; their sewing and reaping; their laughter and weeping; their fashion and passion; their halo of protection and affection unbound by the restraints of time.

And every year around Mardi Gras, around Carnival time, all I do is sew, sew, sew.

A short, cool summer
Stamford, CT 2007

Don't Wish for What You Want

Once upon a time on the night of St. John's Eve a relatively underendowed married man found a green, glass, brass-plated kerosene lamp on a footbridge over Bayou St. John. Being the loving husband that he was and thinking that greater physical proportion would enhance the qualitative nature of his marital coupling, he took his second-linin' hainkachiff and rubbed the lamp. A genie emerged from a cloud of smoke and the man requested "a cock as big as a horse." Just then a great commotion chanced to come about as a giant gamecock emerged from the waters and swallowed him whole.

Later that evening another fellow happened by, saw the lamp and picked it up. Understanding the mysterious, mystical, magical occurrences that often happen on the eve of the celebration of the Feast of St. John the Baptist, he too decided to implore the spirits in the lamp for its necromantic patronage. He stroked and beseeched the lamp to remake him in the image of Hugh Hefner and surround him with every *Playboy* beauty imaginable. In a flash he found himself transformed into a morbidly obese female of mammoth extremities in a vermilion red dress. "What the -- ?!?!!??? I said 'Hugh Hefner,' not 'HUGE HEIFER'!" he protested. Then, an 18-wheeler big rig carrying used *Playboy* magazines sprang from the waters and smashed him to less than recognizable smithereens.

Another fellow sauntered by the bridge, came upon the lamp, brushed it a bit with his snotrag and asked for "a room fulla sapphires." Suddenly, severe winds arose over the waters, whisked him away and he found himself in an inescapable, enclosed space with an aggravating aggregation of disgustingly argumentative colored wimmins for all eternity.

Finally, a woman came across the lamp, and understanding the enchanting legends of the ancestors, caressed it in the folds of her skirt, remembered her mother's and her grandmother's and her great-grandmother's admonition: "Be careful what you wish for; you just might git it."

So she appealed to the powers of the heavens for peace in her heart, and continued on her way to a long life of achievement, joy and happiness.

October 2012
Stamford, CT

Jazz Stories: *From Katrina to Connecticut*

Epitaph

*"Row, row, row your boat,
Gently down the stream.
Merrily, merrily, merrily, merrily,
Life is but a dream. . ."*

-- English language nursery rhyme

    The brick and stucco vault, a somber, yet majestic structure built in the crescent city's unwavering, tradition-heavy *faubourg* during the latter portion of the century before the Great War by a French immigrant bricklayer who was espoused (at least in the eyes of his blooded kin) to a free woman of color in spite of the territory's *code noir*, now contains my pedigree's flesh, bone, and blood that slumber together in the monument that comprises a medley of their diverse, saintly and uncelestial lives, loves and legends. It embodies waning remnants of the fanciful and conventional bygone times of my fantastic forebears and their inheritance of the range of all that is contemplative and comic, delightful and sordid, earthly and exalted.
    Inside there are misers and womanizers, dressmakers and homebreakers, fancy French Quarter sportin' women and church ladies (sometimes they were *both*). Familial lore invariably includes the verbiage that it was built by my great-great grandfather "with his own hands."
    The vault's brick and concrete cadaverous structure, located in an aisle in close proximity to where a melancholy medley of residents including master musicians, patrician politicians, poets, *victimes de l'honneur*, and the daughter of the revered voodoo priestess (who rests eternally in this same tract of illimitable homestead as the soon-to-be-sainted Blessed Mother Henrietta Delille) are entombed, stands unflinchingly on a slab of concrete by a grass pathway and gray pebbled lane of the corrupted decay of the enduring, crumbling Claiborne Avenue burial ground that was consecrated by the eminence of Roman Catholic Church fathers in the early 1800s.
    This aboveground city of the dead is a magnificently morbid, hushed necropolis, the final resting place for heroes and innocents, newborns and decrepits, virtuosos and dunces, the

flourishing and afflicted, the youthful and addicted. There were sisters, brothers (and unspoken others), the lettered and unschooled, the square and the cool. Bookmakers and heart breakers, risk-takers and homemakers are all perpetual indwellers of its blissful permanence.

The chamber's gruesomely poetic entry, with the family surname carefully, lovingly engraved, stands imperturbably alongside a rusted, degenerating iron lace fence and is encompassed by sepulchral monuments of women weeping, praying, and nurturing amidst chunks of fractured gravestones, tarnished metal remembrances and stacks of haunting, redbricked, walled tombs, their dearly departed cargo asleep in mortality's terminal expedition and death's omnipotent legacy. At the entrance is posted the admonition:

VISITORS ARE WELCOME BUT ENTER THESE PREMISES AT THEIR OWN RISK. NO SECURITY NOR GUARDS ARE PROVIDED AND THE NEW ORLEANS ARCHDIOCESAN CEMETERIES DISCLAIMS RESPONSIBILITY FOR THE PERSONAL SAFETY OF VISITORS AND THEIR PROPERTY.

The first occupant to take up residency in the internal compartment of the chamber was the immigrant craftsman's comely wife, a tastefully-manicured, sublimely stunning, honeyskinned beauty with huge, full lips who bore him a dozen dutiful, upright, and pietistic natural children by way of a left-handed marriage. They lived a prosperous life of blissful domestication in their well-attended-to household. Family fable has it that she came to him as a succubus, a dream lover whose physical acquaintance he later made in the flesh of the young servant girl he met while laying brick for a French Quarter dining establishment.

They say he killed a pirate in a duel under the oaks for publicly speaking ill of her in a manner unbefitting a proper lady. She died of the fever and he used his considerable construction skills to erect an enduring monument to the indelible memory of her revered, loving legacy. He never spoke a singular word to anyone, nor did anyone disturb his simmering discontent during the entire span of time he built the memorial in which the remains of his beloved would forever rest in eternity's bosom. As was the custom, every All Saints Day thereafter, until his death at a ripened age, he and his children weeded the area surrounding the vault, painted the stone slab at its entrance white, and beseeched the Creator for her soul to forever repose in peace.

A year and a day after her death, it was rumored, her beauty was so eternal her body never decomposed in the confines of the bronze-fringed, custom-made casket the humble immigrant had purchased for her interment. Family fable still has it that her corpse, unlike the other cadavers that are compressed into the vault's hermetically sealed recessed area (mostly in moderately-priced body bags), is *still* uncorrupted. No one visits the tomb on the anniversary of her parting, and it is said that on those recurrences the Frenchman still stands weeping, for after a life of existential angst he rejoined the eternal flame of his passion in the unyielding grasp of death's boundless expanse.

* * *

The next unanimated lodger in the generational confines was a great-great uncle who was in a group of former WWI colored doughboys and was eventually designated to run the mail in the Negro sections of the city. What we know about him is that he lived an unremarkable life in Corpus Christi parish, paid his bills on time, and was married to a virtuous, incorruptible woman (also entombed alongside him) whose remains are among the most venerable in the family's eternal home.

The elders say she never accommodated any man other than her husband, was a childless lover of children, lived a true Christian life, read her Bible every night of her life, put its words into practice every day, and was surely welcomed by her Maker in a triumphant homecoming. Shortly after her death a baby in the family was born and returned to the ages within minutes of the exquisite pain of entry into the world. The old folks say the infant looked like her forebear and that God brought her back to Him because He didn't want her to suffer the discomforts of the flesh a second time. She was buried in a tiny pink casket, with the clothes and toys her parents had purchased in anticipation of her arrival, nestled at her side.

Uncle Red endured bullets, bombs, and biased brass in WWII as a post-D-Day convoy driver for the Red Ball Express. He didn't survive a cordner barroom humbug in which an errant shot from a .22 caliber pistol, when two men were occupied in a spirited argument over a literal nickel-and-dime game of chance, punctured his head. Neither died, but Uncle Red did. The termination point of the shot's projectory indicated that he was shot by accident and the shooter was walking those same mean streets a few years later.

The native gentleman's parting ceremony included a flag-draped coffin, an army musician playing "Taps" with a *real* bugle (and not one of those pre-recorded contraptions), and a woman who was crying a waterfall of tears for him after making his life more miserable than a berobed KKK leader's would've been at the Million Man March.

We stood silently in awe of her performance in full view of the crush of mourners in attendance at his semi-patriotic homegoing ceremony. His brother, Uncle Sleepy, who suffered from narcolepsy, also survived the epic episode that was the war, but fell victim to the chronic sleep disorder and drove across an Uptown thoroughfare's neutral ground into oncoming traffic and met a rather crushing demise. He was buried in a basic cardboard box in a private, family-only service.

My older cousin, Walter, had the lifeblood of his youth stripped from him in that brilliantly-executed campaign known as the Vietnam War. He was on the track team at Joseph S. Clark High School, but wasn't college material (who *is*?). They gathered his body parts, shipped them home and we set still another flag-covered coffin in its place with those who went before him. Other than the 'Nam, he had never been outside of New Orleans except for basic training and a Parent's Day trip to Alabama to visit me in college. His hauntingly boyish graduation picture sits placidly on many a family fireplace mantel. His mother choked to death on a chicken bone and his father was killed by his second wife when she discovered him in an indelicate position with a woman purportedly of easy virtue.

My cousin, Larry, was the sort of fellow who would take a hand outstretched in friendship and send back a knob. He was a decayed-toothed heroin addict at the age of 15 and was killed by his own father when he came home desperate for a fix one moon-bright night. He attempted to raid my uncle's stashbox, got caught in that (ahem) vein attempt, and engaged the man of the house in a kitchen knife struggle. He came out on the sharp end of the fight and perished from a series of multiple stab wounds.

My uncle moved the rest of that part of the family as far away from New Orleans as one could imagine. Two of his other sons were imprisoned for a murder in an after-hours spot in their adopted hometown. We never heard from that branch of the tree again.

Larry still enjoys the dubious distinction of being the first family member to be cremated. In spite of the objections of some family members who believed that the lustrous idea of ancestry would be tarnished by his presence, his ash-filled plastic urn was placed in the vault with the relics and remains of those who had come and gone before.

Other ripples from that tributary to the bloodline have been described as a lady of whom they whisper died from "sudden coital death" and a huge woman who was conjectured to be a glory girl. All we overheard as children was that she had a big butt, brown bangs, and got stabbed to death Uptown by an unhappy happy-house trick. They say her coffin was so huge that nobody volunteered for pallbearing duties and the funeral director had to substitute his staff. That part of the family wasn't referenced too often.

* * *

Arguably the most (ahem) colorful figure in the family's history was Uncle Freddie or "Fast Freddie" per his street moniker. He was a longshoreman, a seaman who was married but had a propensity for running with a *goumada* or two in a slew of cities worldwide while he was runnin' on the waters. During the war he served on a liberty ship, the John W. Brown, the pride of the merchant marine fleet. He was a travelin' man who favored Brioni custom-made suits, Panama hats with 3-inch broad brims, fine felt fedoras, fitted vests and sporty sunshades (even at night), fishtailed Chryslers (he drove -- even though he couldn't read and had to use landmarks), highballs and hookers, and asking the little fellows in the family things like, "Who would you do first -- Marilyn Monroe, Sophia Loren, or Natalie Wood?"

One Mardi Gras season during Carnival's great illusion he masked as Robin Hood, grandstanding, "I rob from the bitch . . . and give to the hoe!" He constantly bragged about his alleged stable of women: "She ain't got no hair, but she got a car. She love me. She come see me every payday."

After his late-night roustabouting and his wife's usual and customary refusal of entry, he and his kangaroo pouch beer belly would stumble drunkenly over our rented shotgun house's creepy side alleyway's slick bricks to the kitchen, where he would gain back door admittance (courtesy of a key my parents ceded to him), then proceed to gorge himself in a diet-disintegrating ingurgitation of Creole cream cheese and glazed doughnuts followed by unhealthy swigs of any liquid in our refrigerator or cupboard containing alcohol.

The children would anxiously await his stumbling, drunken arrival for the unerring prospect of sharing in some of his delectable gastronomic amusements -- all antithetical to the alleged slenderizing endeavor to which he only occasionally and fractionally dedicated himself. "You gotta die of *somethin'*!" he'd jest during his late night forays into portliness. My parents always inquired about his funeral plans and he'd often respond, "I'ma have all *women* pallbearers. A broad brought me in -- and broads gon' bring me out!"

His appetites extended far beyond the normal vices of some men (drinking, gambling, patronizing whores). He never let his brain move faster than his penis and was always introducing a discordant note to whatever tune. During a serious, instructive discussion about absentee fathers he'd say something like, "I ain't no absentee father. I'm a long-gone daddy!"

I asked him for some advice about college one day and he told me, "Never put your finger in a turtle's mouth." On another occasion when I asked why girls are the way they are, he provided me with the assified adage: "Never trust a woman over 69."

He could tell monumental lies. When we'd catch him sniffing cocaine from a glassine packet he'd tell us that the happy dust was Sal Hepatica. He had a side hustle -- loansharking people in his eyeshades and rolled-up sleeves from the back room of a Basin Street steakhouse. He was ridin' high in the catbird seat. After a contentious divorce, he met that li'l woman from downtown.

The adults referred to her as "Boots" because she was in the world when that Sinatra girl's song was out there. She worked in a shoe store and had every voguish style of boots on the market.

We called her "*Miss* Boots" as was the traditional linguistic sign of respect for our elders. Her real name was Gaye Dix, but it was a rather awkward construct to call her "Miss Dix," so we just said "Miss Boots." (The parents of that era didn't merely *feed* us . . . they *raised* us.) He'd often joke that they were an "owl and pussycat couple". . . "**I'm** the night owl -- and **she's** the pussy!" he'd crack.

She was a high-handed hussy from Transylvania, LA, who favored silky shorty pajamas and lazy little numbers designed to intoxicate and enliven the attentions of her most inebriated gentlemen callers. Eventually she and Uncle Freddie wed, purchased a home in an oaklined subdivision, and settled in for a raucous rendition of a life of celebration and festivity in the land of rum, coke and honey.

In his advancing age he considered his physical condition to be fair-to-middlin'. At a stage in life when his friends and associates were suffering from debilitating physical conditions, he thought himself fortunate to only have rheumatoid arthritis (and one loose tooth) and he spoke theatrically of his marriage as "That time I got shot in the ass by Cupid."

She inevitably tired of his lampshade-on-the-head partying and womanizing, and after her threats of divorce following rumors of his part ownership in an Uptown sporting palace and his auditioning of its requisite carnal pleasures, one of her family members informed her that he had long been involved in a love quadrangle during the entire season of their espousement. She questioned him about the allegation and he replied, "It's my place o' business! I cain't be layin' up at home all the time! I cain't sit on the highway crappin' and make money too!"

She made an appointment with a spirit woman in the Sixth Ward who concocted a potion that would rid her of him and his three-timing affairs, splashed a smidgen of his ruination into a container of his favorite brand of cream cheese, and eventually spent the rest of her life in an upstate prison for his murder. When he died word spread like mice in a cornfield, and he enjoyed one of the most tumultuous second-lining homegoings in the city's history of revelry and festivity.

* * *

On one recent late morning another family member was consigned to the grave. A customary brass band blew a solitary sendoff tune as the present-day, youthful descendants of the immigrant Frenchman and the free woman of color scampered about or stood in silence in their Sunday best, oblivious to their date with destiny. The pallbearers' gloves were placed on the coffin, wreaths of flowers were laid atop and around the vault's awaiting entry, prayers were uttered, and libation and the ceremonial dinner were being prepared for the repast.

As for me, I recalled life's fleeting impermanence, how just yesterday I was a toddler involved with my little Golden Books and toy soldiers (in the playpen near my mother's sewing machine). Now I had embarked on an eternal journey into a greater life force of majesty and completeness as the vault's gaping gateway stood open for my preordained, inseverable interblending with the crumbled dust of my forebears in the beginning of a vision of newer worlds where I would once again harmonize with their haunting, hallowed ranks in memory's ceaseless, unremitting river of ever-renewed beginnings.

August 2012
Stamford, CT

ADAPTATIONS

Professor Arturo

The Pound of Bionic Chronic
(inspired by *The Cask of Amontillado* by Edgar Allan Poe)

> "He causeth the grass to grow for the cattle,
> and herb for the service of man that he may
> bring forth food out of the earth."
> -- Psalms 104:14

A thousand times I tolerated the stunting and fronting in the dastardly drama perpetually perpetrated by Fortuné. I bore his expedient exaggerations, his morbid fascination with the suicidal folly of habitual debauchery, his facade of respectability, the plasticity of his template of rationality and morality, his "inadvertent" purloining of my cigarette lighters, his petty persecutions, his nasty insinuations and ruthless determination to remain permanently maintained by and entrenched in a world of fattened bellies and big cigars; I endured his judgmental, self-hating filth disguised as benign discussion, his sartorial sins, his expedient hyperbole, his flatulence, his scorn and derision, the arrogance and intolerance of his brash individualism and philosophical inflexibility, the strategic inertia and intellectual inconsistency of his villainy and deceit masquerading as savage grace and unguarded optimism, the clothing of his naked treachery in his attempt to seem saintlike, his sneak thievery and corruption of the public good, his perverted sense of inadvertent humor as reflected in his insistence that "OJ didn't do it," his financial fragility, his Peter Lemongello records, his disputations, contentions and his unconstrained transgressions.

I stomached every course of Fortuné's dreadful, iniquitous meal of evil for time without end. I had borne his permanently-imbedded idiotsyncrasies decade in and decade out and had finally tired of enduring the unendurable. If revenge were to take a thousand years it would be revenge taken too quickly, for I had become excessively exhausted at the unresolved consequences of drowning in the toxic gumbo of his mindless madness.

Fortuné was indeed a farce to be reckoned with, a morbidly obese, vulgar, flippant, nefarious scoundrel who persistently failed to honor his sporting obligations. He was as dumb as a bag of bricks and had the credibility of a Mallard Fillmore cartoon. Even on his best days his personality and presence were borderline oppressive. He had an early career as one of those teachers who teach college level English and never see their names in print until they appear in the obituaries.

As a politician he was a serial loser. Every election cycle he ran for the same office, received his relative pittance for splitting the native electorate's vote, and lost each time with unprecedented precision. He was repeatedly threatened with disbarment for his awesome antics in the organized grime of the legal profession and his intemperate remarks were moodier than *Moody's Mood*. He was so slow it took him a week to take a One-a-Day pill.

He was from a "blink-and-you'll-miss-it" backwater Louisiana town and his fourth spousal equivalent was an antiquated creature with drooping jaws on a careworn, pimply, painted and powdered, toad-eating face as old as the pyramids. He had graduated from the school of soft knocks, one of those people who achieved some minimal semblance of success in life who were born on third base and think they hit a grand slam home run. He was so heartless and unfeeling -- he'd fire a New Yorker for missing work on September 12, 2001.

I trusted him no further than I could spit against a hurricane. What masqueraded for Fortuné's mind was a toxic curiosity with a mental capacity that was akin to stupidity on steroids, and he had an habitual indulgence of engaging in the cognitive dissonance of waxing poetic in conversation about the conservation of the aggravation of his constipation; and was in blissful paradise whenever he engaged in his passionate infatuation for chronic, headsplitting, monster marijuana. He was indeed living heaven on earth, but he was going to live hell under it, drawn into an inescapable web of his own making, for the mask of his friendship had become an intolerable burden.

He was a notorious, would-be serial womanizer of high infidelity, with a series of dalliances that proved to be progressions of diminished expectations in the futility of romance. He was under the impression that he was a mack, but he was an uncooked macaroni. He had the personality of a department store clothes dummy and was a repeatedly rejected suitor who didn't listen to Tom or Harry . . . he listened to Dick.

Fortuné's first *gooomah* was a towering woman from Texas who left him for a horse. Then there was the one-legged lady that he invited to hop over to the bar for a drink. She fell while doing so, shattering the bones in her functioning limb -- causing her to have it surgically removed. Then there was the church lady who fingered her glow-in-the-dark rosary beads and recited every known Mystery of the Rosary while they smooched. She claimed she was a bride of Christ and her legs were as locked as the parish rectory doors after the altar boy picnic. There was also the one with the enormous fangs that he was hesitant to kiss for fear of losing that part of his anatomy that caused so much of his life's conflict. After that, there was the substance abuser whose stench was so horrible that he thought bloodthirsty vermin, drawn to the aroma of her less than private parts, would emerge from the walls of her house of chill repute, scaring him senseless at the thought of coupling with her breathing but near-skeletal remains. Sex with her was about as welcome as a vaginal abrasion.

Finally, there was the wife of one of his colleagues, with whom he had taken liberties. After several surreptitious endeavors to bed her she couldn't perform because of a recent hip replacement. The last time he was inside a pretty woman was when he toured the Statue of Liberty. I didn't trust him any farther than a dragonfly could throw a manatee.

The gathering storm of vengeance in my controversially contentious plan grew exponentially as I harkened back to the strange terrain of our social contact. Though the wisdom of my methodology might be determined by some observers to be rather unconventional, I was not acting out of a delusional compulsion. And I would take more than grim satisfaction in finally exacting my revenge and bringing justice to this *Monk Marathon*-watching, porcine prevaricator of gross improprieties, through a frigid dish of revenge I would personally bring into being, for no poison is more potent than one served by a trusted hand.

* * *

I pondered the litany of accusations resultant from our less than fortuitous association and recalled each sordid circumstance with academic dispassion as I quantified the extent of Fortuné's transgressions. I thought of the time he pilfered the currency that was pinned to my shirt at my 4th birthday party; I recalled when he didn't pick me up at the agreed hour to bring me to the airport because he was getting loaded (I had to take my car), didn't answer his phone -- and the parking fee was $240 when I returned from my sojourn.

My infuriated mindset evoked the occasion on which I literally begged him not to ask my neighbor if he could purchase some of the ganja she shared with us, and he proceeded to do so anyway despite my admonition that it wasn't that kind of party -- and that occurrence when he perjured himself by telling that piano player that I was "double-booked" and made me appear as unprofessional as himself when she called the venue, received some information to the contrary and thought *I* was the Great Prevaricator.

I recollected when Fortuné took that footage of my performance and procrastinated its processing for over five years . . . and those times he used my cologne on every occasion he chanced to use my facilities. Also coming to mind was his misplacing my Kool & The Gang cassette and scratching my treasured *Bill Withers Live at Carnegie Hall* CD. His sitting at my computer and massaging his Vienna sausage in the full view of one of my female clients (while snorting copious amounts of cocaine) also arose in my tired, fatigued consciousness.

My long-lingering decision to rid humankind of this useless mass of flesh was additionally buttressed by a remark he made about my daughter's *derriere*, his visits to a medley of porn sites on my computer that resulted in my twice having to summon the Geek Squad to engage in corrective action, his over-fertilizing of my herb plants and their resultant demise, and his lie about his claim to ownership of a pair of trendy cufflinks we found at a deceased friend's home when we were collecting his possessions. He said that our friend had borrowed them and never effected their return, but I had been in the company of the departed when he purchased the upmarket accessories.

Adding fuel to the flame of Fortuné's depraved indifference to truth was when he gifted my landlady with a pedigreeless cayoodle that he told her was a full-blooded Chow Chow; that time he drove off laughing, with the lobster bisque I had the wait staff prepare for takeout; that time he used my Social Security number to open a cell phone account resulting in my credit rating being ruined by four reporting agencies; that time he joined the Rush Limbaugh Fan Club; and those superabundant occasions on which he left doo-doo stains on the toilet seat.

Then he sold me that raggedy car, misused my niece by taking her innocence (while playing it like he was holier-than-Mao), drank the last beer at the party time after time, allowed my lawsuit to languish for years at a glacially slow pace, stole my designer key chain, peed on my marigolds and my colacasia (elephant ear) plants -- and relieved himself on a hornet's nest and we had to jump in the pool to escape the stings of their righteous wrath.

The agony of his deceit grew to even greater proportions when he left all of his incoming messages on his cell phone so I couldn't access him when I called to get that money he owed me; ran into the back of a marked police car (resulting in both of us being assigned three hots and a cot as overnight guests of Sheriff Foti); came to live with me after that fire at his apartment and gave me a TV that was soaked from the firemen's salvage efforts -- then took it back when it worked after it dried out; stole my two vintage console stereos and record collection I had in storage after Katrina; ripped off my yardstick when I was half-asleep (I saw him out the corner of my drowsy eyes); walked away with my roach clip, parked in my assigned space and forced me to park on the side of my own building by the dumpster -- and my car got towed.

Fortuné also ran off with my last $20 on Thanksgiving Day (and I had to watch the game beerless), said something out the side of his face when the stripper next-door came by in a black negligee and with a bottle of vodka, appropriated that money I sent that boy in jail (then absconded to the dope man's house), scooped that cash up that fell from the torn pocket of my robe (and went to the dope house *again*), and stared up and down my oldlady's fine, shapely, sculpted figure like it was a Van Gogh painting.

He made up a phony receipt and charged me $100 more for a tune-up; switched lighters on me -- mine had fluid -- *his* didn't; took that $10,000 from that elderly lady when he settled her account (then declared bankruptcy so he wouldn't have to pay her) . . . and committed numerous other unspecified transgressions far too vulgar to mention in polite company.

It was all I could stand. I couldn't stand any more.

* * *

At the proverbial stroke of midnight the anticipated summons of the doorbell interrupted my foray into the strategic inertia of Fortuné's deficiency of character. I had given my staff the day off, ostensibly to join the partying populace of the Crescent City's Mardi Gras festivities. The gaiety and splendor of the Carnival Day merrymakers and revelers had been dampened by the Gulf showers that arrived unexpectedly from deep, purple clouds that descended on the city like a horde of thirsty longshoremen under a FREE BEER sign on payday.

I peeked through the thick, wine-colored curtain of my mortuary's brightly-lit atrium. Next to the concrete outer wall topped with broken glass was a drenched, tuxedoed figure in an "old school" fur-trimmed parka, waving drunkenly at me, greeting me with an upthrust middle finger. It was Fortuné, his loosely-cemented perception and capacity for rational thinking now even more diminished by the alcohol-inspired debauchery from an obvious series of jaunts to a slew of neighborhood haunts. *The chores of vermin,* I thought.

I was presented with an unpleasant and frightening situation and welcomed the audacious opportunity I finally had to fulfill the destiny of our *folie au deux*. I buzzed him through the outer, iron lace gate. He stumbled up the red brick walkway in the night's pestilential fog and rain towards the funeral home's doors, through which the dead had often made their last passage to the tomb. He was about as slow as a white woman running the hundred yard dash.

"Maulana-Maulana, the funeral man. If you cain't put 'em under, he damn sure can. . ." he sang as I unlocked the heavily-bolted wooden door.

"Where y'at?!?!" I greeted him in customary, common parlance.

"I'm wet as alligator titty," Fortuné joked. I let him into the reception area and he immediately reached for a towel in a nearby veined marble-and-mahogany mirrored dresser adorned by tousle-haired cherubs. He removed his outer garment, hung it on a nearby bank of hooks, and dried his soaked brown flesh and tux as I approached him with an imperturbable soul.

"Alligator titty? I see you've developed an extreme case of lactomania."

"Yeah. The doctor did tell me I been gittin' too much lactose."

"I've been expecting you," I said in genteel toleration of his wobbly-legged presence, his buzz-cut hair and the eraser-sized mole on his right cheek. He stared around the room, at its colossal masonry columns that rose from the building's foundation to its roofline. He gawked at the etched-crystal, Moorish chandeliers and concave, popcorn-finish ceiling, looking dumber than a three-eyed dog.

"Were you busy?" he slobbered.

"Busy? I am shocked that you would ponder such an odious assertion. I was in my *atelier* doing a bit of . . . planning. But I think I know why you're here," I said, with malice aforethought. "You heard I have the chronic."

"The *Chronicle*? The Houston *Chronicle*?"

"The *chronic*. The *bionic* chronic."

"Huh?" asked the ill-mannered bore. "Why don't we order sumthin' to eat?"

"The chronic. I have some. The food can wait. I like to smoke *before* the meal. We'll order a little later. Let's just 'herb up' right now."

"Oh -- herbs! I wish I could cop some. I'm so dry I'm crappin' cotton." I concurred, agreeing with his observation regarding his heightened despair in his effort to procure the top-of-the-line quality product to which I had access.

"I have the chronic, the bionic chronic," I repeated. "A pound of it. It smokes like angel's breath and hits like a casketful of cocaine," I added, appealing to his baser nature. "It's more chronic than Harry Connick!" I quipped.

"I had sumthin' the other day -- we passed it around -- they was five of us -- we passed it around one time and the whole room was high all night," Fortuné boasted, firing up a *Romeo y Julieta* cigar.

"The *room*? What *I* have'll get the whole Superdome zooted -- with just the *sight* of it -- much less the smell!" I embellished. "It's not Panama Red or Acapulco Gold, Orange Crush or Maui Wowee or Skunk or Swampgrass Green or *Dagga*. It's *the* chronic . . . like coke . . . the real thing."

"I sure wish I could hit summa that," he offered sheepishly. I grinned at his less-than-subtle suggestion.

"We can do that, but we can't smoke up here in the front. Cigar smoke is one thing, but the chronic'll linger for days. Let's go in the back . . . where we won't be disturbed."

* * *

"These things gon' kill me one day," Fortuné said as he puffed on the *R & J* while walking as slowly as an aged elephant with a sore foot.

"I don't think you'll die from smoking . . . cigars," I said, offering him a bitter dose of reality. "That won't kill you."

"Yeah. I guess if it ain't killed me by now . . . I'm bored stiff with life."

"How old are you now?" I asked, engaging him in polite repartee. We navigated along the snaking, meandering stretch of the carpeted corridor towards the casket display room, past the front chapel, the viewing room, the gift shop (featuring authentic funerary objects), the side chapel, the kitchen, the lounge and the preparation room.

"Fifty-four."

"Interesting. The U.S. life expectancy a hundred years ago was 47."

"You kill me with your statistics."

"The probability of your being murdered is 1 in 2,000."

"That's my chances?"

"*Probability*. Chance is a fool's name for fate," I said in a rhythmically assertive voice.

"Maulana," he cracked, "you make about as much sense as a propositional phrase."

I unclasped the velvet rope that barred the entrance to the casket display area and turned on the room's muted light revealing an array of caskets in varying sizes, colors, shapes and materials including bronze, copper, stainless steel, cherry, hardwood, mahogany, maple, oak, pecawn, pine, walnut, and cremation-friendly. "Wow!" Fortuné bellowed, "I ain't seen this many coffins since I was in Vietnam."

"Well, when you're certified in mortuary science you see a lot of them." I reached into a desk drawer. The wall to its right was adorned with my black-framed academic and professional credentials. "Would you like to roll an Optimo -- or would you prefer twisting a 'white girl'?" I asked as I offered a pack of rolling papers to him. He lounged back, planting his inebriated body into a chair at the side of the desk as I produced a large plastic bag of the fire herb. *"Voila!"* I said, displaying the bag to him, its contents' aromatic purple, gold, green, orange, and brown-tinted buds glistening in the faint light.

"Wow!" he said. "I thought I'd die before I saw any of this again! You sure this is the chronic? You *lyin'*?"

"Me . . . lie? My Lai was a massacre. Watch what happens when you hit some of this. Roll one and fire it up. This bud's for you," I said, a suggestion that did not fall on deaf ears. In a moment he was taking a cavernous, chest-busting toke faster than you can say "Mardi Gras Mambo."

"It's that delayed action," I cautioned. "Watch out for a coupla seconds."

"*Wow!*" he shrieked as he jumped like a shot deer. The chronic hit his already besotted self in a flash, causing him to drift into jocularity as he giggled and chuckled from the laughter-inducing effects of the git-high. "What kinda breast exam does a black woman git?. . .-- a mammy gram," he answered himself as I looked on at the spirit of the joint venture's proceedings. "That ain't nuthin' but the liquor talkin'," he explained. Then -- "I keep tellin' Bushrod that this is what I'm lookin' for -- when I'm lookin'," he coughed.

"Bushrod? What does Bushrod know about the chronic?" I asked. Bushrod was my chief competitor in the funeral business. "He's no more familiar with the chronic than he is with quality coffins."

Fortuné continued joking and toking, our voices mingling oddly with the intermittent flashes of the lighter he had "borrowed" from me last week. He was as loaded as an aircraft carrier in the Persian Gulf. "Yeah," he said. "I got bipolar mania, chronic dry eye, fybromyalgia, occasional irregularity, mesothelioma, constipation, and irritable bowel syndrome. I could use summa that chronic."

"What about your oppositional defiant disorder and acute alcoholism?"

"I sure wouldn't mind coppin' summa this -- how much?" he asked, ignoring my inquiry.

"It's for my *special* customers," I told him. "I reserve the chronic only for those who patronize my business . . . the bereaved family members and friends of the deceased that we've been serving since 1867."

"What? I ain't got no family -- 'cept for Yvonne. What about *me*? Ain't I your boy?"

"Not if you don't plan to do business with me," I said. "Being 'my boy' doesn't pay the house note. This is about business."

"Business? I'm outa pocket. I ain't got no money!" he protested for the umpteenth time that week. He was so tight he squeaked. He would break your Waterford Crystal ashtray, buy one from the Dollar Store, put it in a Tiffany & Co. box, and swear to its authenticity on his grandmother's grave.

"Okay," I said. "Tell you what -- you do business with me and I'll front you about an eighth of the product -- just for signing up for our services."

"You mean a funeral?"

"Bruh," I said. "I'm not selling used cars."

"Well, what *kinda* services?" he asked in his usually self-righteous, pompous, extremely pugnacious manner.

"A coffin," I said. "Why don't we start off with you signing up for a plan to purchase a coffin? That'd be a good start." I waved the bag of chronic in front of his crapulent eyes. "Look --" I said. "I'm sure we can come to an agreement of mutual reciprocation. I'm not talking about a traditional, horse-drawn funeral with a half dozen jazz bands . . . just something simple. . . . Let's start off with a coffin."

He gazed longingly at the bag I dangled before his ever-widening eyes, now under the spell of both the alcohol and the chronic. "All right. What do I do?" he asked, grinning sheepishly.

"First, try a little more of *this*," I said, offering him some product that he quickly rolled into a colossal joint and lit.

"WOW!" he roared, pulling on the joint. "I'm locked, cocked and ready to rock. OO-*ooh*! This ganja GOOD! My head light as a Seventh Ward boy with a French name! Woo-oo-oo-OO!!! I'm happy as a sissy on Muscle Beach. WOO! WOO! I feel like Frankie Beverly! What do we do? What do we *do*?"

"What we *do*," I said soberly, "is fit you with a coffin," my voice a silky baritone.

"A coffin?" he asked. "Already?"

Professor Arturo

"Yes," I urged the talking head. "*Ipsa loquitor.* It's never too early for these things. We never know when it's our time to go. Just step on over here," I said, taking him by the arms and leading him towards an oversized 20-gauge casket. He stood in front of the box, weaving back and forth, as I heaved, attempting to shove his massive frame towards the prescribed vicinity. I had forgotten that he was so big that when his oldlady was repairing his khaki pants we thought she was making tents for the Boy Scouts, and that he got winded walking from the table to the icebox.

"Park yourself here for a sec," I said as he leaned against the container. "Now lift this leg . . . then *this* one . . . now the arm . . . the other arm . . . then these steatopygiac buttocks. . . *There!* You're all in."

"I feel like I'm in heaven times seven," he smiled, still under the stupefying effects of the day and evening's libation and the night's inhalation. "This is all it's gon' take for me to git the chronic? . . . HEY!!!"

I sealed the lid shut and the descending darkness inside enveloped this ridiculously obtuse bubble of frivolity and intoxication. I began wheeling the coffin out the door of the display room towards the crematorium in the rear of the facility. I could hear him laughing contentedly as my motive, method and means were in full sync towards effecting his ceremonious end in poetic justice of immeasurable proportions. As we rolled through the corridor I could sense him feeling that this was something a bit more than a cruelly deceptive joke. His boozy charm was fading and I felt his faint knocking and heard his affable pleas to cease and desist from my performance. I coldly, calmly ignored entreaties for me to open the confines of his coffin, but continued with my sacrosanct duty to humanity.

I entered the retort, lined with its refractory, heat-resistant bricks, and adjusted the industrial furnace to generate the 1700+ degrees needed to ensure the creature's disintegration. I mounted the coffin on the motorized trolley that would deliver his body to the searing heat as I heard his mounting protests emanating from the container. "*Fortune favors the bold!!!,*" I yelled.

When it was done and he had been reduced to ashes, I rejoiced in the destruction of his mortal cremains and flushed the powdered relics down the toilet where he would join the other feces and assorted filth that dwelt within. The next morning I stood proudly on the balcony in the rear of the facility, savoring the mighty conqueror's glorious triumph over evil and wickedness, smoking a joint of the bionic chronic . . .

. . . and realizing how much I love the smell of chronic in the morning.

August 2011
Stamford, CT

Professor Arturo

Handa Wanda
(from *Cinderella* as told by Jacob and Wilhelm Grimm)

Once upon a time when the goose drank wine and the monkey chewed tobacco on the streetcar line, a young mother dwelling in an unassuming Galvez St. courtyard in the Lafitte Project was dying of an anonymous ailment. As her end drew near, the parish priest administered Extreme Unction to her and (abiding with her last wish) summoned her small daughter Wanda to her bedside in the humble, brick-encased surroundings that was their Sixth Ward home.

The priest left them to their solitude and the child leaned over the bed, caressing her mother while hearing her last words. "Baby," she said to the tearful child, "I'ma die. I know you prob'ly been knowin' that for a long time, but my time done finally come. . . . But you gotta go 'haid on wit *yo'* life. So I done made arrangements for what you gon' do now."

"Yes, momma?"

"I wanted you to go by yo' daddy, but he still out there runnin' the streets after all his li'l wimmins. That wouldn't be good for you, bein' a girl and all, so I been arrangin' with the guv'mint people for you to go live over in the Seventh Ward on Old Prieur Street with yo' daddy' sister -- yo' Aunt Belle. She got two chirren -- and they both girls -- and she can use that check -- so we done filled out the custody papers and she gon' take care o' you and put you in a good school. She wunna them 'bright people,' but I'ma trust her with you."

"Momma --" the girl wept, her tears falling to the blue blanket enclosing her mother's soon-to-be stilled flesh.

"Baby, I done done the best I could. I didn't ask to be bornded po'. I didn't ask for *you* to be. I just want you to git a better life than what we both done had. The Fairy Godmother be in that book. . .not in real life out cheer. Life ain't no crystal stair. Git yo' education . . . *be* sumthin'."

"Momma --" Wanda sobbed again, embracing her mother in an effort to keep her from death's disjointing divide.

"And don't depend on no man for what you wan' do in life. You see what runnin' with the mens done done for me . . . or maybe I done did it to myself for bein' out there with 'em," she reflected somberly from her deathbed, whispering despite the sores and lesions that shrouded her tongue while clutching a set of worn, wooden rosary beads under the covers they had purchased on Canal Street in more contented times. The unparalleled pain in her swollen lymph glands, her coughing, shortness of breath, the diarrhea and rashes, the constant fatigue, the skin spotting all finally made her admit to her child that she would be (in her words) "a gone pecawn."

"Be yo' own woman," she said. "Just be yo' own woman." One of her feeble, gnarled, contorted hands unclasped the rosary beads and gently, lovingly caressed a cluster of her daughter's wiry, plaited hair.

Then she died.

She was placed in a cheap, bottom-of-the-line, imitation oak box and laid to rest underneath a chineyball tree in Holt Cemetery, the potter's field (where the architect of jazz, Buddy Bolden, is said to be interred), adjacent to Delgado Community College and in close proximity to City Park. Some Mardi Gras Indians from the project's Galvez Street court sang and danced deliriously at the graveside ceremony.

Holt, a hushed museum to the departed loved ones of those citizens of less than nominal economic means, was one of the city's more intriguing final resting place sites. Inside its rickety iron fence were personalized acknowledgments left by the living in remembrance of the dead. Adorning the informal topography of the burial plots, which were free (as long as they were maintained by family or friends), were graves garnished with gaily-colored favorite chairs, dog fur, favorite cigars, hand-painted wooden crosses with misspelled names, threadbare clothing, once fashionable shoes, frayed walking canes, dog-eared bibles, strategically-placed whiskey bottles, elaborately-beaded steering wheels, and rusted bicycles. The creativity and resourcefulness of the surviving poor were on perpetual display as evidenced by the white picket fences and multicolored bricks used as gravesite borders, the Mardi Gras-themed memorials, the array of plastic flowers in long ago-faded vases, and the handdrawn pleas to Sweet Jesus to keep longsuffering loved ones in an eternal life of peace and blessings of the Light of the Lord and His faithful care.

Where her love for her mother once was, there was pain. There were tears instead of smiles, weeping instead of laughter, detachment rather than inextricable linkage, and shivers and shakes within and on her dark, youthful outer rather than the thrill and ecstasy of their rapport.

* * *

After the polite conversation and delectable culinary intake at the traditional post-burial feast where her Aunt Isabelle proudly and publicly proclaimed the prospects she had for the girl's future, they went to the project (her aunt called them "housing developments" when certain folks were around). They gathered Wanda's few possessions in a large black garbage bag, and drove (her aunt would say "motored") over to the Seventh Ward.

Isabelle's home was a double-galleried variation of the gable-sided, center-hall residence with the lathed and plastered facade and yellow baseboards: her new home. Her aunt had the child tote the massive bag, dragging it up the front steps, as her cousins, Florabelle and Corabelle, pranced to their room to get out of their dress-up clothes and play with their paper doll cutouts. Once inside, Wanda plopped down on the plastic-covered, faux French Provincial sofa near the French doors to the right of a lace-draped window in the living room.

"What is yo' project-dwellin' behind doin' sittin' on my Hurwitz-Mintz furniture? You triflin' -- just like yo' drunk, ign'ant paw!" Aunt Isabelle fumed as her features turned Creole tomato-red.

"I just wanted to sit down for a minute. I was tired, Auntee," murmured the child, taken aback at her aunt's acidic manner of speech.

"Don't be callin' me 'Auntee' -- you nappy-haid, ashy-legged wench. I don't want nobody to know I'm related to yo' black, pickaninny behind -- not even by marriage. My sister-in-law shoulda aborted yo' stinky, useless tail," she raged as a frown fixed itself on the child's face and tears bubbled from her eyes.

"You best fix yo' face 'fore I fix it *for* you -- and shut up with them crocodile tears 'fore I give you sumthin' to cry *for*. And don't you *dare* call me 'Auntee' again. Don't be embarrassin' me in front nobody. You ain't no relation. You ain't nuthin' but a check to *me*!" she spat. "Git that bag o' gobbidge up and put it where it belong -- and call me 'Miss Isabelle'!"

"Where to put it, Miss Isabelle? In my room?"

"Room?"

"In Florabelle' and Corabelle' room?"

"You must be done lost yo' ugly black mind."

"Where I'ma sleep?"

"-- In the damn washroom, heifer!" Isabelle retorted. "I made a pallet back there by the screen door for you. Git back there and git yo' kinky, empty haid some sleep. You gon' need it! And be sure to wash yo' fonky face 'fore you lay yo' stinky, black tail down!"

"Yes ma'am," Wanda said sheepishly. She carted the bag and its meager contents to her assigned space.

"You best be glad I don't chain yo' sorry, project-dwellin' ass up. . . . You just like yo' ign'ant, dead-ass maw!" her aunt-by-marriage barked.

That night Wanda slept an uneasy sleep, frightened and terrified over what fate had destined for her sorrowed, saddened soul.

* * *

She was awakened the next morning with a stinging slap in the face. "Git yo' lazy black ass up!" Isabelle screeched. "You gotta make breakfast and git them chirren' uniforms ironed for school. The sun done just come up! Git yo' triflin', worthless ass to work! If I could buy you for what you worth and sell you for what you *think* you worth -- I'd be big-time rich. I'd be Miss Rockyfella!"

She instructed the child on the specificity of her chores and the expectation that they would be completed in a timely, proficient manner. She demonstrated how she wanted the girls' uniforms -- white blouses and blue/grey skirts -- to be pressed so that they would appear the epitome of proper Catholic girldom when they entered the grounds of the nearby Corpus Christi Elementary School, a short distance up St. Bernard Avenue to Galvez Street across from McKenzie's Bakery. She showed her how the children's eggs should be prepared and the expected texture of their bacon and toast.

As the sisters tumbled down the Italianate-style stairs for their morning fare, Isabelle handed Wanda a box of Quaker Oats for *her* breakfast and told her, "You know where the water is. You best have yo' skank ass outa here -- on yo' way to school --

by the time I git back, or I'ma slap you into next week," Isabelle forewarned. "And wash them damn dishes!" she added.

A frown almost appeared on Wanda's face, but she thought better of it and quietly went about her assigned tasks. "And if you ain't out here by the time I git back, I'ma slap you into next week! I'ma put so much o' you on the flo' -- they gon' think it's the blood bank up in here!" The front door shut.

Isabelle drove her children to the archdiocesan educational enclave for a stimulating day of learning and social interaction at the historic Catholic institution for colored children.

As for Wanda, she began the long trek through the Seventh Ward to the Sixth Ward for her day of instruction at the school in the same historic area around the projects as Dooky Chase Restaurant and Willie Mae's Scotch House. She went to St. Bernard Avenue then out Johnson Street, where she saw the uniformed Corpus Christi children going about pre-class play within the school's freshly-installed picket fence.

After walking for what seemed like an eternity, she finally, breathlessly arrived at Phyllis Wheatley Elementary School, the 1954-designed, two-story "public institution for colored children" that was touted by smooth-tongued segregationists as one of New Orleans' "pioneering testaments to contemporary structural enterprise" and "a priceless design of provincial modernity." Its location was in the 2300 block of Dumaine up the street from *Marionneaux Maison de Maitre*, a portion of the old Leper Colony. The school was named after the African poet who was then widely acknowledged as the first, black, captive female bard in the United States. The architect originally had the intimidating mission of designing a building that could house some 800 students on two acres -- an area one-sixth the recommendation for that number of students. When it was finished area residents thought it was something out of a sci-fi movie due to its multi-colored outer and huge windows. Teachers were less enthused about the structure when they discovered the blackboard glare and empty stares of young scholars who would pay more attention to goings-on outside those outsized glass outlets -- focusing on real-world perils and menace from which the school was an island of impermanent refuge.

At each opportunity Wanda had throughout the day she crept into a corner of the girls' bathroom and wept.

* * *

On her walk back through the Seventh Ward that afternoon she stopped at Nora Navra Library, the branch of the New Orleans Public Library system a few blocks from her present residence. Nora Navra opened on a temporary basis in 1946 across from London Avenue at the intersection of St. Bernard and Prieur and was one of the first library branches to admit people of color. It became a permanent branch in 1956 when the city's iconic civil rights attorney, A.P. Tureaud, gave a rousing speech in which he said:

> ". . . Public facilities, which are provided on a racially segregated basis, are not only a drain on our economic resources, but are an outmoded relic of a slave psychology. Libraries tend to free the mind of bigotry and prejudice; they are supposed to be a civilizing influence on the community. We need more of them. . . ."

The tasteful brick building was eventually converted to a children's library serving the youth of the city's colored community.

Wanda delved into the stacks of children's books maintained by the repository's librarians, who once were little girls in pigtails, uniforms and two-tone saddle oxfords. She felt at ease with their calming, helpful manner, spic-and-span appearance, and welcoming encouragement as they referred her to books about mothers and daughters and flowers and the happinesses of heaven. She gathered their suggested tomes and read voraciously at one of the expansive wooden tables near the front-facing windows overlooking an isolated green space outside the one-story brick structure. She fancied herself in another time and place as she read of ladies and their knights and the people who were black before they were colored and her school's namesake and where babies came from and the stars and the sun and -- "Oh, Lawd!" she mouthed, sucking in air -- "I gotta git home!" She shut her worlds up, returned the books to the lady at the front desk for reshelving, and scurried back to the torment that she knew lay ahead.

* * *

Waiting for her (after a day of soap operas, smoking in bed and slumber), at the top of the front steps in a muted moo-moo, belt in hand, was her aunt-by-matrimony. "Bring yo' disgustin' rear end here! I'ma beat you like you stole sumthin'! Lazy cow!"

"I just stopped at the library -- "

"Shut up! I'ma knock fire from yo' ass!" she threatened as she menacingly raised THE BELT skyward.

"But I --"

"I said shut up! Don't let yo' mouth overload yo' ass!" she yelped as THE BELT found its mark across the child's neck, then her legs, then her arms and back, then everywhere one could imagine. She ducked and covered while her aunt-by-nuptials went nuclear. She could hear the two sisters giggling in the background as she endured the stinging licks and bruising blows. Her aunt-by-legal-proclamation then dragged her by her bristly hair to the kitchen where she tore open a one-pound bag of rice and poured its contents on the floor.

"Kneel, you li'l witch!" she ordered as she indicated that Wanda should position herself bare-kneed on the grains, hands behind her back with her nose touching the wall. "And you bet' not move!" warned the torturer's rabid voice. "If you move one inch I'ma slap the taste out yo' mouth!" And with that Isabelle left her to her misery.

Wanda knelt silently, almost whimpering, but afraid to allow the slightest sound to spring from her voicebox, for the wrath of the evil one would surely rear its ugly head and obliterate whatever part of her flesh and spirit that hadn't already been razed.

As she knelt, pouting and sniveling hour upon hour, she thought about her mother and the last warm and tender grasp they shared before she passed across that mystical divide between the living and the dead. She thought about her former life in the project, dangling her ashy legs in the wading pool behind the brick-encased housing units at Lemann Park, playing on the monkey bars and stepping in the red ant piles by the fence.

She remembered making necklaces from used spools of thread with her friends, running home just before the street lights came on, building cigar box altars with her mother, playing "sting butt", making bra-zeers with her friends' daddies' hainkachiffs, going to her neighbors' waistline parties, giving mosquito hogs tobacco to make them drunk, and smacking flies with rolled-up newspaper for her pet turtle (the secret was to stun and not smash them).

She recalled skating 'round and 'round -- "poppin' the whip" on the second floor of Phyllis Wheatley in her new bluejeans and Union skates her mother somehow managed to get her every Christmas, scurrying under a slowly moving train on the tracks in back of the project as a rite of passage, leaning over the bannister and naming the cars as they went by, buying penny candy from the sweet shop down the street from the Carver Theater, playing the medley of sidewalk games her mother and *her* mother and her mother before *her* took pleasure in, and . . .

" -- *You best git yo' tail up and git you sumthin to eat!*" stung Miss Isabelle's voice, interrupting her dreamlike trance. "I don't want you starvin' to death! Sweep up that rice and throw it in a pot with some water! That's gon' be yo' dinner for the next coupla days! And I don't mean *all* of it -- you know yo' eyes bigger than yo' stummick -- and wash yo' stinky ass! You smell like a pot o' chitlins! Then go by the door to my room and git that slopjar and empty it! Lawd, if you was a boy I'd put yo' simple-minded ass in a dress and make you sit outside on the front steps -- all day! I know what to do for yo' ass!"

Over the next stretch of weeks Wanda went about her chores diligently, her knees aching and her shoulders drooping. She washed and dried the dishes, emptied the garbage, washed and hung the clothes on the line, ironed everything, staggered to the Circle Food Store on St. Bernard and Claiborne to make groceries, cleaned everyone's bathtub rings, and swept the front steps.

"Didn't I tell you it's bad luck to sweep the front steps after dark!?!?!?" Miss Isabelle reminded her one evening, smacking a piece of hosepipe against her skull. "I don't need no bad luck. I'm 'bout to go over to church to the bingo; then I'm goin' over on Er-leens Street to the gamblin' house -- and I need all the luck I can git -- so git yo' black ass away from me! Don't touch me! And stay yo' greasy ass in the back --'cause I might bring some company home with me."

She found that the only solace and comfort she had was her frequent-as-possible visits across town to her mother's grave under the solitary chineyball tree where she would entreat her departed soul for its intercession in the unpleasant present that plagued and persecuted her. She told her mother how (when she was finally allowed to play with Florabelle and Corabelle) *she* was the one who had to chalk the hopscotch outline on the banket, how *she* was hit the hardest when playing dodge-the-ball, how *she* had to plait their fine strands of hair before attending to her own, how *she* had to wash the walls when *they* marked them up, how *she* was accused of being the one who instigated the use of the brand new clothesline for a jump rope, how *she* was blamed when someone used the last Dixie cup from the dispenser, how the other children went to visit relatives in California and went to Disneyland and saw Nat King Cole's house and *she* stayed home and painted their rooms, how the other children were decked out in little-girl bows and tutus and *she* sported their worn and weary hand-me-downs, how *she* couldn't go to the other girls' birthday parties (but had to clean up after), how *she* was taken to Sunday mass at Corpus Christi Church and made to sit in the last pew, how the daughters gave their mother manicures -- but *she* was assigned the pedicures, how the children would cackle through earsplitting readings of *The Story of Little Black Sambo* so she could hear them, how *she* was always the one who was sent to the corner store to get a pound of sugar or rice in brown paper bags, and how *she* wore yellow rain slicks in the winter while the other girls wore new P-coats.

The children were just as brutal and pitiless as their mother. They would taunt and tease Wanda to tears at playtime (if her chores were completed in a timely manner) with the malice of a primal potentate. At times they would engage in a call and response song that cruelly commented on her late mother, chanting rhythmically as they clapped hands:

"I'm so glad her maw is daid
"Handa Wanda, yo mom-ma
"Layin' in the ground with her legs all spread
"Handa Wanda, yo mom-ma

"Her big, black ass done gone to hell

"Handa Wanda, yo mom-ma
"She makin' the devil' weenie swell
"Handa Wanda, yo mom-ma

"Christmas she changed her dirty draws
"Handa Wanda, yo mom-ma
"Gave that ass to Santy Clause
"Handa Wanda, yo mom-ma. . .

"She went on down to Claiborne Street
"Handa Wanda, yo mom-ma
"Knelt right down and beat her meat
"Handa Wanda, yo mom-ma. . ."

One day Florabelle demanded, "Lemme see yo' hand."
"Why?" Wanda asked.
"That's for *me* to know and *you* to find out," came Florabelle's caustic reply.
Wanda extended a hand, palms down, then Florabelle remarked, "See, Cora -- momma said to watch her -- 'cause she might have light hands, but they black as her big nose. Looka them lips. They so big they look like a suitcase. Look like she goin' on a trip."
On another day they were skipping rope to a newly-discovered rhyme:

"Two-four-six-eight, we don't wanta in-te-grate
"Eight-six-four-two, we don't want no jig-a-boo. . ."

"I'm Florabelle, my sister' name' Corabelle, and she 'Dumbelle'," they would alternately say when introducing her to other children, remaining ever faithful to New Orleans blackfolks' rigid color-caste system. "We ain't like *her*," they'd tell their playmates. "We go to Corpus Christi. She go to Phyllis Weekly. We don't need no hot comb like her; we got *good* hair," they'd say, stroking the colorful *barrettes* her dexterous, dark hands had fastened to their ponytailed tresses. Sometime they would just mess with her just to be messy. "Wanda -- look!" they'd say.
"Huh?"

"I made you look, you dirty crook. You stole yo' momma pocketbook."

One day there was some change missing from the chiffarobe in Miss Isabelle's room. "I know you did it -- where is it? You went and spent it over at the sweet shop on Lapeyrouse? You done gave it to some nappy-haid boy?" Miss Isabelle interrogated her.

"I promise to Gawd I didn't do it," Wanda said, bracing herself for what was to come. That evening she got a beating so ruthless and relentless that its severity would not be repeated until decades later in the Rodney King incident.

The cruelty in the Gulag continued throughout her grade school years.

* * *

She attended Andrew J. Bell Junior High down the street towards the river from her grade school, then went to high school at the home of the mighty, mighty red and grey Joseph S. Clark Bulldogs over on Derbigny and Bayou Road, another colored institution from whence a wide ranging array of black professionals had graduated and gone on to the glory of distinguished careers in politics, the arts, the military, medicine, education and athletics.

The other girls went to St. Mary's Academy, a private, Catholic school (with a focus on training for entry into higher education) located in East New Orleans, a seeming infinity away from the Sixth Ward.

Bell and Clark both proved to be welcome respites from her pained subsistence in the Seventh Ward where she pursued her studies in the dim light of the washroom after her chores were completed. At Clark she discovered a sensitive staff of caring instructors and mentors, many of whom came from similar circumstances to her own. She was growing into the ripeness of young womanhood and bore her pained existence with increasing facility. But one day the sustained agony became a bit too much and she bent her head over her desk at the end of her afternoon homeroom session class and sobbed into her folded hands. Her teacher saw her still sitting there after the last bell had rung and approached her asking what was wrong. Was there something at school? At home? What would make her break down in such a manner?

They sat that afternoon and discussed the predicament she had found herself in after her mother's death. It was a time when parents and guardians had full reign in such matters. Teachers seldom committed the *faux pas* of violating the social taboo of interfering in someone's child-rearing practices and procedures no matter how dreadful their implementation. The age of litigation and *in loco parentis* had not yet come to full fruition. But her homeroom teacher reassured her, telling her of her own unprivileged roots and how she sought her liberation through education. She told her of the legions of the poor throughout history who had *made* their own bootstraps and achieved lives of fulfillment and great magnitude despite being born with wooden spoons in their mouths. They talked of such things until the hour came for her to leave in order to be on time for her evening duties.

"You make me so full," she told her homeroom teacher. "It hurt me to my heart to hafta leave you this evenin'. You make me happy to be nappy!" She laughed.

"Nappiness *is* happiness," her homeroom teacher smiled. It was the first time that someone had showed her affection and understanding since her mother grasped her closely on her deathbed.

Then it was Carnival time.

* * *

Carnival season was in full swing and the city was abuzz with anticipation of the gay parades and colorful, costumed balls at which the *crème de la crème* daughters of New Orleans upper middle class society would be introduced to the public in a series of formal black tie, ankle-length gown events. This year would be *extra*-special because Florabelle and Corabelle were graduating and this would be their last opportunity to connect with promising, properly-blooded young men in a forum that was welcome to their families' pedigree. The mayor's son, an Army Captain, was back from Vietnam and would be the guest of honor at the festivity, an opportunity which afforded some lucky lady a chance to meet one of the city's most eligible bachelors -- even if she were merely on the cusp of marryin' age.

Miss Isabelle spared no expense in preparing her daughters for the Dynamic Gentleman's Annual Cotillion Ball at the I.L.A. Hall uptown for which she had invitations for herself and her two daughters. She had her girls sized and fitted by the most expert *modistes* she could afford. She purchased their shoes at the most upscale Canal Street stores and invested in the most aromatic, man-catching perfumes imaginable. She nervously fretted about, training her girls in the same arts of sitting, standing, walking, and being lovingly ladylike that her mother had instructed *her* in and *her* mother had done before *her*. It was to be a faultless evening of precision and perfection.

"You kinky-haid devil! Don't let yo' black ass rub off on that dress!" she shouted to Wanda on the appointed night. Her daughters primped and primed themselves for their introduction to polite society while Wanda stroked the girls' smooth manes with a footlong, silverplated comb. "In fact -- git yo' black ass from out here," she ordered as the girls prepared for the outing. "*Move* -- or I'ma give you one second to draw a crowd at Canal and Rampart -- then I'ma beat the black off yo' ass! . . . *Go!*"

They left for the ball, leaving Wanda behind -- sorrowful and saddened that she wasn't involved in such a momentous occasion. She watched a little TV, read for a time, then decided to set out for the seclusion and solitude of the grave beneath the graveyard's chineyball tree.

She took the St. Bernard bus to the Broad, then walked up Orleans to Delgado Community College, hit a left and came to the rickety, rusty iron gates of the graveyard. The full, yellow moon lit her way through the hodge-podge of graves and homemade markers to the solemnity of her mother's burial place. She knelt under the shifting shadow of the chineyball tree, her hands clasped in homage to her mother's memory, pleading for relief from the fiendish deeds that caused her so much despondency and discontent.

Abruptly she heard a sound that gave the impression of someone sharply snapping his (her?) fingers. She turned toward the sound and saw a tall figure in a purple velvet tuxedo (with red accents) and the largest pair of pink high heels she had ever seen. She stood back a bit, startled at the sudden spectacle just a few feet away, astonished that anyone else would be out and about on such a night that loomed with preternatural mystery and the dark magic of adoration's embrace.

"Who . . . what . . . who are you?' she asked the lofty figure, who leaned coolly on a red, brass-handled, beaded walking cane.

"Me?" asked the figure in an affected baritone.

"Yes . . . *you*. Who . . . wh-- *what* are you?'

"Who? Who? Well, I'm certainly not an owl," the figure said flippantly.

"But where did you . . . how did . . . ?!?!?!!!"

"I'm the Fairy Godbrother, honey."

"Fairy God*brother*?"

"Didn't you read the book?" (he?) asked. "Oh, I get it . . . you must've gone to one of *those* schools."

"I know about fairy tales -- and *mo'*. My life ain't been no crystal stair."

"I know. That's why I've been summoned."

"Summoned? From where? By who?"

"That's for *me* to know . . . and *you* to find out," he said with a flourishing fingersnap.

"But in the book it was a lady who -- " she started. Then -- "My momma used to read me -- I thought it was s'posed to be a Fairy God*mother*."

"-- Gender equity, honey. . ."

"Don't be gittin' salty with me," the former project-dwelling girl warned.

"'Salty' isn't the word for it," he said, licking his forefinger playfully.

"Then what are you here for?

"Well, baby . . . in my world the bottom rail always comes to the top."

"What does *that* mean?" Wanda asked, surprised that she was even entertaining a conversation with whatever this was standing before her.

"I have no idea, honey. It's just something I picked up on my last expedition."

"But why are you here? In the middle of the graveyard? What are you *doing* here?"

"Well," he said, leaning slickly against the chineyball tree, "I'm here to grant you . . . I'm here to . . . give you . . . Aw, I'm here to get you up off your little tushy and hook you up to go to the ball."

"The ball? I can't go there. I wasn't invited. I don't have an invitation."

"Honey, the way I'm about to lay you out, *you'll* be the only invitation you'll need. Watch *this!*" he said fingersnapping once in the air.

Immediately a nearby milk crate transformed into the latest model convertible, a pink Excalibur with every bell, button and whistle imaginable. Another fingersnap produced properly-prescribed formal shoes, a splendidly-tailored red evening gown (plus tiara and highly wrought hairdo) where her thong sandals, hand-me-downs and nappy, barrette-clasped links once were. Two fingersnaps and a twist literally lifted her off her feet and gently sat her in the Excalibur's passenger seat. Then they were off to the big, bad bash with a double fingersnap and wrist twist.

They arrived at the hall, pulling up to the entrance where he got out, opened her door, and gallantly assisted her in emerging from the convertible's fine leather interior. "Just one thing, honey," he told her as he drove off. "I'll be here to get you at 3AM *sharp*. If you stay out any longer than that then the magic will fade off into the sunset . . . like *me* . . .*"* And the Great Pretender disappeared into the nearest dark street corner's moonlit merriment.

Just outside the hall's entry two uniformed NOPD officers on paid detail were checking invitations and IDs, for there were a number of civic officials and persons of means inside including the mayor and his son, who had single-handedly been responsible for saving the lives of several of his comrades by holding off dozens of Viet Cong and NVA regulars while his men made a successful retreat.

Wanda showed them her invite, then stepped through a chorus of *oohs* and *ahs* towards the ballroom floor that was flanked on either side by ranks of gown-wearing ladies and tuxedo-clad gents. She blended into the grand elegance of the dance, mingling with those entranced by the entertainment hall's trappings of splendor. The sisters and their mother saw her, but didn't recognize the refined, chic lady in red as the target of their malevolence.

She entered a receiving line that wound its way to the young, uniformed war hero captain, curtsying and smiling broadly when he slyly, slickly asked her for a dance. They waltzed and boogied to the beat as the time rolled on towards the wee-est of hours, their eyes drawn to each other like liquefied magnets, oblivious to the delightful peasantry and seasonal royalty encircling and surrounding.

As they swayed and swung and laughed, hitting it off big time, she noticed that the hour was approaching about which she had been forewarned. She blah-zayed a bit more with the handsome warrior, informed him that she had to fix her face and powder her nose, but left the animated gathering through a side door leading to a noiseless side street where the Fairy Godbrother was laid back in the 'calibur's driver's seat awaiting her. Just as the car's clock showed it was quarter-to-three she gave him directions for the Seventh Ward address and they raced off in the moonlight away from the night's fun and frolic.

They screeched to a halt in front of the house as she peered around to see if her aunt's car was there. He let her off with a wave of his hand as the clock struck three and her tiara turned back into the cheap plastic barrette, her shoes became well-worn rubber flip-flops, and her dress shifted back into the drab, colorless hand-me-downs.

She watched the Fairy Godbrother clinging to a flying milk crate as he flew out of sight into the cloudless, starry night sky.

At the dance, the young former combatant was disheartened when she didn't return from her alleged nose-powdering and only found a tuft of brown, kinky hair clinging to his uniform. He inquired of the policemen on the door as to whom she might be, then asked some of the after-partiers if they knew who she was.

The next day Miss Isabelle, ever the opportunist, got wind of his inquiries and suggested to a friend that she contact him and have him meet her daughters, who might know who the lady in red was. In reality she saw such a proposed meeting as an opening to have her offspring meet him on a more controlled basis.

The following weekend he arrived at their home and was greeted by Miss Isabelle and her daughters as Wanda prepared the front dining room table for brunch. After a brief introduction and elucidation for the basis of his visit he removed the ball of hair from a small white envelope and approached Florabelle, but even Ray Charles could see that it was no match for her wavy, cream-colored mane. He then compared the ball of fuzz to Corabelle's silky tresses, but could plainly see that her auburn skin was not the same as the midnight-black, velvety outer of the fancy dancer in the crimson garb. Then he noticed Wanda at the table, as she bent over place settings and finger food she had prepared. Something about her seemed familiar despite the black and white aproned servant's attire her aunt had her wear for the gentleman's visit.

"Let's see if the hair matches *her*," he recommended as he sweetstepped nearer.

"Her?!??" her aunt-by-wedding-ceremony exclaimed.

"Of course. We might as well . . . since we're all in this together."

He held the tiny chunk of hair to her head and *VOILA!!!* It was a perfect match.

The three Seventh Ward witches were shocked that this object of their disaffection could possibly be the damsel desired by the strikingly handsome gentleman and expressed their displeasure at being so insulted by his obviously repugnant choice. He, however, insisted that he and Wanda be allowed to speak unchaperoned, and they were led to a side gallery overlooking an ivy-covered garden. He told her of his intentions towards her, but she informed him that she should speak on the subject in everyone's presence, so they went back into the house, almost catching the sisters as they hopped from a window where they had been eavesdropping. Then she said some things that had been on her mind for a long long time.

"I'm really, truly feelin' good 'bout myself that a man so handsome -- and *rich* -- and from all them connected people in his family is all after me and everything -- pursuin' my affections and such," she said, using some of the vocabulary words that she got from a book given her by her homeroom teacher. "But even though a man' smooth talkin' might mean a lot, they's sumthin' in my life that's mo' important to me right now.

"I got what they call a 'mentor' at school who I been talkin' to . . . about the way I been treated over the years since I been here . . . how y'all all made what shoulda been the most bestest years o' my childhood a livin' hell. . . . The point is -- I don't need you, Miss Isabelle, or *you*, or *you*," she said, indicating her daughters. "And I definitely don't need no man comin' in my life right now and makin' it worse than what it is. . . . What I need is my education. And what y'all don't even know is I been accepted into the Upward Bound summer program at Loyola -- the program I'm gon' finish and git a full scholarship to college.

"I done found over the years that I don't need nobody but *me*. *I'm* the only one done took the whippins. *I'm* the only one done did the cleanin' and cookin'. *I'm* the only one was ever cussed at and *I'm* the only one who know that piece o' paper that's gon' help me help girls like me who ain't never had no help.

"That said, I ain't gon' allow nobody to beat me or tease me or starve me into a skeleton . . . not no mo'. . . . Things gon' change 'round here over the next couple of months . . . 'til I graduate . . .'fore I move into the dorms. If anybody put a hand on me again -- I'm gon' go by my legal rights and have 'em dealt with. I been readin' up on that. . . . If anybody use they mouth to beat me down . . . they just might end up bein' *beat* down. As a young girl . . . as a woman . . . as somebody who's gon' *be* somebody . . . that's all I have to say."

And she cast off the apron as they stood in awe of her words and demeanor.

She successfully completed the six-week Upward Bound summer experience, attended undergraduate school, got accepted to Southern University's School of Social Work where she earned an MSW, received a doctoral degree from Columbia University, lectured widely on child abuse and bullying, founded a nationwide mentoring program for "at-risk" female juveniles, never wedded,

and lived hiply ever after.

August 2011
Stamford, CT

Professor Arturo

The Jewelry
(from *The Jewelry* by Guy de Maupassant)

Mr. LeBlanc became inflamed, entrapped in the heat of the young woman's loveliness like a roach in a microwave oven when he met her at a party given by the Senior Manager of his company's Office of Clinical Excellence Assurance. She was a woman of humble origins, the daughter of a room service waiter at the Roosevelt Hotel just off Canal Street. Her father had been dead for some time and her mother made several clandestine visits to the oak-shaded, Uptown homes of several old-moneyed Garden District bachelors for whom she worked as a domestic in the anticipation that she could snare a provider of some solidity and permanence for her daughter. After the father's death, they were impoverished and reputable, calm and temperate. The young woman appeared to be the epitome of that perfect storm of faith, trust and goodness in whom many young men might invest their future. Her simple, serene Southern beauty had a magnetism of innocence and the playful pout on her duckface lips appeared to be a reflection of her soul.

Everyone who chanced to interact with her intoned praises of adoration for her and insisted that any man who wed her would indeed be fortunate, for there could be no better marriage prospect in all of womanity. She was top shelf quality. Where other women were considered nosey -- she was "impudently curious." Where others drove used cars, she motored "pre-owned vehicles." She considered herself "aesthetically unchallenged" rather than "pretty," and used "body cleansers" rather than soap, "figure enhancers" rather than girdles, and had a "monthly visitor," where others had periods.

Mr. LeBlanc, who was then Assistant Manager in the company's Office of Clinical Excellence Assurance (with a lower mid-level management compensation package), proposed to her, and they became linked in holy matrimony in the church where he had served as an altar boy at several such ceremonies. They learned to relate to each other without the need to dominate, control or destroy.

He was infinitely blissful with her, and she administered the affairs of his home (and his lower mid-level management salary) so efficiently that they appeared to live a life of lavishness and comfort. She transformed the single family *maison de maitre* on Duels Street (which had been willed to him by his father) into an artwork complete with marbleized plastic birdbaths, circa 1880 French bronze, three-light candelabras, and French Provincial, carved elm, double-door armoires. She smothered him with every pleasure imaginable: warm baths and back rubs, gentle embraces, massages, manicures, magnificent New Orleans-style meals, and those midnight marital acts of passion that are inflamed by new romance and refresh old ones. She was indeed ahead of her time, so much that six years after they were married, he loved her even more than he did when he first caught sight of her eye-entrapping outer.

* * *

There were only two things about her with which he found perturbing: her irresistible urge to attend every concert performance in town with "Girlfriend" -- and her addiction to costume jewelry.

She had social contact with the wives of several of his working-class colleagues, who were always gifting her with complimentary tickets to seemingly every concert in town from the Saenger Theater on Canal Street to the UNO Lakefront Arena. She would often convince her husband to accompany her to these performances, where she could secure front-row seats at will. He preferred watching the cable news and falling asleep in his Stratolounger after a demanding day of audit documentation, sales training of entry-level personnel, developing time management seminars to improve daily operations, managing contact sales lists, and performing all other duties as assigned by the Senior Manager. He would entreat her to attend the frequent events with her female associates who would see her safely home after the shows. She was a bit sad about it at first because she thought it might not look too well for a married woman to be about so frequently unaccompanied by her spouse, but she consented to his wishes in order to give him pleasure, an act for which he felt eternally grateful.

Night-tripping to such an extent eventually inspired a desire in her for more of the newest, most fashionable arrivals. Her closet was filled with items that accentuated her uncomplicated allure, but she got into the practice of wearing what she said were two imitation diamond earrings, simulated pearl necklaces, replica gold bracelets, and tiaras with counterfeit precious stones.

Her husband, who was taken aback a bit by her fondness for glimmering, shining baubles and beads, would often say, "Sweetheart -- you have a natural beauty that doesn't have to be gilded. Your beauty is as profound as the summer sun's heat in August and as powerful as the Mississippi's undercurrents. You're blessed with an innate beauty possessed by few women."

She would just smile at him impishly and say, "I like what I like. I know that your intention is meant to be positive, but each to her own. This is what I like. I've just always loved jewelry so much. Don't make me over."

She would then finger the necklaces and gemstones, making the crystals sparkle in the light and tell him, "Look at how well made these things are. You'd swear they were real."

He would merely smile and tell her, "You have the tastes of a St. Charles Avenue fancy woman. Inside, you're just like one of those Garden District ladies."

At times in the evening when they were discussing the day's unevents, she would break out the wooden box they had brought back from their Mexican vacation two summers ago, spill her "stash" on the coffee table, and scrutinize her trinkets and ornaments with ardent glee, as though she were experiencing the throes of orgasm in fondling her jumbles of joy. She was adamant in placing one of the necklaces around her husband's collar while expressing amusement, giggling until she couldn't laugh any longer. She would tell him how comical he looked, then embrace him and kiss him fanatically.

One chilly winter night after a "girls' night out" jaunt to a performance by Sade, she came back running a high fever and complaining of chills. The next day she had a terrible cough and spat blood through her silken, now chafed lips. The tongue that once teased him so flirtatiously became infected and swollen with excretion. Eight days after that, after an extreme weight loss, blood in her urine, night sweats and fatigue, she died.

* * *

Following her death, LeBlanc found himself so grief-stricken that he cried uncontrollably at the thought of no longer seeing her beatific smile, hearing her laughter or enjoying the sumptuous bliss to be had by her pleasurous, velvety lips, and the carefully-choreographed moves of the hidden valley of her aromatic spices. She had taught him a trick or four. He kept her clothes in the closet (just as she left them) in an abortive attempt at retaining some semblance of her presence.

He walked around the neighborhood for days, showing her picture to total strangers who thought him more than a trifle odd. He sat on their bed for hours, gazing expectantly at a ribbon of light from the cracked bedroom, yearning for her to draw close in a sheer, see-through baby doll nightie and regale him with tall tales and stylish evocations of how her jewelry made her feel so majestic and magnificent. His hair fell out and his teeth decayed from disregard. He felt a cosmic imbalance between his body and soul, not knowing which was more wrecked at her departure, as he sobbed unreservedly at work.

He noticed that the bills were coming in like immense, swirling, whirling, swiftly moving clouds before a hurricane. He ended up pawning their car to a moneylender in the East and made regular visits and special novenas to the Shrine of St. Jude, the patron saint of hopeless causes. His earthly appetites were few, but things were askew and he found himself in a quandary of economic anxiety due to his wife no longer being there to tend to their household affairs as proficiently as she had in spite of his lower mid-level management compensation package.

Desperate to alleviate his clogged cash flow, he decided to take some of his wife's jewelry to one of the neighborhood's "special men" that he knew from high school. His old friend would possibly give him money enough for some of the jewelry to at least enable him to eat for a few days or so. That night he closed his fear-filled eyes and slept through a deafening, thunderous downpour.

The next day the last vestiges of the overnight rain had ceased and a fire-red sun was a massive ball of flame against a cloudless skyscape of dauntless blue. It was an unseasonably warm day as he casually entered the front door of an Orleans Avenue gambling den and was escorted to a back room to present what was purported to be a diamond-studded, 24-inch gold herringbone chain he thought might be attractive enough to his friend who (among his legally permissible and prohibited occupations) fancied himself a gemologist. A sunglassed coadjutant leaned against the door, arms folded, a slight bulge in the vest pocket of his suit.

He stood before the special man, who was gumming a cigar while seated in a ten-gallon Stetson and well-tailored suit behind a marble-topped desk under a picture of him shaking hands with Muhammad Ali. "I want to see what I can get for this," LeBlanc mouthed humbly as he reached into the pocket of his blue blazer and handed him the chain.

"What you got there?" his friend asked with a prudent curiosity.

"It's just a little something that my wi -- uh, *I* had around the house," he said through perjuring eyes.

"Yeah-ya right!" his friend said. "Lemme see that." He examined the chain closely, applied some chemicals to it, then used a jeweler's glass to assess the piece's relative value. "Hmmm. . ." he murmured. "Nice symmetry. I don't see any misaligned facets. No imperfections. No blemishes. The proportioning is nice. The purity of the color's *sweet*. The girdle looks good. The finish is superb. You sure this ain't hot? I cain't afford no bid. I'm on probation for this right now."

"It's not hot. It's *mine*," he assured his soberly candid friend.

"I'll give you 12 big ones for it," his friend offered.

"Twelve?" LeBlanc asked, puzzled. "It's worth --"

"All right -- 15! But that's high as I'm goin'! I don't usually keep that kinda green around here all the time."

"Fifteen?" LeBlanc asked him. Then said to himself -- *Fifteen hundred? For a piece of junk jewelry? This is my lucky day.*

"**Let him have it**," the neighborhood "special man" baritoned to his assistant barring the door. "Give him 15 thou." *Fifteen thousand?* thought LeBlanc. *I know we were tight in high school, but . . .*

The warm body in the gun-packed suit walked over to a safe, opened it, counted out 150 Benjamins, and rested the stack in LeBlanc's trembling hands.

"Uh -- you got some mo' o' this, bruh?" asked his friend, desire twitching from his now-widened eyes. "I know somebody who might be interested in summa this. If you can git some mo' o' this -- and it's clean --"

"I can get some more. I can get you all you want."

"Here. Take this number. Ask for 'Big Man.' Tell him I told you to call. I'll let him know you callin'."

That afternoon he took the Broad bus to McKenzie's in Gentilly and ordered a 20-piece chicken box -- with fries. In the evening he fell asleep on the couch surrounded by stripped chicken bones and dried French fries.

* * *

The next day he bagged up some of the jewelry and found himself on the uptown-bound St. Charles Avenue streetcar passing Lee Circle. He daydreamed of a life of good fortune and wisdom in an elegant uptown avenue home if someone would actually be dumb enough to pay such an amount for something with such minimal value. *The DJ doesn't show, but the party grooves on,* he thought.

The friend of his friend was as happy as a sissy with a life sentence in open population when LeBlanc poured the contents of the Schwegmann bag on the dining room table of a well-manicured home. LeBlanc giggled with glee as the glitter and gloss of its blingfest of bangles, necklaces, earrings, chains, anklets, rings, watches and beads met a pair of keen, ravenous eyes. The friend of his friend appraised the spectacle lying before him, did some calculations on his Blackberry and announced -- "TWO HUNDRED AND SIXTY THOUSAND!!!"

"Two-hundred sixty?" quizzed LeBlanc. "Is that all? How about -- " he began to negotiate.

"Okay – three hundred. And that's as far as I'll go."

"*Bet,*" said LeBlanc as he shook his hand. "Cash?"

"*Hard* cash," the friend of his friend agreed. *And I still have even more,* thought LeBlanc, as the friend of his friend handed him several large envelopes swollen with ready money.

* * *

On his way back from Uptown he took a cab instead of hopping the streetcar. Rather than chowing down on an order of fried chicken from one of the local spots, he decided to feast at a touristy, upscale French Quarter dining establishment. After enjoying a sumptuous meal (and complaining about the service and not tipping), he went to a drugstore on Esplanade Avenue to pick up a prescription that had languished there for quite a while due to his previous economically-challenged status.

As he exited the glass doors of the family-owned corner store, an awkward silence entered his heart. His head began to speak volumes of truth to him, truths that had somehow eluded him in his indulgence and dissipation. *The jewelry . . . she got the jewelry from . . . when she was telling me . . .*

His head spun, and he zonked out.

An unknown span of time later he woke up on a bench in the emergency ward of Charity Hospital, reached in his pockets for the money-stuffed envelopes, assured himself that nothing was awry, and left after complaining of the medley of impoverished souls who were waiting for service along with his now-prosperous self. He walked to City Park and stared for a while at a huge statue of P.G.T. Beauregard, the Civil War traitor/general. He was loose as a goose. He called his job and officially resigned -- then thought about going out to one of the strip clubs in the East, but opted instead for some of the gentlemen's clubs on Bourbon Street. *No more office skanks,* he thought, as he engaged in uncivil discourse with a bevy of lap-dancing, busty and bronzed good-time girls while sipping bottomless flutes of champagne.

"Chow belly, baby," he said to them. *WOW! This young stuff is like fresh tuna in spring water*, he told himself in ever-escalating rhetoric. *Old man 'Cain't' is dead -- and I helped bury him!* He rented a sportin' gal and got the handjob of the century in the shadows on the side of St. Louis Cathedral. For two years he was on a constant binge in which he passed the time in wanton desire, insane recklessness, terrifying depravity, and epic debauchery.

He eventually quieted down and met the second Mrs. LeBlanc who talked incessantly, suffered from habitual flatulence and made him the most miserable wedded person in all humankind.

September 2011
Stamford, CT

Jazz Stories: *From Katrina to Connecticut*

The Necklace
(from *The Necklace* by Guy de Maupassant)

She was one of those strikingly natural beauties from the lower Ninth Ward born into a family of porters and chambermaids, domestic workers in the Crescent City's hospitality industry. She had no titled position, no panoramic vision of a prosperous future, no name recognition in the city's elevated social circles. She eventually "married up," to a George Washington Carver High School teacher who wed her in an unpretentious civil ceremony at City Hall.

She made her own clothes (having been taught the art of seaming, stitching and hemming by her mother), dressed fashionably for her station in life as a school teacher's spouse, and found that women of her social order and untitled status could still be favored due to their loveliness and style despite their unprivileged lineage. She was naturally fine, quick-witted, limber of intellect and knowledgeable (in spite of her life's circumstances) and was the equal of any woman of alleged superior extraction and affluence.

She felt that being married to a teacher at an inner city public school was beneath her station and longed for the sumptuousness of the luxurious, laid-back lifestyle to which she had been made privy through her fantasized forays across the seductive, color-slick pages of the glossy home accentuation magazines that graced the Rosenberg's Furniture coffee table in their sparsely decorated living room. She longed for the trappings of other eras that would liberate her from her unfulfilled present: the circa 1800 Georgian inlaid mahogany tallcase clock and the circa 1900 pair of continental silver urns that she saw at an estate auction, the Kimball armoire that was on sale for 30% off at the furniture and accessories store on Royal Street off Canal, the enviable addresses in East New Orleans, ornate valences overlooking authentic Victorian chairs, her neighbor's tufted red velvet psychiatrist's couch, 19th-century quarter-sawn oak dining tables, and Oak Street intellectual gatherings where poets would present their wayward words and wit.

At dinner when he returned from the coaching responsibilities for which he had contracted at the high school, her husband would express his fondness for the simplest meal that she prepared, saying, "This is the most magnificent meal I've ever had," for she would concoct the most upmarket meals imaginable from his school teacher's salary that would pleasure the palate of even the most demanding gastronome.

She had a decent closet but no designer dresses, jewels or gems save for the cubic zirconia ring her husband had given her upon his proposal. Seven years it had been now since he had promised to purchase a ring she thought might be more representative of his perpetual affection for her.

She had a rich girlfriend, her former kindergarten classmate who worked at the school board and married a politician. She habitually visited their two-story, center-hall house with the delicate arched opening, imbibing exotic liquors and foreign wines while the woman regaled her with tales of shopping trips and vacations to far-off locales of which she could only fantasize.

One evening her husband came home from work and announced that he had a surprise for her. He produced a monogrammed packet and told her, "Here is something you might like."

She tore open the covering, hoping there might be a large amount of money inside, but was still agreeably surprised to find an invitation to the Mayor's Ball, one of the most prestigious events to be held that season. The envelope said:

> "His honor, the Mayor of New Orleans, requests your presence at. . ."

After reading the raised lettering on the glossy invitation she casually laid it on the coffee table with an affected glower. "You actually think I can go there . . . in proper finery?"

"Camille," he said. "Every powerful politician and anybody who's somebody will be there. I went through hell and high water to get that invitation. I thought it was the kind of thing that you would wish to do."

"I might wish it," she spat, "but I can't attend an affair like that! I don't have anything appropriate enough to put on my back."

That possibility had never entered his mind and he said, "Just wear the same thing you wear when we go to church. What about the stuff you wear when you go to see your old classmate?"

"Are you for real?" she asked, two bogus tears trickling from her eyes.

"What's the problem?" he asked. "I'm doing the best I can. I went through a lot to get what li'l I got. But if it's going to cost something to get you a new dress, we'll just have to make do. I tried my best."

"Your best isn't good enough," she stammered, stifling the tears. She went to their vintage computer, did some computations, and came up with an offer he couldn't refuse. "I think I can manage a dress, some shoes, and the hairdresser and a manicure and a pedicure for about $800."

"EIGHT HUNDRED DOLLARS?!?!" he protested. "We're not trying to *buy* the place. We just want to *go* there." *There goes my computer upgrade,* he thought. Then -- "Okay, baby," he said, hugging her. "I have enough set aside for what you want to do. I'll have to defer my dream of doing something else, but if it'll please you . . ."

"Thank you. Thank you, darling," she said before giving him the most intense night of pleasure they had shared since their wedding night.

* * *

The night of the ball was almost upon them and she appeared a bit edgy and ill at ease as the hour approached.

"What's up with you?" he asked her one day as she slammed down a frying pan in the kitchen, making him think someone was breaking and entering their humble haven. "What up? You haven't been acting like yourself lately."

"What's up is I don't have all of what I want for the ball."

"But we just paid Lord & Taylor my . . . *our* computer money for you to put something on your back."

"That's exactly the point," she squabbled. "I have something for my back and my feet, but that's all."

"Well, what else do you need?" he asked.

"I need something shiny. I need something shimmering. I need something to accent the dress. If I don't get something -- I'd rather just stay home and watch the Shopping Channel all night."

"Baby," he said, "your beauty is not going to be enhanced by some metal or some rocks on a string. A rose or two in your hair in the Billie Holiday style will do you just as well."

"But I don't want to go there and look like a re-ject hood rat from some ghetto gangsta movie. The other women there will be dressed to the tens. I can't go there looking like just anything with everybody else looking like they'll be looking."

"Tell you what -- why don't you try to go to your rich friend and tell her that you want to borrow some trinket or bracelet or something -- just for overnight -- and you'll return it to her the day after the ball."

"Oh -- " she sighed. "I didn't think of that. I guess that's why I married an educated man," she said as she kissed him smoothly just under his left ear, inviting him to a foray of salacious entrenchment in the delectable delights of the innermost depths of her passion.

* * *

She went to her friend's home the next day and related her dilemma. Her friend guided her to her master bedroom's huge closet and emerged with a fine Corinthian leather-covered case in which she kept her jewelry. "Choose whatever you'd like," she offered as she spilled the contents onto her well-draped, king-sized bed.

Camille scrutinized the shiny spherical shapes before her. A string of pearls caught her searching eyes. She didn't know whether they were cultured or farmed, nacreous or iridescent, from pearl oysters or mussels. All she knew was that they were perfectly round and smooth and would excite the envy of the other ladies present at the ball. She thanked her friend ardently then left to make preparations for the blacknificent affair.

The night of nights finally arrived and she was the finest among New Orleans' finest as she mixed and mingled with the biggest of wigs, delightfully dancing to the orchestra's jazzy rhythms. She was the bubbling belle of all balls as she drifted from table to table, the envy of the other women and the attention of the men, while her husband sat quietly in a corner with three other male attendees whose wives were whirling around the ballroom in their frantic fantasies.

Finally the clock struck the wee-est of hours and it was time to depart to real world truth. The other women were draping themselves with fancy furs while she had only a dime store outer garment from a secondhand shop in Gentilly. She wanted to make a quick getaway from the cloakroom, but her husband told her she should lay back until he hailed a cab, cautioning that she might catch a cold because of the sweat that now saturated her dress. She joined him anyway, going down the stairs and leaving the scene. They walked from the hall to Canal Street, then to Bourbon Street where they would be more certain to contract a cab. They did and were taken to the unassuming home in which they dwelt, as he reminded her that he had early morning classes and was glad to finally get home.

As they were undressing, a painful look came over her painted face. She shrieked, "It's not here! I lost it! I lost it!"

"*Now* what's the matter?'

"I lost her necklace," she said, her voice trembling at the very thought. "I can't find the necklace."

They looked in her purse, her coat, her bra, her pantyhose, everywhere. No necklace. He re-dressed and returned to the hall and asked the janitors if they found anything resembling the pearl necklace, but they denied any knowledge of any such article. He retraced their steps from the hall through Canal Street to Bourbon Street and even found their cab driver. No necklace.

He got back about 7 AM, cancelled the classes at which he was to give examinations, and even went to police headquarters on Tulane and Broad, but came up with nothing. Back home, flustered and frustrated, he suggested that she should simply call her friend, tell her that the necklace was lost and they would make amends in lieu of it not being returned. Her stubborn pride caused her to refuse to do so and worry aged her five years over a week's time.

They went to several jewelers hoping to find a replacement for the necklace, but were disappointed with each inquiry for days of high and low searching. Finally, they came to a shop where they found a similar necklace priced at $180,000. He had a few grand in his retirement account at work and cashed it in. He got a night job as a porter at Harrah's Casino to supplement his income while they scrimped and scrounged every penny they could get to pay for the duplicate. She started cleaning uptown mansions day and night while taking in ironing for some of their bachelor neighbors. They both worked day and night, sold the house and their possessions, then moved to an efficiency rental in her old lower Ninth Ward neighborhood in order to economize what was becoming a mere trickle of a cash flow. They begged, borrowed, and stole every penny they could muster, including a fund his students had set aside for a class trip they intended to take come graduation. They lost weight and also lost whatever friends they had who loaned them money that they never paid back.

Finally they were able to purchase the replacement piece and she proudly brought it to her friend, who didn't seem too bothered that she took a bit more time than promised to return it. She returned to her husband, satisfied in the fact that the indebtedness was paid, and they lived in abject poverty due to accrued debts for nearly twenty years. The smoothness of her skin became wrinkled ridges. Her hands became as seasoned and wellworn as those of a United Farm worker. He often fell asleep in front of his classes because of his night duties at the casino, and they both cursed the day that the wretched piece of jewelry entered their lives.

Many years hence, one afternoon as she was walking with buckets, a broom, a mop and caustic cleaning agents towards a home she tended to on Louisiana Avenue, she chanced to see her friend strolling merrily towards her down the street. The lady hesitated for a second as she gazed deeply at the fractured, limping figure toting the array of cleaning materials. "Camille," she asked. "Is that you? What in the world? What happened to you?" she inquired as she embraced her long lost friend.

"What happened to me? Maybe I should confess."

"What do you mean? Confess what?"

"The necklace. I didn't return it. I didn't really give you back the necklace I borrowed."

"Necklace? What necklace?" her friend quizzed, looking into her hollow, haunted eyes.

"The one you let me borrow for the Mayor's Ball -- years ago. I -- *we've* only had misery and sorrow in our lives ever since then. I lost it and bought another and now I'm . . . we're spending our days and nights paying for it."

"'Paying for it'? What do you mean?"

"We found one just like it. We lost our home, our friends . . . we're up to our grey hairs in debt . . . just to pay you back all the money you paid for that demonic trinket."

"Camille -- " her friend said, clasping her by her shoulders and looking intently into her eyes. "*Gir-ir-ir-irl* -- the necklace I loaned you wasn't a *real* pearl necklace. I caught that string of fake pearls one Carnival -- at the Zulu Parade."

September 2011
Stamford, CT

Professor Arturo

A Mardi Gras Mambo
(from *A Christmas Carol* by Charles Dickens)

It was Lundi Gras, the day before the day of days. Bourgeois and Beauchard Insurance Co., an unpretentious, glass-fronted, one-story brick and mortar building on Claiborne Avenue, sat just off Basin Street across from the Lafitte Project, a mid-20th- century strip of red-bricked, low-rise public housing for economically-challenged urbanites. B & B Insurance, as it was known in its less-than-prime-time AM radio commercials, was a time-dishonored neighborhood institution that offered "total coverage from quote to claim."

The city's pre-Interstate 10 Sixth Ward (when it *was* the Sixth Ward and not generally designated by its natives as "Treme") in which it was located then boasted a thriving urban stomping ground of sumptuously towering oaks, dental and doctor's offices, barbershops, hair salons, cleaning establishments, restaurants, shoe parlors, churches, drugstores, gambling dens, markets, haberdashers, tailor and printing shops, and of course, nightclubs. Jukebox songs were six for a quarter.

In B & B's office, a hollow-faced Billy Bourgeois, a portly man with spook-brown, properly-polished brogan shoes, "pawnshop special" suit, already-thinned gray hair, a prominent mole on his nose, horn-rimmed glasses, and a Snidely Whiplash moustache, sat on a raised platform under a humming ventilation shaft at a makeshift desk composed of cinderblocks and a decrepit door that offered him an uninterrupted catbird seat view of his only employee, his nephew, Freddie. Freddie's back was visible as he went about his conventional, commonplace chores while (Bourgeois hoped) not engaging in non-work related activities on the IBM Selectric typewriter that the company paid a then-unpretty penny for. A bronze replica of Napoleon's death mask sat next to Billy's cereal-in-a-cup lunch near an antiquated black rotary phone and a mini-plaque that said, "A Faith-based Business."

Adjacent to his midday meal was a one-gallon plastic container that he had been refilling with tap water for as long as anyone could remember. Behind him stood a handmade placard that proclaimed "TIME IS MONEY."

Bourgeois, a charter member of DOMEO (Dirty Old Men Eating Out) and lifetime associate of the Metropolitan Slime Commission, was bent over an underwriter's wheel reviewing actuarial details with robotic precision. He had framed the first nickel he made as a child when he charged the neighborhood children five cents to watch a then-state of the art black & white TV in his Sixth Ward backyard. The framed nickel hung to his right, adjacent to a shelf full of business and "Best Practices" awards and memorabilia. To his left, written in red, broad-tipped marking pen ink on a whitewashed wall, was "You can't do business from an empty wagon."

A grizzled old man *sans merci,* his life was a blizzard of statistics. He had a prodigious appetite for money and was indifferent to everything but his own ambition. Some years past Burnell Beauchard, his longtime business partner and only facsimile of a friend, staggered into the now-defunct Club 77 down Claiborne Street on Mardi Gras Day, hit the deck facedown, quaked, tremored and twisted a bit, and died with his spiritless scowl staring from the barroom floor at an array of rank and file, stewed and plastered, costumed observers. The party still didn't stop and they cut loose and buckdanced over and around his remains all night. The autopsy indicated that he died of consumption and gave up the ghost when his body finally wasted away from years of bawdyhouse bingeing and livin' that life. He had a bang-up send-off (paid for courtesy of a B & B policy) and was now long gone, rotten and forgotten by his pitiless progeny who so despised him.

"Hey, Unk!" called Freddie. He smiled through a set of flashing white teeth while jamming to a Mardi Gras anthem on a rickety AM radio. "I just got a call from Miss --"

"Don't call me that," Bourgeois sizzled for the umpteenth time. "Don't call me 'Unk.' We're at work. Let's keep the relationship professional! It's 'MR. Bourgeois.' This is a place of business -- not some second line parade." (Second lines were often impromptu, raucous rituals of street dancing, high spirits, music and mirth that took place at the drop of a brassy note.) "You're not a 'team member.' You're an employee -- and I'm the H.N.I.C. -- the boss. . . the Supreme Being! This is *my* office and you will address me with the proper decorum!"

Freddie reluctantly shook his head north and south in agreement and said, "I just got a call from a relative of Miss Gloria. She -- "

"-- 'Miss Gloria'???? Who is *that*? We don't have any 'Miss Glorias' as a client. Use her correct name. This is a business."

"Gasparini. Gloria Gasparini. . .the one whose house burned down over on Roman Street last week . . . with her in it. They say her gown caught fire while she was standing over a gas heater trying to keep warm in this cold spell we're having. You know how it always gets so unbearably cold right around Mardi Gras time. That's really sad she's going to miss Mardi Gras tomorrow."

"Mardi Gras. Farty Gras. All I want is an item number."

Freddie furiously fingered through a cumbersome, grubby, disorganized stack of unattended-to paperwork for a minute, accessed a dog-eared folder from a nearby file cabinet, and told him, "Policy number 6-3-4-5-7-8-9."

Bourgeois searched in a lengthy grayish-green account book for the digits, reviewed her premium history, and noticed that the last entry indicated that her accidental death and dismemberment policy had been terminated due to non-payment the day before she perished in the flames of the shotgun house in which she was conceived, born, dwelled and died so tragically. "This policy isn't worth the paper it's chickenscratched on," he spat as he stared at the paperwork. "The premium was late. She was a day late and a dollar short."

"But she just died," Freddie protested weakly.

"But? *But*? If butts on chickens were money then we'd all be rich!" Bourgeois grumbled. "I didn't tell her to die! I didn't send her to her maker! I just wrote the policy!"

"But if -- " Freddie started.

"If? If 'if' were a fifth we'd both be drunk right now. I have rheumatoid arthritis, but I'm not complaining!!! There's no ifs, ands or buts! Butts are on cigarettes. Butts are the targets of jokes. Butts shake up and down on those dancing darkies in those parades disturbing my sanity with sordid spectacles of their vanity!!! And turn off that radio!!! If I hear that Mardi Gras Mambo song again I'll explode! And another thing -- please discard your empty cans and bottles in this bag over here," he said, indicating a gargantuan black plastic bag near his workspace. It wasn't that he was a committed environmentalist, Freddie knew. He was just cheap.

"And don't use my cotton swabs any more!" Bourgeois bellyached. "I had 300 at the beginning of last week and now I have 295. I only used two. Somebody else who works here used three . . . that he didn't pay for. Next thing you know you'll be digging in the cash box!"

"You actually counted them?" asked his nephew, again startled at the extent of his uncle's most recent manifestation of chintzyness. He was the tightest of tightwads. His stinginess was legendary. On the rare occasion when the company entertained a thirsty client he'd water down the water. He was so miserly he didn't buy cologne, but scrounged through trashbins near work in search of male-oriented fashion magazines with scented inserts, while also on the lookout for aluminum cans. He would go to McDonald's and swipe fistfuls of napkins and condiments (without placing an order). His penny-pinching was so contemptible that he would leave a goo-gob of dirty dishes out at home so he could wash them once a month (with bar soap). As Freddie told his friends, "He reuses his bathtub water to flush the commode. And he's so tight he can't pass gas. He's got to use FOUR-In-One Oil for the squeaks." He laundered his clothes by hand and hung them on a makeshift clothesline made from surplus strips of cloth. He cut his own hair and hadn't been to a barber since haircuts were 25 cents. Getting a penny out of him was like trying to glue hot wax to a wall. He would use one sheet of (pilfered) toilet paper to wipe his butt. On oppressively hot afternoons he'd pass time in church or at the mall to save on air-conditioning. Instead of purchasing an umbrella or raincoat for the region's monsoon salvos he used a plastic bag and a blanket.

When YOU needed HIM to do something for YOU it was business. When HE needed YOU to do something for HIM it was friendship or family. Although he could afford a more luxuriously appointed residence in East New Orleans, Tall Timbers or other conspicuously prosperous community, he preferred living a life of hermitage in the Old World atmosphere of the French Quarter -- even though he despised the street musicians and performers that were within earshot of his second-story room in the 300 block of Royal Street, a Mardi Gras bead's throw down from the Vieux Carre District police station.

His favorite cartoon character was Boris Badenov, the loathsome Cold War spy in the Rocky and Bullwinkle cartoons. He had fired Freddie for missing work the day of a hurricane, but had to hire him back when nobody else would work for him. He was so mean he wouldn't loan a crippled crawfish a matchstick for a crutch if he owned the whole match factory.

Like many of his professional contemporaries, his primary focus in life was to exploit the intellectual vulnerabilities and lack of business expertise of his unlettered clients. He trusted in neither God nor government and griped and groaned about everything from overflowing ice trays to the size of raw oysters. Some decades prior his twin brother died from wisdom tooth surgery on Lundi Gras, and so Billy had long maintained a toxic relationship with the annual fete. During the Carnival season he prohibited his nephew from wearing clothing in the workplace with the traditional purple, green and gold Mardi Gras colors.

And he was arrogant. His nose was stuck so high in the air that if it rained he'd drown. If someone gifted him with a ton of gold he'd get his BVDs in a bunch because it wasn't in 20-pound bars. He felt more entitled than a strip club fulla Republican campaign delegates and thought himself bred to a higher set of social standing than the ghetto-dwellers to whom he went door-to-door selling low-premium, low-benefit life insurance that would barely pay for a near-sufficient repast for the mourners. There was no cloak large enough to conceal the nakedness of his ambition.

The traumatized narrative that was his life didn't commence with his entry into the world, but with his descent from a lineage of free men of color who believed that a dollar spent is a dollar burned. His dockworking father was cheap, too. When he made 18 his father gave him an 18-candle affair -- no cake, just candles. His dad was never on relief, worked as a rope maker, peddled reams of fabric door-to-door on the city's graveled streets, and took pictures of cowboy-hatted children on a black and white pinto pony for a quarter. At night he played washboard and kazoo on a French Quarter corner.

During the war Bourgeois' father was a Pullman porter on the Sunset Limited between New Orleans and Los Angeles, an "essential" wartime occupation that afforded him 22 deferments. All he knew about his grandmother was that she was a "California widow" (a woman whose husband was runnin' the rails) who shopped at the more pricey Canal Street stores and that his grandfather was a sportin' palace piano professor and Storyville bouncer at a time when drugstores sold cocaine, marijuana joints were three for ten cents, painted women threw mattresses down in cathouse halls to turn tricks, and maids waxed floors by sitting on towels and sliding across the floor on their fannies. During the Great Flood of 1927 his salt of the earth grandfather was "Black Coded," forced to sign a year-long labor contract at a construction camp or be arrested for vagrancy.

His great-grandfather was a Mexican War veteran who carried the law in his holster in a Northwest Louisiana town with a new bank and an old sheriff. Just outside the hamlet's incorporated administrative district was posted:

ALL SAMBOS -- READ AND RUN
IF YOU CAN'T READ . . . RUN ANYWAY
P.S.:
DON'T READ THIS SIGN AFTER DARK

Great-grandpa was a native gentleman immune from the customarily assigned social status of his brethren due to his heroism under fire at the San Cosme Gate of the Battle of Chapultepec's storied "halls of Montezuma" under future general and president and then-Army Lieutenant Ulysses S. Grant. During that battle 90 percent of the Marine officers and non-coms that fought were killed. His heroism was so noted and widely proclaimed that the town fathers favored him as one of their own despite prohibitions against such undemonstrated conduct in that antebellum era. He "slipped the noose" by leaving town one jump ahead of the hangman after the sheriff walked in one night on him, his brother, his cousin and a white glory gal inmate in an array of more than compromising positions in a parish jailhouse cell. Acknowledging his wartime contributions, the sheriff gave him a half-hour to get outa town, but remanded his brother and cousin into custody. The tortured flower of the South, a well-seasoned East Texas tramp working the track in Louisiana, accused them of rape and an unblindfolded justice took its inevitable course when a mob stormed the jail and laid hands on them. They were dragged forth and beaten with bats, axe handles and long whips that could snap a horsefly from a lazy mule's ear. Chains were placed around their necks and they were stripped naked in the town square in the presence of the mayor, sheriff and town fathers (by a crowd the size of which had been previously unseen in the whistle-stop burg's history) drenched in oil, hoisted to a tree, slowly lowered onto a bonfire, and roasted and toasted as they screamed out their innocence.

"Leave the coons' balls for the *rac*coons!" later shouted a domestic terrorist as onlookers scrambled to sever their toes and fingers for souvenirs of the ghastly ritual murder.

Great-grandpa established a carriage building business in the Crescent City, founded one of the state's first black-owned auto dealerships, only got into police trouble once (for rollin' dice), and lived out the remainder of his providential, prosperous life as a New Orleans tobacconist.

* * *

"Unk -- I mean, 'Mr. Bourgeois' -- there's two young ladies here to see you," Freddie announced as his caustic custodian pored over a rickety volume of actuarial statistics and non-standard rates.

"Well, what do they want?" Bourgeois demanded.

"Uh . . . I'll . . . I'll let *them* tell you," his nephew/employee said reluctantly, knowing the bedevilment that would surely ensue if he mentioned the import of their mission. "I'm sending them back," Freddie added in an attempt to avoid being the target of a profanity-laced tirade.

He ushered in two cheerleader-cute neighborhood girls in matching purple and pink jumpers, each toting coffee cans with makeshift labels saying "PLEASE HELP."

"Well, what do *you* want?" Bourgeois snarled, glaring up from a mountain of paperwork.

"We're from the Pretty Babies, a Mardi Gras organization that promotes values, integrity and a sense of duty in young women. We're daughters of the Diaspora who are seeking contributions from area residents and businesses -- " one of them began, bowing to his less than military bearing, as the other shook her coffee can with its load of change they had earlier collected from passersby and other area establishments.

He crassly interrupted her canned presentation. "Mardi Gras!?!?! I don't give a hoot in Hades about Mardi Gras!!! It's gobbidge! Nothing but gobbidge! I have bigger crawfish to berl," he said, nodding at the mound of documentation and portfolios on his desk. "Mardi Gras!!! Farty Gras! You can't even get to your own house because of those police barricades!" He nervously stroked what was left of his hair. "Contribution? For a Mardi Gras group?!???! You've come to the wrong place! I hate Mardi Gras! I hate Rex! I hate ZULU! I hate the truck parades! I hate beads and coconuts! I hate that asinine tomfoolery in whiteface . . . all that cooning and tomming . . . wearing grass skirts . . . throwing worthless junk off a float! Embarrassing!"

"Sir --" the other girl began.

"I hate second lining! I hate those flambeau-carrying spooks and jigaboos!!! And I especially hate you little dancing darkies with your flimsy costumes and trampish, jitterbugging routines!!!" he scolded, releasing a stream of invective. "Get out of my office -- *Now*!!! Or I'll put *this* on you!!!" He produced a Louisville Slugger stashed under his desk.

Startled, the two darling damsels effected a hasty exit as Nephew Freddie shook his head at yet another display of his uncle's frenzied fury. Getting money out of him was like trying to use one's bare hands to pull the back teeth out of a hungry gator.

Bourgeois simmered, fussed and whined all afternoon at the very thought of someone asking that he part with even the most token, miniscule pittance of his legal tender for any cause beyond his own desire to accumulate and hoard all that he could on (as Freddie imagined it) his inevitable journey to hell on a greased sliding board with gasoline underwear.

Just before closing that evening Freddie invited him (again) to the family's annual Mardi Gras celebration that took place every Carnival Day in a balcony apartment of the Lafitte Project on the corner of Prieur and Orleans Avenue, only a chineyball's throw from the office. Rex, Zulu, and the plebeian truck parades passed on Orleans Avenue and the apartment's balcony afforded an unobstructed view of the day's merriment and madness. As usual, he refused.

"You didn't show much sympathy today to those two girls,"

Freddie said.

"Sympathy? You can find 'sympathy' in the dictionary between 'switch-blade' and 'syphilis,'" he muttered.

"Well, thanks for giving me the day off tomorrow. Tineshia's going to enjoy finally having me home on Carnival Day."

"Tineshia? Who in Hades is Tineshia?"

"My daughter . . . your niece . . . well, your great-niece."

"What's so great about her?"

"It's just that her illnesses have been going on for quite a while. I wanted to talk to you about her medical coverage. Is there any kind of way we can upgrade the benefits for more coverage of her Sickle Cell treatment and heart medicine? It's getting quite a bit expensive. My baby's a brave little girl, but those treatments --"

"We all have our problems," Bourgeois snapped. "Before you shoot off your mouth -- be sure your brains are loaded."

Freddie scowled. "Well, 'Happy Mardi Gras' anyway."

"A waste of time, money and misguided sentiment . . . painting faces on coconuts. . . strutting like savages in the middle of the street!!! Gobbidge!!! Nothing but gobbidge!!!" Bourgeois cursed, donning his bowler hat and briefcase as his nephew exited the place of business to make preparations for the next day's elaborately costumed magic and mystery.

* * *

He negotiated the city's narrow, pedestrian-choked streets, snaking his way through the gay, unwashed rabble he so despised, as the Lundi Gras revelers shook their merrymakers under seas of celebratory confetti. No power in heaven or on earth could quell his anger at being shoved, jostled and jammed by the paradegoers' drunken, liquid lunacy and unrestrained mirth in the opening salvos of this latest season of celebration in the city forgotten by care. To get through the crowds he used that old Mardi Gras parade trick: "Pregnant lady comin' through! Pregnant lady comin' through!"

As he passed a Royal Street souvenir shop a group of tapdancing children with bottle caps attached to their tennis shoes played that age-old tourist-targeted game with him and bet him that they could tell him "where you got your shoes." The anticipated response would hopefully be the name of a store, which would invite a snappy retort by the questioner in the form of "On your feet!" and a stretched-out hand in expectancy of beneficence. But he was a bad sport. "Get away from me!! Don't bother me -- you little pickaninnies!!! I'll slice and dice your little behinds," he growled while brandishing a Vietnam-era Buck knife. Grumbling, he trekked on homeward while gazing at the ground for discarded pennies and aluminum cans.

He arrived at his sanctuary, clung to the banister and cursed his arthritic condition while ascending to the veil of isolation that was his sanctuary, and undid the latch and the four safety locks he had installed. Inside at last, he sat by his bed scribbling plans for the next day's workplace enterprises. After working for a while he re-recounted the coins that he kept in a Luzianne 16 oz. coffee can on his nightstand; that way he could grab the loot and scoot in case of a fire. He bathed in the most minimal amount of water possible, donned a bedraggled robe, took his arthritis medicine (generic, of course), ate a meal of Chicken Ramen noodles, and scoured the airwaves of an analog AM radio for the latest business reports. A little later he watched a segment of the national blues, changed into his PJs, and settled back to listen to what he called "grown folks music" (Eddie Jefferson's version of Filthy McNasty) on the one scratchy LP he had ever invested in as an adult. (He didn't want to get the cassette when it came out because he thought the then-new medium was overpriced and refused to purchase the advanced technology needed to play it.)

After listening and relistening to the piece for a while and mulling the evil sideshow that was his life, he retired for a night of respite and grave solitude in the expectation of cursing a dog in the building that had a habit of barking every night just about the time he was intent on a nightlong snooze. But a while later he found that he couldn't sleep, for instead of hearing the matter-of-course dog's barking there was silence. The building was boneyard quiet. He thought he heard his name whispered just outside the door. Or was it from beyond the walls?

He turned over, attempting to resume his efforts at slumbering; then heard the wooden gradation creaking as though a neighbor was mounting the rickety stairs. Then the dog started barking as though someone were indeed coming up the stairway. The commode flushed . . . and flushed . . . and flushed. *Must be some kinda delayed action*, he thought.

Then his coffee can full of change rose in the air, floated to the middle of the room, and dumped its tinkling, clinking contents on his decades-old, second-hand area rug. He momentarily detected a figure in the room's dimness, scanned around for some form of protection, looked again -- but whatever it was was gone. Then he saw a shape emerging from the wall's peeling paint. As he nervously clutched the covers in frenzied fright and impure terror he realized that it was transparent and what could be its face, featureless.

"What is this? Who's there? Who's there?" he babbled at whatever it was before him. "If you're trying to rob me you won't get a thing. It was all in the can."

He gazed closer at the materializing apparition. It appeared to be a pale, bloodless, decomposing body encased in a scraggy, moth-eaten, formerly cream white shroud. He glared, conflicted, at the spectral Frankensteinian presence that floated nightmarishly before him. That countenance. Those ashen spaces that once were eyes. It was his longtime business partner . . . Burnell Beauchard.

"Burnell??? Burnell Beauchard??? But how? You're dead! Long dead! How can you be here? Why?" he stammered, clutching the bedcovers, struggling to comprehend this frighteningly bizarre specter, as he backed up like a crawfish in hot water.

"HOW? WHY? I AM NOT HERE TO RELIEVE YOU OF YOUR VALUABLES, PILFER YOUR TRIFLES OR ABSCOND WITH YOUR PUTRID POSSESSIONS!" the thing moaned in a cadaverously profound, echoing, hollow voice as it pointed an upraised ashen, accusing finger towards Bourgeois. "-- OR TO CHASTISE OR LAMBASTE YOU FOR YOUR GRAVEN, HERETICAL DEPRAVITY. I AM ONLY ONE WHO HAS BEEN SENT TO PROVIDE YOU FAIR WARNING THROUGH THIS DISPLAY . . . OF WHAT CAN LIE IN YOUR FUTURE IF YOU DO NOT EFFECT A PROFOUND EFFORT TO MEND YOUR WAYS. . . . I WAS ONCE YOUNG AND SPRIGHTLY, BUT I CHOSE TO LIVE A LIFE OF JUBILATION AND PLEASURE RATHER THAN ONE OF PRAISE AND BENEVOLENCE. SUCH BEHAVIOR HAS CONDEMNED ME TO A STATE OF ETERNAL ANGUISH IN

THE MOST INFERNAL REGIONS OF THE EVERLASTING FIRES OF TORMENT AND SUFFERING!"

"Sent? By whom? Why you? Why are you sent? Why are you the one sent? From where?"

"IT MATTERS NOT *WHO* SENT ME. IT IS ONLY OF IMPORT THAT I AM HE WHO HAS BEEN SENT. . . . IN OUR EARTHLY AFFILIATION, WE EMBEZZLED, DEFRAUDED, AND DESTROYED EVERY POOR UNFORTUNATE WHOSE DESTINY IT WAS TO BE INVOLVED WITH US IN EVEN THE MOST INSIGNIFICANT BUSINESS TRANSACTIONS IMAGINABLE. WE RUINED LIVES. WE DESTROYED MARRIAGES, STOLE FROM THE POOREST OF THE POOR, SHARED NOT A PENNY WITH THOSE IN NEED. . . . I WAS A DRUNKARD AND WOMANIZER WHO PLACED MORE VALUE ON MY TEMPORAL APPETITES AND CARNAL SATISFACTION THAN I DID ON THE WORTH OF THOSE FELLOW CREATURES WHO INHABITED THE WORLD AROUND US. . . . BITTERNESS AND DEBAUCHERY WERE MY WATCHWORDS WHILE ON THAT MOMENTARY JOURNEY CALLED LIFE -- NOT REALIZING THAT EXISTENCE ON THIS PITEOUSLY TINY BLUE MARBLE IS BUT ONE BRIEF MILLISECOND OF A JOURNEY TO FOREVER. I ONLY COME TO WARN YOU: LIKE ME, YOU HAVE SET OUT ON AN UNSWERVING COURSE OF DESTRUCTION AND DESOLATION. MEND YOUR WAYS, LEST YOU SUFFER THE SAME MISERY AND PATHOS OF THE FATE THAT I NOW BEAR THROUGH THE FRAILTY OF THE FLESH AND THE HOLLOWNESS OF THE SOUL. . . . I MUST NOW RETURN FROM WHENCE I CAME, BUT YOU CAN EXPECT A VISIT FROM THE THREE THAT ARE YET TO COME . . . THE THREE THAT ARE YET TO COME . . . THE THREE THAT ARE YET TO COME. . . ."

That said, what had been Burnell Beauchard dwindled, slowly merging into the places and spaces from which it had come. After the transcendent physical appearance of Beauchard in death returned to the ages, the recluse Bourgeois pondered the phantasmal solicitation and departure in an eerie sensation of mock determination. He sheltered himself under the covers in an effort to ward off any further spasms of agitation and annoyance, and entered the suspended consciousness of the dream world.

* * *

At the wee-est of hours after a vain attempt at sleep, a shadow of distrust enveloped him. Suddenly a bright light hovered over him revealing a sprite, girlish figure clad in purple, green and gold Mardi Gras Indian-feathered regalia and clutching a flaming torch.

"You must be the first of the spirits!" His voice shivered as the dancing, dazzling figure pranced before his stupefied eyes.

"I am the Spy Girl of Mardi Gras Past," the pixyish personification informed him. "My father carried the flambeau." Her bright, blinking, twinkling eyes reflected the shining, scintillating glitter of her sparkling, flashing, handheld beacon. "I am the daughter of a Mardi Gras Queen of the Nation. On Carnival Day I ran ahead of our tribe to determine the whereabouts of the other bands of Indians. Tonight I am here to escort and guide you through times past so that you might fathom some of your outstanding, unresolved issues and reclaim the restorative power of love. I am here to illuminate the way, the truth, and the light."

"Guide me? Illuminate? The way? To where?"

"To where time, the master of all destiny, has long dwelt. To the undisclosed mysteries and memories that linger in the heart."

Suddenly he found himself in a panorama of the past. Uniformed children were at play at recess in St. Peter Claver Academy's schoolyard. He snickered as he watched familiar figures from his youth, running to and fro, playing basketball, shooting marbles, jumping rope and making an ear-splitting melody of disquietude. His heart welcomed the innumerable eruptions of laughter and shouting and he smiled for the first time in his conscious memory. "Yo, Breaux!" he screamed to a noteworthy figure that ignored his heralding.

"He can't see or hear you. None of them can. You can only observe," the Spy Girl of Mardi Gras Past informed him.

The scene before him shifted to berobed children in church (boys on one side and girls on the other) singing the Blessed Mother's praises, their angelic voices rising to the heavens in a beautiful chorus of innocence that inspired a pinch of sentiment in the hardened texture of his innards:

> "Oh Mary, we crown thee with blossoms today,
> Queen of the Angels and Queen of the May. . .
> Oh Mary, we crown thee with blossoms today,
> Queen of the Angels and Queen of the May. . ."

    They filed out of the church building under the watchful eyes (and pointers and rulers) of some of the meanest nuns in the history of Catholic education, circled the block as they recited the Rosary, then ended up back in the church. There an eighth grade girl who had the highest academic average thus far that year performed the crowning of the Blessed Virgin's statue. He remembered with a glazed expression that he was in the Special Class that year and didn't participate, but took grim solace in the fact that he was the school's top saleskid (two years running) in the World's Finest Chocolate sales competition. It was another discordant note in the unresolved trauma that was the tormented existence of his childhood.

    The messenger then transported him to a Mardi Gras fundraiser for his fifth grade class, the purpose of which was to harvest funding for the school's floats to be featured in that year's Mardi Gras celebration. His class would be costumed as Robin Hood (for the boys) and darling little damsels (for the girls). The event was held at the Carver Theater, a neighborhood institution across from the Lafitte Project that was hailed as "America's finest theater exclusively for colored patrons." The board game competitions (bingo, Monopoly, Parcheesi, and Po-Ke-No) were followed by a sock hop and seafood boil/supper.

    A much simpler time, he thought. People enjoyed the most basic pleasures with maximum satisfaction. It was a time when Jon Gnagy's "Learn to Draw" TV program caused many a child to be glued to the black & white TV for session after session in an effort to acquire a minimal working level of artistic achievement. Boys sat in quiet solitude for hours negotiating the most intricate of stitches as they crafted leather belts and wallets. It was an era of the knife-sharpening man, the milkman, the ice man, the vejitibble man, and the rag man (who collected rags, paid you 15 cents or a quarter, then sold 'em to the shipping companies for "wipin' rags." Bourgeois' father once joked that the rag man customarily got more for the white rags than the colored rags.) There was the feed man (who sold feed for chickens), the waffle man, the cotton candy man, the shrimp man, the paper man, and the voodoo lady.

Bourgeois recalled that he almost breathed his last one summer when he was at Indian Village (the Boy Scout camp for the coloreds) as a Tenderfoot Scout after being thrown into ten feet of water by an old-school swimming instructor. He had almost drowned before Beauchard pulled him out. He spied himself playing coon can (a street variant of cricket played with balls, aluminum cans and brooms or mopsticks) and kickball (his contemporaries' version of soccer) in the street while other children were playing "Redlight," engaging in the challenges of "Simon Says," playing jacks, skipping across patterned rectangular hopscotch spaces, spinning tops, yo-yo-ing, and jumping rope on the bankets.

"Do you remember when you were a young innocent, uninformed as to the ways of the world?" the Spy Girl of Mardi Gras Past asked him. "Do you recall that occasion when your father couldn't -- or wouldn't -- buy the bow and arrows you needed for your Robin Hood costume?"

"Yes, of course," Bourgeois acknowledged. "Uncle Willy went out and bought 'em and brought 'em by. I was as happy as an escaped crab from a barrel."

"Interesting analogy," the Spy Girl of Mardi Gras Past said.

The dreamlike sequences brought to mind playing Spin the Bottle and Mommas and Daddies with Betty Jo Johnson, a 'round-the-way girl who eventually developed into a heavenly honey who blossomed with mushrooming breasts and wore well-engineered bras at an earlier age than most of her female peers. She was tall and yummy. At a time when most girls were envying the unattainable figures of their dolls, she had also developed a toothpick-thin, catwalk model waist and a posterior that could crack a coconut. As a child he was not very adept at social intercourse, but her tenderest of mercies -- like that time she let him eat the entire vanilla portion of a bowl of her Neapolitan (aka "three-flavored") ice cream -- invaded his heart with a flight of inspiration that led to true devotion and commitment. He became well-versed in "pretty talk" and kept himself open-casket sharp in his starched khaki school uniforms and his boisterously loud-colored, stylish patterned shirts (in an age well before young men became walking billboards). She was the most welcome song in the soundtrack of his youth and seeing the object of his adoration in her crisp, white blouses and green, meticulously-pressed, pleated skirts constituted a tormented existence for him.

At last, in high school together, he finally mustered up the courage to emit a "Hey, baby" to her one afternoon as she was gathering and packing away her belongings in her hallway locker. The sight of her hypnotic, exotic, erotic, herbal eyes and the magic in her thunderladen thighs brought about a melody of madness in him. She was his first love and his love had not been and would never be tended to by another.

He recalled their daily lunchtime cafeteria meetings, their evening romps to the movie show and the taco place on Elysian Fields near Lake Pontchartrain, his boyish dreams of blissful domestication, standing outside the club coolin' out while leaning on a lamppost like he was Frank Sinatra or somebody, the treasured gemstone he purchased from money he saved from his book cover-making business and his grass-cutting earnings to lavish spontaneously-purchased gifts upon her, her pleasant smile, her permanently-pursed lips, her fluffy gowns and lace-themed blouses, the rich fabrics of her tignons and the rosettes in the front, her cabbage and cornbread, her gravy-smothered poultry, her red beans and rice and her fondness for being called "Baby." She was finger-lickin' good.

One Carnival season she gifted him with a Ban-Lon shirt that he wore with relish. He became the nattiest of dressers and shopped at the city's most accessible and then-priciest men's stores. He purchased his skys from Meyer the Hatter and his bathrobes from Rubenstein's. He fell in love with her with less than an abundance of caution. She became a presumed lady of character and they envisioned a life of gothic soirées and satin sheets as they made plans for connubial bliss and the chatter of a gaggle of little people.

Then his father died and left him a hefty inheritance with which he planned to purchase an Uptown estate, but his plans went awry when destiny's fickle finger pointed towards a different direction and he was drafted to fight a war in a country with a name he'd never before heard: Vietnam.

In the beginning they exchanged letters every week. Then it was biweekly. Then it was monthly. Then bimonthly. Then the letters stopped coming while the bodies stacked like cordwood. He returned stateside, looked her up, discovered she was inextricably and happily wedded to one of their grade school classmates, experienced the sting of love rejected, and made a Faustian bargain to immerse the besotted remnants of whatever heart and soul he had left into the financial services industry and the pursuit of prosperity and plenty.

You, he thought wildly, *you became nuttier than squirrel poo.*

The optic spectacle ceased and he found himself in his bed, thrown into a tenor of discomfiture by the paralysis of analysis of such measure of dysfunctional conflict in the highs and lows of what passed for his life.

* * *

The night of removal from his unpleasant present lumbered on. He quivered and quaked at the otherworldly scenarios to which he had just borne witness. Then a shaking, rattling, rolling sound gave him a start. A hulking, humongous figure clad in animal skins and sizable clattering bones (that seemed to have formerly belonged to huge beasts of burden) materialized before his fright-filled eyes. It was the Bone Man of Mardi Gras Present.

The skeletal makeup of the thing was partially draped by a seedy, scraggly cloak that revealed an intricate outline of intimidating carrion relics and disintegrating, cadaverous remains. It motioned to Bourgeois to join its company, and he was lifted off the bed forthwith and reluctantly drawn to its side.

In a flash they were outside of a dilapidated dogtrot Creole cottage. It was so named, Bourgeois knew, because the structure's two equal-sized rooms were separated by a shared, open passage through which the residents' dogs could be heard "trotting" through the structure's breezeway.

The Bone Man of Mardi Gras Present signaled that Bourgeois should peek inside one of the humble abode's windows. He did and spied his nephew Freddie, Freddie's debilitated daughter, and his wife as they were putting the finishing touches on their unpretentious contribution to their extended family's Mardi Gras Day meal (baked chicken, mashed potatoes and peas) and patching and seaming the costumes they would don in the rawest hours of the next day's laughter and liveliness.

He tittered as he heard the family's conversation. "Daddy, you sure I'll be well enough tomorrow to go to see the parades?" Tineshia asked. Her mother busied herself with her attentive stitching and Freddie to his culinary commitment.

"Well, we still have a couple of pills left. You can take one tonight and I'll save the other for the morning -- and we'll see how well you feel from there," her father reassured her.

"I just wanta see just one parade. I hope I'm strong enough," the sickly child said. "You gon' hold me on your shoulder -- high-high-high like you always do? I wanna go high-high-high 'til I reach the sky and catch all the beads in heaven!"

"I know you do, baby -- and you will. We'll be able to catch all the parades from Aunt Tessie's balcony when we go to the project. They all pass there. Zulu . . . Rex . . . the truck parades. We'll see them all," Nephew Freddie guaranteed her as he prepared a generic packet of boxed stuffing for their contribution to the Big Day's meal.

"Daddy . . . we gon' have lemonade or Kool-Aid tomorrow?"

"I don't know yet. I have to check and see which one we have enough of. We'll have whichever one we have. If we don't, we'll just have to make-do. I had to pay the light bill. Lights cost money."

"That's okay, daddy. As long as I got you and momma . . . and plenny-plenny-plenny beads." She grinned with a wisdom beyond her years, radiating the good fortune of hearth and home.

Bourgeois was DUMB-DUMB-dee-dee-dee-DUMB-DUMB dumbstruck, on the verge of being driven to tears at the harmonious, pastoral scene. He felt as though he was inextricably bonded with the household's inseverable cord of faith and fate. He reached a hand towards them, but was undetected by the family.

He turned to entreat the Bone Man of Mardi Gras Present to make it possible for him to join the fortuneless but convivial pre-Mardi Gras preparations. But it was not to be, for the Bone Man of Mardi Gras Present, the crude colossus, spread his outer covering revealing two gaunt, glaring, glowering human skulls. Tattooed on one was "IGNORANCE." On the other was "AVARICE." The Bone Man of Mardi Gras Present then vanished back into whatever realm from whence it came.

Dazed, Bourgeois noticed a dreamy, hooded figure approaching him in the shadows of the dogtrot Creole cottage's breezeway.

* * *

"Hey, Baby!" a flirtatiously feminine voice called to him, the Cajun moon-bright night giving way to a ribbon of light in the dimness. He eyeballed a chocolate-covered, picture book-pretty pixie clad in a turquoise, split-to-the-hip, peek-a-boo shorty nighty, baby blue bonnet and flaming red platform heels, her embodiment reeking of a seductively magnetic, mancatching fragrance. It was the Pretty Baby of Mardi Gras Yet to Come, her artfully masked face and percolating rhythms beckoning to the most sensual depths of his nature. He gaped wide-eyed and open-mouthed at the rhapsodic frame sashaying in the shadowy night before the early dawn bopped bright. She was brassy, jassy and sassy, her Husband Hunter perfume percolating, oozing through the still night air.

"What are you?" he asked Ms. Sweet Thang. "Are you some sort of succubus, some dream lover here to seduce me in the throes of my self-flagellation? I've been a keystone species for greed all my life, but I implore you -- "

"You have no reason to fear me. I am only here to unmask your future," the Pretty Baby of Mardi Gras Yet to Come assured him.

A veil of wind encompassed them and they were whisked away to a brick-surfaced street corner under a malfunctioning lamp that flickered and fluttered over a pitifully prostrate figure. Two fleshborne demons rifled through the unresponsive man's clothing.

"I know he had a li'l sumpin'-sumpin' on him," one said.

"I hope it's mo' den dis Timex watch. The pawn shop don't even take 'em no mo'." They rummaged further through the cadaver's clothes for any semblance of a morsel of value that they could turn over for a pretty or even petty penny.

"He got bullet holes all over him -- from his haid to his toenails!" the first one said.

"Good. Serves him right. I hope he felt every one of 'em. If anybody deserve to die that kinda def -- he did!"

"Broad daylight yesterday . . . everybody saw it and nobody called the po-leece."

"Serves him right. He got what he deserved. I'm glad he's daid . . . sellin' dat li'l cheap insurance to everybody . . . cain't even pay for the flowers."

Bourgeois and the sassy lassie were then swept away in a whirlpool of wind to a graveyard adjacent to Delgado Community College, the Holt Cemetery. The old folks said that Buddy Bolden, arguably the father of jazz, was buried there amidst paupers, poets and the lovingly crafted souvenir tributes of the surviving poor. There were wood-framed enclosed graves with homemade markers, the deceased's favorite record or chair, meticulously-patterned beadwork and other mementos and memorials of lives lived in hardship and poverty.

The Pretty Baby of Mardi Gras Yet to Come motioned towards a desolate grave in an unattended corner of the cemetery under a decaying chineyball tree. Bourgeois leaned forward in the glimmer of the night's full yellow moon. The Pretty Baby of Mardi Gras Yet to Come pointed a painted finger forward as he inspected a slumping, wooden, decomposing, makeshift grave marker. A web of confusion and apprehension came across his consciousness as he discovered the epitaph carved into the ungainly slab:

BOURGEOIS
A Titan of History

"No . . . that can't be. That can't be me. I won't be buried in a place like this. This is impossible," he insisted. "I have money."

"*Had* money," the Pretty Baby of Mardi Gras Yet to Come corrected. "Money? A pig with lipstick is still swine. There was an extreme weather event that occurred -- that will occur. It was called 'Katrina.' It bankrupted your insurance company and you were reduced to collecting cans and begging for a living until you became just another piece of human debris to be swept away in an act of violence. This is the future I am here to relate."

"But is there anything in the heavens or on the earth that I can do to avoid such a fate as this? Please, Great Spirit -- have mercy upon my soul, the soul my mother bore and brought to this earth. I renounce the reprehensible errors of my wicked ways and pray that my soul . . . my life . . . can be salvaged."

"You alone are the master of your fate. You alone are the one who will determine whether your soul will travel the road to salvation or negotiate the passage to the place of eternal torment. *You* must decide," she forewarned as she faded into the night sky.

Bourgeois found himself in bed, his windup metal alarm clock clanging for him to awake and head to the office for a Mardi Gras Day of toil and endeavor. Upon awakening he came to an inescapable epiphany, found himself tired of dancing at the wrong wedding, pondered the self-inflicted wounds of the heartless fool's errand with which his life was involved, and discovered a renewed awareness of the simmering embers of his discontent and the throes of his ham-handed deeds with deep trepidation. He came to an inevitable recognition that he couldn't walk with God while holding hands with the devil.

No longer would he be the crudest, most wretched of rapscallions and search for loose change under people's couch cushions or forage through his neighbors' trash receptacles for aluminum cans. He would redeem himself, unseal and renew his fate, embrace the refinements of civilization and willingly engage in usual and customary social ritual. He would no longer shy away from family custom by way of controlled embraces and a propensity for being a keystone species for greed with a cruelty of conduct unbecoming of an unmerry gentleman (or an SS Officer). He set about on an ambitious agenda with a short timetable determined to right the overabundance of wrong he had committed during the frayed fabric of his life.

He called a caterer that owed him some premium on his business' contractual agreement, arranged to adequately compensate him for the zero hour request of his services, ordered every type of libation and solid morsel imaginable, gathered himself, and made his merry way to the family's annual festive occasion at Prieur and Orleans to take in the parades on the gaily-decorated Lafitte Project balcony at Aunt Tessie's. On his trek he came upon the two youngsters who earlier visited his office seeking a donation to their Mardi Gras organization. Their wigs flipped when he wrote a walloping check (while actually smiling) and cheerfully forked it over. His family members were shocked and awed at his appearance, for he had been invited for years, never accepted their invitation and had always pegged away at work on Carnival Day.

That afternoon, while taking in Zulu, Rex and the truck parades, they enjoyed a sumptuous feast of dirty rice, peas, green bean casserole, shrimp pasta, fried turkey (with cranberry sauce), baked turkey (with oyster dressing), stewed hen, honeybaked ham (even though a Muslim brother was over there), pot roast, barbecued chicken, smothered chicken, monkey bread, garlic bread, corn, cornbread, cornbread dressing, macaroni and cheese, potato salad, red beans and rice (and a lotta beer on ice), stuffed bell peppers (six for a dollar at Circle Food Store on St. Bernard and Claiborne), gumbo, milleton (they ain't never heard o' no "*mer*liton"), sweet peas, spinach, snap beans, collard greens, broccoli, stuffed eggs, cheesecake with toasted pecawns, yams, sweet potato pie, lemon meringue pie, pecawn pie, lemonade, Kool-Aid, all the liquor they could drink, red gravy, and assorted strains of aromatic herbs.

All day they caught beads and trinkets from their second-floor balcony vantage point, shared laughter, hugged, kissed and reminisced. For the first time in history he even promised his nephew a raise. He was as spry as a newborn roach. The generations all stared in astonishment at his metamorphosis. That night when the paradegoers and party people dispersed and the native indwellers began resting in preparation for the next day's menial subservience, he held little Tineshia, costumed as a papoose, in his lap as he rested on a plastic-covered Barcalounger, varicolored necklaces of beads around his neck. "*Laissez les bons temps rouler!!!*" she beamed.

"Yeah, baby!!! Let the good times roll!!!" he countered.

And he lived nattily ever after. . . .

August 2013
Stamford, CT

Professor Arturo

EJACULATIONS

Jazz Stories: *From Katrina to Connecticut*

Alice in the Afternoon
or *Up For The Downstroke*

"It doesn't matter whether a cat is black or white --
as long as it catches mice."
-Alice

Swedish-blonde hair, freckles, blue/grey eyes, and drunken bubblebaths . . . *Her father was Jewish, but he thought he was Italian.* . . . The girl couldn't help it. Alice reveled in the water, its warmth, the closeness and remoteness of the bubbles, the erotic sweetness of the exotically-scented candles, politely, delicately pointing her unadorned toes ceilingward, reaching through the translucent bath gel for a sea green bottle poised perilously on the outer edge of the bathtub. Her dorm suitemates, she supposed, were off doing what students were expected to be about in the age of the new realism.

She eased back in the tub, picked up a bottle of Panadol, dropped a couple of pills into her lovelaced mouth (now powdered with a dried bubble moustache), and took a swig from the lime-colored bottle of 12-year-old single malt Scotch. The Scotch, proclaimed by its gold label to have been made "the same unique way since 1742," was loudly, proudly, widely, and wildly-touted by most public and closet alcoholics as having "unparalleled silkiness and quality." She peered into the eye of the bottle as she held it aloft in the Indian summer daze' early afternoon light. She stared profoundly into the emerald bottle. Inside was her liquid love. Inside was her friend, ablution, blessing, salvation. Inside was her future and her history. Inside was her present presence. Inside was her momma and her daddy. Inside was her crazy uncle in the attic and his faded Hudson Valley Psychiatric Center T-Shirt. Inside was her great-great grandfather, the Civil War veteran that nobody brought up anymore at Thanksgiving dinner. Everything about her and just about her everything was in the bottle. If they'd bottle pregnant platypus pee, the girl would drink it.

The men in her life were Carlo Rossi, Tom Moore, Jim Beam, Mogen David, Hiram Walker, Johnny Walker, George Dickel, Evan Williams, and Jack Daniels. She preferred Ezra Brooks to Ezra Pound, Bacardi to Baraka, *Gato Negro* to Gato

Professor Arturo

Barbieri, and pitchers of beer to Molecular Biology. Her menfriends were many-many-many. They was her mens, all right . . . and they were all spirits in a bottle.

Oftentimes, when she was the victim (perpetrator?) of a straight-up, stomp-down, no-holes-barred Eastern seaboard jungle lust safari, her womanish parts hell-bent on eroticide, she would partytake of the wickedly notorious *Torada, Spanada,* Matilda Bay Bacardi (light and dark), *Asti Spumante, Riunite, Cabernet Sauvignon, Mouton-Cadet, Fundador!, Drambuie* (and a whole lotta stuff yo' momma cain't pronounce, neither).

The girl drank, gargled, gurgled, giggled and guzzled so much they thought she had some kinda drainpipe stuck up in her. She imbibed royally. She drank Sir Malcolm, Chivas Regal, Crown Royal, and 100 Pipers ('cause 99 ½ just wouldn't do). She had to have a hundred. She was an avid nature lover and often swigged Wild Turkey, Cold Duck, and Grey Goose. She dreamed lazily, gazing longingly, lovingly, at the tiny waves of spirits and the eerily odd vapors seeping from the ghostly, green bottle. She slept. . ..

* * *

She awoke somehow, miraculously escaping death-by-drowning in the now bubbleless bathwater. She rinsed and soaped her soggy skin, dried herself, wrapped her tight, tense, supple, young flesh in the white towel she and her boyfriend pilfered from a hotel in the Catskills last summer, peeked into the suite's "common area," and dashed to her room. After combing her hair and lotioning her freckle-sprinkled outer, she jumped into a pair of brown pants (with matching "leather look" belt), but decided instead on a bleached blue-jean, skin-tight miniskirt, a red halter top with a purple cicada silkscreened on its front side, a pair of fashionably-torn black fishnet pantyhose, and a pair of black and gold 4" closed-toe imitation leopard pumps. She was a young and reckless, Woodstockian-chic, lady of the Eighties trapped inside an avaricious Age of Prevarication (and prolifically pitiable punmanship).

It was hot. Two silent contrails crept across a cloudless, blue sky. She skipped her Two-Dimensional Design class and didn't remember walking past the library, the art building, or the older section of the campus closest to town. She was tired, dog-tired of the "unique academic experience in the shadow of

Mohonk Mountain and its famous tower" where she took courses in ceramics, color theory, and design in a major that explored how color impacts upon every facet of life, including art, attire and persona. Her classes involved hypothesis, observation, communication and laborious learning exercises encompassing the use of dyed paper and paints.

It was hot. She stared glassy-eyed at her fellow scholarly apprentices as they went about their choredom in the cosmically, comically dazzling sun and didn't even acknowledge any familiar faces among the college's warm, student bodies as they hopped, skipped, jumped, bumped, and humped on the green brick road to a classless struggle. She only knew it was hot. It was hazy, humid and hot. It was Indian Summer. The pale face of winter would soon rear its ugly head.

* * *

The Hudson Valley hamlet's Main Street swelled with afternoon traffic. Mighty Mohonk Mountain rested, nestled in a panoramic backdrop landscaped in bright yellows; dancing, flashing reds; swirling, flaming oranges; and brimming, bubbling browns. Alice stood, soaked in a river of sweat, in front of Ariel Booksellers (just across from Barclay's Bank).

An Uppy's taxi driver made the turn off Main Street towards the campus and blew her a kiss. "Dork!" Alice frowned, folding her arms. The driver blew his horn. "Peterhead townie! Pervie! Barf out -- you jizzdribble! Bag your face -- you walking zit!" she shouted, raising a clenched fist.

It was like that. It was Indian Summer. It was a blistering, sizzling, soaring, sweltering heat. It was a blazing, blinding, hot and humid Hudson Valley. *A drink! A drink! My tuition for a drink!* she thought. *I wish I had a cold pitcher of beer.*

Just then she turned and was surprised by a familiar frame. Smiling in the simmering sun next to a table of vendors selling antiques, craftware and homemade baked goods was Peter, the Nehru-jacketed Vietnam vet.

He had finally taken advantage of his benefits and returned to college to pursue a degree in English (with a concentration in Journalism) a decadent, debauched decade after graduating from the 'Nam. Sometimes they called him Casper -- not the Friendly Ghost, but the Holy Ghost. They both worked with one of the campus publications and he was actually enjoying his second opportunity to pontificate and party at this stage of what had been a life of precariously dangling danger and delight. Another incentive was being around more young twat than Chuck Berry, Don Cornelius and Dick Clark could manage. Sweat trickled from his auburn, grey-tinged afro and yellow, butterfly-collared shirt.

"Hey, baby --" he said, "how about a pitcher, Ms. Moorehead? You look stressed out. I already cashed my work-study check. That li'l three-thirty-five a hour burnin' my pocket. The car broke down -- again. I had to come here on my magic carpet. Let's go git a cold one," he suggested, making her an offer she couldn't refuse.

"I usually don't drink this time of the day." She laughed. "I begin much earlier. Let's go!"

As they walked towards Pee & Gee's, the main Main Street magnet for the parched throats of the college's thirsty populace, they noticed Willie Namba, the president of the campus African Students Union, bedecked in his homeland's most profound sartorial finery -- throwing rocks at Barclay's Bank. "What's *that* about?" asked Alice.

"About something bigger 'n' you and me. He wants that bank to stop doin' what they doin' to his country. He still 'bout that disinvestment issue he brought up at the last Student Association meeting. He some mad 'bout what's goin' on over there. Hey, bruh!" Peter yelled, waving at the foreign national.

"I will throw stones at the Devil each and every day at every hour -- until my people are triumphant!" Willie shouted. "Come and join me! Come join the struggle, my brother!"

"I -- I have a meeting," Peter half-truthed. "I gotta git to this seminar on race relations."

"Well, I will see you at the next SA meeting -- if the authorities do not send me to my ancestors first!" he shouted above the hum of the passing traffic in the boiling, burning, early afternoon sun.

"C'mon, baby," Peter urged. "You slow as Christmas. Let's go git stoned."

"Look-- " Alice twirled around "-- a salmon-crested cockatoo!" Then -- "Ooh -- my neck hurts. I was trying to learn how to do the Wop in the mirror in the dorm the other night. I think I need a Panadol. But let's get some beer. We can go Dutch."

"As long as it ain't 'Dutch Afrikaner'," he ribbed.

"Good. Then let's go get de beers!"

* * *

They sat at a table in the rear of the tavern and ordered two pitchers of ice-cold draft. The liquid laughter arrived. "Here's a toast to the boogie," he proposed. "Bottoms up!"

"I'll drink to that," she said as George Benson's *White Rabbit* oozed from the bar's greatly-employed speakers.

"What up?" he asked. "You seem like you're still out of it."

"It's my boyfriend. That peckerhead blew me off. I was supposed to meet him last night at Coochie's, but he didn't show up. I waited for two hours. He's always dumping on me."

"Dumpin' on you?'

"Grossing me out. Out there with a bunch of bimbos and geeks. He doesn't know if he wants to be a Black Panther or a Young Republican -- and he's 22 years old. He has a good job, a trendy wardrobe and a passion for dancing . . . but he's still a yutz -- acting like he's the biggest studmuffin on campus. He thinks he's the campus horndog. . . . He's *meshugana*."

"*Meshugana*?" he asked. "That's some 'fect'."

"'Fect?"

"*De*fect. But what is *meshugana*?"

"Crazy. Nuts. Whacked. . . My father's Jewish, for instance, but he thinks he's Italian," she said, ordering a flute of *Polo Brindisi*. "We're really part Indian. During World War Two my grandmother and grandfather disappeared. The Nazis took them to the camps."

"That's bogue."

"Bogue?"

"Bogus. Counterfeit."

"Oh -- like my father munching Italian food like *bruschetta*."

"What's that?"

"Garlic bread . . . and he just loves *Lombatinadi Vitello*. . ."

"Okay, what is *Lomba* -- whatever?'

"Veal chops. And *Pagano, Gamberi ai ferri, Pollo alla Romana*. . ."

"That ain't nuthin' but roast chicken. I prefer eatin' Chicken Diane -- or grits and ketchup."

"Grits and ketchup? Is that Italian?"

"No. It's not Italian. It's the 'ghetto special'. . . the *American* ghetto," he added.

"No, really -- he actually thinks he's Italian. He's got BIG issues. He's having an affair with one of his patients."

"A lotta doctors do. It ain't no biggy, boo. Is he a psychiatrist?"

"No."

"An MD?"

"No-o-o-o."

"Then what is he?"

"He's a veterinarian."

"Oh --" he choked. To him, the li'l white girl talked more crap than Jane Fonda.

Alice was going on. "After the movie *Private Benjamin* came out -- he wanted me to join the army."

Peter nodded. "After *Superfly* came out all my friends started wearin' platform shoes and takin' bubblebaths with they oldladies. It's like when Pharoah Sanders made a album named *Karma* and everybody started sittin' on pillows like they was *The Maharajah from the 'Hood* -- and my podner in class was tellin' the professor about how rap don't influence or bring about certain behavior in some doofus people."

"Some of my friends don't speak to me anymore . . . because they see me talking to you sometimes."

"Friends? You mean your suitemates? There's always some mess in them dorms. I don't even see how you can drink the water. I heard it's unsafe."

"It's the spring runoff."

"How do you deal with that?"

"First, we filter it."

"Uh."

"Then we boil it."

"Yeah."

"Then we add chemicals to it."

"Chemicals?"

"Then we drink beer!"

"You are a very funny soul," he muttered, shaking his head.

"Far out. You're nothing like my boyfriend. You're so. . .*earthy*," she breathed drunkenly. "I may be young and white, but I'm not slow. I am *not* a bimbo," she Nixoned. "-- And he's such a goonybug. A greaseball. He grosses me out."

"Everybody's got a li'l light under the sun," he quipped. "It take rain and sunshine to make a rainbow. One of the great arts to livin' is the art of forgivin'."

"He was my heart's desire," she moaned.

"Baby --" he started, "there's two tragedies in life -- one is not gittin' yo' heart's desire. The other can be to git it."

"That's morbid. That's sucky."

"Well, the water that float the boat can also overturn it. People be so lonely 'cause they build walls insteada bridges."

"I don't know," she said. "I just like to question everything."

"The first time I questioned *everything* was when the *L.A. Times* announced to the world that the campus poet was dead. But I'm alive! I paid my dues. I'm a flower child that never wilted. That's the first rule -- 'Never surrender'."

"Toe-tuh-*lee*," she agreed. "But I just wish he would go away -- and *stay* away," she pouted.

She never saw Boyfriend again. Things were getting curiouser and curiouser.

* * *

They left the watering hole, explored the area around the corner from the bar, and rambled around the bohemian clothing boutiques near Huguenot Street (reputed to be the oldest street in America) while marveling at its original stone houses. He hummed *Jockomo* and she insisted the Grateful Dead made it first.

They barhopped the circuit, hitting Bacchus, Thesis, and the usual haunts, havens and drinking dens of Collegetown, USA. They ended up shooting pool and downing suds in Snug Harbor (across from the Post Office by Rock and Snow -- the store featuring cross country ski rentals and mountaineering, backpacking and camping equipment). They toasted everything from *glasnost* to *détente*. At this point in their hot fun in the summertime she put the glasses and mugs to the side and was drinking out of the pitchers. She talked incessantly between shots, providing a lifetime landscape of her pedigree. "My uncle is an organic farmer near Lake Katrine. He has fly fishing, skiing, camping, rabbits, goats, chickens, dogs, cats, horses, geese, and ducks," she muttered drunkenly while popping two Panadols followed by a healthy (?) swig of beer.

"You sure you okay droppin' them bullets like that?" he asked.

"I don't have a habit," she said. "I've been taking them for years." Then -- "Oh, I need a big, thick, juicy, long, bun-sized hot dog."

"I need another beer," he deadpanned, ordering more libation.

"I need to dance." She giggled. "C'mon -- let's dance! I have ants in my pants!"

"Are you sure it's okay? People are kinda starin' at us --"

"People?" she asked. "Who needs people? Let's dance. I'd like to learn some of the 'old school' dances. C'mon. Show me. Show me the way."

They took the floor and she began doin' wunna them dances drunk white girls do (*the White Girl?*). An *I Dream of Jeannie* rerun was on the tube above the bar. A Bunny Wailer tune boomed from the box. The music settled down, they re-wet their whistles and got back up to jam to Kool & the Gang's *Open Sesame*, the P-Funk's *Alice In My Fantasies*, and Bootsy Collins' *Point of View*. She showed him some (alleged) dance moves he never saw hide nor hair of before, and he gave *her* a culturally authentic, practical demonstration of the Jerk, the Slide, the Hucklebuck, the Frug, the Funky Chicken, the Hully Gully, and the Bugaloo, taking her on a magic carpet ride, hoppin' and-a boppin' in the history and harmony of his music's ageless era.

After the boogie blended back to the woogie and they tired of pitchers and pool, they sat, dewey-eyed and breathless, discussing the mysteries of the universe and thrashing out the whys, whens and wherefores of learning strategies, aptitudes, and the generalities and specifics of living, breathing and being. They were standin' on the verge of gittin' it on.

"Your hair is so. . .so. . .*different*," she said, leaning towards him and stroking his 'fro. "It's like lamb's wool. It feels like a stuffed toy I once had."

"Yours feels like . . . like . . . like *thread*," he said, fingering her corn silk-yellow strands.

"One of my professors told us that black students can't learn. They only retain information for a little while. She's an airhead, a space cadet. She sucks eggs."

"That's interesting how you use words. You give 'em some amusin' meanings."

"When I use a word it means just what I choose it to mean -- nothing more or less."

"Yeah. It's like the word 'muthafucka' doesn't mean 'a person who has intimate relations with his or her mother.' That's why I fell out with summa them militant cats from the '60s. Talkin' 'bout 'Off the Pig' didn't mean 'Kill the police'."

"Off the Pig!??!? You mean not eating bacon?"

"No . . . no, baby. It's something from the '60s -- 'round the time they were protestin' the war, burnin' bra-zeers and smokin' anything that popped out the ground."

"I heard about the '60s. I heard about dancin' to the music and wild things and 'gimme some skin' and Jim Morrison -- the roots of rock. But what about 'Off the Pig'?"

"There was a trial in Chicago and --" he started. Then -- "Never mind. It was just all about some people gittin' caught out there and tryin' to lie they way through. They need to speak the truth to the people -- whether it's in the radical canon or not. Times change. Things change. Words change. It's like 'rappin'' usta be sumthin' you did on a door or the sweet talk in a song or your romantic verbalizations towards an intended love interest."

"-- or lust interest," she flagged. Then -- "You know what I wish? I wish you would escort me back to my dorm. You just *have* to see my 'Girl and a Bottle' ceramic. My professor called it 'modernistic with classical origins.' Plus, I have to take my herbal supplement. But there's one thing I have to do before we leave." An Ozzy Osbourne tune blasted from the box.

"What's that?"

"I gotta pee."

He stared deeply into the shallow, blue waters of her bloodshot eyes. "You are the craziest li'l white woman I ever met in my life," he said calmly.

"And you have a beautiful set of big, shiny teeth."

"It runs in the family."

* * *

They navigated through the late-afternooners, stumbling through the sunwashed thoroughfare past the rows of bars and scores of sunburned scholars and B.A. and B.S.-seeking students. "I'd like to sketch you when we get to the dorm," she said. "I can do a quick study."

"I really think you're a bit too smashed to even *hold* a pencil -- much less sketch somebody," he whispered.

As they entered the outer area of her suite and she fumbled for her key, he noticed two of her suitemates (who were watching TV) staring oddly at him. He hoped that they wouldn't call the campus police and he'd be arrested for taking advantage of a coed who was so under the influence they'd need an earth mover to recover her. Her suitemates turned off the tube and scurried to the haven of their rooms when the presence of the black plague was realized.

"I hope I don't puke," she said. All I had to eat since yesterday was some Trix."

"I hope I don't have to upchuck, too," he said. A pair of her suitemates' eyes peered furtively through the crack of one of the dorm room doors.

In her room a bucolic poster of the Russian winter countryside signed *"To Alice, with love . . . Vladimir"* graced one wall across from a Mel Gibson poster that stared oddly at them above an orange and yellow Zapotec rug. A tiny model of a sailing ship sat atop a box of Scotch tape near an empty Cutty Sark bottle. Sandwiched on her bookshelf among layers of academic tomes and artsy-fartsy magazines was an instructional manual: *How to Play Gin Rummy*. On her desk near the window was a lava lamp and a painting of apples -- "That's mine, that's my work," she said -- with the words "Delicious Rome, MacIntosh, Baldwins, and Golden Delicious" scripted in bold, black lettering with a blanket of blue skyscape. Two empty beer balls sat silently in a corner near her quilt-covered double bed.

"Welcome to Wonderland," she declared as she motioned towards the bed. "I'll be right back," she said. "I have to pee again."

When she got back from paying her water bill, she lit a joint, stuffed a towel under the door to keep the scent from escaping, nonchalantly sat next to him and removed the stretchy fabric of her halter exposing her purple bra. She leaned over so that her body was in intimate contact with his. "You know --" she breathed, "I remember that time I saw you under your robe." She passed the primo.

"*What* time?" he asked.

"That time we were in your room and you were helping me with my essay. You had your robe on. I know you let me see your giant cock under the table on purpose."

"My *dick*!?!"

"I've been trying to tell you how I've felt for a long time," she confessed. "Why don't I sit on your lap and we'll discuss the first thing that pops up. You know you're a horny toad."

"And you a fly li'l thing."

"I tried to get caught a couple of more times."

"Huh?"

"Like that time I was leaning out the window -- when I was going home and waiting for my parents to pick me up . . . that time when I was leaning out the window in my red bikini panties and T-shirt and you were standing by the door and I told you to come in . . . or that time I came to your room with my tight-tight-tight short-shorts on . . . Being around you is like being in another world. You teach me so much. Your passion is so . . . *rabid*. . . . You're nothing like my boyfriend . . . or my classmates, or my father. You're just so different. You show me so many new things." By this time she had shucked her skirt, panty hose, and matching purple, barely there, more-than-intimate apparel.

"Strange place for a mole," he said as she removed her bra and tossed it on the bed beside him. He picked it up, inspecting it as though it were a priceless work of art. He was like a camel, he thought -- just humpin' to please.

"What *are* you doing?" she breathed. "What are you looking for?"

"I'm a titty man," he owned up. "Mine is just another point of view. I'm just a reflection of you. . . . I'm lookin' for your bra size."

"It's a 38."

"38? But you're so tiny. . . . You wear a 38?"

"Yup. Fill your hands, partner!"

He removed his outer garments and his Fruit-of-the-Looms, then began to suck and nip at her freckle-flecked, bulbous breasts. She was down on her knees and ready to spread -- all around the world for the funk.

"Oh, my -- I don't know-*ow-ow-ow*. . ." she mouthed, shocked at the dimensions of his erection.

"Is everything OK?" he asked.

"No . . . I mean – yes. . . . You're the first black man I've ever been with."

"-- And you're the first li'l young white girl I've ever . . . *touched*," he said.

"Wow!" she screeched, embracing her newfound obsession. "Now *that's* a bone of contention! Talk about affirmative action!" Then -- "Krinchskins! It tastes as good as it smells!" And -- "If my father saw us doing this, he'd kill me," she said as they engaged in their forever and ever foreplay.

"If yo' paw saw what I'ma do to you -- his shotgun would stand up and load it*self. Law-aw-awd . . . if David Duke walked in here right now. . .* he thought, but announced, "Let the fun begin."

* * *

They did the Crab, the Chicken Wing, the Ankles In the Air, the Just Don't Care, the Mutiny On the Booty, the Ten-Minutes-To-Two and the Quarter-To-Three. "Ride yo' pony, baby! Git on yo' pony and ride. . . . Git down on it!" he gasped.

"Wow! Wow-*wee*! This is so rad!" she screamed. The girl was a freak. The girl never missed a beat. There was a whole lotta rithum goin' 'round. They were briefly interrupted from their cummings and goings-on by one of her suitemates who asked her if everything was OK after hearing the cacophonous, carousing racket emerging from her room. "Everything is *wonderful . . . breathtaking*," she said before returning to the afternoon's escapades.

"To the wax! To the max! To the *rear-ear-earrrrr mararch*!" he wailed to the freak o' the week as he shot her with his bop gun while showing her how to do the Juicy Watusi, the Family Stones, the Booty-Wooty and the Come-Here-Li'l-White-Girl-I'ma-Wear-Yo'-Ass-Out -- as he let her have it like a special man. He did some exploring too -- his oral cavity crossing the threshold of her not-so-clandestine basin of bliss -- even though he claimed he ain't never did that (when the fellas was around). *Gimme that chalice, Alice. . . Gimme that chalice, Alice, stretch it out, baby... stretch out dat rubber band,* he chanted breathlessly, knee-deep in her cosmic slop. He just had to git more o' that funky stuff as they were gittin' up for the downstroke, takin' it to the stage, turnin' that mutha out and tearin' the roof off the sucka. It was all the way live. They was *doin' that stuff... doin' that stuff...* on the real side.

* * *

When they were finally exhausted from the jovial jaunt to their lustfilled oasis, he kissed her slyly, gently on her cheek; left her adrift in their thrill upon the hill in the Land of Nod and tiptoed out the door to wherever it was from whence he had come. Later, she awoke in the bubbleless bathtub and wondered how a floating patch of woolly, auburn, grey-tinged hair had gotten there as she fixed her eyes on the eerily odd vapors oozing into the ghostly, green bottle.

About a year later, they nodded to each other at graduation.

August 2011
Stamford, CT

On A Mission

It was their turn to get the beer. They were on a mission.

Fatima Arbuckle, a wayward townie from the heavily-trafficked locale surrounding the Hudson Valley college's oasis of knowledge, knocked firmly on Peter's dorm room door. "What up, Sweet Peter Jeter? What's hoppin', Peter Rabbit?"

A semi-conscious, unshaven figure appeared sluggishly. "What it is?" mumbled his well-read, education-seeking buddy, who had returned to the collegiate learning process after a perilously treacherous stint in LBJ's foreign adventure some years prior. "It's time to git the beer," Fatima pompously decreed. "I got a free coupon from my uncle for the state store."

"Good mornin', my flatulent friend," Peter said, rubbing his unmanaged, woolly head of hair. "The state store? New Paltz got a state store?" he quizzed, picking the sleep out of his exhausted eyes. He'd had quite a night . . . and afternoon.

"No. We gotta drive to Poughkeepsie," said Fatima. "It ain't that far. I ain't got no money, but I got this coupon. It's good at the store over there. I think the truck'll make it."

"*Think*? Either it's gon' make it or it ain't. What's the deal?"

"The deal is -- we don't have no beer," his gumbo pot-bellied podner disclosed. "It's Miller time. The fellas is waitin' by the crib. They sent me to git you 'cause you the only one over 21 -- *wa-a-a-ay* over 21 -- and I'm the only one with the ride . . . a match made in heaven," he kidded.

Peter shat, showered and shaved and they stepped out to the truck, which looked like it belonged in the opening scene of a *Sanford and Son* rerun. As they approached the rusted, formerly red hoopty (with a boom box on the back seat for a radio), Fatima spied a coed walking her four-legged friend. "Mornin'." He tipped his tattered, navy blue NY Yankees baseball cap. "Nice animal you got there."

"Thank you," the yellow-frocked, unhighlighted blonde lass with ocean blue eyes acknowledged.

"I was talkin' to the dog," he gagged, laughing thunderously through the weapon of crass disruption that was his mouth while embracing his outsized tummy-tum-tum.

"Bruh -- what's the deal with you?" Peter demanded. "You cain't be comin' on campus talkin' to them people like that. That ain't no townie. That girl pay tuition to be here."

"I was just tryin' to hit on her. You ain't gotta make sense to 'em . . . just git they attention. Say anything. Wunna my favorite pickup lines is -- 'You got a map? 'cause I'm lost in yo' loveliness.' He who loses is hesitated. The cat ain't *never* had *my* tongue. But it's all right. Children and dogs love me."

"You need to see a proctologist and have yo' head examined," suggested Peter.

"Proctologist? That's a head doctor? Is that like a rumortologist?" Fatima asked. "The ones who be spreadin' rumors?"

"Yeah, bruh. Yeah," muttered Peter, shaking his head.

That was the kind of guy Fatima was. He was a Special Ed dropout with the credibility of a used car salesman at a Liar's Convention. Whatever scientist said that two objects can't occupy the same space simultaneously never saw his asscheeks. Whenever he and his childhood friends played Zorro he'd be Sergeant Garcia. He couldn't type "WWII" (he once said) because he "couldn't find the Roman numerals." He was so slow it would take several millennia for his century plant to bloom. His political philosophy was a blend of Thomas Jefferson and Bill Clinton -- life, liberty, and the pursuit of interns. The infernal combustion engine that was his voice message on his rotary phone said, "If you call and I ain't here -- I went to the store to git the beer."

"That's a nice scene," remarked Peter when they stopped for a light near campus as a man pushed an elderly woman in a wheelchair. "That's a nice picture. It's refreshin' to see that. He looks like he's happy to be out here helpin' her."

"He *should* be happy. He just got out the penitentiary for paralyzin' her."

They weaved through the village of New Paltz and its proclaimed "oldest continuously-inhabited neighborhood in Anglo-America" to the highway interchange that would take them to the New York State Thruway and the opportunity to get tipsy in Poughkeepsie. "C'mon, bruh -- you got some gas money 'til payday?"

"When's payday?" Peter asked.

"I don't know, my 'steamed colleague -- *you* got the job," he said as they pulled over to a gas station. "The dogs bark, but the caravan moves on."

Peter coughed up the capital outlay for the petrol. They gassed up, Fatima squeezed into the driver's seat, turned on the beatbox, and they were off to see the Poughkeepsie-based, morningtime merchant of liquid laughter. "Onward 'til glory," Fatima proclaimed as they took off, reentering the highway. They wove on down the road with its panoramic views of fields, woods and mountains with their celebrated climbing sites and historic times of yore.

"You know what --" Fatima said as the music blasted from the box, "I'm hongry, but I'ma wait 'til we git the beer. If we woulda stopped for food first -- I coulda gave you some gas for free."

"Haw, haw."

"Eatin' without drinkin' is like poo'in without stinkin'," he quipped. "But I still like to eat a lot. That's how I am how I am," he continued. "I like bein' fat. You can call me what you wanna. Just don't call me late for dinner. I ain't got no acid refucks. I'm just fat. They got some advantages to it . . . like that time I rode on the airplane and they gave me a upgrade to first class 'cause I couldn't fit in the coach seat.

"My momma was fat. My daddy was fat. My chirren is fat, and I like my name . . . *Fatima* . . . it got a certain ring to it. When I was born-ded -- they say I was a bundle o' heaven . . . a BIG bundle. . . . My momma named me after her favorite saint . . . Our Lady of Fatima . . . 'Fatima Arbuckle.' It's better than my brother' name -- Fartmore. He stink, therefore, he am. . . . The marines are always the first to fight. He's always the first to fart. . . . Momma gave all of us all names that start with 'F' 'cause that's the grades the older children made in school.

"My momma was fat, too. She was so fat she went to Jenny Craig and they told her: 'Mission Impossible.' And my paw . . . my paw . . . I remember when my paw gave me my first taste o' beer . . . stuck his thumb in the glass and put it in my mouth. Years later I told him I remembered that and he told me, 'That wasn't my thumb.'"

"What you babblin' 'bout? You talk about yo' own momma and daddy like that?" quizzed Peter.

"Yeah. My old, grey maw -- she ain't what she used to be. I know you a acamajician and done read mo' books than they got in the Texas suppository -- but I know my maw and my paw."

"I'm underwhelmed." Peter yawned. "You ain't worth the paper towels you wipe yo' big ass with," he asserted inelegantly.

"It's bigger than both of us," offered Fatima.

"Yes, Your Roundness," said Peter as they chugged along, winding through the seams of interconnecting forks, junctions and straightaways on the yellow beer road to liquid pleasure and delight.

* * *

"Look --" cried Peter. "Look at that dead bird."

"Where?' Fatima asked, peering overhead at the seemingly infinite ocean of blue above.

"By the side o' the highway -- over there --" Peter said, motioning towards a cluster of flowering shrubs. "You blind too, bruh?"

"I don't wan' look *too* hard. I don't wan' be a extracted driver." Fatima gripped the steering wheel with his knees, grabbed a lighter from his crusty bluejeaned pocket, reached in the vehicle's trembling ashtray for an alligator-clipped joint, lit it, and hit it.

"It ain't safe to be tryin' to look for dead birds when you behind the wheel," he cautioned. "And I don't drink and drive -- I pull over and finish the bottle. I wouldn't wan' git caught out here bad like that. That would be a tragedy of justice. That's my New Year's revolution. That would be another sad story in the anals of my life. I ain't gon' *never* do nuthin' no mo' to git *me* locked down," he declared as the pungent scent of marijuana smoke saturated the frayed innards of the scruffy, uninsured motor vehicle. "I'm like my podner, the Rabbi, when it come to goin' to jail -- 'Never again.'"

Just then, right on cue, a patrol car with lights flashing came literally out of nowhere, crept behind them for a slight distance, then sped up as a loudspeaker blared, "PULL YOUR VEHICLE TO THE SIDE OF THE ROAD. PULL YOUR VEHICLE TO THE SIDE OF THE ROAD."

Peter sighed. "You're about as lucky as a onelegged cat in a dog pound fulla hungry canines," he said.

The helmeted officer approached the truck, hand on his weapon, and requested that Fatima produce his license and registration. The unlicensed State of New York motor vehicle operator (and his passenger) were well aware of the danger inherent in even the slightest encounter with a representative of a police agency for males of their pedigree and economic status.

"I SAID -- LICENSE AND REGISTRATION -- TURN OFF THE VEHICLE -- AND TURN OFF THAT RADIO IN THE BACK SEAT!" the officer barked, standing back slightly, his hand poised dangerously on his firearm.

"Mr. Policeman -- " Fatima began, "I . . . I . . . I don't have a license. And even if I did -- I cain't afford no insurance anyway. You see --"

"YOU HAVE ANY ID ON YOU?"

"I got this coupon from the beer store."

"GET OUT OF THE CAR," the officer ordered as he detected the undeniable odor of the Mary Jane. "AND *YOU* -- DON'T MOVE," he yapped at the other American citizen. Fatima complied, while Pete cringed at the prospect of never getting to the nirvana of sudsland due to the intrusion of their present fate as rendered by legal edict.

"HANDS ON YOUR HEAD!" the officer ordered. Fatima placed his hands over his private parts. "ON *THIS* HEAD," the policeman demonstrated, pointing his now-drawn .357 at Fatima's big, empty skull. He frisked him and found a 50-count box of zip-lock baggies in his back pocket. "WHAT ARE THESE?" he asked.

"I . . . I . . . I collect coins," Fatima answered nervously.

"COINS? THIS APPEARS TO BE PARAPHERNALIA USED FOR THE PACKAGING AND DISTRIBUTION OF MARIJUANA."

"-- Marijuana? Weed? Ganja? I ain't no dope fiend! I'm a alcoholic!" Fatima protested.

The policeman shook his head and secured Fatima with a set of plastic zip-tie handcuffs, took his name, proceeded to call in for wants and warrants on him and checked for violations involving the vehicle. Sure enough, Fatima and his truck had scores of unpaid tickets and a laundry list of citations out on it for vehicular violations and infractions including exceeding the speed limit, overtaking and passing a school bus, open container in a motor vehicle, driving under the influence, operating a motor vehicle without a license, operating an uninsured vehicle, possession of marijuana, and driving without a safety belt. The cop added a charge of possession with intent to distribute a controlled substance, bein' stupid, and driving while black (even though they didn't write the last two down).

Other units and a tow truck arrived, and the gendarmes had the vehicle hauled away while Fatima sat squirming, squeezed into the back of a police cruiser. "I thought the statue of eliminations wore out on all that," he told the rollers. They checked Peter's ID, saw he was a veteran and a good, clean college boy, and accepted his explanation that they were just on their way to cop some beer with the free coupon they had. They let him off with a warning to be careful of who he made future beer runs with and shuffled Fatima off to the local lockup.

Peter stood in the late morning heat under a soon-to-be searing sun pondering the long trek back to campus and the ill-fated journey to get the beer.

He was so thirsty and his throat was so parched that he didn't have enough spittle left for a sticka gum.

August 2011
Stamford, CT

Professor Arturo

A Living Doll

"The most terrible poverty is loneliness
and the feeling of being unloved."
-- Mother Teresa

My wife was a living doll.

I had long daydreamed and fantasized about interblending with the heart and soul of such an entity as the eternally beloved object of my affections while tediously toiling away in pedestrian economic peonage as senior assembler at a Louisiana Avenue mannequin factory. It was far from being a coat & tie job, but it paid the rent.

My life was about as cheerful as a slave ship manifest. It was a tragic medley of misadventures. In my early teens I was told by my aunt that my mother committed suicide at a home for destitute women and my father was serving a quadruple life sentence for murdering my older siblings as they slept (I always wondered about my pedigree). I was the Most Valueless Player in the major leagues of life. In high school they said I kept to myself as I did because my father served so much time in "administrative segregation" (solitary confinement) in prison and the greenest apple didn't fall too far from the rotten tree.

Every Christmas Eve I anxiously awaited Santa's arrival, just to have a minimal interaction with another being. I did that until I was 17 and found out his existence was an adult fabrication. I never had a girlfriend or went on a date. I was emperor of the Lonely Hearts Club. The closest I ever got to having sex was somebody telling me "F--- you!" My right hand was my BMF (best male friend), intimately adored ally, aider and abettor. I spent prom night at home with a bejeweled white glove (shadow dancing all night to Michael Jackson tunes).

To say that I was reclusive or a misanthrope is the ultimate understatement. I was lonelier than a far right-wing Republican Southern state senator at a midnight reggae concert; as estranged as a vegetarian at a meat lovers' cookout; as companionless as a peacenik in the Pentagon. Rambling through my sock drawer was a major league adventure. I was so unbefriended that I installed several mirrors in my bedroom for company. I spent many a dystopic, soulless evening memorizing Henny Youngman jokes, watching *Lou Dobbs Tonight*, or mulling over the next day's workplace activities involving the assembly of euphemistically-labeled "male, female, and non-sex- distinguishable fashion display modules."

Mannequins, in a word.

Then one day during another spiritless, repetitious shift of monotonous mishappenings, Providence smiled upon my plebeian presence. While perusing the morning's departmental mail I came across a catalogue featuring what were billed as "The world's finest vinyl rubber blow-up dolls." It was a raucous pictorial rendition of an assorted collection of rubbery, offbeat lookers and hookers. I thumbed through the pages and marveled at the promises of "the perfect companion or wife" who would "fulfill your every fantasy -- and introduce you to newer worlds of passion." I was as hooked as a loquacious largemouth bass in a bucket as I surveyed the booklet's panoramic pictorial representations of samples of dollfaced dreamboats and the captivating captions beneath.

The life-sized dolls (made in China) ranged in every distinction and divergence conceivable and their primping parade of characters originated from every racial, ethnic, religious and cultural background imaginable. There was Bambi Bootylicious (with the pulsating lips and lifelike, molded breasts), the Minaj-4-1 (with cyberskin mouth, removable wigs and hair coloring packets), Alarming Ava (with the vibrating rear, programmable mouth, 25-inch waist, and travel alarm), the Alien Love Doll (far out attachments included), and the Space Age Spinning Doll (complete with astronaut suit and ray gun). There was Shee-Shee the Shemale (with interchangeable parts), the Big Greasy Glenda Doll (complete with extra wide frontal and rear openings), Hero (the Inflatable Horse), and Jazzy Jackie (with built-in prophylactic, rotating private parts and removable multi-speed undulating egg).

The toneless, unchanging recurrences of my day dematerialized as I surveyed the representations of flexible, stretchable honeys that magnified my eyes and elevated (debased?) my lustful reflections. *There she is,* I thought . . . *my future lover, companion and bride* . . . Passionate Perfecta!!!

I was immediately and enduringly blinded by the beauty of her huge, full lips; her potential for bouncing in all the right (and left) places, her three "easily accessible" openings, and her fantastic fleshpillow funbags. I would no longer have to spend joyless midnight masses alone or take solo walks along the levee amidst laughing lovers holding hands. Weekends in my future would be more tolerable with such an unpicayune item in my now-pleasant present. Movies, dinner dates and nightlong conversations would replace previous nights of idiot box idols and their presidential preferences. With the addition of her (and the accompanying $19.95 air pump) in my life I would finally be a conventional and customary human being.

I engaged in the relatively minor annoyances of filling out the order form, speeding to the post office after work in the late afternoon's oppressive heat, and nervously awaiting the arrival of my soft, stretchable, rubberized helpmate. A shred of an eternity later I found myself unwrapping her cardboard and plastic confines and beamed with pride over my mail order bride. I attached the air pump and expanded her seamless skin, her piercing eyes, her sumptuously soft hands, movable arms, and easily accessible multi-entry points. Our cavorting and playful squeezes continued until the wee-est of hours.

I didn't want to deflate her ego by having her think she was mere arm candy, so I presided over our wedding ceremony one Sunday afternoon and we spent our honeymoon at a hotsheet motel on Tulane Avenue over by the courthouse. We even paid extra to have the movies piped in.

I found that Perfecta was indeed the perfect spouse and companion -- and not just because any stick'll do to beat a dog. She was the ideal mate. She was extremely low maintenance (minimal upkeep of a one-time investment in an air pump), was always on time for dates, didn't complain about her weight, didn't ask for my opinion about her clothing, didn't run her mouth incessantly over dinner, had free passage at movies and on public transportation, and afforded me the privilege of driving in the mandatory two-passenger designated lane whenever or wherever we had to. There were no weekly visits to the beauty parlor or the nail shop. A bevy of beauticians wouldn't be sending their children to college on *my* dime. I didn't have to pay for top shelf perfumes. Where other women might have wanted *Jean Patou's 1000*, she was satisfied with *Manhunter*. She had no demand or refusal for late night or early morning sex, there weren't any "girlfriends" or family members all up in our business, and nobody would hit on her at parties. She was the perfect dinner date. I only had to cough up for one (even though she never shared in tipping).

My landlord, however, was a bit taken aback when I asked if I would be charged extra for the additional tenant. He suggested therapy.

The cable guy was a bit more empathetic when I introduced her. He wanted to know how *he* could get one. I got her some courtin' candy and took her to a second line, that orgy of ritual street dancing and carnal romancing that reflects the musical traditions of New Orleans' indigenous urban dwellers. She bounced so merrily to the music that she nearly got blown away. Her hat, which protected her nose from peeling in the blistering New Orleans afternoon sun, was spirited to the skies by her ricocheting, shaking and quaking, but she didn't make any bones about it.

But all good (and horrid) marriages must inevitably come to an end either by death, divorce, or other departure. We were picnicking at Lake Pontchartrain one afternoon when I had to scamper to a cinderblock shelter to use the facilities. While I answered nature's call, the tether I used to secure her became loose and unfastened due to rising winds from the Gulf.

When I returned to our blanket and basket I could see her floating away, far into the distant skies beyond the water's edge, and realized that the melody of memory's magic and the fickle, fleeting nature of happiness would forever pierce my heart.

June 2013
Stamford, CT

Jack Moore (Private Dick)

The Case of the Missing Draws

I'm Moore . . . Jack Moore. I'm a dick . . . an unprivate eye. During my decades as a dick I've been up many a rough road, down many a dark tunnel, and in a who-o-o-o-ole lotta deep valleys. I've always wanted to get ahead in life, and I'm a firm, unshrinking, hardnosed player who doesn't make boneheaded moves, screw around or dig in over my head when I'm getting the shaft from the squeeze of a tight situation or a loose end whenever I'm left swinging in the wind.

When a problem comes along I whip it. I don't shrivel under scrutiny when pressed hard, stuck in limbo, or about to take a licking and hit rock bottom. I hold up well and don't withdraw or jerk around. I tighten up the loose ends and don't peter out. I stiffen up, stand defiantly, suck it in, shoot back at the loyal opposition, hold firm, enlarge my perspective, take a hard stance, stick with it, burst out and come clean.

I've hung in there when I was sometimes stuck on stupid -- and I've often been told to shove it. I've had some significant blows to my career, but once I get the hard evidence I bone up, allow for any slippage, stand erect, take matters firmly in hand, stretch it out, penetrate the wall of silence, get poised for the attack, make a resurgence through a come-from-behind victory, and rise for the occasion -- even though some people might think I'm screwy, cocky . . . or merely nuts.

It was another shadowy, soggy, rainy New Orleans monsoon afternoon as I sat swigging some straight Jack out of a well-blemished coffee cup and smoking a bone at the rustic, wooden Rosenberg's dining table in my office, which is also my Royal Street upstairs studio apartment just down the block from the Vieux Carre District police station. I was prioritizing and contemplating the latest inflow of demands for payment, listening to an antique Barbara Lynn tune on the radio about "losing a good thing," and trimming my salt and pepper chinstrap beard with a set of corroded, dulled antiquarian shears. My AA meeting attendance was an experiment gone awry, my binges were becoming nothing more than selective blackouts, and my singular soul, death, taxes, and inflation comprised my comfortless and secluded congregation of solitude in this most acrimonious of workplaces. My life was so dull that the most exciting thing about it was my euphemism collection.

A cultivated knock at the door interrupted my latest episode in self-abuse. "Come in," I offered while glancing at my leetle friend, the soon-to-be-pawned Colt Woodsman .22 that slept under a grizzled, yellowed, mellowed copy of the New Orleans Tribune.

In stepped the magnificent spectacle of a demurely smiling, pert-mouthed, pouty-lipped enchantress with delicately-waxed eyebrows, a pecawn-brown lacefront wig, and a glimmering grill of toothpaste TV commercial-white teeth. She sported a see-through New Orleans Saints fleur-de-lis'd, hooded poncho; a black lace overlaid blouse, a maroon pencil skirt that exposed more thighs than Popeyes, a pair of classic black pumps, tiny seashell gold earrings, jangling gold bracelets, and a high grade cultured pearl necklace. I fantasized about putting another strand of *liquid* pearls around her refined neck. She was summertime fine with a driblet of hypermammary development and a more than ample apple-bottom booty. I hankered my head being buried deep within her sillycone valleys.

I added her up as one of those women of discerned refinement who would put her mouth where the money was. She seemed like she had a good head on her shoulders. There wasn't a visible tramp stamp on her body. She was healthy . . . about one hot sausage sandwich away from being a "BIG" girl. *What a chunka chocolate,* I thought, contemplating the toxic tonic of her beauty, the extent of her ball-handling skills, and how I would love to run my fingers through her . . . extensions. My crazed desire for this pretty woman was the crab boil . . . not the crabs. For some men, a fine woman was the whole meal. For me, they were the Tabasco Sauce. *I ain't no carpenter,* I thought, *but if I EVER had a shot at that, somebody'd get screwed. I --*

"Mister Moore -- Mister Moore . . ." I heard from somewhere outside myself. "Do you *really* have to stare me up and down like that? I didn't come here to pussyfoot around. I'm about business."

"Didn't you see the sign on the door?" I asked as I rose from the discounted wooden chair and walked towards the entrance.

"*What* sign?"

"*This* one," I said, standing wobbly-legged while indicating the hand-painted words on the door's dangling shingle:

JACK

OFF

TODAY

"Oh --" she said. "I took it as a suggestion."

She was my kinda doll. I motioned for her to sit in one of the canvas camping chairs by the table that served as my seating arrangement for the rare clientele that I might chance to encounter. She removed her outer gear, hung it on a teetering coat rack by the door, and sat her tight-ended tushy on the cushy.

"How'd you hear about me?"

"I just looked on the Internet and found the first dick I could," she offered. "I haven't been in New Or-leens too long. I'm originally from Fort Dix . . . New Jersey. I looked on the Internet for a dick and your name popped up."

I'm on the Internet? I asked myself. Then -- "Of course -- we advertise in a variety of print and electronic media . . . . What's your name?"

"Mrs. . . . .uh . . . *Ms.* . . . Cockburn."

"Talk is cheap . . . money buys whiskey," I quipped. *I wasn't born yesterday. I know the difference between ketchup and catsup,* I thought. "My fee is quite expensive . . . and comes up front," I said, knowing I would take on all comers anyway. Front, back, side, standing, reverse cowgirl. It didn't matter.

"I have money. I have a *lot* of money," she said, dipping into her oversized Chanel tote and coming out with a wad that would choke a swampful of hungry gators.

"Uh. I see you do. Let's talk turkey . . . just the facts . . . just the facts, ma'am."

"My panties are missing."

"Well, I'd better get you a towel. You need to cover up or you're gonna catch cold," I cautioned.

"Gracious sakes, *no* -- don't be redic'," she corrected. "They're *missing*. Somebody's been stealing my panties," she spilled with cuttlefish charm.

"You can't feel it when they do that?" I asked, thinking she was relating some cock and bull story.

"No -- not from my *be*-hind. They're missing from the laundry room in my building."

"Oh -- the washateria!"

"Come again!!??!"

"That's what we call self-service laundry facilities in New Orleans, ma'am," I explained to the transplant. "You have any idea of who might be stealing these . . . items? Could it be your husband? Your ex? I noticed you referred to yourself as 'Mrs.' and then 'Ms.'. Obviously you were married; now you're not."

She began giving me a blow-by-blow description of their whatever-it-was.

"I was married . . . once . . . once upon a time . . . We had a home in Jersey . . . and a condo in Toronto . . . We lived in Pilot Knob . . . in New York . . . for a while . . . " The scenester sighed, gazing out the window at the raindrops tickling the windowpanes. "He was too overbearing," she conceded. "We had relationship issues . . . He had the sense of humor of an overnight shift morgue attendant. He was so lazy I thought he had stationary fever. All he ever did was constantly shoot off his mouth. Talking to him was like conversing with a funerary prayer card. He was a real slippery character . . . always trying to play an honest game with a crooked deck . . . We had a non-exclusive relationship. . . . One night he went out and never came back again. . . . His life was a conglomeration of wrong on *so* many levels. . . . He never really . . . measured up. . . . He was a loser who came out on the wrong end of the final score more than the Washington Generals. . . . His life was a series of unforeseen, unavoidable consequences. . . . I met him when I was fresh off the bus . . . Then he threw me under it. The night I met him he rolled me a nice big one; I did some shots . . . a valium or two . . . and I was cherry dew . . . and married to the dog. . . . I heard he was with some barfly floozy back home. . . . He's dead and I *still* hate him . . . . I *still* hate him. He can eat me from the lowest depths of hell on my wettest day. . . . She had the man, but I have the papers . . . especially the little green ones with the pictures."

"Did you kill him?" I asked dryly.

"He committed suicide in a bowling alley parking lot. They found what was supposed to be his brains where his balls should've been . . . business as usual."

"Never pitchfork the dead," I said. Then -- "You think someone who knew him might be the panty purloiner -- like this is a morbid kind of joke or something?"

"No. He was a Jersey jerkoff . . . for life," she offered. "He wouldn't know anybody way down here."

She insisted that she wanted to keep things on the down-low from the building's co-op board because she didn't want the stigma of being a pestiferous tenant. It sounded like it would be a difficult case, but as I said earlier -- I was the kind of dick who would take on all comers.

* * *

"Okay," I told Babygirl, "I'll take the case. We'll make it a joint effort." I rose from the chair and inched towards her. The fragrance of what I determined to be a 'Lizbeth Taylor original oozed through my wide open nostrils. I stood over her, offering her a hit of the Jack, but she motioned *no* with a practiced wave of her hand. *She's a classy li'l thang,* I thought, *and I'm the Dean of Students.*

"Will you please stop undereying me like that -- and sit down?!!" she blurted. "You're such a dick. I came here for business -- not to get blown away by some armchair detective." It was a boo-coo big bruise to my ego, but money is thicker than honey, so I sat down and stared straight ahead knowing that her case would be a tough row to hoe.

"Okey-dokey," I said sitting erectly.

"Now that's much better." She calmed down. "Don't be so randy."

I dictated my terms to her, scribbled out an agreement on the last vestiges of pages of a decomposing legal pad, and arranged to meet her at her Uptown fourplex the next day. I'd be pulling out at the crack of dawn in hot pursuit of what I thought might be a serial underwear bandit.

* * *

The next day (after cleaning my two-tone wingtips and donning my favorite sweater vest and almost-matching slacks) I arrived at the scene of the grime on Napoleon Avenue, not far from Pascal's Manale Restaurant just off St. Charles. It was a couple of hours after the cock doodle-dooed as a fiery sky ushered in the morning. She greeted me at the Belleville AvantGarde cherry door of a two-level, three-bay late Victorian frame house (with a second-level gallery and full-length augmented arches on every opening). She wore a skintight pair of black leggings, orange brand name sneakers, a yellow poet shirt, and a smile that was the envy of the morning sun.

"*Come in*," she vamped. "You have to excuse the place. I've been working out."

I entered the vaulted portico to the hallway and was ushered to her apartment on the left while noting that the doorless crib on the right was under renovation. "Nobody lives there," she indicated. "They're remodeling. I think they've taken a deposit on it. My only two neighbors live upstairs."

On entering her apartment I immediately discerned that she was an uncompromising perfectionist. It was as though I had walked into a page of *House & Garden:* glittering crystal . . . Daliesque wall art . . . award-winning designer furniture . . . modish lamps . . . super-fine deco accents . . . She ushered me over to a white Arne Jacobsen Ox chair under a Lauritzen "Embassy" chandelier, offered me some coffee, but I chose whatever the brown liquid was in the Waterford Monique Lhuillier Atelier Ships Decanter. All the stuff I dreamed of when gazing so many afternoons into the Hurwitz-Mintz window a coupla steps from my administrative center.

She poured a polite amount of the firewater into a Lismore shot glass, and I downed it in a wink and a blink. She took me on a guided tour of the co-op then showed me where the common laundry area was in the first floor rear of the structure. I examined the set and didn't detect any possible external entrance. It had to be an inside job.

She allowed me to peruse her collection of unmentionables, which she kept in a white Olivia bureau dresser in her walk-in closet. I asked if I could examine her treasures alone so as not to be distracted by her magnetic allure (at least that's what I told her). She left and I was blown away by a kaleidoscope of

Professor Arturo

aromatic colors and a cornucopia of perfumed fabrics of cotton, silk, lace, and satin in all styles of stock and invention. There were Lane Bryant's Passion luxury lace trim hipster panties, Jennifer Lopez's Vintage Glamour Cheeky tangas, Maidenform's lace-trim cheekies, Gilligan & O'Malley's Intimate Apparel, bikinis, monokinis, lacies, comfies, hiphuggers, personal massagers (vibrators), thongs, seamless thongs, supersoft thongs, fishnet lace-up thongs, V-strings, crotchless panties, open crotch panties, granny draws, metallic micros, metallic Y-backs, patterned Y-backs, neon Y-backs, Perfect Performance boyshorts, hanky panky boyshorts, Punish Me specials, booty-wooties, sheer butterflies, Chriss Cross crotchless jeweled G-strings, animal print tie sides, wide side go-go shorts, floral icons, lace minis, gray sassafras shorties, rhinestone-trimmed shimmy fringes, Unwrap Me's, Poetic Lines, red-white-and-blue flaggies, catch-'ems, throwback bikinis, Penelopes, Paisley Pleasures, spankies, lace charmers, stretchables, edibles. . . .

"-- What -- what *are* you doing?!?!!" Ms. Cockburn's voice interrupted me some span of time later as I turned, breathless, exhausted, and sweating like a galley slave in a gladiator movie.

"-- Oh . . . I'm coming . . . I'm coming . . . I was just . . . uh . . . just familiarizing myself with the . . . uh . . . merchandise . . . I'm just doing a little . . . sniffing around," I shucked, dripping with . . . perspiration. "It's -- It's a li'l warm in here," I jived. "I wanted to be able to . . . uh . . . screw . . . uh . . . srcu . . . ti*nize* . . . uh . . . *recognize* the evidence when I uh . . . come across it. It's just a bit hot in here."

"I really wouldn't know." She grinned. "I usually don't stay in there that long."

She gave me the skinny on her upstairs neighbors. One was a nightclub comic, an older dude . . . Willy Lancelot. The other was a pusillanimous pussyfooting, pigtailed hippy remnant . . . Maryjane Clover Dew. *Somebody* was stealing the draws, and I was going to catch the panty thief wet-handed.

* * *

That evening as a light drizzle fell, I gave a magisterial knock to the door of the perennially up-and-coming comedian. I could hear him rehearsing his act to whatever invisible audience. When I flashed my ID at his hightop fade haircut, he greeted me with an unsettled look that reflected the sincerity of an injured,

Jazz Stories: *From Katrina to Connecticut*

sidelined, towel-waving NBA player cheering on his replacement. His hair wasn't "relaxed." It was in Rip Van Winkle mode.

"Whatever it was -- I didn't buy it," he blurted. I assured him that I merely wanted to ask him a few questions about a problem one of his neighbors was having and he let me in. "Detective?!?!!" He grinned. "I thought you was a bill collector." Then -- "Law-aw-aw-awd, them chirren out there next door playin' in that rain . . . them chirren gon' git ammonia!" he mumbled as he looked out the window. As I watched, he removed a plaid leisure suit from a green and white vintage folding lawn chair near a pair of battle-scarred black combat boots. The wall above was dominated by generations of Scotch Tape-secured pictures. "That's my people on the wall. I love my family so much -- " he started, "I got relative humility for 'em."

I sat back in the lawn chair next to a stack of porno mags that included everything from *Barely Legal* to *50Something.* "Who dat?" I asked, indicating a picture of a shirtless, skirtless woman windmilling her legs on a pole with **HARMONY IS BLISS** tattooed across her chest. She could easily pass for an annual lifetime participant in a bad tattoo convention and looked like she fell out the ugly tree -- and hit every branch on the way down.

"That's Harmony, my used-to-be. I ain't with her no mo'. When I *was* it was so nice you had to hit it twice. But *that* parade *been* done passed. See that ring on her finger? It's real. It's a real cubic zirconia," he boasted. "Her new boyfriend got that Niggatitus D. The boy started shrinkin' up so much . . . he got so skinny -- he had to run around the shower to git wet. But I got a new oldlady. She was arguing with me the other day about her career choice."

"Your *new* lady? What does she do?"
"She just bounces around from job-to-job."
"Is she a substitute teacher?"
"No."
"Is she a temp worker?'
"No."
"A private nurse?"
"Uh-*uh*."
"Then what *is* she?"
"She's a plastic blow-up doll."

"Huh?"

"When it comes to havin' sex I believe in do-it-yourself."

I took note of some scribbling on the lady's picture. It said:

Bring on the liquor
Bring on the beer

Where's the beef?
The beef's right here.

LOVE WILLY

I tightened the screws, questioning him about his neighbor, Ms. Cockburn. "I thought she was 'high church'," he said, "but she so tight -- she wouldn't even buy wunna my church's Good Friday fish fry dinners last Lent." He laughed. He was as happy as a gay sex addict with three life terms.

"You think she's attractive?" I asked.

"Yeah. She fine, but she ain't so pretty she cain't catch the bus. I ain't no kinda stalker, but if I was a carpenter -- I'd nail her!" If stupidity were an orchestra he'd be a first chair player. I could see that this was going to be a glacially slow process.

"What kind of work do you do?" I asked. "You have a lot of tenure on the job?"

"*Ten* years? No. I got 42 years. I'm a 63-year-old up-and-comin' comedian. . . . At *my* age I'm trying to *stay* up and comin'. Right now I'm in aluminum . . . recyclables . . . disposables . . ."

"You make a living picking up cans?"

"Yeah. Of course. I'm a . . . collector," he boasted, motioning to a massive stack of overstuffed black garbage bags slumbering against the wall. "But I'm mainly a comedian."

"I can tell," I declared. I could also tell that he once had a regular date with the short, yellow bus.

"I been rehearsin' my ass off. I been giggin' at Sweet Lorraine's and that gay spot in the Quarters -- Club ERECTUS. They keep asking me to git some new material."

"Do you think she's pretty? You like the way she dresses?"

"Yeah. She fine. If she was into science I'd try to teach her the Big Bang Theory. But it's *her* ass -- not *mine*. It'd be mine if I was hittin' it. I'm a man. I'd hit it, but if I hit it -- I'd hit head-on." Then Willy obviously remembered I was a detective. "But she ain't my type. They say that woman got mo' problems than a junior high math book. . . . Ass don't pay the rent. . . . You can buy it, you can smell it, you can eat it, you can sell it . . . you just cain't spend it. Ass is like butter. Either you got a lot or you ain't got none."

After that series of assified adages, I concluded that he was classless and clueless. I erased him from the list of in-house suspects and accepted his invitation to kick back and enjoy the rest of the rehearsal session for his comedy act. "Hold on -- I'm comin' . . . Hold on -- I'm comin'!" he shouted. "Lemme git this snot rag and blow out the horn." He blew a beastly blob of green and brown bilge from his snoot into a formerly white hanky.

He stood in front of a black bi-cast leather floor mirror fronted by a mic stand and upraised an unplugged mic. "The only thing my father ever liked was being a *ba-a-a-ad* mutha . . . My father was the undisputed ruler of the roost. . . . There was only one rooster in the henhouse . . . I was the turkey . . . His favorite music was swing music . . . My head was the band. . . . He had several assets . . . I was the biggest ass. . . . He was so mean he'd sell a meat-eatin' dinosaur a salad . . . If my father was alive today he'd tell me something like 'Hey, son, you're goin' out? . . . Why don't you stop at the store and get some Skittles and some iced tea . . . and don't forget your hoody'!"

"Didn't I hear that one before? You cannibalize your own work?" I asked.

"Cannibals? I don't know nuthin' 'bout no cannibals," he protested, then continued. "Why is yo' maw like PEP Boys? . . . (sing-songish) 'cause she does-every-thing-for-less . . . If the president and the congressional leadership were on a plane and it was about to crash, who'd be saved? . . . the country! . . . A daughter was just home from her first semester at college and told her father, 'Daddy, I ain't no virgin no mo'.' The father gave her a backhand slap across the lips. 'Why'd you do that, daddy?' 'I'm payin' all that tuition money and you still sayin' 'ain't?' . . . What do you git when yo' maw don't show up for the *bukkake* party? Twelve angry men.

What did Linda Lovelace and Monica Lewinsky say when they met? 'Two heads are better than one!' . . . What did Paul Revere say at the orgy? 'The British are coming! The British are coming!' . . . I'm good friends with a politician -- Anthony Weiner. He --"

"Look -- I've been a dick for over 40 years. I've heard all the weiner jokes," I told him.

"Well, check out *mine* . . . My Chinese assistant Hung Wang told me Weiner was running for office again. I asked him who he thought would win the erection. . . . I -- "

"-- Look," I said, "I really have to split --"

"I didn't mean to turn incense into injury!" He grinned.

"I really have to cut," I said. He was dumber than a mouthful of Mississippi mud. I didn't think he was lying. He just had a tinge of a credibility deficit . . . in addition to some other mental afflictions. It was time to make the segue from happy time to hippy time.

* * *

Neighbor # 2 was classic Sixties: a freckled, strawberry-tressed, aging flower child living in a newer moment and era. She sported a revealing, paisley-print camisole, parachute-style M.C. Hammer pants, well-worn clogs, and gold marijuana leaf earrings.

"Hello!" Maryjane Clover Dew greeted me. "I'm no Benedict Arnold," the leftover longhair said dreamily through purple haze-painted lips and blue-embellished teeth. "But there's just not enough activism today. Everyone's occupied. . . ." I could hear a discharge of ultramodern corn (think Kenny G. Gaga) blasting from a sound source somewhere in the rear of the pad. Her eyes were as wide as a newly-released lifer in a strip club.

"I haven't had any Castile Soap . . . not even Octagon . . . since Farleigh Dickenson . . . where I studied Emily Dickinson," she narcotized. "Are you the man from the soap company? I lost all my albums in Katrina, but I still have my cassettes."

She beckoned me in and motioned me to a wicker peacock "Huey" chair positioned next to an easel with a fist-raising Angela Davis poster. Just above it a Yoko Ono knockoff print sat adjacent to a large purple statue of the Buddha. The Buddha's head served as an ashtray for several roachified remnants of former marijuana joints. The sweet, spicy scent of patchouli hung in the air like a mythical fragrance from a preexistent generation.

She offered me some organic tea and gingerly asked, "Are you The One? Are you The One for whom the earth has been waiting?" Her bulging eyes perforated my flesh. "Are you really The One? I want to come together with you . . . to reconcile my thoughts with you. Are you really, really The One? The One we have awaited?"

"No," I responded matter-of-factly. "I'm just a dick."

"A dick? A dick? . . . a real dick . . . Can I offer you some . . . green tea . . . and organic honey?"

"No, I just want to ask you --" I started.

"Then how about honey and lemon?"

"No -- I'm a dick. All I want is --"

"-- All *I* want is no more war. I believe in making love . . . not war . . . making love . . . and you're a dick."

I numbed up, froze, rose, quickstepped to the door and beat it, for my years of accumulated instinct told me that she wasn't the one who stood accused. As a lifelong dick I had been in some pretty tight spaces before and had no desire to probe any further. Interviewing her would be a whole lotta nuthin' gained and a whole lotta time lost. I decided to take matters firmly in hand and employ a direct action initiative to solve this misgiven mystery of insane folly and debauch.

* * *

The next day I asked my client to do some laundering, after which I secreted myself in the rear of the empty first-floor apartment in hopes of busting the panty pilferer in the act. I could hear the motion of the dryer as it swirled and whirled gusts of hot air in and around the endangered undies. It was quite a stretch, but for a dick like me things would come to pass sooner than one might think. Being the dedicated dick I am I'd hang around until something came up.

As I squatted, cocked and ready, I heard a set of footsteps striding toward the laundry room. There was a metallic sound as though something was unceremoniously dropped on the floor. I crept to the building's panel box and disconnected the power. Then I (along with the rod, prepped and poised) wended my way through the dark to catch the thief with his draws down. My eyes became accustomed to the light and I discerned a figure standing over one of the dryers. I snuck up behind him, put the gat to his head, and proclaimed, "I've finally foiled your latest caper -- you draws-stealin', lowlife panty thief!"

The pitiful, odious prey, shaken and stirred, turned around like a flash, staring into the barrel of the .22. *"Panty thief!???? . . . You Idiot!!! This unit has been sucking up everything from socks to Shinola!!! . . . I'm the MAYTAG repairman!!!"*

August 2012
Stamford, CT

Company Man

"Everything was believed except the truth."
(Alexandre Dumas *fils*, *La Dame aux Camélias*)

"I have nothing against the institution of marriage;
I just don't want to live in an institution."
(Groucho Marx)

Just after the Zimmerman trial he faced the incontestable, indisputable certainty that life with his white wife in his native New Orleans was OVER. Their connubial duration had become a dynamic exercise in fruitless futility. They fought more than Popeye and Bluto. Despite the indelicate decadence of their earlier daze, he had all he could stand of her general indignities and just couldn't stand no more.

To him, the trial proved that white women were not prone to be sympathetic, empathetic, prophetic, or *an*esthetic to males of his hue and pedigree in either a criminal justice arena or unholy wedlock, any more than a pissy-drunk Klansman in full-sheeted, coneheaded regalia would be welcome at the city's annual Zulu ball. She had become patently *pa*thetic. He had long tired of her dissonance and discord, her intolerably insulting behavior, and her lack of solicitude for the lower classes, and consequently developed a permanent disdain for her porcelain-white skin; her familial, monolithic lineage; her barren womb, her pithy comebacks, her toxic posturing, her intolerably insulting behavior, her ringing denunciations and allegations, her neo-confederate co-workers, her ghastly peek-a-boo nighties, the muddied memories of the chance encounter of their meeting in grad school back East, her invariably shedding Alpaca sweaters, her A-cup padded bra, her pancake makeup, and her fashion-conscious Michael Kors and Swarovski spending binges. Coupled with that came her monied agendas, her sushi obsession, her demonstrably misleading assertions, her unguarded enthusiasm, her latte-liberal leanings, her presidential voting preferences, her negrophobic upbringing, her casket-ready face, her graceless inability to Second Line, her chic flic fixation, her squeezing the toothpaste tube from the top, her knotting the bread bag rather than using the plastic tie, her not refilling the ice trays, her hesitance in replacing the toilet roll when the sheets were exhausted, her Mel Tormé records, her purple, blue-in-green varicose veins, and her unprepossessing honey-blond hair.

The uncivil union that was his battle-laden, ball and chain marriage to his college sweetheart was an unfortunate adventure amidst a tapestry of pain. He met his future wedded partner when he got into the college's foreign exchange program because he wanted to study a broad . . . a li'l French girl he encountered in History 102. His domestic companion was one of those marriage partners who needed constant reassurance of their desirability (y'all know the kind). Theirs was a romance that had traversed a span of time extending from fountain pen to laptop. They became a part of the aspirational middle class and were a gruesome twosome.

Eventually, any attempt at the most minimal conversation with her was like smoking on hay in the middle of the barn. She had been a runway model-slim young girl of good family when they met many moons ago. Her parents were wealthy, landed and leisured. She didn't fot . . . she farted. Her father was a man of square-jawed cavalier confidence who favored sporting arms and was prone to morning constitutionals and afternoon and mid-evening elaborately embellished concoctions of exotic intoxicants and signature cocktails. They had money out the wang-wang.

Now, as he readied himself for work, brushing his salt and pepper hair after showering, he recollected the muddied memories of growing up with less-than-modest means. All he really knew about the female of the species who bore him (his "mother") was that she fell in love with a no-good man and left him in the care of his grandmother. All he ever heard about her was that she claimed the dubious fame of being the first colored woman to win the cleavage contest at her church's parish fair and was a Bourbon Street fan dancer. His grandparents were prideful people who lived off his grandfather's pension from runnin' the mail. His belt-wielding grandfather was an inoffensive man whose idea of sex education was storing his wellworn *Playboy* magazines in the bottom drawer of the chiffarobe so the boy could "discover" them. He once overheard a conversation about his great-grandmother in which it was mentioned that she often danced nude on the levee around a Papa Noel bonfire and in an assortment of Voodoo ceremonies under the City Park oaks.

In college they were a Beauty and the Beast couple who met one night at a beer-pounding frat house binge. She was wunna dem li'l white girls with the bearing and deportment of a lady who was into being exoticized. He was the dashing football hero and founder of the legendary Sweat Phi Sweat fraternity. She was the homecoming queen who dared to have a daylight affair with one of "them."

Over the decades the fascination of their affiliation's ethnic ambiguity devolved into an unfortunate adventure. Pile-driving her to orgasm no longer worked its problem-solving magic. He married her because he was fond of her cooking and the way she ironed his shirts, but now his life had become an epic tale of disenchantment and their wedded life was merely a dynamic exercise in futility. Her favorite movie was *A Thin Line Between Love and Hate* (the one where the Martin Lawrence character ended up in the hospital). His favorite was Hitchcock's *Dial M for Murder* (except for the ending).

Their relationship was as weak as Bosco and water. Where she once was entranced by his humor, simmering discontent now dwelt. She was wunna dem hipsteristic white women, a pioneering yuppie who confused jungle lust sex with love and good lovin' with a good man. It was a union made in hell.

She favored patches of sunflowers, poolside tiki torches and drama of Hitchcockian proportions ('cept for that movie). Their wedded unbliss was filled with irreconcilable differences. She snored. He had sensitive ears. He was a Saints fan. She was a tried and true Patriot. He was a corporate attorney. She was a kindergarten teacher. She liked prayleens. He liked pecawn candy. He liked bouncin' and boogyin' to the beat. She was into ballroom dancing. But they were legally and inextricably bound and nothing but the unsettling certainty of death could effect their parting. Such an event would be an agreement of mutual satisfaction, for their passion went out the window when their late autumn of life came through the door. Attempting to reason with her was like peeing against a hurricane's howling winds, pushing a boulder up a hill, or climbing a greased, pre-Mardi Gras, iron-laced balcony support pole on Bourbon Street. Her fiery glare was accentuated by a depressingly inept litany of senseless, illogical jabbering:

"You don't value my opinion."
"You think too much of yourself."
"You have low self-esteem."
"We never talk."
"That's all you do is talk."
"That's why we can't have children."
"You never wanted children."
"You don't love me anymore."
"Stop trying to love me so much."
"You haven't bought me anything lately."
"You're always trying to buy my love."
"You're too possessive."
"You don't pay enough attention to me."
"You joke too much."
"You're too serious."
"You're getting old."
"You're so immature."
"Why can't you have another drink with me?'
"You drink too much."
"You're too quiet."
"You're too loud."
"You never consider my point-of-view."
"You can't think for yourself."
"You're too weak."
"You're so overbearing."
"Can you lower your voice?"
"Can you speak louder?"
"You're calling a bit early."
"You're calling too late."
"You never call me from work."
"You call me too much from work."
"I hate you."
"I wish *you* were the one Georgie shot."

For him, sex with her was like getting some Lewinski from a piranha. For her, it was so repulsive that it defied description, metaphor or nightmare. The screaming harpie had the creative flexibility of a Reggae bass player and made his life seem like a bucketful of spilled milk. They were now official members of the old and the reckless, that joyless journey of midlife that blends unsublimely with time, the master (mistress?) of all destinies. She became about as relevant in his life as the two-piece lighted china cabinet in the foyer. Their sex life eventually and inevitably evolved into a "friends-with-benefits" arrangement. As a man who had too often tempted providence, he kept on hopin', but things just weren't changin'.

With an unsettling uncertainty he recalled the delicate decadence of their youthful exuberance, when they were innocent in the ways of the world -- before he sentenced himself to the volunteered slavery of espoused life at hard labor without the benefit of parole, pardon or any act of deferred adjudication.

The atmospheric conditions of her life had undergone a resolutely menacing sea change. She once was sunny and hot, but she had become quite a bit cloudy and cold. The omen of the diamond falling out of her wedding ring just after they moved into their white picket fence-lined, gated community, four-bedroom colonial dream home didn't help. It was a compelling narrative indeed that the officiant at the ceremony when they plighted their troth later committed suicide by hanging himself in the rectory men's room after his dalliances with a chorus of altar boys were discovered by the police authorities. It took them a tragic march of decades filled with dissension and dispute to find out that marriage was more than a towering cake and a pretty eggshell-white dress. All he wanted for Christmas was a non-adversarial divorce.

They made several attempts (however half-heartedly) to salvage what remained of their spousal ties. They sought counseling, attended pre-divorce support group meetings, participated in role-playing exercises at an event billed as "Married Couples Weekend Retreat" (while verbally brawling all weekend before, during, and after the role-playing exercises), and "crawled the stairs" in supplication while saying the Holy Rosary at the St. Anne Shrine on Johnson and Ursulines. They even sat in the front pew on the left-hand side (facing the altar) at Sunday mass at St. Peter Claver Church -- right in front of an androgynous statue of St. Michael the Archangel, his unsheathed sword at the ready, his foot bearing heavily on the neck of a pecawn-skinned, cringing Satan. That really didn't help much and his long-lingering, persistent question of "Why did I do it?" endured.

The times, they weren't a-changin' and he didn't want to vacate the premises because doing so could be legally interpreted as abandonment, so he established sleeping quarters in his Saints memorabilia-embellished man cave with the garage entrance. That way he could enter and exit the premises without sight of her fiery glare or within earshot of her unrelenting verbal harassment. (He especially couldn't stand her establishment- class overuse of words like "paradigm shift," "schema," and "indices.") Theirs was a love quite a bit less than supreme. It was a fonky deal.

* * *

It was another hazy, hot and humid New Orleans morning in the comatose I-10 downtown-bound traffic. His work at the Central Business District-based firm as an (ahem) out-house general counsel included a potpourri of hardly-human clients to which he provided a medley of services including, but not limited to: developing memoranda of understanding, constructing independent contractor agreements, analyzing liability, defending lawsuits, assessing intellectual properties, developing corporate policy, and executing any and all assignments deemed pertinent to and necessary for the healthy business practices of the firm. It was more like being a banker than a barrister. The boy had credentials (the company's generous compensation package helped a bit).

That morning he was scheduled to attend to a slew of job performance reviews for the dozen or so legal interns employed at the office. Instead he locked his office door, adjusted his black-framed glasses as he sat at his custom-designed desk, lit a Monte Cristo cigar, informed his personal administrative professional (she was too highly compensated to be a "secretary") in the figure-hugging pencil skirt that he was not to be disturbed, laid out a few lines of cocaine on the desk's Parnian finish, and began his day. He was on Cloud 10 quicker than you could say "Johnnie Cochran."

Rather than hammer away at his duties as indicated by the usual and customary contractual obligations of his employment, he immersed himself in a jumbled gumbo of "side cases" he was handling without the knowledge, endorsement, or sanction of the company. He reveled with missionary fervor at the opportunity to engage in criminal litigation in defense of the business people, judges, politicos, street pharmaceutical salespersons, and other miscellaneous miscreants who were always pressing the flesh on velvet rope lines or surrounded by a throng of reporters.

There was the hypoChristian minister/preacher/hustler that espoused the "prosperity gospel." He was accused of telling some underage girls in his flock that receiving his sperm on their foreheads was symbolic of baptism by one of the Lord's trusted servants and that the various sex acts he performed with them would prevent them from getting pregnant until they were over eighteen. He (allegedly) gave four of them oral gonorrhea and impregnated two twelve-year-olds. Police authorities still didn't know exactly how many victims there were because of their reluctance to come forward.

Then there was the embattled city council member who ran (and was elected) on a crime-fighting platform, and who embezzled about a half-million city dollars intended to address vocational training for "at-risk" unemployed youth. He once gave a benefit for "elderly, ailing musicians" but ended up using the proceeds to pay a debt he owed to a healthy, young coke dealer. He also had a minor charge for falsely billing his insurance company for the front door of his home (the dealer had kicked it in). He claimed it was worth a grand, but Home Depot records indicated it was purchased for about 1/20 of what he declared. He was the same one who came up with the brilliant proposition of putting the city council members' pictures on posters urging the youth of the city to "read and succeed" instead of using pictures of indigenous community-based and widely-recognized writers.

Another black collar criminal His Dishonor represented was a female member of the Orleans Parish School Board who had a 41-count indictment filed against her for filing false tax returns, conspiracy, money-laundering, wire fraud, and being stupid enough to think she could be so visible and get away with it. Another genius stole an RTA bus to get home about twenty minutes after he was released from Parish Prison. The police arrested him at his baby momma' house about twenty minutes later. Finally, there was the idiot who stole a car Uptown, abandoned the vehicle, forgot his phone, called the police and informed them that he had left it in the front seat, gave them his home address, then provided the officers who arrived at his house with a description of a suspect who could've passed for his twin.

Professor Arturo

The attorney giggled, drunk with happiness, and in his intoxicating haze of cocaine, sniggered with laughter at the idea that they were all either too stupid or too big to jail. He was conducting more gravely dismaying (outside) business than a Baghdad coffin maker and his main contribution to addressing the concerns of his native Sixth Ward was flashing a beaming smile at the annual Kwanzaa celebration at the Treme Community Center. He saw that it was around noon. It was New Orleans. It was time for a drink.

* * *

He took a creep to the Come Again Club, a li'l upstairs jiggle joint on Esplanade over by the French Market, far from the CBD's towers of glass and steel and the maddening legal crowd's vulgar careerism. He considered himself a man of mystery and a quite daring rogue (in spite of his existential angst) and felt oddly at home amidst last night's lingering pee smells and the tasteless tourist traps that passed for the city's culturally symbolic landscape. It was in the same block as a drinkery to which he was denied entry in the city's pre-desegregation-by-legal-prescription times.

Unclad women were romping and rollicking to intense ear-popping, uproarish music on strategically-positioned mini-stages. As usual, the regulars (mostly fast men and loose women) and the music were in full swing. He ambled over to the bar, signaled for service, and was joined by his Lilliputian podner and former high school classmate Diamond.

Diamond was so named because of his decades-old sartorial snafu of wearing a cubic zirconia stickpin in every shirt he wore -- even his hoodies and T-shirts. He was a social undesirable -- one of those brothers who were "deep in the streets." He looked like he had just returned from having intimate relations with his sister in a doublewide trailer and had the sex life of a trench coat flasher.

The out-house attorney grinned as Diamond spread every category of change imaginable on the bar and ordered a rum & coke with the last Mohicans of his total financial worth. The boy needed a modification.

Behind the counter, Black Jack the Bartender (as opposed to White Jack, Red Jack, Big Jack, Li'l Jack, Uptown Jack, Bo Jack, Mack Jack, or Wack Jack) was involved in his usual lyin', philosophyin' and pontificating as he waxed poetic on every manner of topical concern from the Zimmerman case to weaves, baby daddies, twerkin' and chest tattoos. The attorney and Black Jack had bonded as lifelong hang podners way before the Superdome was built and had known each other since the Ninth Ward was nothing but cow pastures. The wit and wisdom accumulated from Black Jack's (alleged) decades of pimpmanship, comprising a carnivalesque concoction of exaggeration and prevarication, spat forth from an immense mouth accented by enamel-challenged lower front teeth that were mostly missing in action. He was as wise as Solomon, hip as Flip, and claimed he had a rod like Aaron. To his friends, customers and even to his spoogie he was "Black Jack the Bartender." He looked like a Mister Clean clone with an iron-gray Afro. His arms were like magnolia tree trunks and the boy feet was so big he had to go outside to turn around.

The lascivious legal representative ordered "something alcoholic, smooth, juicy and fruity."

"Then you don't want a drink," Black Jack kidded. "You want my brother-in-law!" He went about his task of providing the first libation of the bar member's liquid lunch. "Why the long face?"

"-- Cuz he's a horse," teased Diamond.

"No, I'm just hung like one."

Diamond, the attorney knew, didn't have the good sense God gave to a nail. He was a vertically-challenged character who was always runnin' with the bad crowd, a childhood associate from the less prosperous part of the Diaspora. He had wunna them "lazy eyes." You couldn't tell if he was looking at your head or your feet. His life suffered from a perpetual state of unremitting mismanagement and he belonged in a rubber room under chemical restraint and extreme medication. He was a chronically homeless veteran who did odd jobs around the bar, couch surfed or slept on a pool table, and took sponge baths in the men's room (on the rare occasions when he *did* bathe). Diamond, a man of uneasy virtue and plastic pride, was so lazy and trifling that he never shook a stick at a tree. He really didn't do anything in high school. He was just there. His luck was so bad it could be raining titties and he'd get hit in the head by a dick. All he wanted out of life was a woman with an ass like a lowercase 'b'.

Professor Arturo

The first time the attorney met him Diamond asked him for a dime and he gave him a quarter. They had been friends ever since.

"What up, Diamond?" queried the practitioner. "Where's the beef?"

"The beef's right here," chuckled Diamond, grabbing his khaki-covered crotch.

"Some things never change," deadpanned the tavern master as he served the mellow mixture and fronted the perennially money-challenged Diamond another freebie.

"You're making sport of me," the company's legal emissary said impassively.

"Diamond -- don't play games if you don't know how," advised Black Jack.

"Where you git this gumbo from? It ain't got 'nuff strimps in it," grumbled Diamond as he helped himself to his third (cost-free) bowl from a barside casserole.

"You don't like the gumbo? That's from Dooky Chase! That's Dooky Chase gumbo. A whole gallon o' gumbo from Dooky's! And you're complaining?" the company negotiator queried.

"You cain't let the perfect be the enemy of the good," remarked Black Jack the Bartender. "Sick grapes make sour wine."

"No matter how you slice it," asserted Diamond, "this remind me o' dat nowhere whitefolks' food I had when I was stationed in England . . . way over there 'cross the water -- layin' back and eatin' tea and strumpets." Diamond slurped the last of the delicacy from the bowl and released a pronounced gas passing. His noxious breaking of wind was local legend. "Wow! A One-Fot meal!" he proclaimed as Black Jack reached under the bar for a bottle of air freshener and the legal executive fanned the air with a handkerchief. Lust wasn't the only thing that was in the air. They'd been going through this ever since high school. He was still fottin' after all these years.

"I got in a li'l trouble over there when a dude in the pub asked me for a 'fag.' I didn't know he wanted a cigarette!" Diamond disclosed. "I asked 'em for a beer and they told me they ain't had nuthin' but 'pints.' I didn't want no pint. I wanted a 40-ounce!"

"This is why the aliens won't talk to us," quipped Black Jack, nodding towards Diamond and clearing the air.

They were (uh) broad-minded men who spent many a blissful hour within the watering hole's rough-hewn walls engaging in the (sometimes) coherent intellectual tradition of befuddled deliberatin' and conversatin' away from the traditionalist conventions and observations of well-tailored men or workplace women and their overwaxed hair and Chanel suits. They were staunch believers in the Dicklaration of Independence: Life, Liberty, and the pursuit of ass. They were gentleman's gentlemen whose ABCs of viewing the world were beheld through their minimal mindset of Alcohol, Broads and Cocaine. Their rhythm and booze-inspired opinions were about as useful as a worn, rusty disposable razor. To them women were mere objects of the lower extremes of the male appetite that engaged in onstage jigglin', nigglin' and snigglin' to aesthetically barren music under the grubby glow of skanky saloon mini laser stage lighting. They were real role models (toilet roll models, one might say) who were prime proponents of the "lady in the boardroom/whore in the bedroom" theory. They weren't totally classless, but if people were fractions they'd be the most common of denominators. They were "men's men" who faithfully adhered to those life-governing guidelines of male decorum to which all manner of inestimable legions of Irish Spring-using MANLY men (and every man's Main Man) over countless millennia have unquestionably embraced and observed with erect, manly firmness --

THE MAN RULES:

Never send a boy to do a man's job.
Never put the pussy on a pedestal.
Never rob a bail bondsman.
Thou shalt not covet thy neighbor's wife
    ('specially when her husband is an insanely
        jealous gun enthusiast with a fifth-degree
        black belt).
Never block a beer truck.
Never give a woman more than you can afford for
    her to leave you with.

Never hit on (or fornicate with) the help.
Every crowd has a fool: never be the fool in the crowd.
Never try to bullshit a bullshitter.
Never let your left hand know what your right hand is doing (it might get jealous).
Always fry chicken with a shirt on.
Don't let your li'l head rule your big head.
Treat a hoe like a lady and a lady like a hoe.
A hard dick has no conscience.
Don't drop a load where you eat.
Never tell a woman when payday is.
Don't marry "fine" . . . marry "thin" (if you feel you must).
Everything that looks good *ain't* good.
Don't try to make a hoe a housewife.
Never cry in public (even at yo' own momma' funeral).
Never hit on your podner's oldlady.
Never drink the last beer.
Never lead with your dick.
If you cain't get the whole dog -- don't take the turd.
Never drink and drive (pull over and finish the bottle).
Never look in a lady's purse.
Always look in a hoe's purse.
Never let a woman "give" you your freedom – and never let one take it away.
Never foam up the beer.
Never call a bitch a hoe.
Never call a hoe a bitch.
Mind your own business.
Never get your honey where you make your money.
Never get your cream where you make your bread.
Never lend nobody your car, your gun or your dick.
Always obey the "I buy . . . you fly" rule.
Never try to rob a gun store.

> Always get the pussy where you find it – but never trust a pussy (cuz a pussy's a lyin' set o' lips).
> Never admit guilt.
> Never admit anything.
> Never admit that you were wrong.
> Don't admit -- *accuse.*
> There's no such thing as too much money, titty, ass or beer.
> Always call a woman "Baby" when you hittin' it (that way you'll never slip up and say the wrong name).
> Never believe nuthin' a woman says.
> Never come where you shouldn't go.
> Never put cologne on your nuts (*Ouch!*).
> *Never . . . ever . . . never . . . ever . . . NEVER* walk down the aisle. . . .

In another hour or so they were higher than the insurance premium on a suicide bomber and trumpeting up their past exploits and adventures from bygone times of sweaty afternoons on blacktop basketball courts while relating all manner of mayhem, mischief and whoremongering known and unknown to the ancient and modern world. They were men. They were "men's men."

They verbally barnstormed through the memories of a continuing series of swashbuckling, jovial jaunts through unheralded but locally-celebrated neighborhood nightspots, reminiscing about the more raucous bright moments from their past. They eyeballed the counterfeit smiles of the shake dancers on the afternoon set as the girls slutposed, bounced, and primped to the ear-splitting modern melodies of the tavern's clamorous pumpadoo and circumstance, fans of one dollar bills in their garters and their bikini panties ("ass floss draws"), while their male spectators stared sleepeyed through a drunken haze.

"Wow! Looka the ass on dat mule!" Diamond babbled above the booming beats as he swiveled his brainless cranium to take in the prurient maneuvers of another dancing doll. "Wow! Colorado cantaloupes! Looka the titties on dat thing! Dat girl fine from the tip of her nose to the top of her toes! Dat girl fine as frog hair!" he cheered. Her cheap, gaudy jewelry (including a golfball-sized pinky ring), poppy red lipstick, pink leather half-cup bra, aqua-inspired eye shadow, shoulder-length blond "hair," yellow Peter Pan collar, orange dollar store patterned leggings, and purple snakeskin pumps made her look like she'd been attacked by a barrel of Skittles.

She took niggadom to a whole new level, the attorney thought; she was "ratchet" before the term was coined. Her body was an aorta of debauchery with "HEAVEN" tattooed just over her crotch. "HE" was tatted on her left butt cheek and "LL" was on the right. A purplish-red splotch on her chest made her a prime candidate for a tattoo removal commercial. The hood bugar looked like a big brown ironing board with a wig on its head. Her breath stank under water. If there were such a publication she'd be the permanent centerfold in *Skank* magazine. She was so skanky people thought it was a seafood joint when she got on stage. But that's what some men like.

"Liquor holds many secrets and loosens many tongues," cracked Black Jack the Bartender.

"Don't be so niggative," coughed Diamond,

"*In vino veritas*," the counselor counseled.

"What dat mean?" asked Diamond.

"Wine brings out the truth," said Black Jack the Bartender.

"I gotta write dat down," said Diamond. "Anybody got a pencil?" In addition to his drink freeloading tendencies he was also a chronic borrower.

"You know how to write?" asked the out-house legal beagle.

"Writing is like sculpture. The artist takes a concept and caresses, molds and shapes it to his or her vision," Black Jack the Bartender said. "You know what Thaddeus, that li'l poet who lived on St. Philip 'n' Robertson, said, bro? He said, 'The artist blends a vision of colors into the symbolic landscape of her or his imagination.'"

Black Jack waxed poetic. "Writing is like music. Its rhythms abound in and are reflected by the sound image systems of the characters represented. Writing is like magic, for what existed in one sphere is manifested in a newer, more identifiable and recognizable one. Writing is like love, for it is forever orgasmic and everlasting in its pleasures."

"Thaddeus wrote a lot. See what it got *him*," cautioned Diamond. He downed another (complimentary) drink special.

"Well, you keep doing what you always do? You keep getting what you always get," said Black Jack with a wisdom honed by his years of working in public service. "It was just bad to see Thad go out the way he did," he added somberly. "I remember when he showed me his stool. It had nuthin' but blood in it."

"The bar stool had blood on it?" asked Diamond.

"No," said Black Jack the Bartender. "His feces."

"What!?!"

"His *poo*!"

"Oh."

"That AIDS took him out . . . took him out bad."

"Yeah, dat AIDS'll kill ya," said Diamond, downing a double scotch and soda. He liked to mix his drinks. "They said it was cancer to spare the family' name, but he got it from dat li'l broad Uptown. Dat li'l hot twat was juss a li'l too nasty -- and too young for him," he added.

"If they're old enough to bleed they're old enough to butcher," reasoned the barrister.

"Hoes gotta git paid," said Diamond between his latest gulp of free libation.

"You throw out the wrong bait -- you get the wrong fish," said Black Jack the Bartender. "And you might just end up *sleeping* with them fishes . . . *permanently*. Y'all know she gave him that AIDS."

"I first thought he had Assburger's Syndrome," said Diamond. "Dat ass git so big cuz you done ate too many hamburgers -- or gittin' too much ass. The best wimmins in the world? Dem A-rabb wimmins. I got a who-o-o-ole lotta booty when I was stationed in Djibouti. Dem A-rabb wimmins is the best wimmins in the world. I had one in Detroit -- all she did was pray, cook, and sneeze! I didn't have to hit it too much cuz she bust a nut every time she sneezed. I asked her what she was takin' for it."

"Well, what was she taking for it?" asked the company man.

"Pepper."

"You . . . are . . . a . . . fool. You're suffering from age-related dementia," offered the special pleader. *Some people have lives that are about nuthin' but nuthin',* he thought, *and all they can offer is less than nuthin' about nuthin'.*

"I knew something was wrong when he first started looking to the heavens and talking to himself out loud about that woman," lamented Black Jack. "He was whipped. No hanging out with the fellas . . . no late-night sports debating . . . no practicing his music . . . no stopping by the house for a beer . . . never did wanna conversate no more. I knew something was wrong when the boy started talking to her pictures. She wasn't nuthin' but another slutbag with big street feet and flapjack titties. She was so dumb that if a mugger told her 'Stick 'em up' she'd start adjusting her bra. Her li'l AIDS-spreading ass was a hot li'l thing -- whenever she was with him or whenever she was without him. She was giving dat pussado up outa three draws legs. Everybody in the barbershop hit it. Everybody knew about her -- except him. That li'l gal was hotter than fish grease. And she ran her li'l mouth much too much. The only time she wasn't running her mouth was when she was down on her knees . . . and I don't think she was praying. He just liked the way she was playing that skin flute. They're always playing that role. They're always treating the right ones wrong and the wrong ones right -- with their lies by omission. They want to play with those losers all their life . . . then when they run into a winner they start tearing him down so HE can lose. He was one of those 'buy-bitch' niggers. You run out of money and the bitch tell you 'Bye.' A man'll shoot you one time, but a woman will have a machine gun and empty the whole clip on you. That's what happens when you fool around and fall in love with one of 'em."

"Yeah. He fooled around and fell in love," moaned Diamond. "Dat's what love'll do. He gave up his music for dat ass. He started spendin' more time with dat ass den he did rehearsin'. I remember when he used to stand up here . . . right in front the band . . . every night . . . with a glass o' red wine in his hand -- dat Merlin."

"-- *Merlot*," corrected Black Jack the Bartender. "He was a helluva musician, but his mouth was always writing checks his ass couldn't cash."

"He should've just followed the 'two weeks in-two weeks out' rule," offered the mouthpiece. "It takes about two weeks to get to know 'em, two weeks to get in 'em, two weeks to get tired of 'em -- and about two weeks to forget 'em. I wish I would've done that with that saltine I married." He stared at the latest bouncing booty on the nearest dance platform. "His oldlady was out there bad, too. Every time he came in from work through the front door the back door slammed shut."

"Bein' wit wunna them white wimmins beat gittin' hooked up with some nappy-haid nigger woman," suggested Diamond. "I can't stand no nigger woman -- 'specially no big-foot, Daniel Green slipper-wearin', nigglet-droppin' nigger woman. Everything 'bout 'em is fake -- wit all dem weaves, sew-ins, tracks, wigs, fake eyelashes, fake fingernails -- and dem hair products made by folks who could care less den diddly about they bald-haid black ass . . . wit all dem cats on they haids.

"When they don't wan' talk to you -- instead o' tellin' you dat -- they play dat 'mailbox full' game and don't empty they messages so you cain't touch base," Diamond went on. "Then when they wit some other cat it's 'I'm out wit the girls and my phone 'bout to die.' The worst thing Gawd ever invented was the nigger woman. They ain't nuthin' but a buncha draws-droppin', nigger-slave wenches who mistake ass for class and contribute to their own man' downfall. They be runnin' the street all they life and when face and ass wear out and nobody want 'em they find Jesus . . . or Obama. Ain't nuthin' but old hoes' tales. I cain't tell you how to keep one, but I can tell you how to git ridda wunna dem handout hoes. When she call -- answer the phone and make like you thought it was a bill collector -- or wear some anklewhipper, high water pants -- or whip her ass -- I'm from the Slapahoe Tribe. I'll spank dat ass. I'd smack dat ass to Krypton. One thing I learned and one thing I know -- spare dat rod and sperl the hoe."

"A man can work from sun to sun, but a good hoe's work is never done," rhymed the company man.

"Ain't nobody gon' be 'bout hitting no woman 'round *me* --" warned Black Jack the Bartender. "But I'll mollywop 'em. I'll dickwhip that ass."

"I'm juss bein' real 'bout it," replied Diamond. "I'm juss keepin' it real. It's simple. I'm juss bein' real 'bout it."

"Real ain't always rational," rationalized Black Jack.

"But he's right on one thing," said the solicitor. "Women -- they're all out of whatever mind they *think* they have . . . they all accuse *you* of having issues when *they* have the whole subscription. 'No' means 'yes.' 'Yes' means 'no.' 'We need' means 'I want.' 'I love you' means 'You'd better not *think* about another woman.' 'I'm not the angry one' means 'You're a vicious, snarling, psychotic sociopath.' And she come home from work, and you better not be sittin' there drunk. Some of those colored girls *need* to commit suicide."

"A wise man once said, 'Strength of mind rests in sobriety, for this keeps your reason unclouded by passion,'" Black Jack the Bartender weighed in.

"Who dat? Who said dat?" inquired Diamond. He flashed seven fingers to indicate he wanted a (free) Seven and Seven.

"Pythagoras," the innkeeper said with an expressionless poker face. Then -- "Take it easy, bruh. Drinking ain't going outa style. Quit being a schwoog." He mixed then served Diamond another unrecompensed drink. His company was about as welcome as a permanent state of Irritable Bowel Syndrome.

"'Pete Thagoras'?" Diamond swallowed. "He from the Lafitte?"

"No . . . he's from antiquity."

"Antiquity? Dat's in Louisiana?"

"Bruh -- just drink . . . don't try to think," suggested Black Jack the Bartender.

* * *

The talkfest's drunken bellowing and banter among the three amigos continued until mid-afternoon in the shadowy whirl of this bizarro abyss beyond the glitter of Twitter.

"I know there's such a thing as a conscious, independent black woman," admitted the company man, "but that's a rarity. They're about as rare as a Black Panther at a cross burning. I guess that's why I married a white woman. It was just simpler. At first, she took more crap from me than a sister would ever do. Now she's always putting me on the defendant's bench. In the beginning it was just so . . . convenient. One time she found lipstick in my pocket and I told her I was selling Avon -- and she actually went for that! I thought she was a vanity acquisition, but looking back I think she just wanted me for my body."

"She musta been a undertaker," ragged Diamond. "You know you married dat white girl cuz her paw got dat money. You married dat gash for dat cash."

"Gold is only as good as the man digging it," said Black Jack the Bartender. "All that glitters . . ."

"It's just that she's . . . *we're* getting so . . . *old.*"

"'The flowers anew, returning seasons bring,/ But faded beauty has no second spring.'"

Diamond blinked. "Who dat? Who said dat?"

"Ambrose Phillips."

"Well, I had one one time," Diamond confessed. "She was nickel-slick . . . slicker den a newborn allygator. She wasn't a gold-digger. She was a haid-hunter."

"Ain't she the one who had you in jail?"

"It wasn't jail. It was a mental institution. Southeast Louisiana Hospital . . . Mandeville," Diamond explained. "I always had good luck findin' wimmins, but bad luck in keepin' 'em. I juss want 'em to come clean with it or stay away nasty. I 'ventually had to leave her be. The law wanted to charge me with aggravated pimpin', but the statue of imitations wore out. I knows the law! I knows how to interpretate the law! I knows the whole penis code!" he insisted. "I was wunna the first New Awlins people on COPS. They had me all over the TV. They was asking me if it was my bag. It wasn't mine, but I runned away anyway. They caught up wit me and found a pipe on me. It was all about 'game over.' The judge was gon' give me five years, but I tricked with the Assistant D.A. and I got juss two suspended. I even helped my lawyer sue the gun manufacturer in my cousin' case."

"Your cousin? The one who got involved in an exchange of gunfire and expired from penetrating trauma resulting from a gunshot wound to the head?" the Perry Masonite asked.

"'Expired'? He got killt. He was covered wit bullet holes from forehead to feet. We tried to sue the people who made the gun, but they had way mo' money den us. . . . . We lost. It killt us too."

"-- Bet!" the company man and Black Jack the Bartender chorused. "That's how it goes -- you come with it like that -- you go with it like that," Black Jack added.

"You know when the employees in Angola's death house is most happy?" asked Diamond.

"When?"

"-- When they executin' a lawyer!"

"What are your plans for tonight?" the attorney asked Diamond.

"Plan? Plan? My plan is to move in wit you."

"Never ask a question if you don't already know the answer," opined Jack Black the Bartender.

"No, seriously --"

"My plan is to win the lottery. When I win the lottery I'ma go live in San Francisco."

"-- More like San *Quentin*," corrected Black Jack.

"All that money?" the legal virtuoso smirked. "Knowing you, you'll end up being another criminal justice statistic eating baloney sandwiches and drinking Tang in Parish Prison. The sheriff gotta get that money."

It was about time to get hat and make it back to the gig. He bade the brothers farewell, went to the men's room and snorted a toot of blow, took a last gander at the bimboish babes' quavering, agitating asses and siliconic funbags, and stumbled officeward through the sweltering mid-afternoon streets.

* * *

Back at work he engaged himself in a case involving a succession in which he could steal the Sixth Ward shotgun house of a little old lady who had the disadvantage of not having a liberal legal education such as his, and made plans to address several of the creditors (mostly high school classmates and contributors to his last campaign for public office) he had listed on his latest bankruptcy filing in order to avoid paying them. In less than the time it took him to gather time to think about taking time to get another hit of blow it was time to leave the legal premises, get on I-10 East, go boogie with his spoogie and get silly in Gentilly at Yung Ho's on Chef Menteur Highway.

He didn't see his hookups with his favorite dancer, who went by the name of "Titty," as philandering but as "respectful infidelities." He didn't have "affairs." His continuing series of flirtations and frolics were "romantic indiscretions." He just didn't understand (or care about) the chances of a gumbo of possibly injurious catastrophic consequences involved in his unabated appetite for such ardent knavery.

The red people say the name "Chef Menteur" ("Big Liar" in French and from the Choctaw) refers to the French colonial governor Kerlerec due to his not honoring a treaty with them. The white people say that it referred to an Indian chief who was a notorious fabricator of truth and teller of tall tales. Others claim that it was so-named because of the Mississippi River's fickle arteries that became marshlands and bayous in pre-levee times.

Suffice it to say that the lengthy stretch of Eastern New Orleans is a humanscape of fast food spots, hot sheet motels, anything auto-related, drugstores (legal and illegal), old folks' homes ("retirement communities"), schools, churches, graveyards, and seedy, shadowy "gentlemen's clubs" such as Yung Ho's. Yung Ho's was a generationally revered institution of raunch and ratchetness that protected and served every panting, impassioned male with a handful of one dollar bills and a horny disposition. It was located in a scuzzy-looking area of the highway near Little Saigon, an Asian-American island of convenience and culture comprised of the progeny of industrious immigrants who fled their native land in the mid-1970s for an ocean of relative prosperity in New Orleans East. My Blue Heaven, an "extended stay" motel next to the strip club, sat seductively silent next to the spot's well-concealed parking lot. Both malodorous expat- owned and -operated establishments catered to its base of cafeteria Christians and lonely men of lascivious intent who ogled, grabbed and goosed the fleet of floozies while sampling their fantasies of deception (for a mere $5 entry fee or ten bucks an hour). The no-tell motel's geriatric neon sign above its cinderblock-corrugated tin structure occasionally flashed the unerotic dictum: "The Place Where You Come Clean."

The attorney entered the world of woofers and tweeters with modest optimism. An assortment of roof-raising "no money-no honey" tattooed women with names like "Stormy," "Mystique," "Ebony," and "Cat Girl" were jerkin' and twerkin' their hooters and heinies on terraced staging to the soundscape of the minstrel music profession in little more than towering titanium heels. One of them looked like a stack of used tires. He briefly disregarded the carnal exposition of thigh-high boots, twirling tassels, exposed crotches and feather ticklers, and ordered a drink and a Jello shot from a nearby sweater girl.

He peered past the legs flung akimbo and gross lewdness for Titty, his favorite dancer/shot and bottle girl. She was born Eden, he knew, but the floozy moniker was what the puppy-playful, slutty arm candy preferred. It was a professional thang, a non-disclosure agreement. He noticed her giving an uninspired lap dance (euphemized by the club's owner as a "friction promenade") to a client in a semi-private, blue velvet-curtained cubicle and nodded, acknowledging her. She blew him a cheap lipsticked kiss with a mirthless smile, cast a crooked, crazy-eyed grin, and motioned his way indicating that she would join him at the bar near a rectangular wooden sign that proclaimed "SPITTERS ARE QUITTERS."

She didn't have skeletons in her closet, reflected the attorney. She had the whole cemetery and was ign'ant and indignant -- right out of central casting. But that's what some men like. When she was in her teens she was wunna them kinda young girls who daddy or momma had to go in the bar and grab her and drag her li'l hot-in-the-twat behind back home (y'all know what I'm talkin' 'bout). He had seen more ass than a gay proctologist, but she was what he liked.

Eden, or Titty, was born on a kitchen table in Waterproof, Louisiana, a blink-and-you'll-miss-it northeast Louisiana black majority town of about 800 located in Tensas Parish -- the last parish in the state to reluctantly permit black people to vote. She came to New Orleans at an early age, always wore the sheerest of clothing, and could make a young man flirty and an old man dirty. The forecast for her sex life's weather pattern was "steamy, hot and wet." She was wunna them li'l hoochie-coochie women off Claiborne Street that came of age in the Lafitte Project, a cookie cutter housing development in the parallel universe of the city's door-poppin', P-poppin' Sixth Ward. Lafitte was a now-forsaken, structureless, ethnically cleansed, grassy swathe of fenced-in land that the descendants of the Confederate gentry were lobbying to transform into a crime-free (meaning "nigger-free," but they euphemized it as usual) bike path/corridor towards Bayou St. John.

In school when everyone else was dissecting frogs she was opening flies. She was hotter than a hen in a wool basket. She had so many rubbers stuck up in her nookie jar that she got saddle sore, and once ingested so much sperm that her stomach had to be pumped. She was hotter than a six-shooter -- wunna them li'l wimmins who keep a single-edged razor blade under their tongue. She put the "ho" in hostess. But that's what some men like.

She won the "Best Ass Contest" at Yung Ho's for 33 consecutive nights (a bar record), had a body by Fisher and a brain (her most underutilized asset) by Hasbro. She wasn't the brightest bulb in the chandelier and if you read her mind it would be a pretty short book. Her personality wasn't the only thing about her that (to him) was infectious. In spite of her delayed cognitive development he saw her as special and unique -- one of those people who happened by in his life about as frequently as it snows in New Orleans, even though she usually attended to her financial obligations with one dollar bills. She was a hustler: During Katrina she had a side hustle stealing and selling MRE's.

He considered himself a daring rogue who would take on all comers and although Titty's womanhood was (at least arguably) tarnished, he forgave her frequent lapses in decorum and treated her in accordance with the requirements of good manners -- despite her peroxide blonde lacefront "hair," blue contacts, corn-colored teeth (replete with removable gold caps), and the skin lightening cream that caked up under her eyelashes. But she made him better instead of bitter. Some women can do that. It doesn't matter their station in life.

Their relationship (or whatever it was) was an agreement of mutual reciprocation. He was as full as a fat fly and his pants tented up at the slightest rousing thought of her head buried in his lap or of the inviting mound between her most public of parts. She once told him, "Cum in my mouf. Don't git it on my weave. That stuff always git stuck up in it. I paid good money for dat hair."

She had attempted to become a casino cashier, but didn't pass the basic math test. Her criminal background also didn't help much. She once wanted to be a home health aide, but she was deemed too much of a security risk for that. Her present grand ambition in life was to establish the world's record for the most Facebook "selfie" phone photos taken in barroom restroom mirrors. She was the kind of girl that urged him to put his money where her mouth was.

Some seasons earlier the attorney had met her in a barside chance encounter when he peeped that she would do something strange for a piece of change. They gave each other a head-to-toe once-over. He suited up, in steppin' shape, clean as a whistle, stepper sharp and smelling good with a pocketfulla money and a company expense account, and Titty -- in shiny white thigh-high stockings, black "spank me" pumps and an outfit that left less than little to the imagination. It was lust at first sight. He was so horny he would've smacked Our Lady of Perpetual Help on her tush. "You must be a parking ticket," he crooned, "because you've got fine written all over you."

"Don't be runnin' yo' haid like dat to me, Pimp Daddy . . . ain't no need for dat . . . I don't care if you from the itty-bitty-dick-committee . . . you look like you got money. I'm a hoe -- and I gots to git paid," she snapped. "Now don't misconscrew me . . . you gon' git yo' money' worf. I ain't no glory hole girl. I does it *all*."

The game was afoot, so he cut to the chase through a non-incriminating statement that could not be admissible in a court of law (for she might have been a police honey trap): "I need to get a head in life. Can you help me get a head? Show me what you're twerkin' with."

"-- Sho' will," she said leading him by the hand to the bar's back room where all manner of mayhem and merriment came to pass. She lit him up like a Christmas tree. Eventually and inevitably he started talkin' all that Ricardo Montalban smack to her about the full moon . . . the ocean's brisk breezes . . . cobblestone corridors . . . Corinthian leather. It was the beginning of a beautiful friendship through a continuing embrace of slut culture as he unknowingly sowed the seeds of his own destruction.

* * *

He felt he had it all -- girlfriend in one hand and middle finger (to his wife) in the other. She was puppy playful, an amorous antidote to his wifetime blues. When he was with her his impious desire made him feel as full as a tick. She was more than a side chick and wasn't like the office-dwelling Facebook floozies who flashed a li'l ass or shamelessly flaunted wish pics of muscular, towel-clad penis-barers. Her rawness relieved his melancholy.

She was a *real* hoe. She did it *all*. That's what some men like.

They became quite an item. Much to the astonishment of his coworkers he was so smitten with her that he even made the ill-advised miscalculation of mixing his business with his pleasure by inviting her to the company Christmas party one season. She showed up in barely there shorts (that were closer to underwear), a holiday-red "Who's Coming With Me?"-captioned sweatshirt, brass skyscraper heels, and a lime-green boa, smelling of sex-on-the-beach incense. She could pee on him and tell him it was raining -- and he'd believe it, for he saw a uniqueness in the connections he made to his roots through her developmentally awkward linguistic constructs and her garish but girlish innocence. She reminded him of the neighborhood girls of his youth who were now mostly scattered North, East, South and West by the wicked winds of Katrina. She finally finished her capital-related responsibility to her client, got paid, and joined him at the bar.

"Hey, Pimp Daddy! Long time-no see! What you brought me to eat?" she asked, her midriff-baring haltertop revealing her racy bronze breasts. "Chicken? Barbecue ribs? Smoke sausage? I wish dem Islams or dem Reggaes was still sellin' that Whitenin' H & G. That was some goo-oo-ood fishes. Whatever you got, I hope it ain't no can goods. I hope you brought some AL Sauce wit it!"

"AL Sauce?" he quizzed.

"Yeah -- dat brown stuff them whitefolks put on they steaks."

"Oh --" he laughed. "You mean A-1 Sauce. You didn't know that?"

"It's ain't how much you know. It's what you *do* wit what you do know," she countered. Then -- "What you brought me to eat?" she asked. "I don't eat no hot dog. I don't want nuthin' wit no dog in it. I ain't no Chinamans."

She likes to play with fire, he thought, *but she doesn't like to cook*. "I didn't bring anything but the rent money, baby," he confessed.

"Aw-ite. We gon' do the do -- soon as I knock off. I'm up on the center stage next after *her* big ass," she said motioning towards one of the entertainers. "She better update her weave and do some crunches. If she was in the 50 Million Pound Challenge -- 49 million would be hers! She smell like a 300-pound tuna dat been livin' in the desert -- for months! Her big corn-fed behind make too many babies. She ain't thick and sassy. She juss fat and nasty -- wit dat big wraparound pouch. She always packin' meals. Somebody need to Super-glue her legs together. She look like she already on the D-I list."

"The D-I list?" the attorney asked.

"-- The Deathly Ill list," Titty explained. "They need to funeralize her. She bald-haid in the mouf -- got most o' her teefs missin', but you cain't see it cuz they on the side. My momma old as you -- and *she* don't look dat bad. My momma *invented* twerkin'," she boasted. "She the one taught me how to work the track. Bars done always been in my blood. I been workin' in bars since Scooby was a pup," said the perennial up-and-comer. "She ever take wunna my customers again and her momma better go git the black dress ready. All them rug burns on her back . . . I saw in my haid my hand go 'round her neck. I had to have a meetin' wif' myself real-real quick-and-in-a-hurry. But she betta quit pushin' me cuz when they pushes me I smushes 'em . . . up there growlin' and scowlin' . . . tryin' to look hard," she fumed.,"They better git dat black dress."

"Black dress?" he asked, puzzled.

"-- For her maw to wear to her funeral when I finish wif her ass!" Titty clarified. "I'm finna hit dat stage. Den we goin' next do' by my house. Juss the two o' us. I ain't gotta be kneelin' down on that hard flo' in the backa the bar no mo'," said the skanky seductress. "I ain't even brought my knee pads." She then stepped to the stage, dancing a joyful jig, like she was Cleopatra making her triumphal entry into Rome.

* * *

They left the club and were met by a hail of rain as they took a tamp to the motel next door. The wild wind whispered through the dark thrill of the night as oceans of yellow police tape waved weirdly around a gas station across the highway. Inside she lit a kerosene lantern exuding a rose-scented aroma as he sat on the edge of the bed and began disrobing. She went to the bathroom, came out and sat beside him in nuthin' but summa that cheap Canal Street vendor oil perfume, a faux pearl necklace and a hospital wristband.

"Turn on the tube," he suggested. There was a pile of dirty clothes in the ramshackle room that was so tall he could barely see the screen and a multitude of rambling roaches that were so big she shoulda charged 'em rent. It was inniggerating indeed.

"No. Telebision git in my brain at night, but I still cain't," she said. "The baby sleepin'. I gave her some beer. She like beer a lot. It put her to sleep." She nodded toward an open dresser drawer where she had outfitted a makeshift bed for her infant. "I'm glad she small 'nuff to fit in there . . . plus I can cut dem dollar diapers in half. When times git hard you can make a monkey eat pepper."

"You don't worry about her being over here by herself like that?" the attorney asked.

"No. She aw-ite. She a born hoe -- juss like her momma and her granma'. We hoes. We *real* hoes. If you cain't feed 'em -- don't breed 'em," she added, unscissoring her gap and pulling out a crack pipe that was concealed in her snatch. "She sleep all night. She gotta have her proper rest 'cuz she gon' be up ho'in all night when she git big."

Then she got a chestnut-brown rock from under her tongue, reached under the bed for a shoebox filled with assorted paraphernalia including a dozen multi-colored lighters of every known brand, chose one and placed it on a saucer from the box. "They come in all shapes and sizes," she explained, "like dicks!" She used a bent clothes hanger as a pusher to clear the glass pipe, jammed some fresh CHORE BOY in it, secured it with the pusher, crushed the rock with a spoon, and pressed some of the product into the top of the glass. She fidgeted with one of the lighters, lit it, and hit it. The pace of her voice slowed. Her eyes glazed. "I'm thankful to Gawd I got me a card fulla food stamps, a good job and my own house, cuz New Awlins gittin' torned off like a cheap chicken," she said as she lazily exhaled the malodorous vapor. "Gawd got His plan for me." She took another hit. "He help me wif' my self-of-steam."

She was tore-up from the floor up, the attorney thought. She could never be a nun, but she had a heavy habit.

"I know you heard what happened to my friend from City Hall."

"Smith . . . Smitty?" he asked.

"Yeah. The white man I showed you next do'. He done hipped me to a lotta things 'bout how to be a proper lady. I thought he had done died o' beedies, but he had done caught dat AIDS. He shrunk all up. He got skinny-skinny-skinny. He lost so much weight -- looked like he lost two people! He got so skinny he didn't have a belt small 'nuff to hold his pantses up. He had to use a piece o' string or tie rubber bands together. He took a long time to die, but he sho' done died. . . . That hurt me to my heart. I flighted all night the night he died. He wasn't but a two-day-out-the-month man, but he was nice to me. Every two weeks he come runnin' over here to cop some dope and hit dat pearl tongue.

"I always knew when he was lyin' cuz his face used to always twitch. He always had a chimp on his shoulder. He always wan' talk 'bout dem polly-ticks. It was much doo-doo 'bout nuthin'. I could always tell when he was lyin' to me cuz his face was always twitchin'. He was juss too jealous-hearted. He juss didn't pass mustard wit me. I had to tell him 'bout his self one night -- come callin' me a stripper. I ain't no stripper. I'm a *pole dancer*! I stood my ground on him.

"Uh."

"After he died his wife ain't had too much insurance money for that big-old house they had. She had to give it up and go be a beautician. She went to cosmology school. I didn't know you had to go to college to fix people hair."

"I think it's 'cosmetology school,'" he corrected.

"I thought he had Oldtimers Disease."

"Alzheimer's Disease."

"*Whatever*." Titty shrugged. "I still didn't know you had to go to college to fix people hair. I really like-ted him. I don't usually date outside my race. I gots pride. But I ain't gon' cut off my nose to sprite my face. I ain't dat kinda girl. Some mens juss acts too biggity sometimes. Maybe all the mens I meet is too old for me. Maybe dat's why I ain't yoked up to nobody."

"Am I too old for you?"

"You ain't old," she said as she tenderly massaged his graying buzz cut. "I was juss bornded early. You ain't dat old."

"How do you figure that? What evidence do you have to that effect?"

"I counted the rings under yo' eyes. You ain't really been livin' dat long," she said as she tweaked, scanning the floor for any wayward grains of the dope.

"At my age living is all that matters," he said. Then, "You know what I pray for? I pray that we can run off somewhere together one day."

"Why don't you pray we win the lottery?"

"Yes. Why don't I?" he said with a depressingly inept tone.

"Look --" she said, "we gon' nip this in the butt right now. Don't go flippin' yo' lid on me. I'ma take care o' you. A blowjob a day keep the other wimmins away. Ooh! My nipples is so hard they could cut diamonds right now."

"Well, c'mon, baby. Come here, Titty. Gimme summa that generation gap. Bring it on home. Bring it on home to me, baby."

"Ooh! I hear you much. I feel to believe I'm scared o' you! Jump in and hang on," she said, then gave him some of her standard lines: "You gon' ruin me for another man. I'ma suck all the juice out you -- every drop -- den I'ma fuck the shit out you. I'ma fuck you to def. I'ma put sumpin' on yo' ass you ain't gon' *never* forgit," she promised as his unyielding, thick firmness began making the rubber meet the road.

* * *

After a night of bridging the gap they awoke just before the (uh) crack of dawn. That morning he was scheduled to be in Baton Rouge to present a lecture on professional ethics at the Southern University School of Law. Then he had an afternoon appointment with the company physician. National Depression Day was coming up in October and the company wanted all employees to get tested for any physical or psychological concerns related to headaches, shoulder, back or neck pain; poor focus, difficulty resting, being tired all the time, awkwardness, quirkiness, sudden sweating, skin rashes, nervousness, stomach pain or addictive behavior. Since he more or less felt that he had symptoms of all of the above he made certain not to miss the screening upon his return to the office that afternoon. He would be going to New York on business the next day and didn't want any sort of last minute tomfoolery to interfere with his foray into the eastern shore's land of silken honeys. He spirited away from the office on a series of sojourns whenever possible and had more frequent flier miles than Al Sharpton and Air Force One combined.

"Where you goin', Pimp Daddy?" she asked as he took a sponge bath.

"-- Time to do like the scissors and cut out," he said. "I have to be in Baton Rouge today; then I have to get ready to go to New York for a week."

"You takin' the bus? The train? You drivin' way up there?"

"No!" He laughed. "I'm flying. I just want to make certain that everything is right and ready so I can get to the airport without some humbug."

"Airport?" she asked. "I ain't never been to the airport. Dat's so far out there."

He thought a while then said, "One day we'll go on a trip. Maybe we'll go to the islands or something.

"I ain't goin' 'round all dat water," she protested. "Not after Katrina. . . . Juss one thing when you gone . . . what I'ma do for dick? I'ma need some hard dick. *Yo'* dick . . . *my* dick." Every time he said goodbye, she told him, she died a little.

He shrugged, mumbled an intercessory prayer, left her some money, went home, shat, showered and shaved, then resuited up for what was going to be a challenging late morning session addressing a group of future legal practitioners on the ethical issues involved in becoming a member of the esteemed and honored profession. "Where secrecy begins," he commenced that morning, "trouble soon follows. . . ."

* * *

He just couldn't find inner happiness, but his pecker would. It was New York, just like he pictured it -- skyscraper heels and ever'thang. That first day he attended the mandatory boring daytime sessions, then made it back to the lower Manhattan boutique hotel for a proper knife and fork dinner of Porcini Dusted Bone-in Chicken Breast, Mango Mousse, two bottles of Tutankhamum Ale ($52 per) and followed that with a serving of oysters in garlic and cognac sauce and a bone dry martini. He felt so . . . *cosmopolitan.*

After dinner his first stop was at a trendy titty bar in Manhattan called Sheik Djibouti's where the "performers" were decked out in harem pants . . . *just* harem pants. The Arabthemed nightspot featured The Gaza Stripper, Florence of Arabia, and a rather intriguing lady in purple snakeskin pumps with jet black hair and an ass like a Butterball turkey who batted her dark, inviting, exotic eyes seductively at him. She was a nice li'l number with a "You Only Live Once" tramp stamp in the small of her back. He took the bait and didn't spend a night in Tunisia, but he spent some time with Elysia.

That week he played at the Playboy Club and hustled at Hustler's. He had big fun at a spot named Fun City, cleaned his horn at Unicorn, scored at Scores, took up space at Lace, did a falsetto at Stiletto, fingered boxes at Foxes, and spent mucho monies at Honeys. He giggled at Wiggles and got a shtick at Rick's from a bump-and-grinder whom he asked, "Are you always this shy?"

She replied, "-- Always with married men."

"I'm not married," he lied.

"-- Then I'm not shy."

He flirted with another boozy floozy who told him what she liked (and how often she liked it). "I like it infrequently."

"Is that with one word or two?" he jived. He even shot her the tried (and untrue) "You must be Irish -- cuz my weenie's dubblin'!"

He was drifting in an ocean of pleasure and using lines like, "You into science? Because I'd like to teach you the Big Bang Theory" or "Excuse me, miss. I think you dropped this paper with my number on it" or "You're a classy lady . . . and I'm the professor" and even "I'm a professional breast examiner and I've been authorized to give free demonstrations." Like Aldo Cella he was quite a fella.

He told the ducklipped, bubble-butted, neo-burlesque bouncing bombshells that his name was "Dick Hardmore" or "Dick Rodmore" (but his friends called him "Dick"). On other occasions he used "Rod Dickum" (but they could call him "Dick"). His now familiar litany of lies grew to even greater heights when he told them that his name was "Carlos Danger" (but they could call him "Weiner").

He ran through an assortment of adolescent antics via a series of sexcapades and amorous dalliances with a bevy of postcard-pretty, perfumed princesses, hookers and harlots. He saw more G-strings, hose, camel toes, triple-pierced nipple rings, butt-skimming poodle skirts, unitards, corsets, pushup bras, and lace-frilled panties than a lifetime manager at Victoria's Secret.

That week he made a hobby of Bobbi, got chummy with Yummie, and tender with Brenda. He got shady with Sadie and naughty with Claudie, tricky with Nikki, and wacky with Jackie. He made merry with Cherry and got lovey with Dovey then got misty with Christy and wopsy with Topsy. He 69'ed with Starr in the back of the bar, went through hell with Chanel and was in heaven with Devon.

He saw, he conquered and he came. . . .

When his secondmost used organ (his brain) had recovered from his craven behavior he took a red eye flight back to New Orleans, not knowing that he had depleted the well of his opportunity for happiness. After days and nights of ongoing ringing denunciation of his wife's allegations about his immoral relations and resuming his faux duties at the office, the company physician called and informed him that he should schedule an appointment to see her regarding his National Depression Day medical examination.

At the scheduled time he entered the medical center's outer office and was ushered into the doctor's inner sanctum by one of the company nurses. The doctor offered him a seat and opened a hard copy file on her desk. She sighed, adjusted her glasses, and addressed him in clinical monotone. "I have some information I must share with you," she said with grim determination. "We have the results of your National Depression Day blood test. They indicate that you're HIV Positive."

His death was a protracted, painful affair.

August 2013
Stamford, CT

GLOSSARY

Affaires d' honneur -- affairs of honor; duels.

Angola -- Louisiana State Penitentiary at Angola, LA.

Ass -- using one's buttocks to force oneself onto a crowded seat or bench.

Atelier -- workshop.

Drinker (Barbiturate drinker, B-girl) -- a usually drug-addicted female used by French Quarter bar owners to entice male patrons to splurge on drinks.

Banket (from French *banquette*) -- sidewalk.

Baptize the gumbo -- to increase a meal (of gumbo) by adding water when unexpected dinner guests linger or arrive. See *stretch the beans*.

Berl -- boil.

Blah-*zay* -- to comment dispassionately.

Blah-*yay* -- an issue; an overblown matter (a big blah-*yay*).

Bogart -- to forcibly take over a conversation, poetry reading, etc., by utilizing an extreme amount of time.

Bogue -- bogus.

Boissiere -- Treme-based family comprised of widely-known business and political luminaries.

Bone Men -- Mardi Gras Day masqueraders who adorned their bodies with animal skins and bones to present a ghoulish presence to onlookers.

BOO-COO (from French *beaucoup*) -- HUGE!!! MASSIVE!!!

Boss -- fabulous.

Bounce music -- a New Orleans variation of hip-hop music.

Bright people -- term used by some dark-skinned blacks to refer to light-skinned blacks. Terms of more pejorative usage would include "red bone" and "*passon blanc.*"

Broad in the mind -- highly intelligent.

Buddy System -- a much-touted Tulane University football program instituted by coach Buddy Teevens (1992-1996) amid a plethora of media commercials that resulted in catastrophic failure (11 wins, 45 losses in five years).

Bugarbat (also *bugarbear*) -- an unattractive woman (see *tackhead*).

Burn a candle -- to cast a spell on someone using voodoo-inspired candles.

California collar -- looped rope used in a lynching.

Calinda -- a risqué form of erotic dance performed by Afro-Caribbean people in Louisiana and especially in New Orleans' Congo Square (now part of Armstrong Park).

Carver Theater -- designated black movie theater located on the corner of Johnson Street and Orleans Avenue across from what was the Lafitte Project.

Cayoodle -- a canine of undocumentable pedigree.

Character -- an undesirable element; bad company. *I don't associate with such a character.*

Chiffarobe -- armoire.

Chiney -- marble in children's games.

Chineyball tree (chinaberry tree, *Melia azedarach*) -- a species of deciduous tree in the mahogany family. Its fruit, popularly known as a "chineyball," is a drupe, a fruit in which an outer fleshy part surrounds a shell with a seed (kernel) inside that first appears green, turns light yellow at maturity, and hangs on the tree all winter.

Chintzy -- selfish; cheap.

Chirren -- children.

Circle Theater -- designated black movie theater located in the Seventh Ward on St. Bernard Avenue between Galvez and Miro. The site is now a Rally's franchise hamburger stand.

Clabon Theater -- designated black movie theater located on the corner of Claiborne Avenue and Ursulines Avenue during and in the post-segregation era; used as a church in recent years.

Clark -- Joseph S. Clark Sr. High School (located in Treme).

Cock -- female reproductive organ (usu. in African-American idiomatic usage).

Cockhound -- a (usually) male with a high libido who persistently and perpetually pursues the carnal favors of the opposite sex.

Coke top -- soft drink (soda) bottle cap.

Colichemarde -- a thrusting sword often used in duels as a close-range weapon.

Commodity cheese -- a type of cheese distributed by U.S. government social programs during the Reagan era. Many recipients still insist that it was the best cheese for creating macaroni & cheese dishes.

Coo-coo-lah-lah -- insane; crazed.

Cornder -- corner.

Cross (over) the basin -- to traverse the former Carondelet Canal that once joined the French Quarter to Bayou St. John.

Daniel Green slipper -- a popular, affordable style of female footwear.

Dirty draws -- to passionately love someone without reservation or limitation – and even love his or her dirty draws (underclothes). *She dirty-drawsed that man for ten years.*

Dooky Chase Restaurant and Bar -- a longtime, world famous Treme establishment frequented by African-American (then-"colored") stars, civil rights notables, and locals. (Note: "Dooky" rhymes with *bookie*)

Drag, dragged – talking really bad about somebody behind his/her back.

Dump the Hump -- an expression calling for the non-election of then-Presidential candidate Hubert Humphrey.

Dust -- money; run; to run quickly; outrun; leave.

Dyspareunia -- painful sexual intercourse.

Earl -- oil.

Edith Piaf -- iconic French singer-balladeer who spied on Nazi occupiers during WWII.

Ejaculations -- short prayers in the Catholic tradition intended to be memorized and repeated throughout the day; often referred to as "aspirations."

Er-leens -- Orleans Avenue.

Erster -- oyster.

Euell (Gibbons) -- American naturalist (1911 – 1975) and promoter of wild foods and natural diets. His "wild hickory nuts" TV commercial for Post Grape-Nuts cereal made him a worldwide celebrity.

Facta non verba -- Latin; "Deeds, not words."

Fancy woman -- a well-maintained woman of questionable virtue.

Fescennine -- obscene; squalid.

Flambeau(x) -- torch carried during nighttime parades. Originally oil lanterns.

Folie au deux -- a madness shared by two.

Four O' Clocks (*Mirabilis nyctagineal*) -- a garden variety weed originally discovered by French botanist Andre Michaux around 1792 that received its name due to its habit of opening in the late afternoon.

Fred "Chicken Red" Hilton -- 1960s basketball star at McKinley High School in Baton Rouge, LA.

Gallo Theater -- designated black movie theater located Uptown on Claiborne Avenue. It was in operation from the post-WWII era until the 1980s.

Giggly water -- champagne.

Git-It-Girl -- a hairstyle popular among New Orleans' inner city women in the 1990s.

Gittin' ideas -- entertaining prurient thoughts or having intentions of a sexual nature when in the company of one's flesh and blood object of desire.

Go-cup -- a plastic cup given to bar patrons as they exit an establishment so that they can "go" with their unfinished drinks -- only in New Orleans!

GOO-GOB -- a lot, an awful lot.

Goumada -- mistress.

Gown Men -- a group of ghostly, white-robed figures who were reputed to perform ghastly experiments on kidnapped children in the area of Charity Hospital.

Graveyard love -- a relationship in which one is so involved in "romance" that he or she accepts destructive behavior from one's partner, and is thus, doomed to a hastened future in the grave.

Halfa G -- a half gallon of cheap wine.

Happy dust -- powdered cocaine.

H.N.I.C. -- Head Nigger in Charge.

Hoopty -- a (usually) raggedy, non-current model year automotive vehicle.

Hoodoo -- to enchant.

Humbug -- a fight; to fight.

Humbuggish -- having a tendency to settle a dispute by violence.

Iberville Project -- a housing development originally intended for white servicemen that was built on the former site of New Orleans' notorious "Storyville."

Ig -- ignore.

Ignify -- to say something really stupid; a variant of "signify" as in the Signifying Monkey and the toast tradition. See **signify**.

I.L.A. (International Longshoremen's Association) -- historic African-American entertainment venue/dance hall on South Claiborne Avenue.

Indian Fire -- acute acne.

In high cotton -- prospering.

Ipsa loquitor -- Latin; "the thing speaks for itself."

Jazzfest shoes -- the most ragged, tattered shoes of which one has possession; used to attend the New Orleans Jazz & Heritage festival which takes place on the often-muddy infield of a racetrack. Many (mostly local) attendees take pride in the fact that they have worn the same shoes throughout the decades-old history of the festival.

Jazzoetry -- a now-popular performance form of poetic and musical collaboration.

Jazz stories -- fiction featuring "piction" (poetic fiction) marked by extended verbal improvisations, the unconstrained spirit of the jazz idiom, and linguistic solos unrestricted by convention.

JET Magazine -- a black-oriented, weekly mini-tabloid news magazine.

Jitney cab -- an affordable mode of vehicular carriage used as a means of conveyance; gypsy cab; used during transportation strikes in New Orleans.

Jockomo -- a New Orleans tune traditionally sung in story form and played throughout the Mardi Gras season (written by James "Sugar Boy" Crawford in 1953 and sung by the Dixie Cups as "Iko Iko"). The song is regularly performed by New Orleans artists and was often used in verbal sparring contests in the toast tradition.

Kah-*goo* -- crazy; nuts; insane; off one's rocker.

K-B purple -- a distinctly unique, purple corporate theme color of a New Orleans drugstore chain founded in 1905 by Gustave Katz and Sydney J. Besthoff. The chain was purchased by Rite Aid in 1997.

Kick (someone) to the curve (curb) -- to inexplicably and unexpectedly end a romantic involvement.

Lafitte Project -- a former 28-acre housing development located on a 3-mile stretch of Orleans Avenue in New Orleans' Sixth Ward.

Lahopp -- Laharpe Street.

Lash LaRue (1921–1996) -- cowboy star ("The King of the Bullwhip") in the 1940s and 1950s. The Louisiana native (born in New Orleans suburb Jefferson Parish) was an adept guitar player who often joined jam sessions at the Dew Drop Inn, a popular black New Orleans nightspot dating from the post-WWII years to the 1970s that featured artists such as Etta James, Fats Domino, Ray Charles, and iconic New Orleans drummer Earl Palmer. According to Palmer, "Lots of white people wanted to come to the Dew Drop. Most were turned away, but they let a few in. Every time the cowboy actor Lash LaRue came in town, he came by. He played a hell of a guitar and was a regular guy that people liked."

Left-handed marriage -- a legal state of wedlock between two people of disparate social status.

Lincoln Beach -- a "blacks only," segregation era amusement park on Lake Pontchartrain. See *Pontchartrain Beach*.

Long in the tooth -- vampire-like; monstrous.

Loretta Young -- movie/TV star known for dramatic entrances in high-fashioned evening gowns.

Maison de maitre -- "master's house"; an old line, traditional, middle class townhouse; also a town house or village house.

Major Lance (April 4, 1939, 1941 or 1942 to September 3, 1994) -- 1960s soul singer; recorded *Gypsy Woman*.

Make a turn -- to stop by (usually unanticipated and/or unannounced).

Mandeville -- location of Southeast Louisiana Hospital, a 374-bed, state operated psychiatric treatment facility. *You so crazy -- you gon' end up in Mandeville.*

Marie Laveau (1782 – 1881) -- an iconic free woman of color and voodoo priestess.

Maw-*maw* -- grandmother; family matriarch.

Mawfiddice (*MAW*-fi-dice) -- pejorative term used to indicate a male homosexual or a male with perceived effeminate actions or sexuality.

McKeithen, John -- the 49th governor of Louisiana (1964 – 1972), a staunch segregationist who constantly fought with President Lyndon Johnson's Office of Economic Opportunity and supported segregation as the best social system for his state. He took a hard line during racial disturbances in 1967 and threatened to allow police authorities to shoot looters; later became national spokesman for the movement in opposition to integration by busing.

Miss Ginny -- hostess of long running TV children's educational program *Romper Room*.

Modiste -- dressmaker.

Mollywhop -- to slap on the forehead/face with a penis; dickwhip.

Morgus (Dr. Momus Alexander Morgus aka Morgus the Magnificent) -- a mad scientist and iconic late-night TV horror host of "The House of Shock," played by Sidney Noel Rideau (Sid Noel) from the 1950s through the '80s. His assistant, Chopsley, was a huge, ax-wielding, hooded, blundering idiot who often wrecked Morgus's creepy experiments which bookended horror movies of the era. His faithful throngs of fans (Morgussians) were thrilled at his attempted comeback in the early 21st century. Orleans Parish Prison even had an infamous tier that was known as "The House of Shock."

Mosquito hog/hawk -- dragonfly.

Nanann -- godmother.

Neutral ground -- grassy traffic island; median.

Nignify -- the act of saying something that might be considered "niggerish" and/or "ghetto."

Nora Navra Library -- located at 1902 St. Bernard Avenue at Prieur Street in the Seventh Ward, it was one of the first New Orleans Public Library branches to allow people of color to use its facilities. It opened in temporary quarters in 1946, was given the status of a permanent branch in 1956 and eventually became a children's library. During its dedication the famed civil rights attorney, A.P. Tureaud, for whom a nearby thoroughfare is named, gave a rousing address in which he said, ". . . Public facilities, which are provided on a racially segregated basis, are not only a drain on our economic resources, but are an outmoded relic of a slave psychology. Libraries tend to free the mind of bigotry and prejudice; they are supposed to be a civilizing influence on the community. We need more of them. . . ." The library was closed indefinitely after Hurricane Katrina.

Nymphs de pave -- prostitutes.

Out-the-wall -- the practice during segregation of selling goods to African American citizens from an opening/side window at establishments they could not enter due to legal edict.

P-Pop -- an extremely rhythmic dance in which the buttocks are swayed, swung, waggled and wobbled in a sexually enticing manner.

Paddy boys with the wagon -- pejorative for "Irish police officers".

__Parann__ -- godfather. See *nanann*.

Paw-*paw* -- grandfather; family patriarch.

Pecawn -- pecan.

Pecawn candy -- pralines.

Peritonitis -- inflammation of a thin tissue lining the abdomen's inner wall.

Peter Lemongello -- 1970s American singer from New Jersey, best known for his double album *Love '76*, the first album to be sold exclusively through television advertising.

Pink Palace -- the old First District Police station, so named because of its pink outer walls.

Pitty party -- an aura of uninvited sympathy. *I lost everything in Katrina, but I don't want a pitty party.*

Pluck -- cheap wine.

Plushofilia -- sexual attraction to stuffed animals.

Po-boy -- a large, traditional sandwich of New Orleans; originally served free of charge on French bread to motormen and streetcar drivers by Bennie and Clovis Martin of Martin Bros. Restaurant during the 1929 transit strike.

Pocket gun -- derringer.

Pontchartrain Beach -- a "whites only" amusement park on Lake Pontchartrain. See *Lincoln Beach*.

Pontchartrain Park -- a 175-acre suburban subdivision designated for "colored" citizens that included an 18-hole golf course, clubhouse, baseball stadium, basketball and tennis courts, picnic areas, and fishing lagoons.

Powder shop -- structure out of which cocaine is stored, packaged and sold.

Pumpadoo (pompadour) -- an extremely greasy hairstyle popular with entertainers and hipsters; conk; process; gashead.

Quadroon ball -- an 18th and 19th-century festive social event at which white males entered into *plaçage* (from the French *placer* meaning "to place with") with women of color in an extra-legal system that paired them with desirable young females for purposes of concubinage.

Rag -- to dress in a stylish, sartorially resplendent manner.

Ratchet, ratchetness -- Urban form of the word *wretched*: very unhappy, ill, etc.; very bad or unpleasant; very poor in quality or ability. Also a diva that believes she is every man's eye candy. (Unfortunately, she's wrong.) (Courtesy of urbandictionary.com)

Recamier -- a backless couch with a high, curved headrest and low footrest.

Red gravy -- pasta sauce with love potion.

Rep – reputation.

Repast -- a traditional New Orleans after-funeral meal.

Rosenberg's -- an "affordable" furniture store with "1825 Tulane" radio ad jingle (referring to its address) recognizable to any New Orleanian.

Rubenstein's -- an upscale men's clothing store established in 1924 on the corner of Canal Street and St. Charles Avenue.

Runnin' head -- trash talking; boasting.

Runnin'/workin' on the water -- pursuing a career as a seaman/longshoreman.

Saddity -- self-centered; self-absorbed; snooty.

St. Aug. -- St. Augustine High School, a nationally-recognized educational institution (originally founded during the segregation era for African-American boys) with a history of academic and athletic achievement.

St. John's Eve -- the June 23 midsummer celebration before the Catholic Feast Day of John the Baptist, a fixed date that occurs June 21 – 24, six months before Christmas. According to the Gospel of Luke, St. John was born six months before Jesus. The spiritual practice of voodoo via secret societies peaks during this time with bonfires, singing, dancing, food, and ritual.

Second Lines -- Street parades of musicians and dancers, all walking, have an old and sacred origin. Commonly and mistakenly thought to be the line behind musicians, the Second Line as celebrated in New Orleans has its roots in West Africa, where folks still parade with parasols (umbrellas) and handkerchiefs dance. Similar traditions occur in Trinidad, Puerto Rico, Cuba, and Haiti. In New Orleans, this practice dates prior to the city. The first line is one of musicians playing for the mourners going to the graveyard, celebrated in the band playing a dirge; the "second line" of musicians and mourners is on the return from burying the loved one and becomes a celebration of the life lived, that all their worries of this life are over and they are in a better place. This was particularly significant during slavery and Jim Crow, therefore, culturally and racially charged with a spirit of joy. It is this joyful post-burial celebration that has struck a strong chord with visitors to the Crescent City. What has happened in New Orleans is that the "Second Line" has evolved in

popular culture as any street parade out of context of its origins. There's nothing wrong with that, but the definition remains the same, and its origins were for a sacred context and post-burial relief. (Courtesy of author/folklorist Dr. Mona Lisa Saloy, Dillard University, New Orleans, LA)

Set-up -- a drink order that includes a bottle of alcohol (usu. a pint or half pint), mixers, ice, and glasses for patrons. It is much more cost effective than ordering drink after drink.

Shake dancing -- stripping.

Shine -- pejorative term for a person of African ancestry living in the United States.

Shoo-shoo -- to speak disparagingly of another in hushed tones.

Shwoog -- someone who is cheap and/or unfair and constantly uses friends; a trifling person.

Signify -- to participate in an African American street ritual of hyperbolic boasting, bragging, and jocular insulting. See **ignify**.

Sho-ya right -- a phrase indicating strong agreement, affirmation, or a stamp of approval. See *Yeah-ya right*.

Short -- car.

Skatin' truck -- skatemobile; a wooden scooter.

Skep' -- skeptical.

Sky -- to quickly remove oneself from a location.

Slipped the noose -- escaped a lynching.

Slopjar -- chamber pot.

Soft drink -- soda.

Sometimey -- the quality of being fair-weathered; unreliable.

Sperl – spoil.

Spiro Gyra -- mid-'70s jazz-fusion band; reference alludes to Spiro Agnew, Vice President under Nixon.

Spoogie – casual lover; intimate partner; girlfriend, boyfriend (pronounced like the diphthong in "boogie").

States-Item -- a New Orleans daily newspaper circa 1960–70.

Steatopygia -- an accumulation of a huge amount of buttock fat.

Stinkin' (oneself) up -- applying perfume.

Stretch the beans- to increase a meal (usually of red beans and rice) by adding water when unexpected dinner guests linger or arrive. See *baptize the gumbo*.

SUNO -- Southern University at New Orleans.

Tackhaid -- an unattractive woman. See *bugarbat*.

Talkin' underneath someone's clothes -- speaking in a sexually suggestive way (on the sly) about a person in that person's presence.

Tamp – an easygoing, hip walk.

Tangipahoa -- a Louisiana parish (county in other states).

Tchoupitoulas (*choppa TOO luss*) -- a street in New Orleans.

Teenantsy (also *teenantchee*) -- minimally miniscule.

"The hand I fan (with)"-- an expression indicating the favoring of utilizing one hand to perform tasks rather than the other; such as using a particular hand to fan oneself with; favored. *I love that man. He's the hand I fan.*

Third floor, Charity Hospital -- psych ward.

Tighten up -- a greeting; also, *"be cool"*. As a greeting it is similar to *Where y'at?!*

Ticklish -- humorous; having the ability to provoke laughter.

***Tignon* (also *tiyon*)** -- a head tie for women of color prescribed by the administration of Louisiana Governor Esteban Rodriguez Miró in 1785 to enforce "appropriate" public dress for women of color, called the "tignon laws." Many of these women were openly kept mistresses who were in competition with white women in matters of dress, good looks, sophistication and charisma. The wives, mothers, sisters, daughters and fiancées of French, Spanish, and Creole men complained that white males often mistook white women for light-skinned women of color and approached them with inappropriate comportment. A law was effected by Miró, whereas, any slave or free black woman was obligated to cover her hair with a knotted headdress in order to be identifiable as a member of a different class from white women. The women of color circumvented the legal prescription by decorating tignons with ribbons and jewels while using the finest fabric for the covering, in effect re-interpreting the law without breaking it; and still were pursued by men.

Tragedy money -- a pittance allotted for burial from the deceased's Social Security account.

Treme -- one of New Orleans' historic *faubourgs* that boasts a history of African- American institutions, professionals, and artists.

Tulane and Broad -- location of Orleans Parish Prison and the Criminal Court Building.

Tumblesettin' -- cartwheeling; backwards handspringing.

Undereye -- to cast a threatening glance.

Understandin' Henry -- iconic figure in a popular TV loan commercial (circa 1960s).

Vandella -- allusion to a member of a popular '60s Motown "girl group," Martha and the Vandellas.

Vejitibble man -- street vendor with horse-drawn carriage.

Victimes de l'honneur -- dueling victims.

Washington Generals -- basketball team (1952-1995) that frequently played the Harlem Globetrotters (as a foil for the latter's comedy routines) and lost over 13,000 exhibition games.

Whammy -- fake dope.

"Where there's life there's hope." -- theme/motto of the Angola State Penitentiary Lifer's Association.

Where y'at?! -- Hello.

Yeah-ya right -- a phrase indicating strong agreement, exclamatory affirmation, or a verbal stamp of approval (See *Sho-ya-right*).

Zulu Parade -- an African-themed Mardi Gras event under the auspices of the Zulu Social Aid and Pleasure Club.

Previously Published Stories

"Last Time I Saw Jeanine: Confessions of a New Orleans Jazz Poet"

Umbrella Factory Magazine, Sept. 15, 2010 issue. www.umbrellafactorymagazine.com

"The Boy and the Famous French Quarter Lady Writer"

Nola Diaspora (2012). http://noladiaspora.org/wordplace/BoyandFamousFQL_byPfister.html

"The Funeral Poet"

Fresh Ink (2013). pp. 50-56. Naugatuck Valley Community College, Waterbury, CT.

"The Boy With the Cheap, Ugly, Green Army Surplus Tennis Shoes"

Fresh Ink (2014). pp. 25-26. Naugatuck Valley Community College, Waterbury, CT.

About the Author

Professor Arturo, a poet and fiction writer from New Orleans, is a Spoken Word artist, educator, performer, humorist editor, monologist, speechwriter, and recipient of the Asante Award. He received a Master of Arts degree in Writing from Johns Hopkins University and a B.A. in English/Journalism from the State University of New York-College at New Paltz. The Professor, one of the original Broadside Press poets of the 1960s, has collaborated on a medley of projects with a mélange of artists including painters, musicians, photographers, dancers, singers, fire eaters, waiters, cab drivers, and other members of the Great Miscellaneous. The independent performing arts professional has performed his poetry, fiction, toasts and "jazz poems" on a solo basis or with musical accompaniment at Ebony Square, Vincent's City Club, Louisiana Music Factory, the Contemporary Arts Center, the Louisiana Folklife Festival, the New Orleans Jazz and Heritage Festival, the Urban League's Annual Golden Gala, Ashe Cultural Arts Center, Tulane University's Amistad Research Center's Achievement Award Banquet, True Brew Coffeehouse, the Gold Mine Saloon, *Le Chat Noir*, ESPE's, the Maple Leaf Bar, the Jazz Foundation of America (NYC), the Telephone Bar (NYC), the KGB Bar (NYC), Bar 82, the Bowery Poetry Club (NYC), Cornelia Street Café (NYC), Small's Jazz Club (NYC), and an array of public/parochial schools, libraries, bookstores, colleges, nursing/retirement homes and churches nationwide. His work has been accompanied by musical legends such as Benjamin "Kidd" Lambert, Michael Beauchamp, Eluard Burte, Henry Butler, Willie Cole, Davell Crawford, Vinny Golia, Leroy Jones, the Magic Band, Porgy Jones, Kidd Jordan, Kid Millenberg and Earl Turbinton. He has also served as Featured Performance Poet at Sweet Lorraine's Jazz Club and co-founded the performance series "Arturo and Joe's Old Skool Jazz & Poetry Open Mic Night" at New Orleans' legendary Edgelake Bar (featured in the 1958 Elvis Presley film "King Creole").

Professor Arturo, who lists Amiri Baraka, Arthur Prysock, Gozo Yoshimasu and Guy de Maupassant among his influences, has had his work published in an array of diverse publications such as the *New York Quarterly, Fahari, American Poetry Review, Shooting Star Review, Minnesota Review, Gallery Mirror, Ebony, From a Bend in the River, Mesechabe, Word Up, Chicory Review, New Laurel Review,* the New Orleans *Tribune, We Speak As Liberators, Black Spirits, A Broadside Treasury,* and Swapping *Stories: Folktales From Louisiana.*

He has taught at educational institutions ranging from Northeastern University (Visiting Poet for the Africana Studies Center) to Texas Southern University (Writer in Residence). He has served as Academic Instructor for the New Orleans Urban League's Computer Operations Training Center and as Poet in Residence at the Neighborhood Gallery. Prior to Katrina, he was employed by the New Orleans Job Corps as Academic/Pre-GED Instructor. He is presently teaching at Norwalk Community College where he also served as a Facilitator in the Lifetime Learners Institute.

Inquiries about the author's availability for interviews, workshops, readings, collaborative projects, seminars, residencies, and publications should be directed to:
(504) 975-6676   FaceBook (Arthur Pfister)
arthurpfister@yahoo.com

www.ingramcontent.com/pod-product-compliance
Lightning Source LLC
Chambersburg PA
CBHW070719160426
43192CB00009B/1241